Gender Perspectives in Law

Volume 6

Series Editors

Dragica Vujadinović, Faculty of Law, University of Belgrade, Belgrade, Serbia
Ivana Krstić, Faculty of Law, University of Belgrade, Belgrade, Serbia

The series 'Gender Perspectives in Law' discusses all-encompassing gender-competent legal questions. Having a gender-competent approach is required when considering the highest values and normative standards of modern international, European, and national law. Raising awareness about gender equality issues means investing in the creation, interpretation, and implementation of legislation that is more fair, just, and equitable and will also contribute to a comprehensive understanding of social reality, as well as to gender-competent political, legal and economic decision-making and public policies.

The series accepts monographs focusing on a specific topic, as well as edited collections of articles covering a specific theme or collections of articles.

Fabio Macioce • Zara Saeidzadeh
Dragica Vujadinović
Editors

Feminist Legal and Political Practices

The Contemporary Interplay of Gender, Intersectionality and Diversity

Springer

Editors
Fabio Macioce
Libera Università Maria SS. Assunta
Roma, Italy

Zara Saeidzadeh
Simone de Beauvoir Institute
Concordia University
Montreal, QC, Canada

Dragica Vujadinović
Faculty of Law
University of Belgrade
Belgrade, Serbia

ISSN 2731-8346 ISSN 2731-8354 (electronic)
Gender Perspectives in Law
ISBN 978-3-032-02855-6 ISBN 978-3-032-02856-3 (eBook)
https://doi.org/10.1007/978-3-032-02856-3

This Springer imprint is published by the registered company Springer Nature Switzerland AG
The registered company address is: Gewerbestrasse 11, 6330 Cham, Switzerland

Contents

Editors and Contributors

About the Editors

Fabio Macioce PhD, is a full professor of Philosophy of Law and Bioethics at LUMSA University, School of Law, Rome. He held visiting positions at Cambridge University, UK, Universidad de Valencia, and University of Oxford. Since 2019, he has been working as an expert for the Council of Europe in the field of bioethics. His research focuses on individual and group vulnerability; migration, democracy, and legal pluralism; legal feminism; bioethics and informed consent; the relationship between law and religion; and the impact of AI on human rights. He has written and edited several books and journal articles in English, Italian, French, and Spanish. His latest books are *The Politics of Vulnerable Groups: Implications for Philosophy, Law, and Political Theory*, Springer Nature, 2022; *The Law of Beauty. The Troubled Relationship Between Law and Aesthetic*, Routledge 2025.

Zara Saeidzadeh is an affiliate assistant professor at Simone de Beauvoir Institute, Montreal, Canada. She has a PhD in Gender Studies from Örebro University in Sweden where she completed her postdoctoral research project on Violence against Trans* Women in Sweden, funded by the Swedish Research Council for Health, Working Life and Welfare in 2024. Her research is situated in the field of law and gender, emphasising feminist decolonial and intersectional methodologies. Among others, her recent publications include: Trans* Citizenship in Feminist Theories and Practices. In N. Lacey et al. (Eds.), *Reassessing Feminist Legal Theories*. Springer 2025 as well as Trans* Women's Experiences of Epistemic Misrecognition in Swedish Law and Society. *Social Politics: International Studies in Gender, State and Society., 2025.*

Dragica Vujadinović is a full professor at the Faculty of Law (FL), University of Belgrade (UB), teaching Political and Legal Theories at master's and doctoral studies, as well as Introduction to the Political System of the EU within the master's study program Master in European Integration (MEI), and Feminist Political and Legal Theories within the master's study program Law and Gender (LAWGEM). She was the Head of MEI and LAWGEM master's academic studies. She was the

UB coordinator for the Erasmus Mundus Design Measures project (EMDM) (2023–2024), for preparing with Örebro University and LUMSA the future joint master's and for applying for Erasmus Mundus Joint Master (EMJM)—*Law, Gender, Intersectionality and Diversity* (LAWGID). She has been the co-editor of the Springer book series *Gender Perspectives in Law*. She has published 20 monographs and edited volumes, and made many contributions for international and national academic journals.

Contributors

Damir Banović Faculty of Law, University of Sarajevo, Sarajevo, Bosnia and Herzegovina

Thomas Casadei University of Modena and Reggio Emilia, Modena, Italy

Ana Đanić Čeko Faculty of Law, Josip Juraj Strossmayer University of Osijek, Osijek, Croatia

Angela Condello University of Messina, Messina, Italy

Sanja Djajić University of Novi Sad School of Law, Novi Sad, Serbia

Naoual El Yattouti Law Faculty, University of Antwerp, Antwerp, Belgium

Burcu Gumus Aarhus University, Aarhus, Denmark

Jelena Kasap Faculty of Law, Josip Juraj Strossmayer University of Osijek, Osijek, Croatia

Jón Ingvar Kjaran University of Iceland, Reykjavik, Iceland

Višnja Lachner Faculty of Law, Josip Juraj Strossmayer University of Osijek, Osijek, Croatia

Fabio Macioce Libera Università Maria SS. Assunta, Rome, Italy

Benjamin Nurkić Faculty of Law, University of Tuzla, Tuzla, Bosnia and Herzegovina

Mario Reljanović Institute of Comparative Law, Belgrade, Serbia

Lucia Re University of Florence, Florence, Italy

Zara Saeidzadeh Simone de Beauvoir Institute, Concordia University, Montreal, QC, Canada

Lorena Sosa Utrecht University, Utrecht, The Netherlands

Dragica Vujadinović Faculty of Law, University of Belgrade, Belgrade, Serbia

Angbin Yasmin School of Law, Jamia Hamdard, New Delhi, India

Introduction

Zara Saeidzadeh, Fabio Macioce, and Dragica Vujadinović

Abstract This book, part of the Gender Perspectives in Law series, explores the dynamic relationship between theory and practice in contemporary feminisms. As editors, we recognize that theoretical and ideological frameworks must be complemented by critical reflections on the political and legal significance of concrete practices. Accordingly, the volume investigates the longstanding and productive interplay between theory and practice through diverse perspectives and methodological approaches—ranging from empirical legal and political studies to doctrinal analyses, national and thematic case studies, historical and comparative assessments, and both domestic and international viewpoints, as well as conceptual and practical considerations. Thus, the book engages with the historical dimensions of women's political activism and practices, analyzing the factors that have been particularly influential in shaping women's political action and asking which elements of past feminist movements remain relevant to contemporary political struggles. In addition, it examines current legal manifestations of gender-based oppression and systems of privilege, while also exploring emancipatory tendencies within modern law, politics, and culture.

Feminist politics are shaped by the theories and practices developed by feminist scholars and activists. However, as Walby notes, collective activities, practices, and perspectives that do not explicitly identify as feminists but focus on gender equality

Z. Saeidzadeh
Simone de Beauvoir Institue, Concordia University, Montreal, QC, Canada
e-mail: zarasaeidzadeh@gmail.com; dragicav@ius.bg.ac.rs

F. Macioce
Libera Università Maria SS. Assunta, Rome, Italy
e-mail: f.macioce@lumsa.it

D. Vujadinović (✉)
Faculty of Law, University of Belgrade, Belgrade, Serbia
e-mail: dragicav@ius.bg.ac.rs

F. Macioce et al. (eds.), *Feminist Legal and Political Practices*, Gender Perspectives in Law 6, https://doi.org/10.1007/978-3-032-02856-3_1

are also considered feminist projects.[1] Feminist politics emphasize the relationship between theory and practice, recognizing direct and personal experience as the foundation upon which theory is built and enters public discourses. In other words, feminist theoretical perspectives, research, and activism are intertwined.[2] This close entanglement is reflected in the mutual relations between feminist movements and the motto “the personal is political.” This political slogan was popularized by feminists in the 1960s, reflecting the structural and systemic origins of women’s experience of injustices and their struggles for emancipation. The “personal is political” highlights the idea that women’s personal experiences are embedded in the political position they occupy as women. Thus, the “private” and “public” realms are inextricably linked, just as the arena of personal experience and political claims are inseparable.[3]

In a similar vein, the notion of consciousness-raising was developed by many feminist scholars and activists in the 1960s and 1970s (Europe and North America)[4] to illuminate that awareness starts from the individual and the personal—that is, the private—and unites with the social dimension—that is, the public. The method of consciousness-raising was developed by feminists to challenge gender injustice, transcending the theory-practice dichotomy and becoming the vehicle for political claim-making and practical action. Women have asserted that the inequalities and injustices they face are social problems that require social and political solutions. This approach integrates personal experience into theory while shaping theory based on people’s experiences, so continuously refining and modifying it. Moreover, it transcends the dichotomy between public and private, individual and community, as well as between theory and praxis. The legacies of suffragette movements from the nineteenth and early twentieth centuries and the second-wave feminism of the 1960s emerged in the West and were mostly embedded in the realm of white Western feminism. At the same time, the Western-centric nature of this mainstream feminist legacy has been contested due to its inherent limitations related to the universalization of white women’s experiences of gender discrimination, and the consequential oblivion or silence related to the diverse forms of discrimination faced by women in the non-Western world.

Challenging gender injustices has gone well beyond the Western-centric view of feminist theories and practices, a shift that started at the turn of the twentieth century. In the 1990s, influenced by critical legal studies and post-modern political theories, critical race feminism emerged in the USA to address the plight of women of color, including Black, Asian, Hispanic, Native American, or other minority groups.[5] Emerging feminist politics around the globe, global critical race feminism, postcolonial feminism, decolonial and Indigenous feminism challenge the hege-

[1] Walby (2011).

[2] Jaggar (1983), p. 12.

[3] MacKinnon (1982).

[4] Sarachild (1975).

[5] Wing and Pappalardo (2023), pp. 53–54, 64.

monic European and North American feminist agendas, initiating important debates on the interrelation between Global South and Global North feminist knowledge and practices.[6]

We do not suggest that women's movements are always feminist, nor that they originated solely in the West. Since the early 1800s, women in different parts of the world have been mobilizing to challenge all forms of inequalities and injustices visited upon them by variety of different systems of oppression. Women's organizations, campaigns, mobilizations, and activities have impacted societies worldwide. Thus, Feminist movements exist in practically every country in the world in different forms and shapes. In this book, we understand feminist movements as historical and transnational theories and practices, known as one of the most successful forms of contemporary modern social movements.[7] Between the 1890s and 1930s, women's activism around the world was concerned with issues of citizenship, focusing on the right to vote and women's participation in nation-building. Among others, "Ruling elites in countries such as Iran, Turkey, and China also saw the demands of 'modernity' as including increasing individual rights for women. Suffrage organizations pressed their case for women's citizenship so effectively within the world community that although virtually no state extended women the right to vote in 1900."[8] By the 1950s, women around the world founded international organizations with hundreds of activists in their ranks.[9]

Globalization, multiculturalism, and mass migrations have transformed Western societies and reshaped Western and transnational feminist movements. The struggles for recognition of marginalized and unprivileged social groups since the 1970s, along with post-modern political and legal theories as well as critical race feminism since the 1990s, have led to the emergence of manifold feminist movements across the globe. This gave rise to postcolonial feminist movements and feminist intersectionality as the paradigmatic approach to addressing gender issues. It also inspired attempts towards dismantling the universal notions of "woman" and "gender" developed by earlier Western-centric, second-wave feminist movements, which were largely dominated by white, middle-class, elite women.

The deconstruction of Western-centric feminisms has brought on the agenda the intersectional approach, which aims to shed light on the profoundly different modalities of (widely experienced) gender-based discrimination in the context of different classes, races, ages, cultures, religions, ethnicities, educational statuses, (dis)ability statuses, etc. However, a crucial aspect of contemporary feminist approaches, as well as a common feature of all contemporary movements—whether from the Global North or the Global South—is the ability to propose forms of activism capable of combining ideas about multiple gender-based discrimination, feminist discourses, and militant creativity in ways that are unparallel in other social

[6] Felix de Souza (2018), Martinez-Cairo and Buscemi (2021), Ampofo and Beoku-Bettes (2021).

[7] Ferree and Mueller (2004), p. 577.

[8] Ibid, p. 585.

[9] Ibid.

movements. From suffragettes to contemporary feminist movements, women's political practices, as well as feminist elaborations of theoretical frameworks, have disrupted social norms. In other words, change has always been accompanied by intense theoretical activity as well as forms of activism often carried out in provocative and unconventional ways. The implementation of social, juridical, and political practices is thus not only the *consequence* of theoretically advanced demands for change, but the natural arising of ideas that aim to reconfigure social, symbolic, and practical systems in their entirety, combining symbolic acts with explicit demands for gender justice and equality.

In fact, feminist political and legal practices and activism not only foster a critical approach to traditional models and structures that perpetuate gender hierarchies and patriarchal relations, but also enable women to physically and symbolically occupy spaces where authority and power structures are exercised, such as courtrooms, public squares, the media, and various workplaces. Feminist practices disrupt power imbalances and structures of hierarchies, male dominance over women, and gender-based discrimination embedded in the creation, interpretation, and implementation of law, thereby questioning the legitimacy of laws and power and transforming these spaces into contestation arenas. Moreover, feminist practices make it possible to re-appropriate places where traditional power and gender hierarchy are in force, transforming them into spaces where male power and privilege are subverted and reconsidered.

Feminist activism has transformed the social and symbolic prominence of emotions traditionally considered as "weak"—such as silence or passive resistance—into powerful political expressions, reformulating traditional narratives linked to ideals of decorum and passivity historically imposed on women. Hence, boycotts, strikes, and refusals have, over the years, become acts of self-liberation and empowerment as well as paths of personal and collective transformation. In such a context, and precisely because of this ability to politically utilize unprecedented tools and messages, feminist activism has not simply sought to change society but rather aimed to change activism itself. Against the notion that political movements must be rational and composed, and that claims for rights must be articulated via reasoned arguments and demands in public debate, feminist activism has reaffirmed the significance of affect and embraced the body as legitimate and powerful arenas for change. Hence, feminist activism seeks to make visible and elucidate patterns of injustice in institutions, structures, and normative values that are gendered.[10]

In this vein, women who experience conditions of oppression, exploitation, or abuse prove their ability to enter public space, shattering the illusion that it is a regulated and neutral arena where anyone can discuss issues of public importance. Against such a model, feminist movements emerge as alternative public arenas, transforming the notion of public discussion, its rules, and spaces. Most importantly, subverting and proposing new subjects and modes of discourse, new perspectives, and new viewpoints that would otherwise be excluded.[11]

[10] Ackerly and True (2010).

[11] Fraser (1990), p. 66.

Besides, in the context of the struggles of different social minorities and/or vulnerable groups for recognition, including the struggles of lesbian, transgender, intersex and queer persons for recognition have also contributed to overcoming the binary/heteronormative approach to gender relations as the relevant ones. Similarly, self-reflexivity trends have emerged among Western feminist movements in favor of accepting a more inclusive approach, one that is sensitive to differences between women of different races, classes, ages, and sexual orientations, and that consider the unprivileged positions of women and feminists of color from the Global South and from post-colonial countries. Unavoidable as it is, Western feminists have acknowledged the unprivileged position of feminists from former Western colonies, because the legacies of colonial history are deeply embedded in all dimensions of the multiple gender-based discrimination. An intersectional understanding of gender-based discrimination must take into consideration each concrete-historical-political-economic-cultural context, as well as factors such as class, race, age, sexual orientation, etc. However, potential cleavages, conflicts, and misunderstandings challenge the mere essence of feminism, which is the pursuit of gender equality. Consequently, relevant feminist theories and practices seriously consider these differences and disagreements among feminist movements, seeking to identify converging practices despite the observed differences. Therefore, the current struggle for gender equality has been multifocal and contextually varied while still striving to include diverse experiences of women as well as others identifying as gender and/or sexually diverse.

To understand the nexus between gender and diversity in contemporary legal and political practices it is crucial to analyze, for instance, how women's voices are silenced and marginalized in the labor market, judicial system, and state bureaucracy, as well as in debates on citizenship and migration. The discussion on contemporary women's political practices requires considering social norms and behaviors that continue to limit women's agency within the public and social spheres, on the one hand, and political and legal activism related to reproduction, sexuality, bodily integrity, and freedom, on the other. Analyses of reproductive justice are an example of critical feminism and intersectionality, and a place where activism and legal-political reflection meet.

Again, such an analysis of contemporary political and legal practices can shed light, first, on the interplay between feminist movements and anti-capitalist or post-colonialist claims, as well as on feminist critics of contemporary violence and the dispossession of marginalized peoples. Second, it can contribute to a better understanding of women's political agency from an intersectional perspective, exploring the interplay between women's agency and LGBTQI+ movements and claims concerning sexuality, family rules, care labor, etc.

Conflicts have emerged in recent years between feminist movements and approaches based on the question of "difference." The existing conflicts manifest in femonationalism, homonationalism, and gender racism, reflecting the lack of readiness among Western feminists to recognize the position and needs of women from other cultures, regions, and historical/political/economic backgrounds. This resistance is particularly evident in the notion of femonationalism,[12] which refers to the emphasis placed by not only extreme right-wing parties on women of their own nation in contrast to immigrant women, particularly Muslims, but also by those feminists who focus on human rights exclusively.[13] Of course, it is legitimate to focus on human rights and Western values, but the problem comes from ignoring and neglecting the concrete-historical positioning of feminists, and women in general, within non-Western parts of the world. Homonationalism, on the other hand, marks the shift in the neoliberal approach to some (not all) homosexual individuals being worthy of protection by nation-states. Therefore, the main critique of homonationalism is tied to the liberal rights discourse, which guarantees some parts of the population access to citizens' rights at the expense of excluding other communities such as queer, immigrants, and people of color in Europe.[14]

Another consequence of these conflicts is the intersection of structural racism, gender-based discrimination, and sexism, a dynamic that is conceptualized as gender racism. Gender racism highlights power hierarchies among members of different feminist movements (for example, the invisibility of Black poor women issues within first and second wave White feminist movements, or, for example, the invisibility of African descent and Indigenous groups women within Brazilian feminist movements), and between feminist movements of different cultural/political/religious backgrounds. The oblivious stance of White feminism regarding the interconnectedness of Western modernity, patriarchy, racism, colonialism, imperialism, and the related ignorance towards complex, deep rooted gender-based oppression against women from the global South,[15] is an example of gender racism, which can be extended to the experiences of (white) LGBT movements.[16]

These conflicts bring into focus the weight of hierarchies and different systems of power in the context in which women live and act. Consequently, they illuminate the different positioning among them as representatives of feminist movements from different historical, cultural, political, and economic contexts. In other words, it is necessary to consider the position of women in the West within existing systems of power, such as patriarchy and classism, as well as the colonial history, while bearing in mind the weight of the discrepancies between the center, semi-periphery, and periphery in the global context, i.e., the power imbalances between states and post-colonial societies, or between the Global North and South.

Polarizations and conflicts within and between feminist movements in the West and in relation to other regions, cultures, and economic-political-legal systems/contexts are the result of Western-centric or biased approaches towards feminisms from other parts of the world. As Lepinard puts it, feminism is in trouble. Despite the

---

[12] Farris (2017).

[13] Lepinard (2020), p. 2.

[14] Puar (2013).

[15] Espinosa-Minosa (2024), p. 86.

[16] Philadelphia Pride decided in 2017 to include more color in the visual representation of the the well-known flag—brown and black colors that designate people of color, signalizing opposition to racism within the LGBT+ movement (Evans and Lepinard 2020, p. 1).

denunciation of whiteness, racism, colonial aphasia, and islamophobia by voices emerging from feminist movements beyond Europe and North America, these perspectives have remained marginal and marginalized, i.e., they ought to be much louder and sounder. Reinventing the feminist utopian project, which focuses on achieving gender equality, requires a more inclusive, solidarity-driven approach, one that is open to differences, cautious, and willful. This is necessary for feminists globally to achieve a deeper understanding of the various sources of multiple discrimination and unprivileged positions, so equipping them to engage with empathy and tolerance, treating "other" feminists and feminist movements as compatriots rather than "enemies."[17]

Conflicts also arise from the political, legal, and cultural differences between Western democracies, which focus on human rights and women's rights, and non-Western cultures and regions, which often focus on religion, particularly Islam.[18] It is crucial that Western and non-Western feminist movements recognize the common roots of gender inequalities in patriarchal system (independent of the very varied manifestations of patriarchy across different concrete-historical, political, economic, and cultural contexts), and consider the intersectional dimensions of gender-based discrimination, differently expressed across different class, race, culture, and political contexts. To contribute to the common aims and survival of feminism as a progressive future-oriented civilizational project, the various feminisms have the necessity to identify converging elements in their ideas and practices, foster inclusive and solidary actions, and overcome the power relations/imbalances between them.

Gender is conceptualized differently with regard to the variety of feminist theoretical standpoints in the West. A more social, poststructuralist approach understands gender as the product of unequal power relations.[19] In this view, gender is a form of social practice that constantly refers to the body. Meanwhile, feminist postmodern approaches theorize gender as something pre-discursive that comes to the surface through the body's performative act, being produced and reproduced through stylized repetition of acts[20] that are not stable but fluid.[21] However, Monro[22] draws our attention to the critiques of the hegemonic deployment of Western scholarship, which promotes a colonized view of gender and sexuality. It is essential to explore how gender is conceptualized as an analytical and theoretical tool across different countries, where varied political terrains expose and challenge institutionalized gender relations in different ways.

As a consequence, the process of connecting practices and activism with theoretical insights must challenge dominant structures of power and discourse and

[17] Ibid.

[18] Lepinard (2020), p. 2.

[19] Connell and Pears (2015).

[20] Butler (1990).

[21] Butler (1993).

[22] Monro (2018).

allow women in general and various groups to open new arenas of discourse, propose different narratives, and aggregate otherwise marginalized interests and needs.[23] In doing so, individuals and groups of women as well as people from diverse sexual orientation, gender identity and expression can facilitate experience sharing, showing that these experiences are not just related to contingent and individual circumstances but also the functioning of social systems while highlighting the relevance of intersectional approaches. Conversely, they operate as sounding boards calling for recognition, opening up spaces for political action and arenas for discussion and helping in shaping the political agenda for the benefit of individuals beyond their individual subjectivities.[24]

When connected with ethical, juridical, political reflection, and theoretical analyses, feminist scholarship fully becomes a form of political activism. Such a connection reveals what is normally hidden, thus bringing to center stage what is marginalized. Moreover, it encourages those (individuals and groups) whose voice is rarely heard to develop political and publicly relevant arguments, presenting the views and claims of women from the Global South, former colonial countries, non-Western cultures, religious groups, minorities, etc. Challenging mainstream liberal anthropology and the Western-white-cisgender (etc.) point of views, such conjunction between theoretical analysis and practices contributes to subversive public debates. Consequently, it allows feminist movements to raise issues and make claims that cannot be ignored or even dismissed with arguments based on solidarity or equality, which fail to challenge the patriarchal structure of society. It is well known that rights discourse can be an alienated and artificial language that limits political debate when used as a tool for legitimizing existing power structures. But it can also be used as means to articulate new values and different political visions. The way a movement claims rights transforms the rights discourse into an instrument for political struggle. At the same time, rights discourse, when organically linked to political struggle, can help develop a political consciousness in those involved and give impetus to a social movement.

Feminist thoughts, in its many variants, often emphasize this change of perspective; for instance, by reassessing the notion of *vulnerability* as a new form of strength, an alternative to models focused on possession and domination. Hence, feminist thoughts provide places of redemption and present an opportunities to bring about new social relations and models.[25] Looking at inequalities and marginalization from such a dual, and intersectional perspective, entails advocating for empowerment and resistance, legitimizing dissent, and opening new spaces for resistance and new demands for visibility, as well as provoking struggles for recognition.[26]

In other words, in a situation where power is distributed unequally, thereby creating structures of oppression and marginalizing and subordinating certain groups of

---

[23] Young (2000), p. 167.

[24] Fraser (1990), p. 71.

[25] Macioce (2024).

[26] Bernardini et al. (2018).

people (through privileges connected to sex, gender, race, bodily ability, money, etc.), this situation should not be only viewed in its victimizing aspect: it can also serve as a site of resistance to oppression and a context where claims and positive actions emerge. As Butler writes, the condition of marginality and exclusion "becomes a potentially effective mobilizing force in political mobilizations."[27] Different practices, in different contexts, and through different modalities (bodies, voices, writings, artworks…) become a source of critique of the existing power structure and form the basis for claiming rights and responses to oppression.

The activity of claiming is in itself a double-sided action. As Feinberg observes, the fact of *claiming* is crucial in the process of recognizing rights, because it is a practice that *per se* legitimizes and empowers: "To have a claim in turn, is to have a case meriting consideration, that is, to have reasons or grounds that put one in a position to engage in performative and propositional claiming." In other words, the activity of claiming, besides its specific objective, makes for self-respect and respect for others, and "gives a sense to the notion of personal dignity."[28] It is not only the reasonableness of claims that matters but the very fact of claiming, the practice of dissenting, making one's body visible and one's voice audible.

Sandra Fredman[29] situates the act of *claiming* within a practical, four-dimensional framework of substantive gender equality. In this framework, claiming is linked to a participatory approach to overcoming gender-based discrimination, emphasizing the importance of law-making, policy-making, and court rulings that actively listen to victims. It advocates for the rights of those unprivileged and demeaned to be heard and especially to take part in decisions affecting their cases and discriminatory experiences and future. The other dimensions of the four-dimensional analytical framework include overcoming and redressing inequality, addressing and challenging stigma, stereotyping, prejudices, and violence while acknowledging differences and accommodating institutional and structural changes in order to accommodate justifiable differences.

Emphasizing practices over mere theories allows for balancing between the universalistic logic of rights and the radical particularity of needs, highlighting the importance of contexts, characteristics, and specific circumstances for collective projects of emancipation and liberation. Such practices enable subordinated individuals and groups (beginning with the recognition of inequalities) to benefit from public awareness of the specific conditions of subordination. Consequently, they can employ techniques that re-shape social and institutional spaces to attain equal dignity.[30] As Young rightly notes, the democratic discussion is "a process in which differentiated social groups should attend to the particular situation of others and be willing to work out just solutions to their conflicts and collective problems from

---

[27] Butler (2016), p. 14.

[28] Feinberg (1970), p. 260.

[29] Fredman (2016), pp. 712–738.

[30] Casadei (2012), p. 114.

across their situated positions."[31] In other words, focusing on particular individuals' circumstances and reasonable claims makes it difficult for people to recognize themselves as connected by relations or structures that are beyond their will. Even if the system of social, political, and institutional relations is properly acknowledged, only practices elucidate the relevance of such relations for the experience and opportunities of people; only collective practices render them visible, allowing people to collectively make claims.[32]

The analysis of practices, specifically those concerning rights, highlights both the process by which these rights are formulated and the way in which the content of rights is established. It is a process by which rights are developed alongside a collective consciousness (think of the awareness of gender violence produced by movements such as Ni Una Menos, which concurrently brought about legal guarantees in the family, workplace, etc.). In other words, the recognition of rights goes hand in hand with the development of individual and collective consciousness, because it is both a legal conquest and a means of projecting and building awareness within the women's movement.

Movements like Ni Una Menos or the #MeToo campaign are examples of how public articulation of the experiences of wounding, trauma, and violence can become a powerful global movement, a site of political agency. However, the global awareness-raising on gender-based violence and the emergence of the global movement in this regard might conceal the fact that global understanding and combatting of gender-based violence must be considered and dealt with from an intersectional perspective while keeping in mind how differences in class, race, age—whether belonging to the center, periphery, or semi-periphery of the global world—differently determine the intensity of exposure to gender-based violence. Gender-based violence is rooted in patriarchy, both its traditional and contemporary forms, which continue to emerge even today. Gender-based violence is also rooted in the conflict between persistent patriarchal structures, which manifest in various contexts, on one hand, and the emancipatory tendencies that have been manifested since the political and industrial revolutions of the eighteenth and nineteenth centuries, through women's gaining equal rights to vote, entering gradually all levels of education, politics, almost all professions, etc.

A sum of individual voices, sharing a vulnerability in the two senses just indicated, can give rise to a feminist movement for emancipation, justice, and change.[33] Even if some feminist, queer, and anti-racist scholars have blamed some of these movements (#MeToo, for example) for exposure to the risk of whitewashing and the exclusion of trans and queer identities, as well as the prevailing focus on the experience of cisgender (and affluent) women, it is also true, on the other hand, that it has favored demands for visibility and struggles for recognition, occupying public space and making an otherwise inaudible voice heard.

---

[31] Young (2000), p. 7.

[32] Woodly (2015), p. 214.

[33] Koivunen (2018), p. 1.

NUM's charter bears the following statement: "*Nosotras no nos reconocemos como víctimas – hayamos o no sido victimizadas – ni nos dirigimos a otras mujeres, incluso las que sufren o sufrieron violencia, como víctimas, sino como sujetas de creación, potencia de hacer, voluntad de transformación (...) El punitivismo y el manodurismo, por otra parte, son usados contra nuestro legítimo derecho a la protesta social. Decimos: no en nuestro nombre*."[34] As a group, then, individuals who experience conditions of vulnerability prove their ability to enter public space, deconstructing the illusion that it is a regulated and neutral arena where anyone can discuss issues of public importance. In contrast to this approach, they enter this space as alternative publics, changing the conceptualization of the public debate process, its rules, and spaces. Most importantly, women challenge the mainstream public discourse by introducing new subjects, modes of discourse, perspectives, and viewpoints that would otherwise be overlooked or excluded.[35]

The critical issue is that these movements, along with other feminist practices across the world, have the potential to implement intersectional and transnational approaches, reassessing legal and political notions, and proposing different narratives of violence, vulnerability, privilege, power, and oppression. Within these narratives, gender and sexual violence are linked not only to patriarchal structures and the state, social inequality and justice, but also capitalism, transnational processes of exploitation, religious issues, racial and class differences, cultural struggles, and sexual orientation and identity, as well as to all the specific dimensions in which power and privilege are differently experienced between the Global North and South.

We have divided the contributions to this book into three parts.

Part I provides theoretical and historical readings of feminist practices, including the origins of various feminist movements addressing women's political and social agencies for change in the past and present.

Lucia Re discusses feminists' critical analysis of laws and legal systems by reviewing historical developments of feminist theories and formulations of different social and legal practices. Discussing theoretical standpoints of difference feminism, cultural feminism, equality feminism, and radical feminism, Re explains how the collective history among feminist theories has denounced unequal and male patriarchy of law and how it has instead adopted gender perspective in the legal system to broaden the notion of women and womanhood. This has not prevented the use of the category of woman to refer to multiple forms of oppression and discrimination. Thus, Re proposes to follow a path of linear development and plural revolution to allow for the integration of different perspectives, fostering critical contribution rather than building oppositions.

---

[34] Ni Una Menos, Carta Orgànica, at: https://niunamenos.org.ar/quienes-somos/carta-organica/ (We do not recognize ourselves as victims—whether or not we have been victimized—nor do we address other women, even those who suffer or have suffered violence, as victims, but as subjects of creation, power to act, and will to transform (...) Punitivism and manodurism, on the other hand, are used against our legitimate right to social protest. We say: not in our name).

[35] Fraser (1990), p. 66.

Thomas Casadei's historical account of theories and political activism in promoting women's emancipation focuses on the work of Anna Kuliscioff, a cosmopolitan and prominent figure in the history of Italian socialist feminism in the nineteenth century. Casadei's reflection on the concept of borderless feminism emphasizes the complexity of feminist perspectives, including governance feminism, institutionalized feminism, liberal feminism, and critical race feminism. Casadei discusses the diversity of feminist practices in different time periods. Thus, the evolution of theoretical concepts in feminist movements from relational capacity and care work to qualified education and work is rooted in the emergence of new demands. Along this axis of development and theoretical re-elaboration, pathways have become clearly visible, in light of the various contributions of feminist theories, seeking to expand, explore, and transform common definitions of gender and sexuality. However, this process of opening among various groups and subjects was foreshadowed by the work of Kuliscioff.

Angbin Jasmin's chapter provides an in-depth analysis of textual resources and legal documents about the status of women during the Mughal period. Jasmin's careful reading of the medieval texts and historiography of Islamic jurisprudence shows how Muslim women, as legal entities, demonstrated agency and enjoyed certain rights with regard to divorce, marriage, and property ownership, and were protected against violence. Jasmin argues that women were present in court as plaintiffs and defenders, were aware of the value of documents and testimonies, and demonstrated the power of agency under this legal system. However, the flexibility and dynamic nature of Sharia law is argued to be manipulated and misused by some groups to exercise power against women.

Part II brings together the work of scholars who study matters related to the provision of rights and discrimination in areas such as the labor market, and EU policies.

Mario Reljanović explores feminist movements' possibilities to impose ideas of gender equality and equity in highly neoliberal and individualistic societies. Reljanović focuses on how feminist collective ideas and actions can be promoted in the neoliberal labor market with broad inclusivity and intersectionality, cooperating with trade unions as well as national and international actors. Feminist theories and practices have had important effects on trade unions as they share significant similarities in their methodologies of action. Reljanović explains that although there are positive stories about the incorporation of feminist ideas and goals into trade unionism, and their implementation through collective bargaining, it seems that there is much greater potential that would have to be realized in the future, in order to create a stronger solidarity front against the devolution of workers' rights in general, as well as the more specific protection of women workers who are often the first to be impacted by the restrictive measures of neoliberal legislators or employers.

Burcu Gumus and Jón Ingvar Kjaran's critical examination of Turkish immigration, asylum and refugee regimes highlights the gradual transformation of hospitality to hostility towards people coming from the Middle East. Their study focuses on the labor market conditions among Syrian refugee women who work in textile workshops in Istanbul. Their analysis of qualitative interviews with these women, through the lenses of feminist violence studies, reveals how much cultural and legal barriers in Turkey have intensified Syrian women's experiences of precarity within economic and social contexts, leading to multiple forms of violence, including verbal abuse and physical assault perpetrated the employers.

In their chapter on the importance of gender equality at the national level in Croatia, Jelena Kasap, Višnja Lachner, and Ana Đanić Čeko discuss discrimination perpetuated against women in the labor market that is manifested in gender segregation where women are employed in "female sectors" such as education, health, and social welfare services. Moreover, women face a glass ceiling in the labor market, which has significantly lowered the number of women in managerial high-ranking positions. Regardless of the normative framework in Croatia based on the Constitution of the Republic of Croatia, the Law on Gender Equality, and the Labor Law, the underrepresentation of female presence on the boards of directors of the largest publicly listed companies as well as in the highest levels of administrative position are the most important indicators of the existence of hidden gender discrimination at the national level. Thus, the authors argue for the adoption of a new national policy to explicitly improve the position of women in the labor market and to increase the political representation of women in the processes of decision-making.

Part III concentrates on various conceptual and methodological issues within feminist theories and practices including bodies, identities, emotions, and practices of care.

Naoual El Yattouti and Benjamin Nurkić explore how the European Court of Human Rights (ECtHR) handles cases on religious symbols, such as headscarves, in comparison to other religious signs. In this investigation, El Yattouti and Nurkić shed light on how Muslim women are treated in the ECtHR, criticizing the Islamophobic and orientalist views affecting these women's access to resources and participation in society. The authors bring our attention to the intersectionality of discrimination imposed on Muslim women with different ethnic, socio-economic, class, and (dis)ability backgrounds.

Angela Condello problematizes the contradictory relations between laws and practices in countries with more egalitarian legislation and public policies where social and political inequalities are on the rise. Thus, Candello argues that achieving social justice cannot be realized without gender justice. Drawing from Marxist feminist ideas, the emphasis is paid to the relationship between demands for justice and difference as well as the work of care, both of which provide a critical examination of subjects before the law accounting for socio-economic status, class, ethnicity, age, and (dis)ability.

Sanja Djajić's chapter criticizes the lack of attention to issues of vulnerability and gender by the European Court of Human Rights (ECtHR) in relation to cases of child abduction. Cases before the Court involving the Hague Convention on the Civil Aspects of International Child Abduction (1980) are numerous and reveal certain factual and legal patterns that often go unaddressed. Statistics on international child abduction cases show that the majority of so-called "abductors" are mothers.

These mothers are foreign nationals and often the primary caregivers with custody rights, yet they typically find themselves in precarious situations in a foreign country. Hence, Djajić argues for a gender-sensitive approach combined with the application of the vulnerability in the Hague Convention cases before the ECtHR to ensure protection of human rights. Moreover, the Court is well equipped to undertake this approach that is aligned with human rights standards.

Loren Sosa's analysis of the term intersectionality highlights the limits of applying intersectionality, particularly in relation to structural inequality and discrimination. Sosa explores how a focus on human bodies can enhance legal and social understanding of intersectional discrimination by proposing a body-centered framework, positioning bodies as the material embodiment of intersecting inequalities. This approach views sexuality and reproduction not only as biological phenomena but as socially and culturally defined practices, offering insights into the socioeconomic, political, and interpersonal factors that shape discrimination and exclusion. Moreover, it underscores the symbolic representation of bodies, arguing that inclusive representation and meaningful participation can challenge stereotypes and reshape the social construction of differences. Sosa studies cases from the Inter-American Court of Human Rights on violence against trans women, applying a body-centered approach that highlights how an intersectional perspective that is rooted in corporeal experience can make visible the structural and systemic forces that perpetuate inequality, providing legal and theoretical tools to challenge entrenched biases within law and policy.

Damir Banović brings two conflicting concepts—queer theory and law—in dialogue to explore the conceptual and methodological nuances of their relationship. Focusing on the institution of marriage from both radical feminist and queer perspectives, Banović examines their intimate, economic, and sexual dimensions. According to Banović, while same-sex relationships have been normalized via social acceptance and legal recognition, the institution of marriage itself remains criticized for being rooted in unequal power relations and essentialism. However, the legal recognition of LGBT and queer relationships through registered partnerships or same-sex marriage around the world challenges the critical approach of queer and feminist theories towards marriage. Additionally, a wide range of other forms of intimate private relationships remain excluded from legal recognition.

References

Ackerly B, True J (2010) A Feminist research Ethic Explained. In: Ackerly B, True J (eds) Doing Feminist Research in Political and Social Science. Bloomsbury, pp 21–39

Ampofo AA and Beoku-Bettes J (2021) Producing inclusive feminist knowledge – Positionalities and discourses in the global south. J Adv Gender Res 31

Bernardini MG, Casalini L, Giolo O, Re L (eds) (2018) Vulnerabilità, etica, politica e diritto. IF Press, Roma

Butler J (1990) Gender Trouble. Routledge, London

Butler J (1993) Bodies that matter: on the discursive limits of sex. Routledge, London

Butler J (2016) Rethinking vulnerability and resistance. In: Butler J, Gambetti Z, Sabsay L (eds) Vulnerability and resistance. Duke University Press, Durham
Casadei T (2012) Soggetti in contesto: vulnerabilità e diritti umani, in Diritti umani e soggetti vulnerabili: violazioni, trasformazioni, aporie. Giappichelli, Torino
Connell R, Pearse B (2015) Gender: In World Perspective, 3rd edn. Polity Press, Cambridge Uk and Malkden, MA
Espinosa-Minosa Y (2024) A decolonial critique of feminist epistemology critique. In: De Suoza Lima L, Otero Quezada E, Roth J (eds) Feminisms in movement – theories and practices from the Americas. Transcript Verlag, Bielefeld, pp 79–90
Evans E, Lepinard E (eds) (2020) Intersectionality in feminist and queer movements. Routledge, London
Farris S (2017) In the name of women's rights: the rise of femonationalism. Duke University Press
Feinberg J (1970) The nature and value of rights. J Value Inq 4(4):243–260
Felix de Souza NM (2018) Gender in the global south: disturbing international boundaries. Spec Iss Contex Int 40(3)
Ferree MM, Mueller CM (2004) Feminism and the women's movement: a global perspective, The Blackwell companion to social movements, pp 576–607
Fraser N (1990) Rethinking the public sphere: a contribution to the critique of actually existing democracy. Social Text 25/26:56–80
Fredman S (2016) Substantive equality revisited, Oxford University Press and New School University School of Law. I*CON 14(3):712–738. https://doi.org/10.1093/icon/mow043
Jaggar A (1983) Feminist politics and human nature. Rowman and Littlefield
Koivunen A (2018) Vulnerability as a political language. In: Koivunen TA, Kyrölä K, Ryberg I (eds) The power of vulneralibility. Mobilizing affect in feminist, queer and anti-racist media cultures. Manchester University Press, Manchester
Lepinard E (2020) Feminist trouble. Oxford University Press, Oxford
Macioce F (2024) Reassessing the notion of vulnerability: the feminist debate. In: Lacey N, Jovanović MA, Spaic B, Zdravković A (eds) Reassessing feminist legal theories. Cham, Springer
MacKinnon CA (1982) Feminism, marxism, method, and the state: an agenda for theory. Signs J Women Cult Soc 7(3):515–544
Martinez-Cairo B, Buscemi E (2021) Latin American decolonial feminisms: theoretical perspectives and challenges. https://doi.org/10.4000/alhim.10153
Monro S (2018) Sexualities studies: the last 20 years. Sexualities 21(8):1229–1233
Puar J (2013) Rethinking homonationalism. Int J Middle East Stud 45(2):336–339
Sarachild K (1975) Consciousness raising: a radical weapon. Redstockings, Inc
Walby S (2011) The future of feminism. Polity
Wing AK, Pappalardo C (2023) Critical race feminism: a different approach to feminist theory. In: Vujadinović D et al (eds) Feminist approaches to law – theoretical and historical insights. Springer, pp 53–72
Woodly D (2015) Seeing collectivity: structural relation through the lens of youngian seriality. Contemp Polit Theory 14(3):213–233
Young IM (2000) Inclusion and democracy. Oxford University Press, Oxford

Zara Saeidzadeh PhD in Gender Studies, is an affiliate assistant professor at Simone de Beauvoir Institute, Concordia University, Montreal, Canada. Her research focuses on law, gender and violence, emphasizing feminist decolonial and intersectional methodologies. Her recent work examines trans people's socio-legal recognition, building on theories of recognition and trans citizenship. Among others, her recent publications include: Trans* Citizenship in Feminist Theories and Practices. In N. Lacey et al. (Eds.), *Reassessing Feminist Legal Theories*. Springer 2025 as well as Trans* Women's Experiences of Epistemic Misrecognition in Swedish Law and Society. *Social Politics: International Studies in Gender, State and Society* 2025.

Fabio Macioce PhD, is a full professor of Philosophy of Law and Bioethics at LUMSA University, School of Law, Rome. He held visiting positions at Cambridge University, UK, Universidad de Valencia, and University of Oxford. Since 2019, he has been working as an expert for the Council of Europe in the field of bioethics. His research focuses on individual and group vulnerability; migration, democracy, and legal pluralism; legal feminism; bioethics and informed consent; the relationship between law and religion; and the impact of AI on human rights. He has written and edited several books and journal articles in English, Italian, French, and Spanish. His latest books are: The Politics of Vulnerable Groups: Implications for Philosophy, Law, and Political Theory, Springer Nature, 2022; The Law of Beauty. The Troubled Relationship Between Law and Aesthetic, Routledge 2025.

Dragica Vujadinović is a full professor at the Faculty of Law, University of Belgrade, teaching Political and Legal Theories at master and doctoral studies, as well as Introduction to the EU Political System at master's study program Master in European Integration (MEI) and Feminist Political and Legal Theories, Methodology and Practical Skills, and Gender Competent Family Law at master's study program Law and Gender (LAWGEM). She was the Head of MEI and LAWGEM master academic studies. She was the UB coordinator for the Erasmus Mundus Design Measures project (EMDM) (2023–2024), for preparing with Örebro University and LUMSA the future joint master and for applying for Erasmus Mundus Joint Master (EMJM)—Law, Gender, Intersectionality and Diversity (LAWGID). She has been the co-editor of the Springer book series Gender Perspectives in Law. She published 20 monographs and edited volumes and made many contributions for international and national academic journals. Her list of publications is available at: http://ius.bg.ac.rs/nastavnici/драгица-вујадиновић/

Historicity of Feminist Legal and Political Theories and Practices

Law, Rights, and Gender: Where Do We Stand?

Lucia Re

Abstract In recent decades, the gender analysis of law has gained visibility and importance internationally and in the European area. It has, however, partly distanced itself from the original feminist approach. The emergence of a gendered perspective on law is therefore criticized as much by those who would deny its prominence as by those who fear that it distorts the original feminist claims. Contemporary feminism is a plural movement that presents different approaches as much to the concept of gender as to the relationship between gender, law, rights, and jurisdictional claiming strategies. The essay aims to examine these different approaches in the light of the history of feminist analyses of law, questioning the need to accommodate the critiques of some currents of feminism, without, however, renouncing the language of rights. This is understood as an indispensable tool that nevertheless cannot be considered a panacea and must be enlivened by practices of activism.

1 Introduction

In this chapter I propose an exploration of feminist legal thought, tracing its evolution and highlighting its contemporary significance. I begin by addressing the increasing visibility and importance of gender analysis in law. I then underscore how this analysis has transitioned from its original feminist roots to encompass broader perspectives, prompting both critique and adaptation. A central theme discussed is the plurality within feminism itself, showcasing diverse approaches to the concepts of gender, law, rights, and strategies for claiming justice. These varied perspectives are examined in light of the historical trajectory of feminist legal thought, addressing the need to integrate critiques from different feminist currents while preserving the language of rights. This language, although not a panacea, is

L. Re (✉)
University of Florence, Florence, Italy
e-mail: lucia.re@unifi.it

F. Macioce et al. (eds.), *Feminist Legal and Political Practices*, Gender Perspectives in Law 6, https://doi.org/10.1007/978-3-032-02856-3_2

positioned as a vital tool that must be animated by activism and contextualized within social practices.

By framing the discussion within this dynamic and pluralistic context, the chapter highlights the relevance of feminist theory in reshaping legal systems and its potential to foster transformative changes, including in the constitutional models, that respond to the complexities of contemporary gender justice. Sometimes different feminist visions lead to conflict and, in particular, leaving aside the legacy coming from some less recent currents of feminism. I argue that we should not allow disagreements to lead to the dissipation of theoretical, political and legal valuable guidance. In particular, the key lesson of the feminist movements of the 1970s and 1980s lies in the self-reflective nature of feminist thought, the integration of theory and practice, its emphasis on singularity, and its focus on women's freedom understood as the pursuit of self-expression beyond gender stereotypes. These characteristics provide valuable insights for legal thought and practice. Similarly, the attention to specific cases, the framing of rights within relational contexts, and the prioritization of care—understood both as labor and as a broader activity aimed at maintaining social bonds—are significant contributions that we should take up in order to counter the pushes to disintegrate the model of the constitutional State and revive, including on the gender equality front, the full implementation of the principle of substantive equality, which, as I will try to show, is pivotal as much for the constitutional State as for human rights theory.

2 Feminist Reflection on Law

The history of western feminism is conventionally distinguished into three different "waves" that have gradually overlapped: (1) "equality feminism", which has ancient roots but became more visible in the modern age, particularly within liberal and then socialist thought. This current of feminism aims to obtain the same rights for women as men. It focuses on equality understood as sameness; (2) "difference feminism", to which U.S. "cultural feminism" is assimilated. It has developed since the 1970s in the West, when claims for greater equality between men and women had made inroads into theoretical debate and political discussion, to the extent that it led to major reforms. This current believes it is wrong to equate women with the male model of patriarchal origin and intends to value "sexual difference". This is sometimes understood as natural, sometimes as a socially constructed difference, but one that has an important cultural and political significance; (3) the "third-wave feminism" in which different orientations converge, united by the critique of both the men/women dichotomy (so-called gender binarism) and the construction of a uniform category of "women", which does not take into account the different conditions in which women from different backgrounds live. It includes postmodernist, black, postcolonial and decolonial feminism, transfeminism and queer currents that not only embrace a conception of gender as a social construct but also highlight its unstable character. Like any historiographical convention, the representation of "waves" simplifies the complexity of the feminist debate and its historical development, but it is useful in highlighting some relevant caesuras.

Smart (1992), partially distancing herself from the image of feminist waves, identified three phases of feminist reflection on law, arguing that it emphasized: in a first phase, the sexist character of law; in a second phase, its male character; and in a third phase, its gendered character. The first phase corresponds to the claims of "equality feminism". In the second phase, feminist theorists denounced the not only unequal but properly male character of law. This argument was already present in the writings of Olympe de Gouges, regarded as the initiator of legal feminism. As Facchi and Giolo note,[1] in rewriting the *Déclaration des droits de l'homme et du citoyen* as *Déclaration des droits de la femme et de la citoyenne*, including rights such as that of every woman to declare who is the father of her children born out of wedlock, de Gouges "(...) does not simply call for the 'enlargement' of the entitlement of rights to the point of including women". Rather, she

> 'splits' the subject, declining the Declaration itself in feminine terms: in this way, it becomes clear that it is not enough to 'implicitly' include women, expanding the meaning of the given notion and thus the scope of rights, but, for inclusion to be effective, it is necessary to transform that very subject of rights, which had not previously considered women.

However, the denunciation of the male character of law was made explicit and deepened by the radical feminism of the 1970s, Feminist Legal Studies, cultural feminism, including the ethics of care, and European difference feminism.

Radical feminism is usually included in the second wave that has emerged since the 1970s. It has had an important development in the United States, where it is also referred to as "dominance theory". Like difference feminism and cultural feminism, it rejects the approach based on claiming formal equality between men and women. Rather, it focuses on the systematic oppression of women within the patriarchal system, male violence against them and sexual exploitation. For these feminists, the problem is thus not so much one of making men and women equal, but that of overthrowing patriarchal power, working as much on the level of the critique of the institutions and the legal tools that contribute to its consolidation as on the level of "cultural hegemony", to make women aware of the domination they have internalized and invite them to break free of their chains. In the United States, leading theorists of radical feminism include Catharine Mackinnon and Andrea Dworkin. In Italy, radical feminism is traced back to the *Rivolta femminile* group, animated in particular by Carla Lonzi, whose thought, however, also inspires "difference thinking".

Feminist Legal Studies—or Fem-crits—arose within the Critical Legal Studies developed, especially in Anglo-American circles, since the 1980s, and inspired by the desire to unmask the power relations that law reflects and, at the same time, reinforces.[2]

---

[1] Facchi and Giolo (2023), p. 60. Translated by the author.

[2] See Minda (1995).

"Ethics of care" refers to the strand of feminist analysis inaugurated by psychologist Carol Gilligan (1982) with the essay *In A Different Voice*. This orientation, aimed at denouncing the invisibilization of knowledge and practices developed by women and the false universalism of dominant liberalism by placing the value of care at the center of reflection, has extended to different fields of knowledge: from education, to ethics, politics, health, and, to a lesser extent, law.

Finally, "feminism of difference" has spread, in particular, in France and Italy since the second half of the 1970s and during the 1980s. Among the main authors ascribable to this feminist current one should mention Luce Irigaray, to whom we owe a theory of "sexual difference" aimed, on the one hand, at highlighting the male character of Western philosophical thought and psychoanalysis,[3] and, on the other, at making "sexual difference" the ontological basis on which to build an ethics and politics that would allow the emergence of the "woman subject".[4] However, different positions have always existed within feminist groups that refer to "sexual difference". In particular, some feminists disagree with the ontological foundation of it proposed by Irigaray and focus on the heuristic value of "difference" and its nature as a social construct that induces political positioning.[5] Among the French groups, *Psy et Po* may be mentioned. Among the Italians, the *Diotima* collective, the group linked to the *Libreria delle donne di Milano*, and the *Gruppo del mercoledì*.

If some of the currents traceable to the second wave, following de Gouges' inspiration, have yearned for the construction of a "universalism of specificities",[6] that is, to maintain the universalist horizon by enriching it through the specification of differences, others have focused, rather, on the valorization of "sexual difference" within an identity politics that rejects all forms of universalism. The ones have promoted some legal reforms, yet without taking this strategy as central to feminist struggles. The others intended to work toward a subversion of the patriarchal system that would also pass through a radical modification of legal and institutional structures.

For radical feminists and Feminist Legal Studies, law is forged within a gender structure that oppresses women. It is therefore not blind to sexual difference, although the metaphor of "blindness" to gender, color, etc. is at the heart of liberal legal rhetoric. Law, in fact, sees sexual difference very well, since it is constructed as an instrument of domination to keep women in a subordinate position to men and authorize their exploitation. It is then a matter of overthrowing this domination, also making use of the legal instrument, which must, however, be redesigned taking into account the needs and experiences of women. Emblematic in this regard is the trajectory of Mackinnon, who has dedicated her work and commitment as an advocate to the fight for women's rights and to counteract male violence against them: from denouncing harassment in the workplace as a form of sex discrimination, to fighting

---

[3] Irigaray (1974).

[4] Irigaray (1984).

[5] See Boccia (2002) and Melandri (2012).

[6] Loche (2021), p. 26. Translated by the author.

against pornography that spreads a degrading image of women and fosters violence against them, to defining wartime rape as an act of genocide, affirmed in defending Croatian and Bosnian women who were victims of rape during the war in the former Yugoslavia. For Mackinnon:[7] "Law is not everything in this respect, but it is not nothing either". It is therefore a tool for women to use, shaping it so that it can meet their needs. Law has non-negligible material and symbolic power and can therefore serve to fight against oppression. To ignore it, on the other hand, would mean to accept that it operates in the service of patriarchal domination.

In turn, authors traceable to Feminist Legal Studies, although aware of the power relations behind legal institutions and guiding policies, have dealt with laws on violence against women, those on workplace discrimination, reproductive autonomy, social rights, and family law, also proposing new methods for legal analysis and legal education.[8]

Exponents of cultural feminism, but especially European difference feminists, while often contributing to the debate on legislative reform and legal interpretation, have instead shown a distrust of law as a useful tool for women.

Equality feminism and radical feminism have guided the developments that have occurred in international, European, and many national legal systems, especially since the 1970s, leading to the recognition of women's human rights and the spread of gender mainstreaming, aimed at including in every policy adopted an assessment of its impact on gender relations. These are approaches that international and European institutions have increasingly taken seriously, fostering important legal and social changes. Gender mainstreaming was defined in the following terms by the Beijing Declaration and Platform for Action, adopted in the 16th Plenary Meeting, at the UN Fourth World Conference on Women, on September 15, 1995 (§ 202):

> In addressing the issue of mechanisms for promoting the advancement of women, Governments and other actors should promote an active and visible policy of mainstreaming a gender perspective in all policies and programmes so that, before decisions are taken, an analysis is made of the effects on women and men, respectively.

It was then defined also by the European Commission in 1996, as a way of mobilizing all general policies and measures specifically for the purpose of achieving gender equality (Brussels, 04.03.1998 COM (1998) 122 final). The principle was incorporated into the Amsterdam Treaty (art. 2 and 3) in 1997.

From a perspective focused on women's rights, however, there has been a gradual shift to a focus on gender equality, referring to both men and women and attentive to the rights of LGBTQIA+ minorities. The words "sex", "women", and "gender" are then used in legal norms sometimes as equivalent or overlapping terms, although on the theoretical level they are considered to refer, respectively, to biological sex (which is also considered by many feminists as an object of cultural interpretation), to the historically discriminated group of women (also defined from

---

[7] Mackinnon (1987), p. 116.

[8] Cf. Menkel-Meadow (1988).

their sexual identity), and to the construction of male and female roles, corresponding to social expectations.

The use of the term "gender" has become widespread in academic studies and policy-making in the 2000s, to accommodate the perspective that considers gender as a social construction and that intends to broaden the protection historically provided for women to sexual minorities as well. As it will be further explained below, according to some scholars and activists, this broadening of perspective is necessary and should lead to the abandonment of the category "women" and, where not strictly necessary, of the reference to biological "sex". According to others, however, such an outcome would correspond to the return under a new guise of the universal "neutral" which, in societies still strongly marked by patriarchal domination, corresponds to the male (cisgender).

If these are the concerns of those who turn to law as a tool for achieving gender justice, however, it must be pointed out that even today there are feminist perspectives that declare themselves wary of the use of law. In particular, distrust and suspicion of the feminist strategy based on claiming rights is still manifested today in feminist positions that, although with different accents from those of the second wave, criticize not only the "equality model", but also the lack of radicalism of this strategy. Indeed, it would entail accepting the existing institutional structures and the prevalence of liberal ideology. Moreover, it would lend itself to consolidating the ethnocentric universalism that characterizes the genesis of human rights theory and the way they are used *ex parte principis* in different areas of the world to impose Western dominance. Finally, it would contribute to the formation of a female *élite* that would re-propose hierarchies only formally different from those typical of the ancient patriarchal system, including hierarchies between different feminisms coming out from different regions of the world.[9]

The contemporary landscape thus sees the coexistence of different feminist theories that have different attitudes toward law, the relationship between law and gender, and the jurisdictional claiming of rights.

3 The "Sexual Contract" and Women's Rights

To understand contemporary feminist reflection on law, it is appropriate to take a step back and dwell on the modern roots of law, politics, and the State. In particular, it should be noted that within modern Western liberal legislative States,[10] inspired by the principle of isonomy and hinged on the protection of individual rights,

[9] Cf. Arruzza et al. (2019); Gordon and Rottenberg (2023); Rottenberg (2018); Spivak (1996); Lepinard (2020).

[10] I use this expression to distinguish between the legislative State of liberal origin, born in the West between the eighteenth and the nineteenth century, and the constitutional State, i.e., the model established by the experience of the Austrian Constitution of 1920 and then taken up by post-World War II European constitutionalism (cf. Ferrajoli 2002; Santoro 2008).

women's access to citizenship rights has been severely limited. Despite the participation of some intellectuals, starting with de Gouges herself, in the debates developed during the Enlightenment and the prominence of women from different social backgrounds in the eighteenth-century revolutions,[11] women were ousted from the social contract by a form of gendered constitutionalism that, according to Ruth Rubio Marín (2022), can be called "exclusionary". Indeed, the liberal era opened with the consolidation of the distinction between the private and public spheres and the exclusion of women from the latter.[12] This form of constitutionalism ensured the "constitutional embedding of the breadwinner family order".[13] The stabilization of an unequal gender regime occurred, then, not against law, but through law, starting with civil law.

For the history of women's rights does not in fact apply the usual distinction between generations of rights, according to the scheme proposed by Thomas Marshall (1950), whereby civil rights were first established and then were political and social rights. Women's status has long remained linked to their role in reproduction, understood in both a sexual and a social sense,[14] and some civil rights were acquired much later than important social and political rights. Sexual difference, understood as a hetero-imposition, naturalized and linked to the role of wife and mother, has thus been, within the modern constitutional model, a cage that has prevented women from full participation in social, political, and economic life. Such a constitutional model arose out of the eighteenth-century liberal constitutions and developed, in the European continent, through the nineteenth-century codifications. In this framework, women's inclusion in the social covenant came about through the institution of marriage, which placed them under guardianship, handing them a halved citizenship.[15] A similar development is present in the coeval evolution of common law.[16]

Even today, the reflection of the modern constitutional model is present in legal systems and jurisprudential interpretation, even in countries that have formally recognized gender equality. On the judicial interpretation of national and local courts, many examples could be given. Great controversy has been aroused, for example, in Spain and Italy, by rulings on cases of sexual violence in which the autonomy of the woman was not recognized because of stereotypes assumed by judges as the basis for their decision, so as to lead to the secondary victimization of the woman who

---

[11] See on the subject Marand-Fouquet (1989); Godineau (1988); Rossi Doria (2007).

[12] See, *ex multis*, Baer (2022).

[13] Rubio Marín (2022), p. 132.

[14] "Social reproduction", in the lexicon suggested by Marxist feminism, means all activities aimed at maintaining and reproducing the labor force and thus, primarily, care work. This work, invisibilized and devalued, has historically been delegated to women. It represents the lynchpin of the development and functioning of the capitalist economy, but it has been treated as a private matter of little importance (cf. Fortunati 1995).

[15] See, *ex multis*, Facchi and Giolo (2023).

[16] See Baer (2022), p. 10.

had reported the violence.[17] From the perspective of the family and couple model crystallized by legislation, consider a country like Italy where only since 2022 it has been possible to choose the maternal surname in addition to or instead of the paternal one, thanks to a Constitutional Court ruling that declared the previous automatism illegitimate (Constitutional Court No. 131 of 2022). Moreover, in Italy parental leave laws are designed having the mother as an almost exclusive reference. This family model is also present in the legislation of other European countries, albeit in a less pronounced way.[18] Social organization revolving around a stereotypical idea of the mononuclear family, in which women continue to be given priority in caregiving duties, means that marriage often proves to be a trap for women. As Susan Moller Okin wrote,[19] "Marriage has a long history, and we live in its shadow".

A central juncture in legal history is the construction of modern social and political organization. Indeed, the society of individuals, conceived as free and equal, which we have inherited from the Enlightenment and liberal traditions, rests on a gender hierarchy that is presented as the natural result of sexual difference.[20] Within modern contractualist reflection, women have not been thought of as parties to the social contract. They may, however, be parts of the "sexual contract", which, while being the very basis of the social covenant signed between "brothers" who conceive of themselves as free and equal, is concealed on the theoretical, political and legal level. As Carole Pateman wrote:[21] "Liberty, equality *and* fraternity form the revolutionary trilogy because liberty and equality are the attributes of the fraternity who exercise the law of male sex-right". And also:

> Sex is central to the original contract. The brothers make the agreement to secure their natural liberty, part of which consists in the patriarchal right of men, the right of one sex. Only one sex has the capacity to enjoy civil freedom. Civil freedom includes right of sexual access to women and, more broadly, the enjoyment of mastery as a sex (...).[22]

It was through this contract, then, that the ancient patriarchal structures were redrawn in the modern era, on the basis of the distinction between the public and private spheres, through which issues of social reproduction were depoliticized. The very meaning of the "individual", understood in an abstract sense as a disembodied subject, is grasped only as long as the internal dichotomies within civil society between natural and civilized, private and public, women and individual remain

[17] On gender stereotypes and law, see, *ex multis*, Bernardini and Giolo (2024). On the Spanish Court controversial decision in the case called "La manada" (Segunda Sección de la Audiencia Provincial de Navarra, Sentencia n° 38/2018 de 26 de abril 2018), see e.g. Pozzolo (2019). On the Italian case-law see e.g. Di Nicola Travaglini (2021).

[18] See Minello and Nannicini (2024).

[19] Okin (1989), p. 140.

[20] Emblematic in this regard is certainly the thought of Jean-Jacques Rousseau.

[21] Pateman (1988), p. 114.

[22] Pateman (1988), p. 125.

intact.[23] Pateman[24] also notes that: “The men who (are said to) make the original contract are *white* men, and their fraternal pact has three aspects; the social contract, the sexual contract and the slave contract that legitimizes the rule of white over black”.

For Pateman, as for most second-wave feminists, however, it is not only a matter of denouncing the fact that women are “the second sex”,[25] that is, they are structurally subordinated to men who embody the neutral subject. Therefore, it is not enough to break the cages in which women are constrained, but it is also necessary to claim their full participation in social, political and economic life as bearers of different experiences, knowledge and points of view, which must be recognized and valued. On this point, however, radical feminism, on the one hand, and cultural feminism and difference feminism, on the other, have been somewhat divided. The latter two, while showing great caution in the use of the legal instrument, have worked toward the construction of “a law for two”,[26] which would take into account the diversity of men’s and women’s experiences, particularly in the spheres of family law, rights over one’s own body, exposure to violence, and submission to social and criminal control. They pointed out the existence of both social and legal norms that systematically disadvantage women, claiming the need for a radical change—cultural and political in nature—that starts with women themselves. The proposal of the ethics of care theorists, in particular, has been to bring the women’s model of care into the public space, favoring a transformation of labor laws, welfare models, criminal laws, etc., but without considering legislative reforms as a priority.[27] At the same time, legal theorists close to this perspective have been working on the formulation of new interpretive criteria, which would take into account the “women’s difference”, challenging those established by tradition and inspired by the model of the “reasonable man”.[28] This work is still ongoing and particularly complex—think of the still frequent debates about the reactions of women victims of violence, which affect the determination of their consent.[29]

Radical feminism has moved in a partly convergent direction—particularly with regard to male violence against women and its criminalization—in part divergent, as it has held that the “difference vs. equality” dilemma nevertheless keeps women anchored to the male model, whether it is taken as a standard to be achieved or as a

---

[23] The point is emphasized by Pateman (1988) although partially differently from how I have taken it up here. The author also, while appreciating constructivist reflection on gender, adds to the dichotomies that allow the meaning of the term “individual” to remain intact the one between sex and gender, 225.

[24] Pateman (1988), p. 221.

[25] Beauvoir de (1949).

[26] Pitch (1998). Translated by the author.

[27] Among the main theorists of the ethics of care one can mention Carol Gilligan, Virginia Held, Joan Tronto. Among the legal theorists who are close to the ethics of care one can recall Jennifer Nedelsky.

[28] Hébert (2007).

[29] See footnote 17.

parameter from which to "differ"[30]. In the eyes of radical feminists what matters is the power differential between men and women. From this perspective, cultural feminism risks reinforcing gender stereotypes and fostering women's internalization of domination. Harsh, for example, is Mackinnon's[31] assessment of Gilligan's work. She writes:

> Women value care because men have valued us according to the care we give them, and we could probably use some. Women think in relational terms because our existence is defined in relation to men. Further, when you are powerless, you don't just speak differently. A lot, you don't speak. Your speech is not just differently articulated, it is silenced. Eliminated, gone. You aren't just deprived of a language with which to articulate your distinctiveness, although you are; you are deprived of a life out of which articulation might come. Not being heard is not just a function of lack of recognition, not just that no one knows how to listen to you, although it is that; it is also silence of the deep kind, the silence of being prevented from having anything to say. Sometimes it is permanent. All I am saying is that the damage of sexism is real, and reifying that into differences is an insult to our possibilities.

Despite polemical accents and important differences in approach,[32] it should be noted that cultural feminism and difference feminism as well as radical feminism have criticized not only the exclusionary framework of eighteenth and nineteenth-century liberal constitutionalism, but also the assumptions of the "inclusive gender constitutionalism"[33] that was established, in the West and, in particular, in Europe, in the aftermath of World War II. This began to recognize women's rights by equating them with men, but only in some respects, as it maintained a strong division of care work and crystallized traditional gender roles that placed women in an inferior position to men.

If on the level of diagnosis there is a common ground between second-wave feminisms, on the level of prognosis there is, however, a significant divergence. For cultural feminists—and at least for part of European difference feminism—it is indeed a matter of rediscovering and enhancing the importance of care and related women's knowledge through two different strategies: on the one hand, by making women's voices heard in the legal professions (particularly in the judiciary) and, on the other, by encouraging the adoption of laws and social policies directed at recognizing care work, including by resorting to special forms of protection (maternity leave, flexible working hours, part-time work, etc.). Laws that include a women's point of view have also been invoked, particularly by the theory of law inspired by cultural feminism, in the areas of business and tax law, in order to better support care duties and family responsibilities, or in that relating to legal liability, e.g. advocating the creation of tort duties to assist strangers who are in peril.[34]

---

[30] See Mackinnon (1987), p. 34.

[31] Mackinnon (1987), p. 39.

[32] On how Mackinnon criticizes, and misunderstands, European "difference thinking" and Gilligan's theses, I refer to Re (2015).

[33] Rubio Marín (2022).

[34] For a concise review of these positions and the work of leading jurists attributable to this orientation see Turnier et al. (2009).

For radical feminism, on the other hand, it is necessary to liberate women from the yoke of care, making them aware of the exploitation they have been victims of for millennia. These currents of feminism have particularly clashed over policies directed at protecting motherhood and reconciling outside work and family work. While cultural feminists considered it important to value and protect motherhood, liberal feminists viewed special forms of protection as an expression of paternalism aimed at keeping women at a disadvantage in competition with male workers, and radical feminists denounced the trap of motherhood viewed as the fate of women.

As a whole, second-wave feminism called not for a mere inclusion of women in the social, political, legal and economic system forged for men, but for its refounding to take into account sexual difference by fostering women's full participation. The contribution of these feminist orientations was thus instrumental in the transition from "inclusive gender constitutionalism" to a "participatory gender constitutionalism",[35] also characterized by greater international projection, which recognized women's role in society and the political sphere.

4 Law and Gender

The overcoming of a binary conception of gender corresponds to the third phase of feminist reflection on law, highlighted by Smart (1992), in which feminists also see law as a malleable tool that can be reshaped. Overcoming in a constructivist sense the categories of gender and the man/woman opposition makes it possible to hold together the claim to equality, not only formal but also substantive, with the valorization of differences, breaking both the identity cages constructed by patriarchal culture and the excessive homogeneity of the category "women", which, as U.S. black feminists and postcolonial and decolonial thinkers have pointed out,[36] risks perpetuating other forms of oppression, such as class and racial domination.

If law can be declined from a gender perspective as a social construction, it can be as much an instrument of oppression as it is an instrument of emancipation. Smart (1992) enthusiastically assesses this development. Yet, it risks erasing from culture, politics, law, and theory the "unforeseen subject" that radical feminists, theorists of sexual difference, and the first ethicists of care had made visible after millennia of oblivion. The "unforeseen subject"[37] that radical feminists, theorists of sexual difference and authors traceable to the first school of the ethics of care had helped to make re-emerge. It is worthwhile, once again, to cite Pateman's analysis[38] which, as mentioned, positively evaluates the adoption of a constructivist notion of "gender". Indeed, she notes that:

---

[35] Rubio Marín (2022).

[36] Cf. Hooks (1984, 1989); Mohanty (1984); Spivak (1996).

[37] Cf. Lonzi (2010), p. 47. Translated by the author.

[38] Pateman (1988), p. 225.

> 'Gender' was introduced as a crucial weapon in the struggle against patriarchy. The patriarchal claim is that women are naturally subject to men, subject, that is, because of their biology, their sex. To refer to gender instead of sex indicates that women's position is not dictated by nature, by biology or sex, but is a matter of social and political contrivance.

However, immediately afterwards she adds:

> True; what men and women are, and how relations between them are structured, depends on a good deal more than their natural physiology and biology. It is also true, however, that the meaning of men's and women's natures, even the depiction of male and female skeletons and physiology, has depended on the political significance accorded to manhood and womanhood. To use the language of gender reinforces the language of the civil, the public and the individual, a language that depends on the repression of the sexual contract.[39]

That of the relationship between the construction of gender and women's political and legal subjectivity is indeed a challenge that contemporary feminism must be able to face, since feminism has taken its cue from the struggles of women who, in the name of an anti-patriarchal vision, have denounced their own subordination to men. The category "woman" itself, while being aware that it must be constructed from the different conditions of women, can thus be understood as "an antagonism that breaks the identity imposed on women by masculine domination".[40]

The constructivist perspective has challenged the categories of "woman" and "man" and their centrality in political, social cultural and legal discourse, paving the way for overcoming gender binarism. At the same time, as Pateman denounces, if one completely disregards the notion of "women" and the highlighting of inequality between men and women, the risk is to lose reference to the specificity of the oppression to which women have been and, to a large extent, are still subjected. This specificity has mainly to do, as noted above, with the "sexual contract" and the division of labor between men and women that has shifted the burden of social reproduction onto the latter. This should not lead to obliterating the fact that some women bear this burden more than others, nor should it lead to underestimating, ignoring or, even worse, denying the various forms of oppression faced by people who identify as LGBTQIA+.[41] Keeping the reference to "women", in politics as well as in law, however, allows us not to forget the specific forms of discrimination and violence against women that have been invisible for millennia. At the same time, it allows us to continue to value certain genealogies and experiences of women that second-wave feminism had brought to light.

On the level of critique, women's political and legal subjectivity and constructivist gender perspectives can be reconciled, including through theories such as those that today suggest a broadening of the very notion of "women" to include transgender people who identify as such and a reinterpretation of the definition of "second sex" in a plural sense as referring to the "second sexes", i.e., all those—e.g., women,

---

[39] Pateman (1988), p. 225.

[40] Rudan (2023), p. XVI.

[41] As is the case in the controversy opposing trans-exclusionary-radical-feminists (TERFs) and transfeminists.

trans and queer people—who, for gender-related reasons, do not enjoy the "male privilege" that ensures that cisgender men still occupy key positions of power, both economically and politically, and are not subject to systematic gender-based violence. They also still represent—as Simone De Beauvoir pointed out more than 75 years ago now—the referent for the human being understood in a neutral sense, compared to which "others" are conceived as exceptions and occupy a subordinate position.[42] This theory is certainly interesting on the level of critique and offers insights for the construction of new political subjectivities and new alliances among discriminated and marginalized groups.

On the level of the proposal, projects aimed at embracing a constructivist notion of gender range from the pluralization of gender (and sex) itself, through the recognition of the existence of different genders (and sexes; a perspective that often calls into question scientific research, including genetic research),[43] to its fluidization, from a queer perspective which rejects stable gender identifications,[44] to an "a-gender" or "gender neutral" perspective, which, by eliminating all reference to gender, at the same time erases the discriminations that are linked to this social construction considered obsolete, freeing subjects and bodies from a normativity—both social and legal—judged oppressive.[45]

Some of these projects, however, in the name of overcoming gender binarism, risk eclipsing any reference to the sexed body—which is, to be sure, itself socially interpreted, but is no less relevant—and again silencing women's emergence as a political subject. They accuse of essentialism those who still refer to the category "women", as if it were simply a legacy of the past, which must be overcome in order to develop a discourse free from the use of normative categories.[46]

"Woman" is a category that refers to oppression and the multiple forms of discrimination and exploitation in which it is embodied, but which, as has happened repeatedly in the history of feminist thought and struggles, can be re-signified: from a label forged to justify subordination to a political subjectivity that fosters liberation. This does not mean, as mentioned, that all women are oppressed equally and that liberation strategies are the same or even convergent for all, nor does it mean denying that some women may oppress others or may oppress some men who are subjected to processes of racialization and marginalization.[47] It does mean, however, to note that without the rupture acted by the thought of sexual difference, that has opened a breach in the patriarchal order, denouncing the false neutrality of the male model and showing the existence of different genealogies and different epistemes, not even the thematization of other gender identities or gender fluidity would have

[42] Cf. Bottici (2022), p. 275.

[43] Cf. Fausto-Sterling (1993), who argues for the existence of at least five sexes.

[44] For an introduction to these debates see Fineman et al. (2009). With particular reference to international law, see Otto (2018) and Gilleri (2024).

[45] Cf., e.g., Gheaus (2012); Verdu Sanmartin (2023).

[46] Rudan (2023), pp. XIV–XV.

[47] Cf. Hooks (1984, 1989).

been possible, as it is evidenced in part by the theoretical journey of an author like Judith Butler.[48] Butler is regarded as a leading exponent of contemporary queer feminism for her theory of the performativity of gender, according to which gender is not an essence but is a doing. However, in her reflection the feminism of difference has had a significant impact, as evidenced by her interest in Luce Irigaray's theory.[49] On Butler's relationship to "sexual difference" there is an interesting debate that moves particularly from the pages of *Undoing Gender* (2004). I find convincing the interpretation given by Lorenzo Bernini (2016), according to which Butler does not deny "sexual difference", but, viewing it as the place from which to interrogate the relationship between the biological and the cultural datum, proposes that it remain open, that it not be defined once and for all. In this sense, Butler also appears close to the most interesting theories of Italian "sexual difference" thought, which focus on self-consciousness and reflection from the self.

The challenge of holding together the constructivist perspective and the legacy of second-wave reflection is political but also legal, because it invests the way of conceiving rights and law, affirmative policies, distributive policies, gender mainstreaming, the question of an "equal democracy",[50] the fight against gender-based violence, etc. Thus, it is not a matter of choosing an abstract paradigm, the result of theoretical speculation, but of using theoretical reflection to forge legal instruments, both at the level of policy-making and of judicial interpretation. And this is precisely one of the main lessons of feminism—and feminist legal theory—which has always drawn attention to the inseparability of theory and practice.

Rubio Marín[51] assessed favorably the advent of a constructivist notion of gender and the beginning of its reception in legal systems and jurisprudence. This shift coincided with the advent of a fourth phase of constitutionalism, that of "transformative gender constitutionalism", which aims to disavow the foundational gender order of patriarchal constitutionalism and places women's freedom from gender-based violence, women's reproductive rights and care work at the center of the constitutional agenda. It also broadens the perspective of women's rights by claiming recognition of diverse gender identities.[52] "Transformative gender constitutionalism" thus reflects a new social order that has taken shape and is connected to a symbolic imaginary that rejects sexism and compulsory heteronormativity[53] as the ordering principles of social relations. It is composed of a range of social practices

---

[48] Butler (1990, 2004).

[49] Cf. Butler (2015).

[50] i.e. where genders are equally represented at political and institutional level and where they all participate to political activity and debates (cf. Casadei 2017; D'Amico 2020).

[51] Rubio Marín (2022), p. 21.

[52] Among the most innovative constitutions in this regard cited by Rubio Marín are: the Ecuador Constitution of 2008, the Bolivian Constitution of 2009, Nepal's 2015 Constitution, and Cuba's 2019 Constitution.

[53] i.e. the organization of every sphere of society on the basis of a gender division that recognizes only the dichotomy between males and females. For a critique see Butler (1990, 2004) and Wittig (1992).

that include normative production, claiming rights, legal interpretation, etc. It thus reinterprets universalism from the recognition of differences and defends a substantive conception of equality, drawing attention to the effectiveness of rights.

The notion of substantive equality was already present in continental European post-World War II constitutionalism. One thinks of article 3 of the Italian Constitution, which explicitly contemplates formal equality and substantive equality, committing the Republic to "remove obstacles of an economic and social nature, which, by effectively limiting the freedom and equality of citizens, prevent the full development of the human person and the effective participation of all workers in the political, economic and social organization of the country".[54] Due in part to this explicit formulation in the Constitution, Italian constitutionalist doctrine, jurisprudence and legal philosophy have provided numerous accurate interpretations of the principle of substantive equality that cannot be explored here.[55] However, it is interesting to note that the concept, although in a more controversial form, is also present in the legal, jurisprudential and philosophical thinking of other areas of the world, including the United States, Canada, and England. In this regard, of interest is the reflection of Sandra Fredman (2016) who, to better define substantive equality, proposes a four-dimensional approach. According to her, the right to substantive equality should aim (1) to redress disadvantage; (2) to counter prejudice, stigma, stereotyping, humiliation and violence based on a protected characteristic; (3) to enhance voice and participation, countering political and social exclusion; (4) to accommodate difference and achieve structural change. These dimensions incorporate redistribution, recognition,[56] social inclusion[57] and solidarity.[58] They encompass non domination[59] and capabilities[60] theories as well. The four dimensions should be combined in order to fulfill the principle of substantive equality. At the same time, one must be aware that this multi-dimensional approach requires synthesis and compromise, since the different dimensions can be at least partially in conflict with each other. Discussions and interpretations are then always needed. One could add to Fredman's analysis that such discussions and interpretations should always be contextual in order to address concrete needs.

The principle of "substantive equality" is pivotal in the discussion of gender equality both at national level and in international human rights law.[61] "Transformative gender constitutionalism", as it was identified by Rubio Marín, aims to fully accomplish this principle, interpreting it in the light of a broad conception of gender discrimination and advocating for legislative reforms and jurisprudential evolution

[54] Translated by the author.

[55] See, e.g., Gianformaggio (2005), Mazzarese (2006), Ferrajoli (2018).

[56] See Fraser and Honneth (2003).

[57] See Collins (2003).

[58] See Barnard (2004); Rodotà (2014).

[59] Young (1990).

[60] Sen (1999); Nussbaum (2000).

[61] See e.g. Fredman and Goldblatt (2015).

capable of removing the obstacles still linked to previous conceptions—patriarchal and maternalist—of gender constitutionalism. Fredman, too, referred precisely to the transformative nature of gender equality, driving to a redistribution of power and resources and a change in the institutional structures that perpetuate women's subordination.[62] She highlighted that change must be structural and should not be limited to changing the behaviors of individuals perpetrating discrimination.

5 Where Do We Stand?

Rubio Marín warns that the types of constitutionalism she identifies only partially correspond to the historical stages of constitutionalism, from the beginning of the modern age to the present. However, one can consider "transformative gender constitutionalism" as a form of constitutionalism that spread in the 2000s, affecting not only European and Western countries, but also some South American, African, and Asian countries. This does not mean that the other models of constitutionalism have been definitively superseded. In fact, the types overlap, at least in part, with each other. There are, however, more pronounced features depending on historical eras. Today, for example, alongside the spread of "transformative gender constitutionalism" we can detect numerous signs of regression. One thinks of the cases of Chile or Argentina, where the reforms inaugurated in recent years have come to a screeching halt.[63] And yet, the "transformative" movement can be said to be underway as much within some legal systems as at the regional and international levels.

Indeed, in the daily mediation between international, regional, national and local institutions, between public actors and nongovernmental organizations, between political and cultural forces, as well as in jurisprudential interpretation, one can glimpse the laborious making of new gender models that aim at broadening the protection of rights and the protection from violence. One can e.g. think of the interpretive strategies deployed to broaden the protection of CEDAW beyond the category of "women" for whom it was originally designed, or the interpretations of the category of "sex" offered by The Human Rights Committee of the United Nations, the Inter-American Court of Human Rights, and the European Court of Human Rights.[64]

---

[62] Fredman (2003), p. 115.

[63] For Chile, I am referring specifically to the rejection of the constitutional reform prepared as of 2019 to replace the 1980 Constitution adopted during the dictatorship. The draft had been the result of grassroots mobilizations and was considered particularly advanced in terms of gender rights and the perspective of care. In Argentina, where feminist mobilizations have multiplied especially since 2016, obtaining reforms such as the legalization of abortion approved in 2021, the new government, led by Javier Milei seems intent on taking a series of steps backward on women's rights and representation.

[64] See Gilleri (2024), especially pp. 86–87; 91–96. For more case-law examples see Rubio Marín (2022).

It is important to emphasize how the forms of "gender constitutionalism" that were mentioned here should not be understood in the strict sense as models for "accommodating" "gender issues" within legal systems. Indeed, Rubio Marín's reflection that has been taken up here aims not only to identify the position and rights of women within constitutionalism, but also, and more importantly, to reveal how precisely "gender issues" are constitutive of different forms of constitutionalism.

I therefore agree with the optimistic judgment that Smart (1992) made more than 30 years ago, and which can be confirmed, despite the strong "backlash"[65] we have been experiencing in recent years. However, there are some theoretical and political obstacles that cannot be circumvented. They must be addressed by taking up some of feminism's—and legal feminism's—reflections at their roots, in order to renew them where necessary and make them useful for the present. In particular, ways should be found to reconcile the need to preserve a specific focus on discrimination against women with the broadening of protection to LGBTQIA+ persons. Such reconciliation can be done on a case-by-case basis in gender policy design, constitutional making and legal interpretation. At the same time, it is useful not to dissipate the legacy of reflection that has been handed down by second-wave feminism, which offered a novel look at gender relations and identities, showing how they cut across every social sphere.

The great lesson of difference feminism lies in its self-reflexive character, the conjunction of theory and practice, the focus on singularities, the emphasis on women's freedom understood as free self-seeking beyond gender stereotypes. These features offer valuable tools for legal reflection and practice. Similarly, the focus on concrete cases, the framing of rights in terms of relationships, and the centrality given to care, understood both as work and as a more general activity aimed at preserving the social bond, are important legacies of the reflection carried out in the field of first ethics and then political theory of care. Despite often emphasizing the rejection of the language of rights and the opposition between women's politics and law, on the one hand, and between ethics of care and rights-based ethics, on the other, these currents of feminism help us to rethink law, rights and justice from a participatory and inclusive perspective, taking up that "universalism of specificities" already invoked by Olympe de Gouges.

As Tamar Pitch, an influential feminist legal sociologist, close for part of her life to difference feminism, has argued:

> Law and rights are tools, not ends in themselves. Often indispensable, sometimes misleading. But it must be clear that outside legal norms there is no vacuum, just as there is no elsewhere from institutions: outside legal norms there are other norms, many of them equally hetero-imposed, and therefore more difficult to see and challenge.[66]

Law, rights and institutions shape relations among people and between people and the State, both horizontally and vertically. I think, therefore, with Pitch, that law

[65] See Faludi (1991).

[66] Pitch (2008), p. 275. Translated by the author.

and rights are "tools to be used sparingly, aware of the possible unintended and perverse consequences of their use. Tools, in some, or even in many cases, indispensable".[67]

After all, law is a social practice. It lives in the activities of claiming, in the interpretation of the courts, in the fiduciary relationships people build and maintain. Law and rights are thus subject to constant resignification. That rights are important and that there is an ongoing struggle for their definition is evidenced by the many oppositions that the assertion of gender rights encounters from those who would like to preserve the patriarchal order. Increasingly, conservative movements are shifting their struggles to this terrain, not only by opposing reforms or promoting laws that dismantle rights that have already been recognized, but also by raising conflicts—even jurisdictional conflicts—between gender rights and other fundamental rights. One thinks of the right to religious freedom, often invoked in education to promote heteronormative models; the right to freedom of teaching, claimed to evade the demand to program teaching initiatives aimed at promoting gender equality and countering homotransfobia; maternity protection norms that are used explicitly or implicitly to oppose an equitable distribution of care work in families and lead women back to the stereotype associated with the "male breadwinner" model, since they privilege the mother, regard paternity leaves as merely complementary, and/or consider care as a prerogative of heterosexual couples and not as a social and institutional responsibility.

Neoliberal culture and politics, in turn, do not directly attack rights. On the contrary, they often champion gender rights, especially when they refer to the recognition of sexual minorities or reproductive freedom.[68] And yet the neoliberal project aims to "undo" the assumptions of contemporary (inter)national constitutionalism[69] and, as Wendy Brown (2015) has pointed out, puts democracy itself at risk. In this scenario, civil rights are often played in opposition to social rights. They are "trump cards" to be used in the market game. Neoliberal culture and politics use rights in precisely the way that a part of feminism—I am thinking in particular of the critiques of the theorists of the first school of the ethics of care—had denounced, that is, as entitlements of sovereign individuals, unrelated to each other and in competition. Their relational character is denied and the conditions under which rights can (or cannot) be exercised are neglected. Within this framework, even the traditional progressive narrative about advances in gender equality in the West (and in many areas of the world) risks functioning as an ideological veil hiding the true state of gender issues. As Beatrix Campbell (2013) has shown, neoliberal policies, such as privatization, deregulation and cuts to public services, foster the emergence of a

[67] Pitch (2008), p. 294. Translated by the author.

[68] Some women's rights, especially freedom from gender-based violence, are also central to the rhetoric of conservative and sovereignist forces. However, these use them according to the paradigm of femonationalism (Farris 2017) to demean immigrant populations and fuel Islamophobia. See also Scrinzi (2023).

[69] This expression, translated from Italian by the author, was coined by Tecla Mazzarese (2018) to underline the inextricably national and international character of post-WWII constitutionalism.

neopatriarchy in which the burden of care and social reproduction is more and more shifted onto households, where women—and we could add especially minority and immigrant women—bear the majority of responsibilities. Not only, but the spread of violence in neoliberal societies and new forms of war more often victimize women.

If we ask ourselves, where do we stand now, we can therefore answer that we are not following a path of linear development, but are in a "permanent"[70] and plural revolution. This pluralism has also been accentuated by the connections that have been established between feminisms and struggles present in different areas of the world and the critical reflection of black and decolonial feminism. This pluralism is an asset, as it allows the limits of different perspectives to come into focus. It also represents a challenge, as it can be a source of conflict.

The goal, however, cannot be to seek a synthesis among the different theoretical and political orientations of feminism. Rather, it is advisable to maintain an openness to different critical contributions and to avoid as far as possible a logic of opposition. The life of law can only derive nourishment from a lively confrontation in which different actors engage, as long as this takes place within the pluralist and democratic framework drawn by (inter)national constitutionalism, which today, despite the attacks it receives, is traversed by a vital transformative current.

6 Conclusion

In this chapter I explored the trajectory of feminist legal analysis, highlighting the three phases outlined by Carol Smart: the critique of law's sexist character, the denunciation of its male-dominated structure, and the reflection on gender. Each phase represents a crucial moment of evolution, from recognizing inequalities to addressing structural critiques, culminating in a constructivist approach that transcends traditional gender binaries.

A pivotal theme in the discussion is the emphasis on "transformative gender constitutionalism", which seeks to dismantle the entrenched patriarchal order in historical constitutionalism and promote substantive equality. This paradigm, in addition to safeguarding women's rights, expands to include diverse gender identities, striving to renew legislative action and legal interpretation through an inclusive and pluralistic lens. The law's adaptability to complex social contexts is demonstrated through examples of judicial and legislative reforms addressing concrete needs, such as those related to gender-based violence and reproductive rights.

At the same time, I underscored the legacy of second-wave feminism, highlighting the importance of maintaining a focus on the specific forms of oppression faced by women. However, the reflection also opens up to the need for balance between safeguarding this specificity and embracing gender diversity, an objective pursued

[70] Pulcini (2006). Translated by the author.

through dialogue among diverse theories and practices, such as black, postcolonial, decolonial feminism and queer thought.

In conclusion, law and rights cannot be seen as a panacea but rather as "instruments" to be used with awareness. Feminist legal theory, with its self-reflective and practical method, provides the tools and suggest an innovative approach for reinterpreting concepts of justice and equality, valuing differences and promoting a "universalism of specificities". Only through continuous and open engagement among various feminist currents can change be nurtured and the transformative potential of the law maintained within a democratic and pluralistic society.

References

Arruzza C, Bhattacharya T, Fraser N (2019) Feminism for the 99 percent. A manifesto. Verso, New York

Baer S (2022) Constitutional law and gender. In: Davinić M, Kostić S (eds) Gender competent public law and policies. Springer, Cham

Barnard C (2004) The future of equality law. Equality and beyond. In: Barnard C, Deakin S, Morris GS (eds) The future of labour law. Liber Amicorum Sir Bob Hebble QC. Hart Publishing, London

Beauvoir de S (1949) Le Deuxième Sexe. Gallimard, Paris

Bernardini MG, Giolo O (eds) (2024) Giudizio e pregiudizio. Gli stereotipi di genere nel diritto. Giappichelli, Torino

Bernini L (2016) La "teoria del gender", i "negazionisti" e la "fine della differenza sessuale". About Gender 5(10):367–381

Boccia ML (2002) La differenza politica. Il Saggiatore, Milano

Bottici C (2022) Anarchafeminism. Bloomsbury, London

Brown W (2015) Undoing the demos. Neoliberalism's stealth revolution. Zone books, New York

Butler J (1990) Gender trouble: feminism and the subversion of identity. Routledge, London

Butler J (2004) Undoing gender. Routledge, London

Butler J (2015) Senses of the subject. Fordham University Press, New York

Campbell B (2013) The end of equality. The only way is women's liberation. Seagull Books, Kolkata

Casadei T (2017) Diritto e (dis)parità: dalla discriminazione di genere alla democrazia paritaria. Aracne, Canterano

Collins H (2003) Discrimination, equality and social inclusion. Mod Law Rev 66(1):16–43

D'Amico M (2020) Una parità ambigua. Costituzione e diritti delle donne. Raffaello Cortina, Milano

Di Nicola Travaglini P (2021) La mia parola contro la sua. Quando il pregiudizio è più importante del giudizio. Harper Collins, Milano

Facchi A, Giolo O (2023) Una storia dei diritti delle donne. Il Mulino, Bologna

Faludi S (1991) Backlash. The undeclared war against American women. Crown Publishing Group, New York

Farris S (2017) In the name of women's rights: the rise of femonationalism. Duke University Press, Durham

Fausto-Sterling A (1993) The five sexes: why male and female are not enough. Sciences 33(2):20–25

Ferrajoli L (2002) Lo Stato di diritto fra passato e futuro. In: Costa P, Zolo D (eds) Lo Stato di diritto. Storia, teoria, critica. Feltrinelli, Milano

Ferrajoli L (2018) Manifesto per l'uguaglianza. Laterza, Roma-Bari

Fineman M, Jackson JE, Romero AP (eds) (2009) Feminist and queer legal theory: intimate encounters, uncomfortable conversations. Ashgate, Burlington

Fortunati L (1995) The arcane of reproduction: housework, prostitution, labor and capital. Autonomedia, Brooklyn
Fraser N, Honneth A (2003) Redistribution or recognition. A political-philosophical exchange. Verso, London
Fredman S (2003) Beyond the dichotomy of formal and substantive equality: towards a new definition of equal rights. In: Boerefijn I et al (eds) Temporary special measures. Accelerating de facto equality of women under article 4(1) UN Convention on the Elimination of all forms of Discrimination Against Women. Intersentia. Antwerpen, Oxford
Fredman S (2016) Substantive equality revised. I.CON 14(3):712–738
Fredman S, Goldblatt B (2015) Gender equality and human rights. UN Women, New York
Gheaus A (2012) Gender justice. J Ethics Soc Philos 6(2):1–24
Gianformaggio L (2005) Eguaglianza, donne, diritto. Il Mulino, Bologna
Gilleri G (2024) Sex, gender, and international human rights law, Contesting binaries. Routledge, Abingdon
Gilligan C (1982) In a different voice. Psychological theory and women's development. Harvard University Press, Cambridge
Godineau D (1988) Citoyennes tricoteuses: les femmes du peuple à Paris pendant la Révolution française. Alinea, Aix-en-Provence
Gordon N, Rottenberg C (2023) From human rights to a politics of care. Humanity J 14(3):327
Hébert LC (2007) Why don't "reasonable women" complain about sexual harassment? Indiana Law J 82(3):711–743
Hooks B (1984) Feminist theory from margin to center. South End Press, Boston
Hooks B (1989) Talking back. Thinking feminist, thinking black. South End Press, Boston
Irigaray L (1974) Speculum. De l'autre femme. Editions de Minuit, Paris
Irigaray L (1984) Éthique de la différence sexuelle. Editions de Minuit, Paris
Lepinard E (2020) Feminist trouble. Intersectional politics in postsecular times. Oxford University Press, Oxford
Loche AM (2021) La liberté ou la mort: il progetto politico e giuridico di Olympe de Gouges. Mucchi, Modena
Lonzi C (2010) Sputiamo su Hegel e altri scritti et al. Milano
Mackinnon CA (1987) Feminism unmodified. Discourses on life and law. Harvard University Press, Cambridge
Marand-Fouquet C (1989) La femme au temps de la Révolution. Stock, Paris
Marshall T (1950) Citizenship and social class, and other essays. Cambridge University Press, Cambridge
Mazzarese T (2006) Principio d'eguaglianza e diritti fondamentali: una (ri)lettura dell'articolo 3 della Costituzione. In: Maniaci G (ed) Eguaglianza, ragionevolezza e logica giuridica. Giuffré, Milano
Mazzarese T (2018) I migranti e il diritto ad essere diversi nelle società multiculturali delle democrazie costituzionali. In: Cerrina Feroni G, Federico V (eds) Strumenti, percorsi e strategie dell'integrazione nelle società multiculturali. ESI, Napoli
Melandri L (2012) Differenza e le sue aporie. In: Marchetti S, Mascat JMH (eds) Femministe a parole. Grovigli da districare. Ediesse, Roma
Menkel-Meadow C (1988) Feminist legal theory, critical legal studies, and legal education or "the fem-crits go to law school". J Leg Educ 38(1/2):61–85
Minda G (1995) Postmodern legal movements: law and jurisprudence at century's end. New York University Press, New York
Minello A, Nannicini T (2024) Genitori alla pari. Tempo, lavoro, libertà. Feltrinelli, Milano
Mohanty CT (1984) Under western eyes: feminist scholarship and colonial discourses. Boundary 2(3):333–358
Nussbaum M (2000) Women and human development. The capabilities approach. Cambridge University Press, Cambridge
Okin SM (1989) Justice, gender and the family. Basic Books, New York

Otto D (ed) (2018) Queering international law: possibilities, alliances, complicities, risks. Routledge, Abingdon
Pateman C (1988) The sexual contract. Stanford University Press, Stanford-CA
Pitch T (1998) Un diritto per due. Il Saggiatore, Milano
Pitch T (2008) La libertà femminile può passare per i diritti. In: Buttarelli A, Giardini F (eds) Il pensiero dell'esperienza. Baldini Castoldi Dalai, Milano
Pozzolo S (2019) ¿Vulnerabilidad personal o contextual? Aproximaciones al análisis de derecho en perspectiva de género. Isonomia 51:1–28
Pulcini E (2006) Luci e ombre di una rivoluzione permanente. Sessant'anni dopo il voto alle donne. Iride 49(3):455–466
Re L (2015) Lo stereotipo della 'differenza sessuale'. Analisi di un fraintendimento in Catharine A. MacKinnon. In: Casadei T (ed) Donne, diritto, diritti. Prospettive del giusfemminismo. Giappichelli, Torino
Rodotà S (2014) Solidarietà. Un'utopia necessaria. Laterza, Roma-Bari
Rossi Doria A (2007) Dare forma al silenzio: scritti di storia politica delle donne. Viella, Roma
Rottenberg C (2018) The rise of neoliberal feminism. Oxford University Press, Oxford
Rubio Marín R (2022) Global gender constitutionalism and women's citizenship. A struggle for transformative inclusion. Cambridge University Press, Cambridge
Rudan P (2023) Woman: history and critique of a polemical concept. Brill, Leiden and Boston
Santoro E (2008) Diritto e diritti. Lo Stato di diritto nell'era della globalizzazione. Giappichelli, Torino
Scrinzi F (2023) The racialization of sexism: men, women and gender in the populist radical right. Routledge, London
Sen A (1999) Development as freedom. Oxford University Press, Oxford
Smart C (1992) The woman of legal discourse. Soc Leg Stud 1(1):29–44
Spivak GC (1996) "Woman" as theatre. United Nations conference on women, Beijing 1995. Radic Philos 75:1–4
Turnier WJ, Johnston Conover P, Lowery D (2009) Redistributive justice and cultural feminism. Am Univ Law Rev 45:1275–1399
Verdu Sanmartin A (2023) The concept of gender in law. In: Vujadinović D, Álvarez del Cuvillo A, Strand S (eds) Feminist approaches to law. Theoretical and historical insights. Springer, Cham
Wittig M (1992) The straight mind and other essays. Beacon Press, Boston
Young IM (1990) Justice and the politics of difference. Princeton University Press, Princeton

Lucia Re is Full Professor of Philosophy of Law at the University of Florence, Italy, where she teaches Philosophy of Law and Politics of Globalization and Human Rights. She is a member of the teaching staff of the Doctoral Program in Legal Sciences at the University of Florence. She is the editor of *Jura gentium, Journal of Philosophy of International Law and Global Politics*. She is part of the editorial board of the journal *Studi sulla questione criminale*. Her research interests focus on sociology of deviance and social control, democracy and the rule of law, legal feminism, the political theory of care. The list of her publications is available at: https://cercachi.unifi.it/p-doc2-2012-200005-R-3f2b3429322c2a.html

Against the "Monopoly of Man": The Ante Litteram Intersectional Approach of Anna Kuliscioff and Borderless Feminism

Thomas Casadei

Abstract The struggles against various forms of violence and oppression—starting with domestic violence, which imposes despotic forms of relationships by men—encompasses struggles for the right to education and access to all forms of knowledge (including scientific and technological knowledge). It also includes demands for economic independence, decent working conditions and equal pay, new forms of territorial, mutualist and community-based social assistance, self-determination and motherhood. More generally, it is a fight for civil, political, and social rights—*against all forms of gender-based discrimination*, which shows a version of feminism capable of continuously crossing boundaries, of transcending borders. The aim of this chapter is to illustrate, first and foremost, how this feminist perspective diverges from forms of feminism that confine themselves within the institutional framework. Drawing on the work of Anna Kuliscioff—a cosmopolitan and prominent figure in Italian socialism and feminism at the turn of the nineteenth and twentieth centuries, this chapter illuminates how her work can be regarded as a rediscovered precursor, anticipating what is now recognized as an intersectional perspective. Kuliscioff's life, as the "doctor of the poor" and "of rights", the "lady of Italian socialism", was always guided by *freedom*: the freedom of her choices—practiced not only for herself but also advocated for other women and, in general, for all human beings—sustained and supported her unwavering commitment against discrimination, exploitation, and oppression. She fought tirelessly and relentlessly, not only for universal suffrage for women of all classes and social conditions—the "main goal" of emancipatory feminist battles—but also for the dignity of labor, health, and education for all women.

T. Casadei (✉)
University of Modena and Reggio Emilia, Modena, Italy
e-mail: thomas.casadei@unimore.it

F. Macioce et al. (eds.), *Feminist Legal and Political Practices*, Gender Perspectives in Law 6, https://doi.org/10.1007/978-3-032-02856-3_3

1 A "Borderless Feminism"?

The international debate of recent years reveals the complexity of the framework of feminist perspectives.

In various contexts, there has been the rise of an "institutionalized" feminism, which has been defined as *Governance Feminism.*[1] This form of feminism is highly influential in certain circles connected to the European and Western media and press and is also central to disciplinary fields more aligned with normative standards. It is based on *gender mainstreaming*[2] and other tools such as *diversity management* or microcredit.

Besides this, within a radical critique of the systems in force, which are still seen as deeply rooted in patriarchal culture,[3] there are so-called "movement-based" approaches, which revive Foucauldian and deconstructive categories[4] and stylistic elements, and which, in reality, seem to limit the political scope of feminism, confining it to the realm of "mere" critique.[5]

Additionally, a specific and certainly relevant domain is the one that has gradually been structured around "anti-discrimination law",[6] emerging from the insights of *engagées* feminist legal scholars and movements closely connected to *Critical Race Feminism.*[7]

In order to understand these processes and their theoretical-political and theoretical-legal implications, it is essential to engage in some sociological-political reflections; after all, feminist perspectives are always characterized by their strong political charge, while at the same time revealing how dominant conceptions are themselves always deeply imbued with ideology and politics.[8] Social systems and political forms change over time and are influenced by the political relations and conflicts given within cultural and economic contexts.

From this perspective, the 1970s were the years in which feminism expressed itself, sometimes provocatively, breaking the foundation of many stereotypes about women.[9] Later, in many European countries (such as France and Italy), the

---

[1] On which reference is made to Walby (2011); Halley et al. (2006).

[2] The discussion on *gender mainstreaming* within various feminist perspectives is heated. For some interpretations the reference is made to Bacchi and Eveline (2010). Cf., also, Vida (2020), pp. 37–44.

[3] Mies (2014); Strid and Hearn (2022). Cf. Ortner (2020).

[4] For an accurate overview of these trends, within a broader examination on "various contemporary feminisms' answers to neoliberalism", please see Casalini (2015).

[5] One example, among many, which nonetheless demonstrates the strength and the importance of the critique, is the offered by McRobbie (2009).

[6] See Atrey (2020); Fredman (2009). Cf., also, Vantin (2018).

[7] Here too, by way of example: Wing (2003); Wing and Pappalardo (2023).

[8] For a comprehensive overview: Geoghegan and Wilford (2014).

[9] With reference to Italian context: Dau Novelli (2010), pp. 39–62; Lussana (1997), pp. 471–565; Stelliferi and Voli (2023). More in general, for the theoretical implications of these political processes: Tucker (2011).

movement positioned itself in more peripheral and less visible spaces: less present in the streets, it carried out its actions more within universities, bookstores, study groups, ultimately creating "its own" institutions, with its own key figures, its own lexicon (admittedly not always immediately accessible to the general public), and its own interpretation of the world, society, and relationships. In short, it seemed more focused on structuring its own, particular perspective and emphasizing its boundaries than engaging systematically and continuously within a political struggle for hegemony (to use the term in a strictly Gramscian sense[10]).

These were the years of study, with the introduction of specific disciplines within university departments, the advancement and articulation of the theoretical framework, and the structuring and creation of national and international networks.[11]

With the new millennium, it was widely believed that women had, from many perspectives, achieved their liberation once and for all, being able to reach various goals, particularly from an *individualistic* perspective, characterized by a vocabulary where words like *choice* and *empowerment* played a central role.[12]

If, on the one hand, the reality of their success was emphasized, the question remained open as to whether a different, more inclusive and solidaristic society had been built, a society that, on closer inspection, seemed more like an aspiration than a concrete reality pursued through effective actions to bring it to fruition. It is precisely in this context that some have spoken of the diffusion of a "post-feminist sensitivity",[13] the result of an unprecedented convergence between neoliberal demands and the programmatic goals of so-called "liberal" feminism.[14]

In another direction, however, in contrast to post-feminism, its narratives, and its rhetoric,[15] a new wave of struggles and protests has emerged: in recent years, it has involved dozens of countries (from India to Argentina, from Spain to Poland, to name but a few), opening a new phase for truly feminist politics and its relationship with international and global dimensions.[16]

---

[10] Cf., most recently, Frosini and Giasi (2019), who precisely illustrate the new frontiers of Gramscian studies in the global world (Europe and the United States, but also Asia and Latin America). Cf., for a gender perspective, Minervini (2019).

[11] Cf. Giolo et al. (2022).

[12] Hence the narratives and rhetoric of post-feminist thought, and the neoliberal discursive system clearly described in Vida (2020). Previously: Vida (2016, 2017).

[13] Post-feminism is widely regarded as a "false feminism" that assumes women's equality as an already achieved fact, leaving room for a femininity where freedom is reduced to free choice, particularly in a consumerist sense: see Casalini (2015), p. 5, who focuses, among other things, on the critique of these findings McRobbie (2009).

[14] The expression was already present in Gill (2007). For a sharp critique: Rottenberg (2018). See also Diamond et al. (2017). Furthermore, see Casalini (2018), pp. 37 ff. For an analysis in relation to other perspectives such as the radical and socialist ones: Álvarez Medina et al. (2001).

[15] The rhetoric space, as the feminist epistemology has taught us, determines the perceptual framework within which "matters of concern", the things to which value is attributed, are situated: Cf. Code (1995).

[16] As observed (Álvarez del Cuvillo et al. 2023, p. 64), "Some authors identify a fourth wave of feminism, from 2012–2013 to the present day, that implies a new impetus in the movement. This

An important confirmation of the expansion of this vision, connected to the international strike that has been held every year on March 8, since 2017, bringing together dozens of countries worldwide, is also represented by the volume/manifesto *Feminism for the 99 Percent* by Cinzia Arruzza, Tithi Bhattacharya, and Nancy Fraser,[17] which was published simultaneously in several countries in 2019.

Along with the resurgence of national assemblies and the construction of a supranational network, several key elements have become established: the expansion of an increasingly broad and diversified gender approach; the claim for an attention-seeking that goes far beyond the sectoral demand for rebalancing political representation; the focus on care work and social reproduction as central to a structural analysis of society,[18] often accompanied by the proposal of a basic income, more precisely referred to as a "self-determination income".[19]

It is no longer just the greater "presence" of women in the public, political sphere, in courts, and in decision-making spaces that accounts for the changes that have occurred (an aspect often highlighted by institutionalized feminism, presenting it as a definitive point of arrival); what is being claimed is the adoption of concepts related to *relational capacity* and *care*, as well as to *qualified education* and *decent work*, accompanied by continuous and respectful guarantees of "life time", as Joan Tronto has effectively described through the concept of *caring democracy.*[20] In many parts of the world women have become less vulnerable and, at the same time, are under attack; they have become freer but still face both old and new challenges, and there is no contradiction between these two conditions.

The outcomes of this resurgence of the women's movement in a transnational scenario also depend on the ability to understand the origins of these new demands, to know the places and people, the stages and key moments of a "long march" that is certainly not yet finished but has made significant progress.[21]

The divide between the perspective of *emancipation* (or equality), recently reabsorbed into equal opportunity policies, and that of *sexual difference* (or, in this case, of transcending freedom or liberation) has long persisted[22] and, it seems, risks weakening the driving force of the broader process of expanding women's rights and, at the same time, recognizing their specific demands, needs, and aspirations.

---

is mainly concerned with diverse online/offline forms of gender violence (domestic violence, rape culture, sexual harassment), body shaming, and women's representation in the media and Internet. Online activism and social media are particularly important in this wave, providing rapid global dissemination to initiatives such as the #MeToo movement. Intersectionality is still highly relevant in the fourth wave, perhaps even more so than in the third wave": see Munro (2013), pp. 22–25; Negar and Kharazmi (2019), pp. 129–146. More generally: McCann and Kim (2013); Verza (2023).

[17] Arruzza et al. (2019).

[18] Bhattacharya (2017); Lynch (2021). Cf. Rigo (2022).

[19] Morini (2021a, 2021b).

[20] Tronto (2013).

[21] In this perspective: Cf. Arruzza, Cirillo (2017). Previousely: Legates (2001).

[22] Verza (2009), pp. 257–296, thoroughly illustrates the implications on the legal and legal-philosophical levels, as well as more specifically on the political-institutional level. See also Vujadinović et al. (2022).

Moreover, recent feminisms express a *need for diversity*—cultural, lifestyle, in choices about self-determination and body image[23]—and make *intersectionality* an essential aspect, both theoretically and methodologically.[24]

As has been aptly observed, the theoretical elaboration of the intersectional approach provides a significant and original key to "grasp the systemic dimension of discrimination": "the notion of intersectionality between identities and personal conditions, understood as the coexistence of multiple specificities within the same subject, represents at this point a cornerstone of philosophical-legal reflection on rights".[25]

At the level of social processes, as has been highlighted,[26] diversity also seems to characterize active political participation in recent years on an international scale. This is a sign of the reactivation of forms of active citizenship after a long phase of disenchantment.[27]

Along this axis of development and theoretical re-elaboration, pathways have become clearly visible that, in light of the various contributions of feminist theories, seek to expand, explore, and transform common definitions of *gender and sexuality*. These efforts include, within an open scope of action corresponding to a broader theoretical perspective aligned with the lines of intersectionality, discourse on *migrant women*, *queer* and *postcolonial theories*, and *disability studies*.[28]

What seems to be unfolding is a process of opening that, incidentally, had already been observed—in various forms—in the 1970s (at the height of the theoretical and practical expansion of feminism), with reference to the conditions of children, the elderly, and people with disabilities, that is, various groups and subjectivities that had previously been ignored and made vulnerable by their contexts.[29] However, as will be shown, this process was also foreshadowed earlier by particularly forward-looking figures, such as Anna Kuliscioff, a cosmopolitan and prominent figure in Italian socialism and feminism at the turn of the 1800s and 1900s.

---

[23] On the "multiplication of recent feminist thought", within a broader process of "internationalization": Restaino (2002), pp. 54–75. Indicative of this trend, in the Italian context, is the collective work edited by Marchetti et al. (2012), a sort of reasoned dictionary, the result of dialogue between feminists with diverse experiences and backgrounds.

[24] Carbin and Edenheim (2013), pp. 233–248. On the notion of "intersectionality": Romero (2023); Davis and Lutz (2023). Cf. Bello (2020).

[25] Giolo (2014), pp. 387–338.

[26] Magaraggia (2015), pp. 23–34, 24.

[27] With reference to the Italian context: Guadagnini (2000). On these aspects, I refer to Re and Giolo (2014).

[28] As has been highlighted, "Gender is not the only factor that determines social position, discrimination, and privilege. In fact, it interacts with other personal characteristics, including, but not limited to, social class, race or ethnic origin, age, disability, sexual orientation and gender identity. Experience modulated by the intersection of different categories or social circumstances is not merely the sum of these categories. In that context, *intersectionality* is the analytical perspective that takes into account the combination of different aspects of people in order to understand their position in the social structure" (Álvarez del Cuvillo et al. 2023, p. 62): cf. Crenshaw (1989), p. 140.

[29] Cf. Macioce (2023).

2 Anna Kuliscioff: An "Intersectional Approach" *Ante Litteram?*

Anna Kuliscioff (1855?–1924), who lived between the late nineteenth century and the early decades of the twentieth century, developed and implemented several strategies and initiatives aimed at promoting female emancipation, opposing all forms of exclusion.[30]

Of Russian origin, she was a citizen of the world "by experience"; her cosmopolitanism played a central role in shaping her ideas, her vision of society, and her political and social engagement.

[30] Anja Moiséyevna Rosenstein (or Rozenstein)—this is Anna Kuliscioff's birth name—was born in Simferopol, in the peninsula of Crimea or, according to another tradition, in Moskaja in the region of Cherson (both territories are part of the current Ukraina) in a rich family constituted by Jewish traders. News regarding her early years of life are scarce, almost nonexistent (it still remains the uncertainty even regarding the date of birth, indicated at January, 9, in an year between 1853 and 1857) and, consequently, her very first education.

She was a truly multifaceted woman: revolutionary and subversive, and for this reason incarcerated four times; a student and researcher of medicine, a scientist, intellectual, and journalist; a leader and prominent member of a political party; a supporter of innovative reforms; an independent woman, lover, and mother; a socialist (after an initial adherence to anarchism) and a feminist.

One trait that stands out from her life—which spans from Russia to Switzerland, from France to Italy (where she arrived in 1878)—is her being "first": just to give a few examples, she was among the first girls to enroll at the University of Zurich; she was among the first women to graduate in Medicine in Italy (in Naples); she was the only female honorary assistant to Professor Achille De Giovanni (her name appears in the 1887–1888 Yearbook of Professors and Assistants of the Faculty of Medicine and Surgery at the University of Padua); she was the first woman to give a lecture at the Philological Circle in Milan (in April 1890), dedicated to the Monopoly of Man; she was one of the first members of the Journalists' Association in Italy.

Her being "first" should be understood as the one who, "first," paved the way for other women. Kuliscioff was able, with great authority, to create around her a network of women, with whom she formed both personal and friendly relationships, but above all political connections, a sisterhood with the common goal of improving the condition of all women.

She fought tirelessly and relentlessly for health, the defense of labor, universal suffrage for women of all classes and social conditions. She had a European vision of the workers' issue and the condition of women: in August 1891, she participated as a delegate of the Milanese Socialist League at the Brussels Congress of the Second International. There, together with other women, she "drafted and signed the resolution, which was then almost unanimously approved, calling on 'the socialist parties of all countries' to assert firmly in their programs the complete equality of the sexes and to demand, above all, the abolition of all laws that place women outside common and public law" (Tarozzi 1996, pp. 118–121, 120).

She was a keen observer of reality, able to combine thorough and scientific study (her clinical studies on the pathogenesis of puerperal fevers are fundamental) with an innate sensitivity to the needs of people, starting with the most vulnerable: children, women, and the subalterns (cf. Tita 2018, pp. 105–11).

Fascinated by the idea of medicine and science serving the emancipation of the most humble, the marginalized of society, Kuliscioff—who would be called the "doctor of the poor" and also the "Lady of socialism" (Casalini (2013))—theorized and put into practice a humanitarian and human, social and socialist, feminine and feminist medicine.

As it has been stated, "her open-mindedness and thirst for knowledge led her to explore and assimilate ideas and perspectives from various intellectual traditions that she encountered during her travels across Europe and through her interaction with diverse cultures and realities. Above all, her ability to listen, connect, and network stood out. Over time, she developed a gaze marked by a deep curiosity, an extraordinary capacity for observation and critical analysis, and a keen interest in social dynamics and otherness. Her attention to and constant updates on international events and dynamics continued to shape her worldview. Despite changing cities and contexts, the dynamics of oppression that Kuliscioff observed remained the same. She did not merely acknowledge and translate this into a political creed; she lived it".[31] In this sense, Kuliscioff can be said to have truly embodied—with her existence and her fights—that "feminism without borders" perspective,[32] which in more recent times has seen forms of structured theoretical elaboration, such as the one proposed by a leading figure of postcolonial feminism like Chandra Talpade Mohanty.

In confirmation of this, she held an international perspective on the labor question and the condition of women: in August 1891, as a delegate of the Milan Socialist League, she participated at the Brussels Congress of the Second International.

There, together with other women, she drafted and signed a motion, then almost unanimously approved, calling on "the socialist parties of all countries to vigorously affirm, in their programs, the complete equality of the sexes and, above all, to demand the repeal of all laws that placed women outside common and public law". Her entire life, after all, was dedicated to political engagement within the labor and socialist movement, with a constant focus on the legal and institutional dimensions, starting from the social conditions of the most vulnerable subjects.

Throughout her journey, she was constantly building networks with other women.

In fact, Kuliscioff was able of authoritatively creating a network of women around her, with whom she established personal and political relationships (not without controversy, differences of opinion, and even disputes): what emerged was a *sisterhood* united by the common goal of promoting female emancipation *against all forms of exclusion.*[33]

Her name is linked to those of many activists who made significant contributions to improving women's material conditions. Among them were Angelica Balabanoff (1878–1965),[34] Argentina Bonetti Altobelli (1866–1942), and Maria Goia

[31] Scapocchin (2024).

[32] Cf. Mohanty (2003). On the theoretical basis and the manifestations of these processess, please see also Bacchetta (2015), pp. 21–34.

[33] On this point: Tita (2018), pp. 105–111.

[34] Balabanoff had a whirlwind life through some of the most intense phases of twentieth-century history, coming into contact with Vladimir Ilyich Ulyanov Lenin, Benito Mussolini, Filippo Turati, August F. Bebel, Clara Zetkin, Rosa Luxemburg, Antonio Labriola, and Lev Trotsky. She left her mark in many countries, from Belgium to Switzerland, from Bolshevik Russia to the United States, from Austria to Sweden, from the town of Chernihiv, near Kyiv, where she was born around 1878, to Italy, where she died in Rome in 1965. She was a prominent figure in the first half of the twen-

(1878–1924), with whom she shared her activism within the Socialist Party,[35] deeply intertwined with the advocacy of women's and workers' rights;[36] Linda Malnati (1855–1921) and Giselda Brebbia (1878–1920), with whom she founded the magazine *La difesa delle lavoratrici* in Milan in 1912; and Rosa Genoni (1867–1954), promoter of the first committee for Italian fashion in 1909 and founder of the magazine *Per la guerra o per la pace?*, a symbol of women committed to peaceful relations between states in the early decades of 1900s. Additionally, together with Eva Kuhn (1880–1961), Ernestina Paper (1846–1926), Maria Bakunin (1873–1960), and Balabanoff herself,[37] Kuliscioff was among the Russian women, often of Jewish origin, who arrived in Italy between the late nineteenth and early twentieth centuries, driven by *cosmopolitan ideas.*[38]

Her lively debates with Anna Maria Mozzoni (1837–1920) on the subject of emancipation, as well as with her comrades Andrea Costa (1851–1910) and Filippo Turati (1857–1932) on women's rights and suffrage, are well known.

Her perspective, particularly influenced by Marxist ideas in the early stages of her intellectual and political journey,[39] stemmed from a sharp critique of what she defined in a fundamental 1890 essay as the "monopoly of man"[40]: it was from this radical stance on what she called "the core of the issue" that her objectives for struggle took shape. These were, first and foremost, the struggles of socialist women, and later they became the struggles of the Italian and international socialist movement. Roots of her intersectional approach, which brings together the question

tieth century: in 1912, she worked alongside the revolutionary socialist Mussolini as co-director of *Avanti!* (Later condemning him harshly for his support of war and then fascism); in 1919–1920, she was Secretary of the Third Socialist International, but in 1921, she broke with Lenin after the Kronstadt Rebellion. For further details on her journey, see Toscano (2024).

[35] Balabanoff and Goia, together with Kuliscioff, were part of the Socialist Committee for Women's suffrage established in 1911.

[36] For a comprehensive overview Taricone (2020). Cf. Degl'Innocenti (2017); Kuliscioff (2024).

[37] Annaratone (2003).

[38] On Kuliscioff' Jewish origins: Shepherd (2009). Cf., more generally, Hoock-Demarle (1995); Bilski (2005); Modena (2021).

[39] Along this line, a text that remains important is: Vogel (1983). As recently highlighted, "*Marxist feminism* relates women's oppression to the social relations of production that cover basic human needs in all societies. Although classical Marxism is indeed concerned with women's subordination, this topic has usually been subsumed under class oppression, which implies that gender relations have often been ignored or marginalized in classical studies. However, subsequent studies in the last decades have used Marxist analysis to address the situation of women as a central political issue. It should be remembered that, in Marxist theory, the material basis of society is constituted not only by the production of material goods, but also by the reproduction of human life. In that vein, the subjugation of women would be related to the division of productive and reproductive labor that implies some kind of appropriation of the domestic and reproductive work of women. Marxist feminism is also called *Socialist feminism*, although some Socialist theories are not particularly linked with Marxist methodology": Álvarez del Cuvillo et al. (2023), p. 65. Cf. Bryson (1992), pp. 232–260.

[40] Kuliscioff (2020). Cf. Cagnolati (2012).

of class, along with that of patriarchy, economic discrimination, and gender-based discrimination, can be found here.

Kuliscioff stated: "All men, with few exceptions, and some social class, for a multitude of reasons unflattering for a sex deemed strong, regard their gender privilege as a natural phenomenon and defend it with remarkable tenacity, calling upon God, the church, science, ethics, and existing laws, which are nothing more than the legal sanctioning of the dominance of a class and a gender. And this is why, despite the close relationships between various problems, I thought I could isolate the issue of the social condition of women from all other pathological phenomena of the social organism, largely generated by that terrible drama of life, which is the struggle for existence".[41]

The international perspective of Kuliscioff's denunciation of oppression and "male tyranny" is clearly evident in her writings: "All the dispossessed, all the pariahs of society are beginning to move, to also ask for a little light, air, and a life in accordance with human dignity; and it is therefore natural that, in our century, a serious and vast movement has emerged among the last and most numerous of the pariahs, who make up half of humanity, that is, among women".

"In all of Europe and America"—Kuliscioff continues—"armies of women are forming, fighting for their emancipation and to shake off the age-old yoke imposed upon them by men. And, although this struggle of women is not as manifest—because, for a multitude of physiological and psychological reasons—it can never assume the harshness and hatred that characterize the struggle between social classes; it nevertheless can have no other meaning than the tendency to overthrow the privilege of men and to shake their power".[42]

Starting from this awareness, that is, the persistence of male dominance, Kuliscioff was an astute observer of reality: she was able to combine thorough and scientific study (her clinical research on the pathogenesis of puerperal fevers is fundamental) with an innate sensitivity to the concrete needs of people, starting with the most vulnerable: women, children, and the subordinate classes.[43] She took care of their conditions and material lives, focusing specifically on education, labor, health, and medical care.

In this perspective, her commitment, together with the socialist party, of which she is one of the most prominent figures, laid the foundation for the first law in Italy

[41] Kuliscioff (2020).

[42] Kuliscioff (2020).

[43] The expression, introduced by Antonio Gramsci in notebook 25 of the *Prison Notebooks*, has been notably taken up in the context of postcolonial studies, particularly by the Indian historian Ranajit Guha and by one of the most prominent names associated with the movement, Gayatri Chakravorty Spivak, in his famous "Can the Subaltern Speak?" (1983). The semantic range of the term has evolved since its first use by Guha, following Gramsci, to refer solely to peasants who had not been integrated into the industrial capitalist system. It now refers to any person or group of inferior rank or status, whether because of race, class, gender, sexual orientation, ethnicity, or religion.

to protect women and children in the workforce (including the reduction of their working hours): Law No. 242 of July 19, 1902.

As has been emphasized, Kuliscioff was aware that at those times, girls bore the brunt of school dropouts because they were considered “more expendable” than their male counterparts due to a range of stereotypes and deeply rooted prejudices against female lore.[44] The denunciation of the exclusion of girls from classrooms gained public traction, also thanks to the attention given to the issue by certain journals connected to the world of female associations, including *La difesa delle lavoratrici,*[45] founded by Kuliscioff herself. These journals often featured articles promoting education as a necessary means to break the cycle of deprivation, abuse, and exploitation to which many girls were subjected at the time: from the “piscinine” of Milan (apprentice seamstresses often tasked with deliveries), to the young factory workers in manufacturing industries, and the young women working in the rice fields.[46]

On several occasions, Kuliscioff referred to the *space of care*, that is time and energy released from Work to dedicate to the relationship with the kids, that she believed mothers had the right and duty to reserve for their children as a space “denied” (both to the women themselves and to their children) due to the brutal working conditions in factories and on farms.

Following Nancy Fraser,[47] one could say, as has been aptly pointed out,[48] that in what Kuliscioff defines as a space “denied” lies one of the contradictions of capitalism at every stage of its development: on the one hand, social reproduction is a fundamental condition necessary for the accumulation of capital, while on the other hand, capitalism’s drive for unlimited accumulation leads it to “cannibalize” the very socio-reproductive activities on which it depends.[49]

According to Fraser, liberal competitive capitalism attempted to overcome this contradiction by establishing “separate spheres”, removing women, even working-class women, from the places of “production” and relegating them mainly to

---

[44] Fanlo Cortés (2025). Cf. Covato (1991).

[45] «La Difesa delle Lavoratrici» (in english: “The Defence of female Workers”) is the first socialist national newspaper, published in 1912 and strongly advocated by Anna Kuliscioff; in the magazine’s pages—which aims to capture the attention and the consensus of less alphabetized female workers—everyday issue are addressed: the insufficient salary, goodness of the cooperatives to support strikes, workplace mortality, precariousness, risk of hunger.

[46] On this point: Seveso (2018). As Isabel Fanlo Cortés (2025) has noted, “less explored, at least in Kuliscioff’s reflections, is the further question of how to educate girls, which is also relevant from a perspective of social discipline and control”. In this regard, the issue of “coeducation” is central, around which an intense debate developed in Italy starting at the beginning of the twentieth century. “A debate”—Fanlo Cortés continues—“often polarized, with one side advocating that the cultural and professional education aimed at girls should not differ from that provided to their male peers, and the other side arguing for the inescapability of teaching domestic economy or other subjects considered essential from a perspective of gender socialization”.

[47] Fraser (2022), pp. 61–62.

[48] Fanlo Cortés 2025.

[49] Fraser (2022).

activities related to social reproduction. However, this contradiction is destined to resurface in changed forms and conditions, even in today's financial capitalism, where the model of the *male breadwinner* is in the process of being overcome, and is expressed in what Fraser has called the "crisis of care".[50]

With an approach that could be described as "intersectional" *ante litteram,*[51] Kuliscioff demonstrates her keen awareness of class differences and their impact on gender inequalities: in an important 1892 conference entitled *Proletariato femminile* (Female Proletariat), she emphasized how, for the working woman, there was "neither physical weakness, nor family, neither motherhood, nor education for her children",[52] since she

> is a convenient tool for labor, docile and silent; it is part of the machine and becomes a machine itself [...]. Capitalism imprisons millions of working women like white slaves in mephitic fumes, without air and without light, it takes them away from their families, and the working woman abandons her children. She cannot take care of her miserable corner, where after 16 or 14 hours of work she returns to quickly eat soup, sleep for a few hours, and return again at four in the morning to the forced labor chain. And this, in bourgeois language, is called preserving the family, nurturing motherhood, and educating children. And wherever women work, in large or small industries, they are always the most oppressed, the greatest victims of bourgeois exploitation.[53]

The quoted passage, in addition to being another significant testimony to the presence of women, at least women belonging to the working classes, in the so-called productive sectors—a presence that was constantly "invisibilized" and devalued despite female labor being a fundamental pillar for the economies of various national states[54]—hints at the reasons that had driven Kuliscioff to advocate for protective legislation for working women (mothers).[55]

---

[50] Fraser (2021). Previousely: Fraser (2009, 2013).

[51] This way, Fanlo Cortés (2025). The intersectional reading of the thought and work of figures like Kuliscioff and similar ones is, moreover, widespread in international literature. These interpretative readings can be situated within what Nina Lykke (2010) identifies as "implicitly intersectional." See, in this regard, Everard et al. (1999); Modena (2021); Zichi (2022).

[52] Kuliscioff (2015a).

[53] Kuliscioff (2015a), p. 71. The same words would be pronounced in a speech addressed by Kuliscioff to the *Alle operaie della manifattura tabacchi* (1898): Kuliscioff (2015b).

[54] Pescarolo (2019), p. 80.

[55] This law, at least in the intentions of Kuliscioff and the socialists, "was not meant to merely protect women's reproductive capacity in the interest of the nation, but rather to free them from the "excessive tyranny of the workshop" and from their condition as "machines" at the mercy of capital, giving them the time to organize and participate in proletarian struggles and, if mothers, to care for their children, especially in the early months of life. This would be achieved through reducing the working hours to 48 per week and providing mandatory maternity leave, which female workers would be entitled to both in the 6 months before and after childbirth, receiving a subsidy equal to 75% of their daily wage, funded by a newly established Maternity Fund financed partly by the state and partly by contributions from employers and the workers themselves". Contrary to these aspirations and objectives, "the final version of the 1902 law primarily aimed to ensure the hygienic, sanitary (and moral) conditions necessary to safeguard the health of the new generations. At the same time, the goal was to avoid discouraging women's employment outside the home, which

The defense of the primacy of this role found support in at least two circumstances, as has been duly noted[56]: the first is that the protection of female labor had been limited by Parliament to the postnatal period through the sole mechanism of leave (without, that is, the recognition of forms of economic support for mothers, unlike what was provided for in the socialist project); the second is the exclusion of certain important areas from the scope of the law—domestic and family work, in addition to agricultural work—where it was evidently believed that women could continue to be exploited without limits or fear of state intervention, as these were considered "private" spaces (or reconstructed as such precisely by liberal and capitalist ideology).

From a general point of view, there are crucial elements of Kuliscioff's thought that demonstrate a profound break with a patriarchal vision[57] and, moreover, exempt her from the critique that part of subsequent historiography has directed, rightly or wrongly, at reformist socialists, or at least at those, like her, who had fought for "protective" interventions in women's and children's labor. Namely, the critique that they had become "entangled with the issue of motherhood", too often allowing themselves to be drawn into ambiguous references to the need to strengthen the species and, above all, lingering in justifications based "on the indisputable identification between women and the maternal role".[58]

There is no doubt that traces of a naturalization of this role can also be found in Kuliscioff's thought: in the famous 1890 conference on the *Monopolio dell'uomo*, motherhood was characterized not only as "one of the most elevated duties of women in social life", but also "one of the most satisfying of her psychological tendencies and the most suited to the development of her body",[59] and the feeling of motherhood was described as "a powerful force", a kind of natural instinct that seemed to characterize the female gender as such.[60]

However, these elements must be read in the context of the time, which did not allow Kuliscioff to explore the impact that social conditioning might have on the choice to become a mother in a cultural context traditionally dominated by the "myth of motherhood", nor to realize that even the feeling of motherhood, understood as an emotional attachment to the offspring, as Philippe Ariès' studies would later teach",[61] has, at least in part, a historical origin.

In any case, these elements are not sufficient to make Kuliscioff a supporter of the identification of femininity with motherhood (in its dual biological and social

industrialists were strongly interested in, without, however, compromising the predominant family role assigned to them in a social context of complete subordination and dependence on men" (Fanlo Cortés (2025)). It is worth remembering that until 1919, marital authorization was still in effect in Italy: on this matter, see Bartoloni (2021).

[56] Ballestrero (1979), pp. 25–26. Cf. Fanlo Cortés (2025).

[57] On this crucial aspect: Röwekamp (2023).

[58] Covato (1991), p. 65.

[59] Kuliscioff (2020), p. 96.

[60] Kuliscioff (2020), p. 37.

[61] Fanlo Cortés (2025). The reference is to Ariès (1975).

dimension): an idea implicitly underlying the "Carcano law" (n. 42/1902),[62] which greatly disappointed her expectations as a woman, a socialist, and a feminist.

In addition to the themes of labor and education, Kuliscioff also paid specific attention to the field of healthcare and medical treatment. She was one of the very first women to graduate in Medicine, the first at the University of Naples.[63] Here, she embraced the ideal of the "social mission" of medicine, which was emerging in those final decades of the nineteenth century in Europe: an idea of medicine and science at the service of the 'last' (a sort of "medical socialism"[64]) that would, in the coming decades, form the basis of concepts such as "public health" in the Anglo-Saxon world and "sanità pubblica" in Italy.

After graduating, she applied to practice at the Ospedale Maggiore in Milan, but this opportunity was denied to her. Along with the philanthropist Alessandrina Ravizza (1846–1915), the "Lady of the Desperate", she started a medical practice at 18 Via San Pietro all'Orto. "*La dottora*" as she was nicknamed, spared no effort; with humility, she walked the streets of the city, including those of the slums, to take care of the humblest women: orphans, widows, outcasts, prostitutes, anyway all of them poor.

When her illness worsened and bone tuberculosis took over her debilitated body, Kuliscioff was forced to abandon her medical practice. From that moment, medical practice gave way to political activism and journalism, always and still in the name of women and their rights.

If today we can count Kuliscioff among the *pioneering women* of medical practice in Italy and Europe, she can also be considered—precisely because she made the female universe the 'privileged' subject of her care—a forerunner of a new 'branch' of medicine that emerged from the 1990s: "Gender Medicine" or, as it is now commonly called, "gender-specific medicine", the study of biological differences (defined by sex), and socio-economic and cultural influence and differences (defined by gender), on each person's health and illness.

---

[62] Anna Kuliscioff's contribution to the long process of preparation and discussion that led to the approval of the law between the end of the nineteenth century and the early twentieth century was decisive (Passaniti 2016). The political growth of the women's emancipation movement and the increasing labor demands (in which female workers also participated, often in significant numbers) during those years facilitated her efforts aimed both at greater involvement of the working class, traditionally wary of any state-protective intervention in social matters, and at expanding the discussion to include women's labor, which had been excluded from specific protections in the previous 1886 legislation. In the final text, however, there is little trace of socialist demands: with the interests of industrialists prevailing, the minimum age for admission to work is set at 12 years (with the exception, moreover, of the agricultural and family sectors, where it is understood that even younger children can be employed without restrictions), night work is prohibited only for underage women, and it is stipulated that to perform unhealthy and dangerous work, it is enough to be 15 years old.

[63] When she arrived there in February 1884, after enrolling in the Faculty of Medicine in Bern, Switzerland, the previous year, she was the only woman "in a crowd of 400 students".

[64] Zazzara (2019).

Kuliscioff's perspective was thus, in many respects, a far-sighted one, constantly striving to go "beyond patriarchal time",[65] aware that to achieve this goal, it is crucial to break the "monopoly of man".

3 The Daily Life and the Counter-Hegemonic Fight: The Need For "Convergences"

The fact that Kuliscioff had a far-sighted perspective, capable of focusing on the major issues concerning the social condition of women, can be demonstrated by several arguments. In particular, at the Copenhagen Conference (1980), the discrepancy between rights nominally guaranteed and women's ability to exercise them[66] led to the identification of three specific areas in which targeted actions were deemed necessary: "equal access to education", "equal access to job opportunities", and "creation of adequate healthcare services".

Education, work, and healthcare are three fundamental areas of definition (and intervention) on social rights. These are still crucial areas politically and institutionally, and they are strongly impacted by the current "neoliberal order" and the "neoliberal law" that supports and structures it.[67]

It is precisely "the feminist lens of care and social reproduction"—to borrow Casalini's words, in line with the most recent feminist theories on the subject—that can help to deeply understand the effects of the cuts in public resource implemented over the past two decades, and to suggest an alternative path toward the creation of democratic forms that are indeed care-centered.[68]

As for political rights, they seem to be reduced for women, as it has often been emphasized, to the mere right to vote, with a significant practical reduction in the right to be elected or, in any case, with a constant difficulty in addressing the issues of a possible feminist agenda.

---

65 Taricone (2025).

66 On this point: Barranco Avilés (2019).

67 Giolo (2020b).

68 Re-launched in the context of the COVID-19 pandemic. In this regard, see *The Care Manifesto. The Politics of Interdependence* (2020) and the appeal *Towards a Democracy of Care* (April 2, 2020) (http://www.ingenere.it/articoli/verso-una-democrazia-della-cura). The latter emphasizes the need to "move towards new forms of democracy, largely yet to be developed with an exciting collective effort; forms of democracy in which care—care for people, relationships, and the environment—is a crucial aspect. This means, among other things, rethinking and reevaluating the largely unrecognized work of those who daily care for their family members, friends, and neighbors for free, as well as the work of those who perform these activities professionally, such as domestic workers, caregivers, and babysitters. This means developing new synergies capable of overcoming the oppositions between public and private, families and institutions, in view of greater individual and collective well-being: in short, a true caring democracy".

These types of problems fall within what Luigi Pannarale has described as a broad process of "rights regression",[69] which does not concern only women but certainly affects them the most. It began with "highlighting how rights, all rights (not only social rights, such as the right to education, health, and housing, but also freedoms) have a cost in economic terms, which is the reason why criteria must be identified that allow for a reasonable selection in their recognition and ownership. It must be acknowledged that the recognition of some rights for certain subjects inevitably entails the sacrifice of other rights for others".[70] In this scenario, not only is equality—something women have fought for since suffragism and through various social and economic achievements[71]—called into question, but more importantly, the foundations of the social bond are denied, or "circumscribed within an increasingly narrow scope that revives those nation-states that seemed to be in slow but inexorable decline, while artificial oppositions are invoked, preventing the possibility of conceiving rights that are inclusive of the entire human species".[72]

In order to identify potential footholds for anchoring a counter-hegemonic perspective, it is important to emphasize that "oppositions always concern the weak links of the social chain and never pit marginal groups against privileged classes, in fact, the gap between rich and poor continuously increases without prompting redistributive interventions".[73]

It is, after all, the spaces of everyday life—on which widespread culture is based and from which individual and social identities are constructed—that continue to reflect a deeply asymmetrical image between men and women, determined by the effects of that monopoly of man that Kuliscioff focused on and which has not yet been abolished.

From the awareness of ongoing regressions, but also of the centrality of "material life" in defining and constituting identities and relationships—as Kuliscioff had well understood—a perspective could emerge that, deeply rooted in the achievements and collective heritage of feminism and women, comes to recognize *the multiple* differences (rather than *the single* sexual difference), giving rise to a "plural", "radical", and "inclusive" democracy—to borrow some of Young's expressions—capable of using *intersectionality* and *contamination* in an unprecedented way as practices that can nurture imaginaries and political struggles[74] and give space to "intersecting voices".[75]

[69] Pannarale (2019), pp. 24–26.

[70] Pannarale (2019),

[71] Cf. Casadei (2019); Giolo (2020a).

[72] Pannarale (2019).

[73] Pannarale (2019).

[74] Cf. Demaria (2003).

[75] This is the perspective suggested by Young (1997).

4 Towards a Caring Democracy In a Responsive State: The Legacy of Anna Kuliscioff

This specific positioning seems appropriate to recover an overarching vision that connects multiple pathways—which are too often overlooked—united by underlying affinities, thus generating *convergences.*[76] The implications can be significant not only on a sociological level[77] but, more importantly, at the political level.

In recent years, women mobilization practices have introduced gestures different from those known in the past: online activism; flash mobs; empty seats left to stigmatize male violence against women and femicide; public denunciations of sexist behavior, including through the massive use of digital technologies and social networks with viral campaigns;[78] public acts and behaviors aimed at subverting traditional forms of struggle, removing them from the "oppositional logic of confrontation, which is instead instrumental to the processes by which power legitimizes the need to resort to violence and the repression of law enforcement forces".[79]

This is where the most interesting potentials of the combination between demands for *equal democracy*, proposals for *radical democracy*, and the realization of a *caring democracy* lie: the internet strengthens a global, "borderless" community, inspired by feminist demands (but also forms of engagement at local and national levels), that discusses, organizes, mobilizes, and contributes to defining the agenda of public debate, revealing new possibilities for expression and mobilizing energies against the regressive processes mentioned above.

Everyday life and its needs, as already in Kulisioff's perspective, thus becomes a source of ideas capable of activating political participation and, at the same time, an object of renewed attention to stigmatize practices of discrimination, inequality, and oppression stemming from the persistence of that "monopoly of man" that Kuliscioff sought to attack at its core.

This refers to promotional actions as well as, in a framework that connects the legal-normative and political spheres, the issue of the effectiveness of equality actions[80] through a renewed centrality of public policies and the specific activities of the constitutional rule of law: interesting considerations, in this perspective, are,

[76] Orsetta Giolo emphasizes, in this regard, that the various feminist configurations and perspectives "can be understood as different elaborations, all attributable to the shared interest in the recognition of the political and legal subjectivity of women": Giolo (2015), p. 46. See also, in the same direction, Casadei (2020).

[77] For a very recent overview: Kaufman et al. (2024).

[78] Chandra and Erlingsdóttir (2020). Cf. Bello (2024).

[79] Magaraggia (2015), p. 27.

[80] On the importance of guarantees for a "legal feminism" that does not abandon the institutional dimension, the arguments contained in Ferrajoli (1997) remain valid. See also Cain (1988); Naffine (1990); Barnett (1998); Casadei (2015).

for example, those contained in the work of Martha A. Fineman, particularly her idea of a *responsive State.*[81]

The idea of a responsive State is based on a specific conception of vulnerability and in many respects recalls the institutional vision prefigured by Kuliscioff. The State must aim to assure substantial equality, starting from the awareness that inequalities result from structural conditions and institutional factors. Therefore, the task of the State is to provide individuals with support structures, that contribute place them in a condition of equality.

According to Fineman, following Kuliscioff, the ultimate ideal of the State is to guarantee the aspirations of equality for the subjects in a vulnerable condition. It must therefore be active and responsive in encouraging the autonomy of every citizen: in Kuliscioff's terms, this means breaking the monopoly of man and putting at the end to subordination of women.

From a cultural perspective attentive to social processes, this entails a constant counter-hegemonic struggle that adopts the feminist lens of care and social reproduction[82] as an overarching and, as much as possible shared vision: this follows in the wake of Kuliscioff's insights into the links between gender and class and extends them to encompass today's subaltern groups.

Furthermore, it is in this context that the forms of what could be called, as has been suggested, a "feminism of conflicts-rights"[83] also seem to resurface, namely, within the framework of arguments that are gradually consolidating, a perspective inspired by *feminist legal studies*: this is a feminism that is not afraid of positioning its claims within institutional contexts[84] and forums, once again reclaiming the transformative power that figures like Kuliscioff attributed to the role of law and legislation in the fight against oppression and inequalities.

Also in light of these phenomena, an original conception of institutions as a whole and of the relationship with political representation may emerge, that is a different conception of egalitarian democracy, energized by the democracy of care and practices of interdependence.[85] This conception can make it possible to go beyond the opposition between exclusively "movement-based" feminism and "institutionalized" feminism: and this was the perspective already indicated by Kuliscioff, who, through her struggles and writings, sought to combine women's demands and claims, in the spheres of work, school, and family life, with legislative production (as shown by her proposals on equal universal suffrage, education, and women's working conditions, particularly in the field of healthcare).

The envisioned project is (historically) thinkable and possible only—this must be clearly stated—after the epochal result of women's self-reflection, their practices

[81] Fineman (2014), pp. 251–275. Cf. Re (2019). On these aspects, please see also Kohn (2014).

[82] On this point: Bhattacharya (2017).

[83] Baeri (2007), p. 91.

[84] I recall here some considerations developed in Casadei (2020).

[85] Well described in the already mentioned The Care Collective (2020).

of liberation, their movements for emancipation and rights, and their achievements in the recognition of specific—and unmissable—needs.

If it is up to the women of today to reclaim this "memory" and broaden its horizons (in terms of environmental challenges, old and new forms of poverty and exclusion, the reconfiguration of workspaces, starting with domestic work and extending to often underpaid and exploited labor), it is up to *new* men to become diligent participants, recognizing themselves, indeed, in a project that can take on precise forms of sharing, as advocated in 1966 by a refined French intellectual like Simone de Beauvoir and, today, among others, by Nigerian writer Chimamanda Ngozi Adichie, who is highly attentive to the dimension of transnational and borderless communication.[86] Therefore, one should not limit oneself to specific claims, in the words of de Beauvoir's, but "broaden their extent", fighting for "a general change in society".[87]

It is time for *convergences*: after all, it is precisely those actions driven by convergence and alliances—the very actions figures like Kuliscioff pursued throughout their lives—that are most feared by those who seek to maintain the *status quo* and consolidated power structures, as they have the potential to make (counter-)hegemony a reality and thus transform the unexpected into real cultural and social change and, ultimately, into consolidated practice.

Even on this point, Kuliscioff's foresight retains its powerful promise: "It is not a condemnation of the other sex at all costs that women demand; on the contrary, they aspire to obtain the conscious and active cooperation of the best men, those who, having at least partially emancipated themselves from sentiments based on custom, prejudice, and especially male selfishness, are already willing to recognize *the just reasons women have for occupying a dignified place in life, having earned that right*".[88]

From these demands, which concern the sphere of life (education, family, work, care's spaces, health, political dimension), contemporary manifestations of borderless feminism draw nourishment, as well as the interrelation between the latter and the intersectional approach, and thus the possible convergences between different feminist currents and practices.

It is from the breaking of the monopoly of man that autonomy and authentic freedom of all women can emerge, at every latitude of the planet: for these reasons Anna Kuliscioff, who was cosmopolitan, socialist, and feminist, can be considered a pioneer, *ante litteram*, of an intersectional approach, which today fully reveals its potential.

---

[86] See respectively: de Beauvoir (1966) and Ngozi Adichie (2014). Interesting insights toward a convergence between women and men in the recognition of mutual solidarity can be found in the previously mentioned Gaag (2014).

[87] De Beauvoir (1966), p. 76.

[88] Kuliscioff (2020), italic mine.

References

Álvarez del Cuvillo A et al (2023) Feminist political and legal theories. In: Vujadinović D et al (eds) Gender-competent legal education. Springer, Cham, pp 57–94

Álvarez Medina S et al (2001) Feminismo liberal, radical y socialista. In: Beltrán Pedriera ME, Maquieira d'Angelo V (eds) Feminismos. Debates teóricos contemporáneos. Alianza, Madrid, pp 75–126

Annaratone D (2003) Due rivoluzionarie russe in Italia: Anna Kuliscioff e Angelica Balabanoff a confronto. Libreria CLUP, Milano

Ariès P (1975) L'enfant et la vie familiale sous l'ancien régime. Seuil, Paris. (1re éd. 1960)

Arruzza C, Cirillo L (2017) Storia delle storie del femminismo. Alegre, Roma

Arruzza C et al (2019) Feminism for the 99 percent. Verso, London

Atrey S (2020) Intersectionality and comparative antidiscrimination law: the tale of two citadels. Brill Res Persp Comp Discrim Law 4(1):1–86

Bacchetta P (2015) Il femminismo transnazionale: aprirsi alle alleanze di genere. In: Bacchetta P, Fantone L (eds) Femminismi queer postcoloniali. Ombrecorte, Verona, pp 21–34

Bacchi C, Eveline J (2010) Mainstreaming politics: Gendering practices and feminist theory. Adelaide University Press, Adelaide

Baeri E (2007) In: Ribero A (ed) Glossario. Lessico della differenza. Regione Piemonte, Torino, pp 85–91

Ballestrero MV (1979) Dalla tutela alla parità. La legislazione italiana sul lavoro delle donne. Il Mulino, Bologna

Barnett H (1998) Introduction to feminist jurisprudence. Cavendish Publishing Limited, London

Barranco Avilés M-C (2019) Anna Kuliscioff. Femminismo, socialismo e capacità di agire delle donne. Materiali per la storia di una cultura giuridica 1:185–210

Bartoloni S (ed) (2021) Cittadinanze incompiute: la parabola dell'autorizzazione maritale. Viella, Roma

Bello BG (2020) Intersezionalità. Teorie e pratiche tra diritto e società. Franco Angeli, Milano

Bello BG (2024) What can an intersectional perspective tell us about the #MeToo and #BlackLivesMatter movements? In: Davis K, Lutz H (eds) The Routledge international handbook of intersectionality studies. Routledge, London, pp 76–289

Bhattacharya T (ed) (2017) Social reproduction theory: remapping class, recentering oppression. Pluto Press, London

Bilski ED (2005) Jewish women and their salons. The power of conversation. Jewish Museum-McMullen Museum of Art, New York-Chestnut Hill

Bryson V (1992) Feminist political theory: an introduction. The MacMillan Press Ltd, Houndsmills

Cagnolati A (2012) El monopolio del hombre. La reflexiòn de Anna Kuliscioff sobre la desigualdad de las mujeres en el mundo laboral. In: Clavijo M (ed) Mas igualdad, redes para la igualdad. Sevilla, Arcibel, pp 111–120

Cain PA (1988) Feminist jurisprudence: grounding the theories. Berkeley Women's Law J 4:191–214

Carbin M, Edenheim S (2013) The intersectional turn in feminist theory: a dream of a common language? Eur J Women's Stud 20(3):233–248

Casadei T (ed) (2015) Donne, diritto, diritti. Prospettive del giusfemminismo. Giappichelli, Torino

Casadei T (2019) Eguaglianza. Un concetto controverso e sovversivo. In: Andronico A et al (eds) Dimensioni del diritto, cit, pp 153–180

Casadei T (2020) "Convergenze": lotta per l'egemonia, contro il postfemminismo. In: Verza A, Vida S (eds) Postfemminismo e neoliberalismo. Aracne, Roma, pp 129–155

Casalini M (2013) La signora del socialismo italiano. Vita di Anna Kuliscioff. Editori Riuniti, Roma

Casalini B (2015) Neoliberalismo e femminismi. Le diverse risposte dei femminismi contemporanei al neoliberalismo e le conseguenze delle politiche neoliberali sulla vita delle donne. Jura Gentium 1:1–39

Casalini B (2018) Il femminismo e le sfide del neoliberismo. Postfemminismo, sessismo e politiche della cura. IF Press, Roma
Chandra G, Erlingsdóttir I (2020) The Routledge handbook of the politics of the #MeToo movement. Routledge, London
Code L (1995) Rethorical space. Essays on gendered locations. Routledge, New York, London
Covato C (1991) Sapere e pregiudizio. L'educazione delle donne fra '700 e '800. Archivio Guido Izzi, Roma
Crenshaw K (1989) Demarginalizing the intersection of race and sex: a black feminist critique of antidiscrimination doctrine, feminist theory and antiracist politics. Univ Chic Leg Forum 1:139–168
Dau Novelli C (2010) Il neofemminismo: riflessioni critiche. In: Bonacchi G, Dau Novelli C (eds) Culture politiche e dimensioni del femminile nell'Italia del '900. Rubbettino, Soveria Mannelli, pp 39–62
Davis K, Lutz H (eds) (2023) The Routledge international handbook of intersectionality studies. Routledge, London
de Beauvoir S (1966) Quando tutte le donne del mondo. Einaudi, Torino
Degl'Innocenti M (2017) L'età delle donne: saggio su Anna Kuliscioff. Lacaita, Manduria
Demaria C (2003) Teorie di genere. Femminismo, critica postcoloniale e semiotica. Bompiani, Milano
Diamond E et al (eds) (2017) Performance, feminism and affect in neoliberal times. Palgrave Macmillan, London
Everard M et al (1999) Forgotten intersections. Wilhelmina Drucker, early feminism, and the Dutch-Belgian connection. Revue belge de Philologie et d'Histoire 77(2):440–472
Fanlo Cortés I (2025) Anna Kuliscioff e la cd. questione minorile. In: Taricone F (ed) Oltre il tempo patriarcale. La lungimiranza di Anna Kuliscioff. Preface by Th. Casadei. Tab editore, Roma
Ferrajoli L (1997) Differenza di genere e garanzia di eguaglianza. In: Bimbi F, Dal Re A (eds) Genere e democrazia, Genere e democrazia. La cittadinanza delle donne a cinquant'anni dal voto. Rosenberg & Sellier, Torino, pp 93–100
Fineman MA (2014) The vulnerable subject and the responsive state. Emory Law J 60:251–275
Fraser N (2009) Feminism, capitalism and the cunning history. New Left Rev 56:97–117
Fraser N (2013) Fortunes of feminism. From state-managed capitalism to neoliberal crisis. Verso, London
Fraser N (2021) Gender, capital, and care. In: Browne J (ed) Why gender? Cambridge University Press, Cambridge, pp 144–169
Fraser N (2022) Cannibal capitalism: how our system is devouring democracy, care, and the planet - and what we can do about it. Verso, London
Fredman S (2009) European Union non-discrimination law. Routledge-Cavendish Abingdon, Oxfordshire, pp 105–122
Frosini F, Giasi F (2019) Egemonia e modernità. Gramsci in Italia e nella cultura internazionale. Viella, Roma
van der Gaag N (2014) Feminism and men. Zed Books, London
Geoghegan V, Wilford R (2014) Political ideologies: an introduction. Routledge, London
Gill R (2007) Postfeminist media culture: elements of sensibility. Eur J Cult Stud 2:147–166
Giolo O (2014) Conclusioni. Il patriarcato adattivo e la soggettività politica delle donne. In: Giolo O, Re L (eds) La soggettività politica delle donne. Proposte per un lessico critico. Aracne, Roma
Giolo O (2015) Il giusfemminismo e il dilemma del confronto tra culture. In: Casadei T (ed) Donne, diritto, diritti. Prospettive del giusfemminismo. Giappichelli, Torino, pp 41–60
Giolo O (2020a) Il ritorno della disuguaglianza e le trasformazioni del diritto. Filosofia politica 1:61–78
Giolo O (2020b) Il diritto neoliberale. Jovene, Napoli
Giolo O et al (2022) Tra società e diritto. L'impatto degli studi di genere. Riv Fil Dir 2:289–304
Guadagnini M (2000) La stagione del disincanto? Cittadine, cittadini e politica alle soglie del 2000. Il Segnalibro, Torino

Halley J et al (2006) From the international to the local in feminist legal responses to rape, prostitution/sex work, and sex trafficking. Four studies in contemporary governance feminism. Harv J Law Gender 29:335–423
Hoock-Demarle M-C (1995) Femmes, nations, Europe. Publications de l'Université Paris 7, Paris
Kaufman G et al (2024) Research handbook on the sociology of gender. Edward Elgar Publishing, Cheltenham
Kohn NA (2014) Vulnerability theory and the role of government. Yale J Law Fem 1:1–27
Kuliscioff A (2015a) Proletariato femminile (1892). In: Kuliscioff A (ed) Scritti. Fondazione Anna Kuliscioff, Milano
Kuliscioff A (2015b) Alle operaie della manifattura tabacchi (1898). In: Kuliscioff A (ed) Scritti. Fondazione Anna Kuliscioff, Milano
Kuliscioff A (2020) Il monopolio dell'uomo (1890). Ortica editrice, Roma
Kuliscioff A (2024) Non sono la signora di nessuno. Corriere della Sera, Milano
Legates M (2001) In their time: a history of feminism in Western society. Routledge, London
Lussana F (1997) Le donne e la modernizzazione: il neofemminismo degli anni Settanta. In: Barbagallo F (ed) Storia dell'Italia repubblicana, 2 vols. Einaudi, Torino, pp 471–565
Lykke N (2010) Feminist studies. A guide to intersectional theory, methodology and writing. Routledge, Abingdon
Lynch K (2021) Care and capitalism. Why affective equality matters for social justice. Polity Press, Cambridge
Macioce F (2023) The politics of vulnerable groups implications for philosophy, law, and political theory. Macmillan, Palgrave
Magaraggia S (2015) Il moto ondoso dei femminismi: abbiamo avvistato la quarta ondata? In: Magaraggia S, Vingelli G (eds) Genere e partecipazione politica. Franco Angeli, Milano, pp 23–34
Marchetti S et al (2012) Femministe a parole. Grovigli da districare. Ediesse, Roma
McCann C, Kim S-K (2013) Feminist theory reader: local and global perspectives. Routledge, London
McRobbie A (2009) The aftermath of feminism. Gender, culture and social change. Sage, Los Angeles
Mies M (2014) Patriarchy and accumulation on a world scale: women in the international division of labour. Zed Books, London
Minervini D (2019) La violenza della cultura. Dominio e emancipazione di genere in Bourdieu e Gramsci. In: De Feo A et al (eds) Scienza e critica del mondo sociale: la lezione di Pierre Bourdieu. Milano-Udine, Mimesis, pp 133–152
Modena LLD (2021) Baronesses and revolutionaries: the activism of foreign-born Jewish women in Liberal Italy. J Mod Jew Stud 21(2):148–171
Mohanty CTD (2003) Feminism without borders: decolonizing theory, practicing solidarity. Duke University Press, Durham
Morini C (2021a) Life is mine. Feminism, self-determination and basic income. BIN – Basic Income Italia. https://www.bin-italia.org/life-is-mine-feminism-self-determination-and-basic-income/
Morini C (2021b) Take care: society of care and self-determination income. Cogut Institute for Humanities, Brown University. https://blogs.brown.edu/humanities/archives/344
Munro E (2013) Feminism: a fourth wave? Polit Insight 4:22–25
Naffine N (1990) Law and the sexes: explorations in feminist jurisprudence. Allen & Unwin, London
Negar S, Kharazmi ZN (2019) The fourth wave of feminism and the lack of social realism in cyberspace. J Cyberspace Stud 3:129–146
Ngozi Adichie C (2014) We should all be feminists. Anchor Books, New York
Ortner SB (2020) Racializing patriarchy: lessons from police brutality. In: Fenstermaker S, Stewart AJ (eds) Gender, considered. Genders and sexualities in the social sciences. Palgrave Macmillan, New York, pp 137–163
Pannarale L (2019) La fraternità dei diritti. In: Anastasia S, Gonnella P (eds) I paradossi del diritto. Saggi in omaggio di Eligio Resta. Roma, TrePress, pp 21–26

Passaniti P (2016) Lavoro e cittadinanza femminile: Anna Kuliscioff e la prima legge sul lavoro delle donne. Franco Angeli, Milano
Pescarolo A (2019) Il lavoro delle donne nell'Italia contemporanea. Viella, Roma
Re L (2019) Vulnerabilità e cura nell'orizzonte dello Stato costituzionale di diritto. Notizie di Politeia 35:183–197
Re L, Giolo O (eds) (2014) La soggettività politica delle donne. Proposte per un lessico critico. Aracne, Roma
Restaino F (2002) Il pensiero femminista. Una storia possibile. In: Cavarero A, Restaino F (eds) Le filosofie femministe. Bruno Mondadori, Milano, pp 54–75
Rigo E (2022) L'impatto degli studi di genere sul diritto. Riproduzione sociale, lavoro non retribuito e cura sotto la lente della pandemia da Covid-19. Rivista di filosofia del diritto 2:319–338
Romero M (ed) (2023) Research handbook on intersectionality. Edward Elgar Publishing, Cheltenham
Rottenberg C (2018) The rise of neoliberal feminism. Oxford University Press, Oxford
Röwekamp M (2023) Challenging patriarchism in the family: law reform and female protest in nineteenth and twentieth century Europe. In: Vujadinović D, Álvarez del Cuvillo A, Strand S (eds) Feminist approaches to law. Gender perspectives in law. Springer, Cham
Scapocchin A (2024) Cosmopolitismo. In: Maestroni V, Casadei T (eds) Medicina, emancipazione, politica. Anna Kuliscioff e noi. Mucchi, Modena, pp 77–80
Seveso G (2018) Il diritto delle bambine all'istruzione sulle pagine di due riviste dell'inizio del Novecento: "Unione Femminile" e "La difesa delle lavoratrici". Diacronie. Studi di storia contemporanea 34. https://journals.openedition.org/diacronie/8214
Shepherd N (2009) Anna Kuliscioff, 1855–1925. Shalvi/Hyman Encyclopedia of Jewish Women. 27 February. Jewish Women's Archive. https://jwa.org/encyclopedia/article/kuliscioff-anna
Stelliferi P, Voli S (eds) (2023) Anni di rivolta: nuovi sguardi sui femminismi degli anni Settanta e Ottanta. Viella, Roma
Strid S, Hearn J (2022) Violence and patriarchy. In: Kurtz LR (ed) Encyclopedia of violence, peace and conflict, 3 vols. Academic, Cambridge, pp 319–327
Taricone F (2020) Politica e cittadinanza. Donne socialiste fra Ottocento e Novecento. Franco Angeli, Milano
Taricone F (ed) (2025) Oltre il tempo patriarcale. La lungimiranza di Anna Kuliscioff. Tab editore, Roma
Tarozzi F (1996) Anna Kuliscioff, la "signora del socialismo italiano". In: Zarri G (ed) La memoria di lei. Storia delle donne, storia di genere, con la collaborazione di C. Pancino, F. Tarozzi. Società Editrice Internazionale – SEI, Torino, pp 118–121
The Care Collective (2020) The care manifesto. The politics of interdependence. Verso, New York
Tita M (2018) Logiche giuridiche dell'esclusione. Sui diritti al femminile tra Otto e Novecento. Giappichelli, Torino, pp 105–111
Toscano A (2024) Camarade Balabanoff: vie et luttes de la grand-mère du socialisme. Colin, Malakoff
Tronto J (2013) Caring democracy: markets, equality and justice. New York, New York University Press
Tucker E (2011) Feminist political theory. In: Gibbons M (ed) The encyclopedia of political thought. Wiley Blackwell, New York, pp 1033–1036
Vantin S (2018) L'eguaglianza di genere tra mutamenti sociali e nuove tecnologie. Percorsi di diritto antidiscriminatorio. Pacini, Pisa
Verza A (2009) Le correnti femministe. Il difficile equilibrio tra eguaglianza e differenza. In: Campesi G, Pupolizio I, Riva N (eds) Diritto e teoria sociale. Introduzione al pensiero socio-giuridico contemporaneo. Carocci, Roma, pp 257–296
Verza A (2023) Violencia contra la mujer en el ámbito relacional-afectivo. In: Castañeda Rivas ML (ed) Hacia la igualidad y plenos derechos para las mujeres. Editorial Porrùa, Ciudad de Mèxico, pp 721–740

Vida S (2016) Identità precarie. Il soggetto neoliberale tra incertezza, governamentalità e violenza. Materiali per una storia della cultura giuridica 2:479–506
Vida S (2017) Postcapitalismo e neoliberismo: il presente e il futuro della crisi. Ragion Pratica 2:299–325
Vida S (2020) Postfemminismo reazionario. In: Verza A, Vida S (eds) Postfemminismo e neoliberalismo. Aracne, Roma, pp 27–74
Vogel L (1983) Marxism and the oppression of women. Toward a unitary theory. Pluto, London
Vujadinović D et al (eds) (2022) Feminist approaches to law: theoretical and historical insights. Springer, Cham
Walby S (2011) The future of feminism. Polity Press, Cambridge
Wing AK (2003) Critical race feminism: a reader. New York University Press, New York
Wing AK, Pappalardo C (2023) Critical race feminism: a different approach to feminist theory. In: Vujadinović D et al (eds) Feminist approaches to law: theoretical and historical insights. Springer, Cham, pp 53–71
Young IM (1997) Intersecting voices: dilemmas of gender, political philosophy, and policy. Princeton University Press, Princeton
Zazzara F (2019) Anna Kuliscioff. Donna, rivoluzionaria, medico. Storia della dottora dei poveri nella medicina del suo tempo. Biblion Ed., Milano
Zichi P (2022) Paolina Schiff and the making of a global women's rights and peace agenda (1841–1926). In: Schüler-Springorum S (ed) Jahrbuch für Antisemitismusforschung, vol 31, 1st edn, pp 111–132

Thomas Casadei is full Professor of Philosophy of Law and Director of Interdepartmental Research Centre on Discrimination and vulnerabilities—CRID at the University of Modena and Reggio Emilia (www.crid.unimore.it), Faculty of Law. He obtained his Ph.D. (2003) at the University of Pisa, Faculty of Political Science. In the academic year 2023–2024 and 2024–2025, he has been Visiting Professor at the Facultad de Derecho, Sevilla University. He teaches several courses, including Theory and Practice of Human Rights, Theory and History of Public Opinion, Didactics of Law and Media Education, Legal Informatics, and Sexual and Cultural Differences: Legislative Aspects. He was also a member of the Project team of the Horizon 2020 EQUAL-IST "Gender Equality Plans for Information Sciences and Technology Research Institutions". He is a member of "Red Iberoamericana de Investigaciòn sobre Formas Contemporaneas de Esclavitud y Derechos Humanos". As an expert in human rights and legal feminism, he is involved in many projects run by various organizations and institutions. He has published monographs, textbooks and more than 160 articles in philosophy of law, international human rights law, children's rights, equal opportunities and non-discrimination, contemporary forms of slavery, digital justice, artificial intelligence, as well as the history of legal thought.

Women as Chattels or Women with Agency? A Study of the Legal and Civil Rights of Women in Mughal India

Angbin Yasmin

Abstract This paper analyzes Mughal textual sources, such as court chronicles and legal documents, including *nikāḥnāma* (marriage contracts), sale deeds, and gift deeds, to understand the legal status of women during the Mughal period. It highlights certain rights that women possessed in the past and provides a foundation to strengthen the position of women in today's society. I will discuss women's rights in marriage and divorce, issues related to violence, and property rights enjoyed by women from the fifteenth to the seventeenth centuries. Farhat Hassan rightly points out that "social groups exploited the flexibility and lack of fixedness in *shari'a* to manipulate it to protect their interests." This flexibility therefore served as a useful tool for women to resist their oppression. The examination of legal documents indicates that women from various religious communities across the empire frequently engaged with the Mughal legal courts. This was true not only for Muslim women but also for non-Muslim women who understood *shari'a* and the procedures of the legal courts. Women recognized the importance of records and testimonies, demonstrating their agency within this legal system.

1 Introduction

As society and the state developed over time, people recognized the need for organized justice administered by the state to maintain public peace. Different communities in India, be it Hindus or Muslims, attach supreme importance to the principles of their faith. Their sacred scriptures serve as guides to regulate their social relations and political organization. The current legal corpus is predicated upon these sacred scriptures, which emerged over time.

A. Yasmin (✉)
School of Law, Jamia Hamdard, New Delhi, India

F. Macioce et al. (eds.), *Feminist Legal and Political Practices*, Gender Perspectives in Law 6, https://doi.org/10.1007/978-3-032-02856-3_4

Given society's patriarchal nature, laws have typically been created by and for men, resulting in legal outcomes that favor male interests and concerns.[1] Additionally, it is argued that law is inherently male-oriented, reflecting masculine values and assumptions.[2] In India, it has been primarily upper-class and upper-caste men who wielded the privilege of lawmaking, often relegating women and other marginalized groups to subordinate roles. This marginalization was accompanied by legal disabilities that some modern scholars argue were divinely legitimized.

This chapter does not set out to examine the historical marginalization of communities or establish how the suffragist movement influenced the legal discourse in India. While acknowledging the contribution of our foremothers in this regard, I focus instead on how these debated disabilities have become a political tool in contemporary times, particularly for demonizing specific communities, especially Muslims. Muslim women have been portrayed as victims of veil, triple talaq (divorce), polygamy, etc. and are often presented as having a deficit of rights because of Islamic law. The events of the 1980s saw the rise of the Hindu right-wing and its appropriation of feminist positions.[3] Controversial issues such as triple talaq, the wearing of headscarves, and maintenance rights became focal points for debate.

The justification for exploiting legal systems to "save Muslim women from Muslim men" has often served the agendas of political groups, evident in legislation like the Muslim Women (Protection of Rights on Marriage) Act 2019. This act has faced criticism for being redundant and arbitrary. Scholars argue that the criminalization of triple talaq, which can lead to a 3-year imprisonment sentence, is excessive, unjustified, and lacks a solid theoretical foundation.

Thus, it becomes crucial to prevent Hindu communalists from using women's rights issues as a means to incite communal hatred against Muslims and other minorities, rather than seeking to create legal safeguards for women. As MacKinnon emphasizes, achieving equality requires a new jurisprudence and a fresh perspective on the relationship between life and law. This raises the question: could there be insights from our past? What if women in history had navigated their circumstances more effectively by understanding and asserting their legal rights? The fact that equality cannot be achieved by law alone and inequality cannot be changed without law becomes important here. Therefore, MacKinnon's method of consciousness-raising shows women's situation in a way that affirms women's ability to change their situation not despite the law but by engaging with the law.[4]

I, in this chapter, argue on the lines of MacKinnon that legal consciousness not only facilitated women's engagement with the law during the medieval period but also provided economic and social stability. This occurred despite the state's effort to uphold the patriarchal norms established by men. My focus will primarily be on the middle and ordinary-class women who exercised legal agency during the Mughal

[1] Conaghan (2013), p. 75.

[2] Robin & Cynthia (2019), p. 63.

[3] Phadke (2003), pp. 4567–4576.

[4] MacKinnon (1989), pp. 161–162.

period, specifically from the fifteenth to the seventeenth century. Although these women came from the non-elite section of society, they were aware of the law and attempted to navigate and manipulate it to their advantage. To understand the context in which these women operated, it is essential to familiarize ourselves with the legal framework and the conditions of the time. I will first examine Islamic jurisprudence and imperial canonization to understand what constituted *shari'a*, and further discuss the prevalence of legal pluralism that facilitated women's access to the law. Given that the state is a patriarchal institution, the second section will address the ambiguous position of the state, illustrating its dual role: on the one hand, showing benevolence toward women and, on the other, enforcing patriarchal norms. This analysis will help us determine whether there was a patriarchal bias in judicial decisions. The third part of the chapter will address the issue of legal personhood. Here, I will demonstrate that women were recognized as legal persons during medieval India by highlighting the legal agency exercised by women in matters pertaining to marriage and divorce. I will also question the contemporary debate surrounding the need to "save" Muslim women, drawing on perspectives from Lila Abu-Lughod:[5] Do Muslim women need saving?

2 *Usul i fiqh* (Principles of Islamic Jurisprudence) and Legal System Under Mughals

The Mughal legal system, an intricate blend of Islamic jurisprudence and customary Indian laws, established a foundational legal framework throughout sixteenth to nineteenth century India. Recognised for relying on the Quran and Hadis, it intricately weaves the *shari'a* with local traditions, ensuring administrative consistency across the diverse Mughal empire. The Mughal legal system emerged with the establishment of the Mughal empire in India. It was a blend of Islamic jurisprudence and pre-existing legal tradition. The system evolved over the centuries, adapting to the changing landscape of the empire.

Muhammadan law, as it exists today, is the result of a continuous process of development over centuries.[6] The law in Islam is called *fiqh*; it is the name given to the whole science of jurisprudence. *Fiqh* literally means 'intelligence' and *faqīh* (plural-*fuquhā)* is a 'jurist', a person skilled in the law. The field of *usul i fiqh* (Islamic Jurisprudence) embodies theoretical discussions of the nature of the religious law and its derivations from the Quran, Sunnah or Hadis (practice of Prophet Muhammad as transmitted through sayings actions and approval), *ijmā* (consensus of the scholars), and *qiyas* (analogical deductions from these three). *Fiqh* implies the exercise of intelligence in deciding a point of law in the absence of a binding

[5] Abu-Lughod (2013).

[6] The term Islamic law is used synonymously with Muhammadan law. As it is a useful expression as far as India is concerned.

naṣṣ (command) from the Quran or sunnah. It emphasises that interpretation plays a substantial role in the development of *shari'a* law. This need arose due to the application of the principles of the Quran and the teachings of the Prophet to the complex, growing and changing society. It was found necessary for the advocates and judges to interpret and reinterpret these principles and teachings. From the earliest times, Muslim scholars had been active in producing legal opinions, which became the base from which the ruler could draw inferences in formulating laws. These advisors were *fuquhā,* men skilled in the study of jurisprudence (*fiqh*), who provided *fatwās,* or legal judgements to questions put to them by the *qazis* (judge) in the courts or the general populace.[7] Thus, various approaches to the sources of Islamic law, the *shari'a,* and the role of reason in deciding matters of law led to the development of several schools of law. The *Shari'a* as interpreted by all the schools, retained a dynamic character for it to be adapted by theorists and practitioners to meet the needs of the evolving Muslim communities. Of the important schools, leaving aside the Shia and Khariji sects, which were founded as result of political cleavage, one can mention the four major schools of law: The Hanafi School (founded by Abu Hanifa), The Maliki School (founded by Malik ibn Anas), The Hanbali school(founded by Ahmed ibn Hanbal) and, The Shafi School(founded by Muhammad Ibn Idris ash Shafi).

Fiqh scholarship on the Hanafi School dominated Central Asia and found its routes to north India during the medieval period.[8] Initially, Muslim scholars or the ulama relied on the rulings of Hanafi scholars in Central Asia and the Middle East. After a while, they also began to produce their compendiums first being the *Fatwa-i Ghiyathiyya* ascribed to Sultan Ghiyas ud din Balban.[9] It was followed by other corpora commissioned by reigning emperors or their nobles demonstrating the expertise of the individual scholars in the matters of law, for example, *Fatawa- i Tatar Khaniya* produced at the request of Khan i Azam Tatar Khan a noble during the reign of Firoz Shah Tughlaq.[10] During the reign of Aurangzeb, two *fatwa* collections besides the *Fatawa i Alamgiri* were produced[11] one by Moinuddin Muhammad bin Khwajah Mahmud al Naqshband and one by Mufti Abul-Barakat bin Hussam al-din Dihlawi in 1698.[12]

The most salient feature of Mughal legal ideology as argued by Corinne Lefevre[13] is the absence of a unanimously agreed version of *shari'a* (Islamic Law) throughout the Muslim world in general and in Mughal India in particular: even though the Hanafi school is often said to have prevailed within the empire, the events described by Abul Qadir Badauni during the reign of Akbar, about the discussion about

[7] Ahmad (1970), p. 2.

[8] Guenther (2003), pp. 209–230.

[9] Islam (1966), pp. 223–241.

[10] Islam (1966), p. 230.

[11] Qadri (1966), pp. 188–199.

[12] Qadri (1966), p. 191.

[13] Lefevre (2017), pp. 116–141.

polygamy, indicate the inner diversity of Islamic law.[14] *Shari'a*, therefore, was not a rigid legal system. It was a polysemous system, that indicated flexibility by assimilating local norms and customs. To put it in a nutshell, at least three normative frameworks coexisted within the Mughal empire: *shari'a*, *dharma* (Hindu law encompassing cates-*jatidharma*, regions- *deshadharama* or kingdoms- *rajadharma*) and *zawabit*(state legislation). Besides all of them had to accommodate the local customs and usages (*'urf-u-'ada*) ingrained in the countless villages, towns and cities. As rightly pointed out by Syed Ali Nadeem Rezavi in his article Civil Law and Justice in Mughal Gujarat,[15] the term *shari'a* connotes "law" and not necessarily "Islamic law". Therefore the invocation of the *shari'a* was meant to be understood as "rule of law", which once entered into, had not to be violated. This diversity and flexibility, therefore, worked in the favour of women, which we will see in the next section. Needless to say, that patriarchal society had taken sexual violation of women seriously and, as a precautionary measure, imposed restrictions not only on mobility but also defined the code of conduct of women. By defining the code of conduct for women in the didactic literature during medieval India, the state tried to uphold the normative behaviour laid down in these ethical treatises. Hence, transgressing from the defined and established norms for women could invite reprimand from the state, which draws legitimacy from the sacred literature upon which these laws were predicated. To cite a few examples: Numerous ethical treatises have, over time, outlined standards of moral conduct for women during medieval India. Among these Nasir Uddin Tusi's *Akhlaq i Nasiri* is the most popular, which has a separate section on the chastisement of the wives.[16] *Tuhfa Nasaih* by Yusuf Gada is another similar text that contains prescriptions for wife obedience.[17] These two influential prescriptive/didactic literatures from the medieval period established the foundations of what an ideal woman looks like.

3 State's Benevolence and Violence Against Women

The laws (Hindu and Muslim) legitimized the use of violence against women to address any perceived deviance or transgressing the norms defined in the conduct manuals. For instance, the provision in Islamic *shari'a* to chastise wives by 'beating them lightly' for 'disloyalty and ill conduct' provided justification for domestic violence,[18] so much so that women had to insert a clause in the *nikāḥnāma* (marriage contract). I will discuss this further under the sub-heading Legal personhood. Additionally, the State played a dual role, promoting moral conduct while also

[14] Badauni (1864-69), vol. II, pp. 211–213.

[15] Rezavi (1993), pp. 189–199.

[16] Wickens (1964), pp. 161–166.

[17] Cf. Digby (1984), pp. 111–112.

[18] Bano (2020), pp. 129–136.

enacting regulations to safeguard women. For instance, since a woman had to be virtuous and chaste therefore, it was expected of them not to be found running about the lanes and bazārs of the town and, while doing so, either did not veil herself or allowed herself to become unveiled or that if a woman was worthless and deceitful, she was to go to the quarter of the prostitutes and take up the profession.[19]

While showing his concern regarding the practice of Sati (widow burning), Akbar appointed an official to ensure that while those who wished to commit sati might be allowed to do so, they should prohibit and prevent any forcible sati.[20] Abū'l Fazl (the court historian of Akbar) also records a remark made by the emperor in the *ibadatkhana*. Akbar does not criticize the practice but registers his concern and censures husbands who obtained their wives' destruction by spreading false reports of their deaths.[21] He also expressed his dissatisfaction with the share in the inheritance that Muslim law allows to women—though more generous than Hindu or Christian laws. He felt a lack of justification for allowing a smaller share and argued that a woman's supposed weakness warranted a larger share. He highlighted patriarchal anxiety surrounding daughters moving to their husband's households, fearing property would pass to outsiders (meaning outside the family).[22]

Additionally, the State offered protection to women against its armies. Instances of sexual violence against women during rebellion are mentioned in Badauni's account[23] wherein he condemns those who, in military campaigns, dishonored women. 'Abū'l Fazl refers to an imperial order issued by Akbar around 1562–63 prohibiting imperial soldiers from taking captive the women, children, and kinsmen of the opposite soldiery and then selling them or keeping them as slaves. Later, Jahangir ordered that soldiers should not alight in any house but should pitch a tent outside the city, thereby offering protection to women from possible abuse and harassment.[24]

Cases of violence against women are well documented in the court chronicles and travellers' accounts, highlighting the state's immediate action. For instance, 'Abū'l Faẓl and Nizāmuddin both describe a dreadful incident regarding the daughter of Bibi Fātima, who had been in service in the *ḥaram* of the late emperor Ḥumāyūn who had married her daughter Zuhra Aghā to the half-brother of Ḥamīda Bāno Begum(wife of Humayun), Khwāja Muazzam who in the words of 'Abū'l Faẓl, on various occasions was an example of immoderation and Bibi Fātima knowing his barbarity and wickedness continually in grief sought Akbar's help. Nizāmuddin says Khwāja, without any reason, was determined to put that helpless woman to death. Knowing that, the Emperor sent some men to rescue her, Khwāja,

[19] Badauni (1864-69), p. 391.

[20] Cf. Habib (1992), pp. 300–310; Badauni (1864-69) vol. II, p. 376.

[21] Fazl (1939), vol III, pp. 449–450; Fazl (1939), vol II, p. 45.

[22] Fazl (1949), vol II, p. 235.

[23] Badauni (1864-69), vol II, p. 155.

[24] Khan (1965), p. 187.

in a fit of rage, stabbed her to death. He was later captured and punished.[25] In the case of such domestic violence, one may argue that the impunity comes from the legitimacy men get from the religious texts. The provision in *shari'a* to chastise wives by beating them lightly for disloyalty and ill conduct gave them the authority to punish. Surprisingly, the state ensured that wives were not allowed to argue with their husbands and bad-tempered wives were abhorred by men. Badauni notes that Akbar implemented a regulation that if a woman quarrelled with her husband, she was made to take up the profession of prostitution.[26]

In the case of sexual misconduct, legal documents refer to any sort of sexual misconduct as *chamchori* (literally theft of the body) and make it difficult to differentiate between adultery and rape. In some cases, the term *joravari* is prefixed to *chamchori*, which implied rape. There are several cases of intra-family *chamchori* where the daughter-in-law was victimised by the father-in-law. There were other cases of incest involving brother and sister, father and daughter recorded in Farohi documents.[27] It is not clear how such offences were perceived by the local communities and the families of the persons involved due to the paucity of records. Nonetheless, the state's involvement and subsequent actions are well noted, as it often acted against male perpetrators in these cases. But, it is difficult to say that the same yardstick was used for all classes/castes. As we know, people from privileged backgrounds in terms of caste or class position enjoyed certain privileges.

Irfan Habib rightly argues that gender exploitation was intertwined with class oppression in medieval times.[28] Jahāngīr, in his *Tuzuk*(memoir) alludes to a complaint that a widow made against Muqarrab Khān. She accused Muqarrab Khān took her daughter by force in the port of Cambay. Upon enquiring, he told the mother that her daughter had died of unavoidable circumstances. Jahangir ordered an inquiry into the matter. After much search, he discovered that one of his attendants had been guilty of this outrage and ordered the attendant's execution. He also reduced Muqarrab Khān's *manṣab* by one-half and made an allowance to the woman who had been thus injured.[29] This incident demonstrates how the severity of punishment was influenced by the class position of those involved.

Another incident mentioned in *Maasir ul Umra* supports this observation. Shahnawaz Khan writes when Akbar was returning from Kabul and halted at Safed Sang, it was brought to his notice that a soldier had dishonoured a peasant's daughter. The accused got a capital punishment. However, the noble Muhammad Sharif involved in the matter who had considerable influence, was merely censured and punished.[30] This illustrates that safeguarding women, was part of the state's project for a just rule, keeping in view the socially accepted class, caste, and gender norms.

---

[25] Ahmad (1939), vol. III, 288–289; Fazl (1939), pp. 217–219.

[26] Badauni (1864-69), vol. II, 391; Ahmad (1939), pp. 436–438.

[27] Singh (2010), p. 291.

[28] Habib (2000), p. 3.

[29] Jahangir (1909-14), p. 172.

[30] Khan (2003), pp. 625–629.

Patriarchy ensured women's dependency by imposing certain disabilities. Fear of sexual violence was instilled in their minds, and the social stigma restricted their mobility and access to resources. Additionally, societal preference for male offspring over female children furthered women's vulnerability through reproduction.[31] By creating dependency (both physical and economic) on men, women were made susceptible to abandonment. One such case is reported by 'Abū'l Fazl, where a woman was threatened to be divorced if she was unable to reproduce a boy. 'Abū'l Faẓl recounts the birth of a noble Saif Khān and says that his mother had only daughters, and when she was pregnant with Saif Khān, Her husband threatened to divorce her if the child turned out to be a girl. She complained of this to Akbar's mother and Akbar, then a child, told her husband that he would incur his displeasure if he should do so, besides predicting, however, the birth of a boy. The mother looked upon Prince Akbar's words as a divine prophecy, and eventually, Saif Khān was born.[32] The expectations from a woman were not only limited to reproducing a male child or to being a subservient wife, it went beyond that. Nizāmuddin reported when Mulla Mir Kalan Hariwi was asked why he had not married, he replied that he feared his wife might not act in as per his mother's wishes.[33] This indicates that a woman's duty was not confined to producing male children or being submissive; she was also expected to obey her mother-in-law, which could lead to further violence against her. This incident reveals the hierarchical order within the household, highlighting the mother's authority over the wife, who was expected to be subordinate. Here, one may agree with Kumkum Sangri, "Patriarchies are resilient not only because they are embedded in social stratification, division of labours, other political structures, religious cultural practices institutions and categories, but also because of the contractual and consensual element in them, which along with patriarchal systems is open to constant and consistent reformulation." Furthermore, she asserts that, "unless certain distributions of power are made within patriarchal arrangements it is difficult to imagine how any degree of consent from women can be obtained."[34]

The above-mentioned cases demonstrate that the state acted when women were subjected to extreme forms of violence. They also show that, despite the limitations enshrined in *shari'a,* women of certain classes had access to courts. This reflects the legal agency of women at a time when legal personhood, by its foundational presumptions, was the domain of men.

[31] Chakravarti (1993), pp. 579–585.

[32] Fazl (1939), p. 375.

[33] Ahmad (1939), pp. 694–695; see also Badauni (1864-69), vol III, pp. 151–152.

[34] Sangri (1993), p. 868.

4 Legal Personhood and Women

Legal Personhood which is a foundational concept of Western law, has been used for centuries to deny legal agency to women via labels of hysteria and mental illness.[35] They often did not enjoy separate legal personhood from men (fathers or husbands); instead, the law viewed women as objects, and these men held the power to make legal decisions on their behalf. However, quite interestingly when it comes to matters pertaining to marriage, divorce and property during Mughal India we find a different practice altogether. Marriage (*nikāḥ*) in Islam is a contract (*'aqd*). If we study *nikāḥnāmas* (marriage contract) from Surat and *Munshat i Namakin* compiled by the imperial employee Saiyid Abu al Qasim alias Namakin (d.1609/10), we find women exercising legal agency.[36] Therefore, I argue that women of this period were very well recognised as a person of law at least during the fifteenth to seventeenth century. Thus, it contradicts the very foundations of Western law that denied legal agency to women and other minorities. However, with time, the format of *nikāḥnāma* changed and took away women's right to impose certain terms and conditions.

In this regard, I would like to cite examples from the *Munsh'āt i Namakīn*, which contains a large number of legal and contractual documents that throw considerable light not only on legal procedures that were followed during that period but also inevitably reflect the conditions obtained in the contemporary society. There are documents relating to *nikaḥ* which provide noteworthy information on the institutions of marriage. Besides mentioning *meḥr* (the sum of money or other type of property or surety to which the wife becomes entitled by marriage) four very significant conditions are mentioned in the marriage contract and all these are in favour of women. These conditions are referred to in the documents as the four conditions of *shari'at*, which are well-known among Muslims. This would mean that these were the usual terms of marriage contracts during that period. First, the man would not enter into a marriage contract with any other woman. Secondly, the man would not stay away from the woman for one complete year in a manner that her maintenance would not reach her and in case this happens, the woman would be entitled to terminate the marriage with one final *talāq* (*talāq i bain*). The husband was required to provide his wife with basic necessities, to survive, clothe and lodge her. In some cases, women acquired a written testimony in which their husbands would promise to provide the listed item and amount of money to their wives at a designated time. Thirdly, unless warranted by some serious offence or perfidy committed by the woman, the man would not beat her in such a manner that leaves its impression on any part of her body. In case of the materialization of any of these conditions, the woman would be at liberty to dissolve the marriage with one final *talāq* (*talāq i bain*) from the man who is guilty of a religious crime (*mujrim i shara'i*) whenever and wherever she desires and the settlement amount would be payable to her. The

[35] Kerslake (2024), pp. 103–134.

[36] Zilli (2017), Docs no. pp. 205–206, 333–335; Namakin. A Munshat i Namakin Maulana Azad Library, AMU, no. farsiya 26

fourth condition is that the man would not bring a concubine of any description upon her, be it Indian, Armenian or of any other description. In case he brings a concubine, she would be free to sell the same at the prevalent price and keep the price as part of her marriage settlement. It was only with these stringent conditions that a marriage was solemnized.[37]

Similar conditions of marriage are mentioned in a series of documents belonging to the late seventeenth and eighteenth centuries from Gujarat. Shireen Moosvi analysed these documents and went on to show that these conditions, as earlier mentioned by Abū'l Qāsim's *Namakīn,* were not aberrations but prevailed all over the century and were quite known and popularly understood up to at least the eighteenth century.[38] This further informs us about the socio-economic condition of women during the period.

There are also references to individual conditions in a few *nikāḥnāmas* of Surat, which a wife might impose over her husband and take surety from him that in case of non-compliance, she would be deemed legally free to divorce him. In one document dated 2 November 1633, we find a husband, a cook by profession, giving surety in the court that he had abstained from consuming liquor for 1 year. In case he is found indulging in future, he nominates his wife as *wakīla* (representative) to approach the law and get a decree of divorce. It shows that drawing up conditions even after marriage was quite common.[39]

The conditions mentioned in the documents do not appear to be only theoretical, as there are cases where women were given divorce due to their husbands' violation of these conditions. For example, a woman named Ḥabīb Bāi got her divorce in 1628 as her husband Isḥāq failed to provide any maintenance and was absconding for a long period.[40] A similar case was seen in 1633 when a woman whose husband had not returned to her for 10 years, not only terminated her marriage but also secured another husband.[41] In 1632, we find Maryam Jī declaring a slave girl independent in lieu of 30 *mahmūdīs*,[42] and getting rid of her.[43]

The concern of lower-class women was more for maintenance, as reflected in one of the documents from 1619 concerning Maryam and Muḥammad Jiu. As stated above, the husband was obliged to provide maintenance to his wife, and if he failed to do so, the wife had the right to seek divorce automatically. Maryam left him, and after a certain period, the husband returned and asked her to come back. She refused. Muḥammad Jiu, therefore, approached the court asking for restitution of conjugal rights. She, in turn, produced before the court the written contract and asserted that she did not receive any maintenance for 5 years, on which the court turned down the

[37] Zilli (2017), pp. 69–70.

[38] Moosvi (2012), pp. 275–287.

[39] Surat doc, ff. 205 (a)–(b).

[40] MS. Blochet, Supp. Pres.482, Surat Doc. fff.195 (a)-196 (a).

[41] MS. Blochet, Supp. Pres.482, Surat Doc.f.205 (b).

[42] Mahmudis were coins prevalent during the Mughal period.

[43] MS. Blochet, Supp. Pres.482, Surat Doc. f. 194(b).

appeal of Muḥammad Jiu and ordered that she had a right to divorce, and thus gave the verdict in her favour. It appears that she ultimately chose not to divorce him and agreed to remain his wife as we find that 2 years later, a person named Ibrahim takes a surety before the *qāẓi* (judge) on behalf of Muḥammad Jiu for his payment to her maintenance.[44]

Thus, it is apparent that the poor women had no respite even after incorporating these conditions and getting divorced from a penurious husband, or perhaps it was difficult to find an appropriate and generous husband for women of Maryam's class. It also implies that the women had easy access and adequate knowledge about the legal process followed in the court in case of failure on the husband's part in providing and fulfilling the conditions laid out in the *nikāḥnāmas*.

However, worth noting is that, as a non-muslim wife, they were also entitled to *meḥr* (dower). In one of the documents (d.11Februrary1686) *baināmā-cum-hibanāmā* (sale deed cum gift deed), a *baqqāl* (banya/grain merchant)[45] purchased a residential building at Cambay for Rs. 701/– *Ālamgīri*[46]—for the payment of *meḥr* of his wife and gave it to her along with gold and silver jewellery, utensils etc.[47] Another such document (d. 16 October 1660) records a woman named Phūlan to have a share in the ownership of a house from her husband as *meḥr*.[48] One may, therefore, observe the existence of jurisprudential pluralism and 'flexibility of sharia'[49] provided these women with opportunities to avail the benefits of *shari'a*. Also, *meḥr* is typically an Islamic practice, and its prevalence in Hindu marriages reinforces the point of the assimilative characteristic of *shari'a*.

A document of 1550 refers to a Muslim family of Bilgram where we find a daughter and daughter-in-law of the family share the same residential plot of land (*zamīn i sakni*) in a way that one having inheritance[50] from the father and the other in *meḥr* from her husband.[51] In the *nikāḥnāma*, the marriage gift promised by the groom at the time of marriage was divided into immediate and deferred portions.[52] The *meḥr* thus could be of two kinds. It could be in cash or kind. It was further divided into *meḥr i mu'ajjal* and *meḥr i muwwajjal*. *Meḥr i mu'ajjal* was usually 1/third of the actual agreed amount, which had to be paid immediately. *Meḥr i muwwajjal* was the deferred dower and had to be paid later. It was generally 2/third of the actual dower.[53] Generally, the deferred amount was paid either upon the wife's divorce or at the death of her husband. If the husband died

[44] MS. Blochet, Supp. Pres.482, Surat Doc. ff 206 (b)-207 (a)-207(b).

[45] Rezavi (2004), pp. 277–303.

[46] Alamgiri were coins prevalent during the Mughal period.

[47] NAI 2695/1-44, Doc. No. 8.

[48] NAI 2695/1-44, Doc No. 26.

[49] Hasan (2004), p. 71.

[50] Bilgrami (1987), p. 265.

[51] Documents from Bilgram (Awadh), Transcripts in Dept of History, Aligarh, No. 6.

[52] Rapoport (2009), p. 52.

[53] Bilgrami (1987), p. 264.

without paying *meḥr*, the wife had the full right to claim it from the deceased's property. When Bi Ayisha, widow of Haji Qirmani, petitioned before the *qāzi* (judge) that her husband died without paying 1000 *ibrahimis*,[54] the *qāzi* ruled that the widow had the full right to obtain it from the property of her deceased husband.[55]

There are also several instances of women acting as *wakīl* (representative). A perusal of these documents shows that the civil suits could be filed, argued and fought on behalf of the deponents; as it was only in 1671 when Aurangzeb formally appointed *wakīl i shar'i* (lawyers) in all the towns and *sūbās*.[56] The earliest evidence for the appointment of a *wakīl* from the documents of Gujarat is from 1621 when a husband authorised his wife to be his *wakīlah*.[57] However, the term here appears to stand for a representative rather than a lawyer. Another document from 1629 reflects the same practice of representation where a mother appointed her daughter as her *wakīl* over her property; she was then given the right to either mortgage or sell the house as per her need.[58] Not leaving the men behind in this genre, there is an instance of a husband acting as the *wakīl* of his litigant wife, and fighting the case on her behalf.[59] Furthermore, a case of 1692 shows three men acting as *wakīl* on behalf of their sister in the court of the Qāẓi of Cambay.[60] Old women and mothers could also have their sons fighting their legal battles as their *wakīls*.[61]

Where such liberties and privileges were enjoyed by the women of that period, there are also references to some reaping the benefits of civil liberties granted to Muslim women in *shari'a* (considering the liberal provisions in *shari'a* compared to others). A case of April 1736 is evidence for the same. Bel Bāi, is seen to be converting to Islam to get a share in the property of her deceased father, as per the *shari'a*. Mirza Muḥammad Ṭaqi filed a suit on behalf of his wife on the ground that Nāthi, the woman's mother declined, saying that as her daughter Bel Bāi had converted to Islam, the demand could not be acceded to. The dispute was handed over to the *'ulama* (doctors of law) who gave the ruling that to give the share would be in contravention of the *dīn* (faith) as the *wirsa* (law of succession) does not apply to her. Therefore, Bel Bāi had to withdraw her claim, and ultimately, due to the intervention of certain individuals a sum of Rs. 10/– was given to her mother given her poor condition.[62]

[54] Ibrahimis were coins prevalent during the Mughal period.

[55] Blochet Suppl. Pers., No. 3, ff.198a-b; Cf. Moosvi (2012), pp. 277–279.

[56] Khan (1925), vol. II, 249, 253; Khan M (n.d.), Tarikh i Shahjahani (Rotograph in Dept. of History, AMU), f.148 (a)-(b).

[57] MS. Blochet, Supp. Pres.482, Surat Doc, ff. 207 (a)-(b).

[58] MS. Blochet, Supp. Pres.482, Surat Doc, ff. 202 (a)-(b).

[59] NAI 2695/1-44, Doc no. 5, p. 29; Sura doc. ff 200 (b)-(a).

[60] NAI 2695/1-44. Doc no. 12.

[61] NAI 2695/1-44, Doc 2, p. 20.

[62] NAI 2695/1-44, Doc. No, 29.

5 Conclusion

Thus, we find that the plasticity of *shari'a* and the pragmatic eclecticism practiced during medieval India allowed women to resist the conditions of their oppression. It was open-ended and inclusive. The study of legal documents indicates that women from various religious communities across the empire frequently attended the Mughal legal courts. One can also assume that non-Muslim women understood *shari'a* and the workings of its legal courts. This implies that the courts may have been effective in upholding the rights of women as ordained in *shari'a* law. Women were skilled at suing and defending themselves in court. They recognized the value of documents and testimonies and demonstrated the power of agency within this legal system. When the law failed women, there were instances where they transgressed legal boundaries through retaliation, both individually and in groups, against the violence they faced. For example, a wronged wife took revenge by reporting her husband's treachery to his master, who then had him killed.[63] Hence, women understood what was best for them. These women were not merely a herd of chattels whom men could abuse at their convenience but individuals of substance who exercised their agency when necessary. Moreover, this also substantiates Lila Abu-Lughod's argument, 'Do Muslim women need saving?' Or perhaps we just need to take a look at history and learn from it. The format of *nikāḥnāma* of contemporary times does not stipulate any conditions. Thus, adopting the format *nikāḥnāma* prevalent during the medieval period would allow women significant power and agency in the marital relationship. This may explain why, in the nineteenth century, the British disentangled *shari'a* and transformed it into a rigid legal code that applied solely to Muslims, while also demonizing the community to serve their interests. As a result, women's issues have become political propaganda not only in India but elsewhere as well.

References

Ahmad N (1939) Tabaqat i Akbari tr. Brajendranath De. The Asiatic Society, Calcutta

Badauni A (1864-69) Muntakhab ut Tawarikh. In: Lees WN, Ahmad A (eds) 3 vols; eng.tr. vol. I G.S.A Ranking; vol. II W.H Lowe; vol. III Wolseley Haig. Atlantic Publishers, New Delhi

Fazl A (1939) Akbarnama 3 vols eng.tr. Beveridge H. The Asiatic Society, Calcutta

Fazl A (1949) In: Phillott DC, Blochmann H (eds) Ain i Akbari. Low Price Publication, Delhi

Jahangir (1909-14) In: Beveridge H, Rogers A (eds) Tuzuk i Jahangiri (Memoirs of Jahangir). Low Price Publication, Delhi

Khan K (1925) In: Kabiruddin A, Haig W (eds) Muntakhab ul Lubab. Asiatic Society of Bengal, Calcutta

Khan SM (1947) Maasir i Alamgiri eng.tr. Sarkar. Asiatic Society of Bengal, Calcutta

Khan A (1965) In: Lokhandwala M (ed) Mirat i Ahmadi. Oriental Institute, Baroda

Khan S (2003) In: Prasad B, Beveridge H (eds) Maasir ul Umra. The Asiatic Society, Calcutta

Khan M. Sadiq (n.d.) Tarikh i Shahjahani Rotograph in Centre of Advanced Study in History, AMU

Namakin. A Munshat i Namakin Maulana Azad Library, AMU, no. farsiya 26

[63] Khan (1947), pp. 188–189.

Secondary Works

Abu-Lughod L (2013) Do Muslim women need saving? Harvard University Press, Harvard
Ahmad A (1970) The role of ulema in Indo-Muslim history. Stud Islam 3:1–13
Bano S (2020) Keeping women under subjection: laws and norms in Mughal India. Stud People's Hist 7(2):129–136
Bilgrami R (1987) Property rights of Muslim women in Mughal India. PIHC 48:261–270
Chakravarti U (1993) Conceptualizing brahmanical patriarchy in early India: gender, caste, class and state. EPW 28(14):579–585
Conaghan J (2013) Law and gender. Oxford University Press, Oxford
Digby S (1984) The Tuhfa i Nasaih of Yusuf Gada: an ethical treatise in verse from the Late Fourteenth Century Delhi Sultanate. In: Metcalf BD (ed) Moral conduct and authority: the place of Adab in South Asian Islam. University of California Press, London, pp 91–123
Guenther M (2003) Hanafi Fiqh in Mughal India: the Fatwa-i Alamgiri. In: Eaton RM (ed) India's Islamic traditions. Oxford University Press, Oxford, pp 209–230
Habib I (1992) Akbar and social inequities a study of the evolution of his ideas. PIHC 53:300–310
Habib I (2000) Exploring medieval gender history symposia paper. IHC, pp 263–275
Hasan F (2004) State and locality in Mughal India: power relations in Western India, c.1572–1730. Cambridge University Press, Cambridge
Islam Z (1966) Origin and development of fatwa compilation in medieval India 12(2):223–241
Kerslake A (2024) The right to legal personhood of marginalised groups: achieving equal recognition before the law for all. Oxford University Press, Oxford
Lefevre C (2017) Beyond diversity: Mughal legal ideology and politics. In: Thomas E, Gijs K (eds) Law addressing diversity pre-modern Europe and India in comparison (13th–18th centuries). De Gruyter, Berlin, pp 116–141
MacKinnon C (1989) Towards a feminist theory of state. Harvard University Press
Moosvi S (2012) People, taxation, and trade in Mughal India. Oxford University Press, Oxford
Phadke S (2003) Thirty years on: women's studies reflects on the women's movement. EPW 38(43):4567–4576
Qadri A (1966) The Fatwa i Alamgiri. J PHS 14:188–199
Rapoport Y (2009) Marriage, money and divorce in Medieval Islamic Society. Cambridge University Press, Cambridge
Rezavi N (1993) Civil law and justice in Mughal Gujarat. PIHC 54:189–199
Rezavi N (2004) Mercantile life in Mughal India. PIHC 65:277–303
Robin W, Cynthia B (eds) (2019) Research handbook on feminist jurisprudence. Edward Elgar Publishing
Sangri K (1993) Consent, agency and rhetoric of incitement. EPW 28(18):867–887
Singh D (2010) Regulating the domestic: notes on the pre-colonial state and the family. In: Bhargava M (ed) Exploring Medieval India II sixteenth to eighteenth centuries culture, gender, regional patterns. Orient Blackswan, pp 285–306
Wickens G (1964) The Nasirean ethics by Nasir ad-Din Tusi. Routledge
Zilli I (ed) (2017) Mughal State & Culture 1556–1598: Selected Letters & Documents from Munshaat-i-Namakin. Manohar Publisher, Delhi

Angbin Yasmin is an Assistant Professor of History at the School of Law, Jamia Hamdard, New Delhi, India. She holds a PhD from Aligarh Muslim University (AMU), India. Her thesis is titled 'Profiling and Imaging Women in Mughal India: The Persian Texts, Travellers' Accounts, Legal Documents and Miniatures'. She specializes in Medieval Indian History. Her research interests are Gender History, History of Sexuality, Legal History, Mughal Miniatures, and Women's Writings.

Feminist Approaches to Policies and Practices for Socio-Legal Changes

Neoliberalism and the Principles of Feminist Collectivity and Solidarity

Mario Reljanović

Abstract Neoliberalism encourages individuality as the only virtue, which has a significant impact on the field of work but also on contemporary feminist action. Putting the individual at the center of production relations implies that the employer and the state are absolved of responsibility for emerging and/or persistent inequalities in the labour market. Neoliberalism is blind to the difference between equality and equity, and the only anti-discrimination measures recommended are those that can pass the economic cost-effectiveness test. The research is focused on the position of feminist movements in described conditions and exploring possibilities to impose ideas for the discussion of true gender equality and equity in a neoliberal environment. Relations of feminist movements and trade unions are examined, as well as their possible cooperation in revitalizing the principles of collectivity and solidarity. The possibility of the influence of feminist ideas on the results of collective bargaining is also part of the analysis, as well as the contemporary rebellious ways of fighting for the rights of women workers, through protests and strikes. The basic hypothesis under study is the possibility of promoting the feminist agenda in the neoliberal labour market by returning to the classical principles of collective action, but with new tactics of broad inclusiveness and intersectionality, with the support and cooperation of trade unions and various other national and supranational actors.

This work is a result of research within the project "Adapting the Legal Framework to Social and Technological Changes with a Special Focus on Artificial Intelligence," carried out in 2025 by the Institute of Comparative Law with financial support from the Ministry of Science, Technological Development and Innovation (contract number 451-03-136/2025-03/200049).

M. Reljanović (✉)
Institute of Comparative Law, Belgrade, Serbia
e-mail: m.reljanovic@iup.rs

F. Macioce et al. (eds.), *Feminist Legal and Political Practices*, Gender Perspectives in Law 6, https://doi.org/10.1007/978-3-032-02856-3_5

1 Position of Women in the Neoliberalist Labour Market

At the first glance, neoliberalism and feminism are not mutually exclusive. Both stand for freedom of choice—a point of overlap that has served as a support for the development of the neoliberal feminist narrative. However, this joint feature is more of a point of separation, than of connection. Neoliberalism is essentially based on social conservatism, which does not perceive women's empowerment as a relevant political goal. In this sense, feminism is perceived by neoliberals as an undermining element of the established patriarchal structure of neoliberal society. There are two particularly contentious elements in making the case that neoliberalism is good ground for the feminist idea.

First, in practice, the freedom of choice in the (unchanged) patriarchal society (and the corresponding labour market) is distorted into its ugly neoliberal twin—the "freedom" to remain on the margins of society. Neoliberalism will use the mantra of freedom only to the extent necessary to economically exploit the female population (as well as other groups); nothing beyond that is the focus of neoliberal capitalists. Aronson ironically but very punctual names this process "the privatisation of hope".[1]

Second, neoliberalism as a political concept has been promoted as a victory of individual freedoms. Everyone is capable of designing their own life path in a completely free society and succeeding in it. No one else is responsible for his achievements and/or failures, especially not the state. Neoliberalism basically does not recognize the essential difference between equality and equity (also referred to as "substantive equality"), that is, it considers them to be the same. However, the term "equity" is used to emphasize when resources are shared based on what each person needs in order to be substantially equal with all other persons in the same circumstances/situation, regarding the concept that some individuals have unequal starting positions and need more resourced in order to be truly equalized with others. The term "equality" is considered in its traditional meaning, when there is equal sharing of resourced regardless of starting positions. Committee on CEDAW in their General Recommendation 28 stated some points in order to explain terminological differences and preferred usage of terms: "The principle of equality between men and women, or gender equality, entails the concept that all human beings, regardless of sex, are free to develop their personal abilities, pursue their professional careers and make choices without the limitations set by stereotypes, rigid gender roles and prejudices. States parties are called upon to use exclusively the concepts of equality of women and men or gender equality and not to use the concept of gender equity in implementing their obligations under the Convention. The latter concept is used in some jurisdictions to refer to fair treatment of women and men, according to their respective needs. This may include equal treatment or treatment that is different, but which is considered equivalent in terms of rights, benefits, obligations and opportunities."[2] Ignoring this difference however builds a simplistic view of social

[1] Aronson (2016).

[2] Committee on the Elimination of Discrimination against Women (2010), para. 22.

inequalities which does not give people from marginalized groups the opportunity to succeed in their usual social roles (including the role of workers, i.e. equal access to the labour market), but also has a devastating effect on the collective rights of workers that had been fought for in the twentieth century. The individuality on which the economic idea of neoliberalism is built ignores—one would say it even deliberately omits—the notions of collectivity, solidarity, joint action. This is not accidental, because it is the workers' collectivity that brought forth the struggle for workers' rights (and thus became the main point of struggle for capitalists in neoliberalism). Workers' resistance is never individual, as a rule it is organized and collective. That is why it has no place in the neoliberal idea of labour exploitation. However, this creates an antagonism towards feminism as a solidarity and mass movement, fundamentally invalidating those ideas that feminists cultivated and promoted during their struggle for equality and equity.

To reconcile the apparent disagreement with the ideas of feminism, neoliberal teaching focuses on the promotion of gender equality. The messages that are sent vary, and often they are completely inadequate. Namely, the promotion of women's equality comes down to the economic benefit from greater participation of women in decision-making processes and is part of a larger campaign that can be reduced to the used catchphrase "diversity is good for business". As Périvier and Sénac noticed: "Contemporary public debate includes a number of ideas such as: "women do politics differently, women manage differently", "more women at decision-making level in private companies provides added value", "diversity is good for business", "tackling discrimination is profitable", etc. Are these arguments part of an effective and well-meaning pragmatism, or are they part of a conservative ideology that has been revamped to make it appear more respectable? Is this type of argument part of a strategy adopted by defenders of equality to circumvent neoliberal ideas by using their own arms against them, or, on the contrary, is it the sign of a victory for neoliberal strategies?"[3]

Furthermore, equality and equity in the neoliberal world are viewed through the prism of cost-benefit factors,[4] so the end result of supposedly anti-discrimination efforts may not be positive at all.[5] For example, even just a cursory analysis of the emerging right to menstrual leave shows that there are significant dilemmas as to whether this right is significant for the overall positioning of women at work. And while certainly the natural, reflex response to the question would have to be that it is necessary to enable the true equity of women in the work process by recognizing their specific biological needs, the neoliberal discourse—apparently concluding

---

[3] Périvier and Sénac (2018), p. 2.

[4] "The economist Stephanie Seguino shows that in 'semi-industrialised countries with open economies that are heavily involved in globalisation (e.g., Thailand and Taiwan), discrimination in the workforce stimulates economic growth. In these countries, the difference in male-female wages is higher than the gaps in productivity between the genders, which makes these countries attractive to foreign investment. The lower labour costs of women are therefore a source of profit." Seguino (2005), cited by: Périvier and Sénac (2018), p. 10.

[5] Ging-Dwan Boyd (2016), p. 153.

that this right will be "too expensive" for employers—goes in the opposite direction, pointing out that recognizing the right to menstrual leave will only deepen the differences between female and male workers. Not to mention the fact that it ignores that the discussion about the right to menstrual leave has to be just a small part of a larger campaign to introduce rules to protect women at work when it comes to their reproductive health.[6] That topic is apparently taboo for neoliberal authors, because simply put, it is not profitable—hence, the basic flaw in the neoliberal design of gender equality is revealed.

On the other side, as the examples show, countries with a dominant neoliberal orientation will easily give up social programs that they estimate are not profitable in the long term, while those programs that survive are primarily aimed at preparing individuals for access to the labour market, where discriminatory relations already rule. In other words, the "calculation" of social programs is realized through the achievement of political goals by choosing the cheapest means, and not the means that will guarantee true equality and equity.[7] Thus, one concludes that neoliberalism fundamentally does not understand the concept of equality and equity: it cannot be counted through economic indicators, but represents a civilizational achievement of a culture of respect for human rights. On the other hand, neoliberalism strongly rejects everything that creates additional costs, so any social support or anti-discrimination measure will potentially encounter significant obstacles if it does not prove to be profitable.

In such circumstances, it is only logical that discrimination at the labour market prevails. And more, it comes in different shapes and forms, including intersectional discrimination. It can even be said that the neoliberal climate is ideal for the development of intersectional discrimination, because by forcing the "entrepreneurial spirit" without help from the side that would guarantee an equal starting position on the labour market, the hypothetically available "freedom of success" in the economic world is in fact specifically denied to those groups who suffer multiple discrimination. Thus, women from rural areas cannot rely on state assistance in order to succeed—for example—through education in improving their starting position on the labour market. It is the same with disabled women, refugee women, and the like. Although working conditions and social security are among the main factors when workers decide to leave their home labor market and engage in jobs abroad,[8] they will very often find themselves in a position of being discriminated against—for female workers, this type of discrimination only builds on the already existing multiple factors that influence their unequal treatment. The "freedom" that is promoted in this way practically eliminates the need for state interventions on the labour market, which does not only prevent women workers from marginalized

[6] Reljanović and Rajić Ćalić (2024).

[7] "Neoliberal changes such as the gradual dismantling of welfare services, the precarization of working and living conditions, the privatization of social services such as health care and education have affected women's (and men's) lives in all parts of the world, albeit in different ways…". Korolczuk (2016), p. 32.

[8] Reljanović (2023), p. 139.

groups from accessing the labour market on an equal basis, but also comes into direct collision with a several international instruments on human rights.[9]

The idea that the only path to emancipation is for women to "independently become independent" through the placement of labour on the open market is misperceived, while consciously ignoring the fact that many women are denied access to the labour market through prior discrimination and patriarchal patterns of division of household work. Even when the access is open, they are often offered discriminatory jobs and working conditions—thus making emancipation significantly more difficult than it should be, and in many cases impossible. It is also actively ignored that a woman's work activity does not indicate her emancipation, as is the case with men, if the conditions of decent work are not met, as well as if the work role of a woman is simply added to her "traditional" family role regarding unpaid housework.

On the others side, there is a notion of collectivity as an important standpoint of both workers' and feminists' fighting for dignity. Collective action at work has always implied special weight, rallying workers around a unified social and political aspiration for better working conditions and a fairer distribution of newly created income. It is clear that in such an atmosphere, the collective interests of working women can be organized and defended, first through a clear sense of belonging to a collective, and then through a connection to the core values of the feminist movement. "Collective identity is a common feeling, a 'we' feeling or bond shared by members of a particular group; it can also be defined as an experienced sense of belonging to a group. Collective identity develops through a conscious effort to construct a common feeling and shared interests amongst members of a group. It brings with it a sense of common purpose and shared commitment to a cause that enables individual activists and / or organisations to regard themselves as inextricably linked to other actors, not necessarily identical but surely compatible, in a broader collective mobilisation."[10] De Souza and Gupta show the strength of collectivity through experience ("stories") shared by the women themselves, which become part of the collective consciousness about common problems.[11] Common problems and common ideals about the world as it should be, constitute a collective driving force that manifests itself through the struggle for such an ideal model of society. Collectivity is therefore an extremely important part of feminist action in all periods of feminist action, and especially regarding the working-class women struggle. "Political feminism should try to formulate alternatives to neoliberalism and be attentive to its potential danger of being appropriated for and playing into neoliberal reasoning and processes of neoliberal restructuration."[12]

There is also the issue of intersectional discrimination against women and questioning the concepts that led to it. "Intersectionality allows for reflection on gender

---

[9] See: Reljanović (2022).

[10] Malehoko Tshoaedi (2008), p. 37.

[11] De Souza and Gupta (2023), p. 198.

[12] Kauppert and Kerner (2016), p. 7.

inequality with regard to different experiences of structural discrimination and power hierarchies ... Reflections on questions and concepts of difference have a long-standing tradition in feminist theory and have contributed to many theoretical debates within and outside social movements to this day. These movements criticize power regimes that are organized along conditions of recognition and that are at work in manifold mechanisms of the othering of those who are placed and perceived as beyond these norms. Recognizing difference and the challenging of normative settings are important steps towards gender equality, as well as regarding legal systems and the distribution of resources and access to positions of power and authority."[13]

Because of all that has been said, the research is directed towards the study of collectivity and solidarity in contemporary feminist movements, in the conditions of the global dominance of neoliberalism. The basic hypothesis is that through joint action of women around the world, as well as their national and supranational connection, some of the basic goals of feminist action can be achieved. The focus is primarily on the position of women as workers, i.e. the possibilities to influence a series of negative trends that neoliberalism inevitably sets up, through participation in collective forms of workers' actions.

To this end, the analysis of the association of women in movements, the actions of women in trade unions, as well as the participation of women in collective bargaining and in organizing and conducting strikes, is specifically in focus. How realistic and possible it is to promote feminist ideas in these activities, how important is collectivity in the women's labour struggle and what are the results of women's collective actions so far, are some of the questions that are specifically answered during the research. Conclusions critically synthesize basic messages about joint actions and women's solidarity as a possible—and recommended—course of action for feminists around the world.

2 Feminism and Solidarity in the Neoliberal Surroundings

Zimmer emphasises that there is internal and external component of solidarity. Internally, solidarity is social relation based on the principle of responsibility and cohesion through dependencies. Externally, solidarity is a political tool, support to certain groups and their political goals, which incorporates of various reactions and collective actions. Also, she considers so-called "exclusive solidarity", which is practised for the benefit of a particular group, potentially at the expense of others, and "inclusive solidarity", when the group concerned has on the one side a common concern, but the actual interest is not homogeneous, nor is the group in itself homogeneous.[14] All these findings are important in order to comprehend how the principle

[13] Zimmermann and Binswanger (2021), p. 2.

[14] Zimmer (2022), pp. 45–46.

of solidarity can benefit feminist struggles in the neoliberal surroundings. Namely, solidarity as one of the basic principles of the traditional struggle for workers' rights, and it represents one of the few effective elements of feminist efforts to ensure gender equality in the field of economic rights. Neoliberalism teaches that every individual is important, and that collectivity should be abandoned as an overcomed concept. The collective rights of workers, however, arose as a direct result of the struggle against the owners of capital and the state that protected that capital, and represent a standard of enjoyment of the human right to work confirmed by international instruments, in a manner guaranteed by the International Covenant on Economic, Social and Cultural Rights,[15] and a number of other international instruments.

This is why it is important to see how the principle of solidarity, on which the collective rights of workers have been built, functions in the neoliberal environment of the feminist struggle for economic rights. In other words, in order to establish a platform for further solidarity action, it would be necessary to examine how the neoliberal influence in feminism did succeed in undermining the sense of collectivity and solidarity, and to what extent these principles are still relevant in the feminist struggle today. This will be most easily seen through the analysis of the collective forms of action of feminists in the world of work: through the action of (labour) movements and trade unions, as well as through the participation of women in solidarity labour actions, collective bargaining and strikes.

2.1 Social Movements/NGOs

The power of collectivity is undeniable. This is why Batliwala emphasises: "Building their collective power through movements helps women convert their quest for their human rights, for equality and justice into a political force for change that cannot be ignored by their families, communities, governments, or society at large. While resistance or rebellion by individual women is easy to squash or isolate, resistance by large numbers, acting together on a common agenda of change, is not easily suppressed. Such larger-scale struggles can also protect women from the backlash that usually follows, or at least ensure that any form of violence against them does not occur with impunity or in silence. … Movements are often the most effective way for particularly stigmatized, marginalized and socially excluded constituencies of women to become visible and have their voices heard."[16]

Historically speaking, movements had a significant role in shaping of the feminist concept of gender equality at work, including problems of educational opportunities, better working conditions, strike movements, body and sexuality politics,

[15] UN General Assembly (1966).

[16] Batliwala (2012), p. 7.

international solidarity, and others.[17] This is not surprising, because movements' activists gather around common ideas that form the ideological backbone of their actions and policies. The emancipation of women in the field of work was certainly one of the basic goals of feminists. And more than that. As Batliwala rationally observes, feminist movements include not only women as such, but women of certain identities, and even women as workers. These movements were launched by women not essentially around their identity as women, but as women of particular identities, categories and circumstances, such as women of particular ethnicities / social groups (Roma women, Dalit women, indigenous women); women facing particular forms of exclusion or voice lessness (sex workers, disabled women, lesbian women, mothers of young children, poor grassroots women), in particular occupations or economic situations (domestic workers, picqueters, sex work), or in particular political circumstances (Iranian women, Sudanese women, Palestinian women).[18] However, the significance of the movement can be viewed from another (historical) angle, which is equally significant today. Namely, Helfert rightly points out that the movements had many modes of action. That breadth of action made them equally reactionary and proactive: they could react to daily issues, the implementation of regulations and policies that were not in line with the principle of substantive equality, but they could actively oppose proposed steps that led to new discriminatory policies, practices and regulations. Also, behind their activities as a rule there were more or less defined long-term policies, i.e. the direction of policy changes that the movement aspired and advocated for. This made the movements attractive to those women who were already expressing their feminist convictions through other means of influence—such as trade unions.[19] That development further led to a convergence of the work of the movement and the unions on feminist issues, as well as an overlap in membership that was of great importance for the potential coordination of activities. Again, as a consequence of such personal interweaving, movements could closely cooperate with trade unions and other organizations with which they shared some values, or a certain narrow strategic goal, as well as organize joint actions.

Korolczuk points to the need for indiscriminate membership in feminist movements. They cannot, or rather must not if they want to be successful, limit themselves to one category of women and one issue that is related to the problems of a relatively small group of female workers.[20] It is quite clear that the movements, in accordance with the classic tactics of action, will push the micro issues that they consider to be significant. But as Korolczuk observes, there is no obstacle for fathers, or persons who are not (and will not be) parents, to join the movement for the issues of the regulation of motherhood at work. The inclusivity and intersectionality of the movement are necessary not only because of the idea of universality of rights for which it is advocating, but also to make it more sensitized and to encour-

[17] Helfert (2024), p. 107.

[18] Batliwala (2012), p. 65.

[19] Helfert (2024), p. 102.

[20] Korolczuk (2016), pp. 39–40.

age an internal dialogue about the policies for which the movement stands in principle. This observation can be applied to any area of activity of the (feminist) movement, but it is especially important when talking about specific topics related to workers' rights.

How has the neoliberal environment affected feminist movements as a whole, including those that arise in terms of realizing women's rights at work and on the occasion of work? It seems that the dominant criticism is directed towards the so-called NGOization of feminist movements, that is, the reduction of the movement to a kind of "enterprise" that follows certain trends and rules that are more characteristic of profit-making, market entities, than those directed towards the struggle to achieve general, altruistic goals around some ideas that bind them together. In other words, the criticism goes in the direction of loss of solidarity and dedication to action (at any cost), at the expense of sustainability and economic (business) logic of long-term running of the "movement" NGOs. As Korolczuk notices,[21] NGOization is a complex process that results in some added value to the movement, but at the same time that could be seen as a danger to the preservation of its originality and commitment to its original goals. NGOization thus leads towards professionalisation, institutionalisation and sustainability of movement's social actions. But it also leads towards de-politization of the movement's agenda and gradual moving away from the true social activism. It will often result in donor dependency and accountability to the funders rather than to constituencies they claim to represent, which ultimately results in diminishing the capacities of the movement to express itself openly about the ideas around which it came together in the first place. Batliwala also adds to this complex equation one more negative consequence of the NGOization: loss of focus of the movement.[22] They will dominantly focus on topics (projects) that are considered as most important for the community not by their members, but by their donors—and these two perceptions do not necessarily overlap, and sometimes they will not even have points of contact.

It is clear that neoliberalism has significantly influenced contemporary feminist movements. This influence does not have to be exclusively negative, although NGOization is certainly a term used in a predominantly negative context. Nevertheless, the sustainability of the movement through project and donor funding is not the worst possible way to maintain the basic ideas and agendas around which the movement was originally created. In the field of labour, and economic rights in general, modern movements have traditionally played a significant role. This is logical, because the economic empowerment of women is one of the most important goals of feminists and, on the other hand, through the neoliberal understanding of labour rights in general, it is clear that many important aspects of gender equality and equity at work will not be implemented if they are not imposed by external actors who have sufficient strength to advocate for changes of dominant policies. It can be said that in the era of neoliberalism this is more difficult than ever, since

[21] *Ibid.*, 34. See also: Kauppert and Kerner (2016), p. 4.

[22] Batliwala (2012), p. 12.

modern capitalism has long since abandoned its (short-term) concept of the "system with human face", and that through individualism it is precisely trying to weaken the strength of collectivity—of every organised group defending and fighting for workers' rights, including women's movements. That is why many authors see the action of the movement in symbiosis, or perhaps complementary, with the action of other actors in the field of work—primarily thinking of the trade unions.

2.2 Unionisation of Feminists

It is difficult to imagine a feminist campaign for the rights of working women without their participation in trade unions. Historically, trade unions along with feminist movements, were the first ways of channelling feminist goals in the field of work. The emancipation of women meant, among other things, their financial independence, which made the position of women on the labour market one of the primary and most important themes of feminist action. Trade unions were also a suitable place for the association of women in the so-called "women's sections" and their action on the education of women workers, so quasi-movements were formed within the unions themselves. Nevertheless, the action of feminists within the trade union was far from harmonious. Trade unions were considered a "patriarchal domain", and they first had to be changed from within, so that the struggle against external influences on the labour market could continue. Trade unions eventually played a major role in promoting the rights of women workers and their path to true equality with male workers. However, it is unlikely conclusion that trade unions around the world are equally committed to the feminist agenda and to issues that are of importance for the substantive equality of men and women workers. Contemporary unions, although they should not be generalized and their actions depend on many local factors, often rely on the politics of the *status quo*, without the essential energy to fight for certain principles, and in (futile) attempt to protect previously acquired positions. This is where the contradiction of their highly bureaucratized decision-making mechanisms, as well as watered-down policies in relation to the protection of human rights in general, and attempts to preserve the dynamism of feminist action through the union struggle, comes in.

In the twenty-first century, trade unions are going through a significant crisis. Neoliberalism has always been against unionization and this antagonism has never been hidden. On the contrary, the emphasis on individualism among workers and the dogmatic positioning that each individual is the sole master of his own destiny, that is, freedom of work (but not freedom of association and collective action), are primarily aimed at weakening trade unions. After the golden age of trade unions in most of the second half of the twentieth century, they have been in stagnation for several decades—both in terms of the number of members and in terms of real influence on the policy makers in the field of economic and social rights.

The question arises, how feminist currents in trade unions can manage in such conditions, when the solidarity and unity of the workforce are being replaced by different principles, promoting there is no place for collectivity anymore? Brener claims in 1989 that "Mainstream feminism's success in legitimizing the ideal of equality and the massive entry of women into waged work have created the conditions for the development of a working-class feminism, one that integrates itself not only politically but organizationally with other movements of the exploited and oppressed."[23] Indeed, the participation of women in trade unions brought to these structures a quality that they did not have until then—close cooperation with other actors in the field of politics, civil liberties, rule of law, social movements for equality. It also brought a new degree of internationalization of trade union activities, as women workers united at different levels around the world, gathered around the same problems they faced and the same goals they aspired to.[24]

The choice of acting through trade unions seemed logical for the feminist movement. As Wånggren points out, "feminist definitions of work include activist work: trade union organizing is one such kind of work".[25] Fighting against sexism, misogyny, and racism in the unions themselves, women workers refined and modernized the unions—not only by increasing the number of members, but also by emphasizing progressive policies that went beyond the traditional topics that unions dealt with. Trade unions stepped forward—many of them reluctantly—into dealing with social issues and policies that, among other things, were of exceptional importance for the functioning of the labour market, but until then were not perceived as their domain of interest. By putting a series of "unpleasant" topics on the agenda, women in trade unions not only increased their popularity, but also developed them into politically minded structures that no longer shied away from topics such as women's reproductive health of women, abortion, maternity leave, sexual harassment at work, unpaid housework, and many others.

Why is this important in contemporary conditions of trade unions' actions and feminist movements within trade unions? First of all, because feminism promotes and is based on collectivity. Neoliberalism abolishes the idea of collectivity in its very essence; feminism can be defended against it through the action of trade unions. "The notion of finding strength in a collective is itself and has always been crucial to any feminist or social justice movement: working in communities and as part of collectives rather than as isolated individuals makes possible an analysis of structural oppressions and injustices. It is also a more effective way of changing the state of relations: unity is strength. The collective nature of trade union organising can be used to counteract the individualising impulse or 'responsibilisation' of neoliberal governmentality, which signifies a shift of responsibility from the structural to the individual."[26] Feminism can be a unifying and pulling factor in trade union revitalization. Unions chronically suffer from a reduction in the number of members, that is, unionisation coverage. Fewer members mean not only less trust in

[23] Brenner (1989), p. 254.

[24] See: Helfert (2024), p. 112.

[25] Wånggren (2018), p. 108.

[26] Wånggren (2018), p. 108.

unions by workers and less space for the dissemination of their ideas and actions, but also less financial resources available to finance unions' activities. Therefore, it is important to increase union membership coverage, which can be achieved by fighting for the right to join unions for workers in atypical forms of work, as well as by attracting such workers to realize their potential for association. Bhardwaj states that Waterman sees one of the key factors in the union's recovery precisely in the unions' interest in unorganized workers.[27] This is particularly important, bearing in mind that a large number of precarious workers who are (formally or *de facto*) denied unionisation are women. Franzway has developed this idea into a plan: "Unions have the resources to bring together women from different countries and different sectors of the economy to exchange information about their experience of globalization and to build new forms of transnational labour solidarity. It must be a solidarity that does not ask women to repress the differences among themselves, but rather encourages the productive use of these differences to expand our ideas about democracy and human rights. … Transnational labour advocacy networks provide material and virtual spaces, where union feminists come together with feminists from other social movements, and with feminist NGOs."[28] Feminists methods of complex association and action of different entities, can prove to be crucial for the revitalization of trade unions. Castro argues that new trade unionism model includes "engaging with social movements in working class neighbourhoods and with women's movements, for example."[29] But there is actually more to this idea, and Peers and Mwamadzingo point out the great potential of trade union in mobilisation of women workers: "A second dimension of trade union revitalization is the ability of trade unions to introduce innovative services and extend their membership to traditionally under-represented groups of workers, such as workers in the informal economy, platform workers, migrant workers, domestic workers, workers in the rural economy, and so on."[30]

The complexity of the relationship between feminist movements and trade unions is the subject of reflection on the future of feminist thought in trade unions, but also the future of trade unions in general. Korolczuk notices: "While the cooperation between feminist groups and worker's unions did not bring immediate results, it was an important attempt at re-interpreting the notion of solidarity in the local context and to make social movements against neoliberalism truly inclusive."[31] … Unions, in turn, have begun to shift their strategies and modes of organising to recapture lost power and to adapt to the flow of capital and labour under globalised neoliberalism. This has given rise to increased social movement unionism (SMU),which often manifests in coalitions and alliances between trade

---

[27] Waterman (1993), cited by: Bhardwaj (2019-2020), p. 15.

[28] Franzway (2004), p. 15.

[29] Castro (2018), p. 89.

[30] Peels and Mwamadzingo (2022), p. 7.

[31] Korolczuk (2016), p. 38.

unions and NGOs, non-profits, and community organising and activist groups.[32] Franzway also emphasizes that "new players from the non-profit sector … and activists from other social movements … are joining with unions as strategic partners in growing transnational labour advocacy networks."[33] It seems that the form of the future way of functioning of the trade union is emerging which has not only accepted the feminist idea and platform, but is actively dealing with it, promoting it and developing it through national and international coalitions. This (un)expected course of action reaffirms what is undoubtedly the common point of action of trade unions and feminist movements: the idea of solidarity as the primary basis for uniting different interests, as well as collective activities as the basic strategy in actions to oppose a more powerful political opponent.. Another common point is the fight against neoliberal individualism, which not only undermines the basic idea of the existence of trade unions, but through individualization tries force the concept of impunity both of the employer and of the state, for the unequal treatment of women on the labour market.

2.3 Feminists in the Collective Bargaining

Collective bargaining is a way to create rules that are binding for employers and workers and are not established by the state but through a specific process of cooperation between social partners. Collective agreements, due to their prevalence and the importance of social dialogue in modern labour law, represent the centre of the system of autonomous labour law. Rules are created by ones who will apply them. A large number of countries have a long and well-founded tradition of collective bargaining. Collective bargaining is considered to be the main channel of collective participation and industrial democracy.[34] The state authorities deliberately leave a lot of room for social partners to negotiate—only the basic international labour standards are regulated by the imperative norms of the law, and they must not be modified to the detriment of the workers.

As Kovačević states, trends of gender inequalities at the labour market "could not be eradicated by building a legal and institutional framework for protection against gender-based discrimination. Although such legislation is important in raising consciousness on discrimination issue, it cannot alone alter women's position at work. That change is not possible without the participation of all stakeholders in that process. Therefore, all citizens must participate in the process of combatting gender-based discrimination in the world of work, and a special responsibility, in addition to the state, lies with the social partners. In this sense, there is a need to strengthen the role of trade unions, employers and employers' associations in this

[32] Bhardwaj (2019-2020), p. 14.

[33] Franzway (2004), p. 8.

[34] Liukkunen (2019), p. 1.

area, primarily through strengthening (bipartite and tripartite) social dialogue on the issue of gender equality."[35] Bearing in mind the nature and importance of collective bargaining, it is certain that collective agreements can be seen as a channel for the realization of feminist goals and the agenda of women's empowerment in the field of work. In this sense, participation in collective bargaining can be seen as an expression of the power of the feminist idea in the negotiating trade union. However, there are various obstacles in realizing the idea of feminist participation in collective bargaining.

The first limitation is systemic. Namely, many female workers are "invisible" to the national labour law system, and their work does not fall into the categories recognized in the legislation. Therefore, they cannot be members of trade unions, nor participate in or influence collective bargaining in any way. And more than that, their problems may be abstract and unknown to the negotiating trade unions, so they will remain completely side-lined and marginalized, beyond any reach of collective agreements. International Labour Organization tried with the Employment Relationship Recommendation No. 198 of 2006,[36] to extend the scope of protection of workers by the national labour rules to any employment-like relation, thus covering multiple vague and undefined types or labour engagement characteristic for the neoliberal era. However, it lacks more precise definitions and potential for its application is fairly limited.[37] It is also non-binding document for the states that didn't explicitly accept its transposition into national legal systems, so many categories of marginalised workers still fall out of national legislations of most states. Some additional efforts were made by the United Nations' Committee for Economic, Social and Cultural Rights and its General Comment No. 23,[38] regarding application of basic labour standards on all workers, whichever their legal position is according to the national law, which emphasized that: "The right to just and favourable conditions of work is a right of everyone, without distinction of any kind. The reference to "everyone" highlights the fact that the right applies to all workers in all settings, regardless of gender, as well as young and older workers, workers with disabilities, workers in the informal sector, migrant workers, workers from ethnic and other minorities, domestic workers, self-employed workers, agricultural workers, refugee workers and unpaid workers".[39] However, many countries occupied with the implementation of the neoliberal agenda of the devolution of workers' rights do not follow these recommendations—because of this, a large number of workers are in a position where they cannot achieve even the most basic labour rights, including the right to unionisation and the right to collective bargaining.

---

[35] Kovačević (2023), p. 123.

[36] International Labour Organisation (2006).

[37] Novitz (2022), pp. 17, 21. Novitz, among other, states: "… it is perhaps ironic that an organisation devoted to regulating the conditions of 'labour' has devoted so little attention to the definition of 'work' and thereby the coverage of the standards that it promotes".

[38] Committee for Economic, Social and Cultural Rights (2016).

[39] Committee for Economic, Social and Cultural Rights (2016), para 5. More about the term "everyone" used in the Covenant, see: Reljanović et al. (2023).

It can therefore be concluded that the currents of neoliberal development of the labour law, which tend to exclude as many workers as possible from the possibility of exercising basic rights based on their labour, have had a very negative impact on collective bargaining in general, and therefore on the participation of women and the possibility of employment feminist policies and ideas through collective bargaining processes. The strategy of excluding workers from their rights dominantly affects marginalized groups of workers who find themselves in atypical work models, and in which women predominate.[40]

Second limitation refers to the male dominance in trade unions, especially at the decision-making levels, which effectively narrows possibilities of women trade unionists to join collective bargaining teams and impose their feminist views and ideas. This has changed over decades of patient feminist activism within trade union, which led to developing policies, strategies and overall conduct which is much more sensitized to gender equality and diversity at work, but also in the trade unions themselves. Trade unions showed signs of both proactive and reactive actions, and worked on issues including sexual harassment, domestic violence and the gender pay gap.[41] However, such evolution is far from over, since there are numerous issues that trade union do not perceive as relevant for their fight, some of them closely linked to the position of women in the labour market.[42]

Despite these obstacles, it can be said that feminist influences in collective bargaining in the recent past have led to some significant developments in the understanding of the importance of various issues related to the position of women at work, which were not given (enough) attention in the past.

Denial of the right to women (and/or other specific categories of workers) to organize in trade unions, in certain situations, leads to reconsider the closeness between the movement and the rebellious actions of resistance of women workers against employers, which in the end result are quite reminiscent of the original actions workers that led to the emergence of collective bargaining at the end of the nineteenth century. Backer describes the situation in which women workers in the textile sector gathered around the international "Right to sit" movement branch in India fought for the right to sit during the work process, instead of standing as was the "tradition" (although the work process did not require such a positioning of the workers). The employer's rationale was almost unreal for the twenty-first century: "She says that the manufacturers and local officials considered women as sitting in the house and engaged in crocheting to pass their leisure time, thereby devaluing their labour. She says that the maintenance and propagation of the housewife ideology structured in the sexual division of labour and society lead to the extreme exploitation of women."[43] Nevertheless, such an explanation fully fits in with the

[40] "...much of the precarious and informal work often performed by women and marginalized groups, for instance in the home-based services sector, is not included in collective bargaining", Elomäki and Kantola (2021), pp. 40–41.

[41] Cullen (2021), pp. 37, 141.

[42] Elomäki and Kantola (2021), p. 40.

[43] Backer (2023), pp. 233–235.

multiple discrimination that women suffered on the labour market,[44] which included job loss (and subsequent impossibility of employment) in case of pregnancy, as well as significantly lower wages for the same value of work compared to men. The movement founded by women workers, which was very directly called "Right to sit" through mass protests and very broad solidarity support of the public, led to negotiations with employers, who eventually relented and accepted the women's request to sit while working. This is a small victory, and the goal reached should be considered something normal in the world of modern labour. However, in a situation where a strong patriarchal community disposes of capital and is only in charge of decision-making, where women are treated as less important human beings, and everything is aimed at the cruel exploitation of women's work, every step taken in the right direction is important. Although it is very unfortunate that the progress was made through some mixture of the labour movement actions, public campaign (also supported by trade unions) and protests—which in all certainly resembles the primary strategies of the workers' struggle 150 years ago—this victory is actually a symbol of what can be done through collectivity, solidarity and unity, as well as a clear sign to employers and state authorities that the emancipation of women at work is not only a reality, but also an inevitable future.

2.4 *Feminism and Workers' Strikes*

In labour law, a strike is usually perceived as a type of rebellious collective action to achieve certain goals related to workers' rights or labour or social politics. Feminists, however, view the strike from a wider, more important angle, as a way of mobilizing women (and generally like-minded people) in order to fight for certain issues, but also as a way to point out to the general public certain problems that women face at work. The feminist strike is therefore not only a means of female workers' struggle, but also a political mean. Even when pointing out the difficult position of women and their labour exploitation by a specific employer, such an example can serve as a reason for wider action and the association of women workers at the national or regional level. Hence, in the analysed literature the strike was identified as a tool of connection for joint activities, which points out the solidarity in the original sense of the meaning of that term.

Strike was one of the basic ways of fighting against employers in the nineteenth century. After workers successfully fought for their rights, including the collective right to strike, work stoppages were regulated by precise rules as a rebellious way of expressing disagreement with certain actions or policies, but devoid of the violent elements that the initial strikes were known for. In the modern era of twenty-first century neoliberalism, strike often remains only mean of rebellion against employers and state policies that increasingly serve as a service to capital owners, ignoring

[44] See: Reljanović (2022).

the previous achievements of labour struggles. However, easier exchange of information and the connection of workers, including women workers, as well as easy public sharing of basic goals of their rebellion on various social networks, led to the emergence of a wider acceptance of strikes as an occasion for connecting different actors on the labour market—unions, movements, individual workers, non-governmental organizations, international organizations, and others. Thus, the strike has been reaffirmed as a mobilization tool that can bring together workers from different spheres throughout the field of labour, and even beyond the borders of a single country, all in a short period of time. This type of solidarity is unprecedented in the history of workers' actions, but it is a logical consequence of very similar neoliberal policies in many parts of the world, which force workers to respond sharply and collectively. The same can be said for feminist ideas, which receive support that far exceeds the basic target groups. "Since the mid-2010s, large and small-scale feminist strikes have been among the most powerful forms of protest in many places across the world. The broad mobilization generated by some of these strikes has been due to the strategy of interconnecting the questions of bodily integrity and control (in the contexts of domestic violence and femicide) to issues of economic exploitation (precarious labour, feminization and abuse of care work, lack of legal protection), racism and exploitation of migrant labour, as well as extractivism and environmental depletion."[45] In Island, more than 100,000 women took part in an organized general strike in 2023, with the aim of pointing out gender inequality, primarily in relation to the principle of equal pay for equal value of work, as well as the unpaid care work which is predominantly conducted by women. The (female) Prime Minister of Iceland joined the protest.[46]

In such way, the feminist strike can be seen as an expression of true solidarity and the feeling of collective belonging to certain values which overcomes territorial distance, political differences, and similar obstacles. The knowledge that there are groups of women who protest or strike against policies that are present in other countries, against ideas that are common to different authorities that are nominally presented as extremely different—but their actions inevitably lead to similar outcomes for working women—are of great importance for connecting these women, but also for mobilizing the entire public (or at least a large part of the public) who are familiar with these problems in various parts of the world. However, this type of solidarity is not based only on the same occurring problems, but also on the same or similar principles on which solutions to the challenges posed to feminist action in neoliberalism are built.[47] Also, it is not only important to know that there are women who share the same obstacles, but in this way the transfer of knowledge and experiences in the fight against common neoliberal principles of capitalism, traditionalism

[45] Neuman Stanivukovic et al. (2023), p. 4.

[46] See: Kenedy (2023); Bryant (2023).

[47] For examples of strikingly similar obstacles for women around the world in seemingly different conditions and cultural patterns, see: Campbell (2013), pp. 29–53.

and patriarchy, is achieved. Global solidarity in this sense becomes an interesting and useful phenomenon in the further struggle for women's rights at work.[48]

3 Conclusions

Neoliberal individualism had serious consequences for the principles of solidarity, collectivity, joint action of workers. Under the monopolistic teachings of neoliberalism, over the past three decades we have seen a decline in the number of trade union members, coverage by collective agreements, but also a different perception of the position of the worker as an individual within the work collective. There is nothing bad or wrong in the idea that a worker can progress professionally with his knowledge and commitment. But when this idea is used to deny the importance of collective action of workers and the purpose of the existence of trade unions, then there are obvious negative consequences—workers today are fighting to preserve their achievements of the twentieth century on the enjoyment of the human right to work.

How does modern feminism fit into these new circumstances? First, we should look at the importance that feminist ideas and movements had on trade unions. Cullen rightfully asks the question whether trade unions are feminised or feminist.[49] Although logically the first address for feminist workers to channel feminist agendas in the field of women at work, trade unions have often created resistance to these changes, legitimizing themselves as conservative and patriarchal,[50] even as women's share in their membership has grown significantly. With the complete dominance of the neoliberal understanding of work, this characteristic of trade unions is becoming relevant again, so it is not possible to say with certainty how much they have contributed to the true promotion of feminist programs in the last two to three decades. Or perhaps it is better to ask ourselves did they advocated some ideas about gender equality at work as politically pragmatic, without an excessive dose of sincerity and faith that they will be consistently applied? Although this is a legitimate question, it seems that the new neoliberal market circumstances, which are not favorable to the activities of trade unions, have actually stimulated their interest in many new fields of conduct, such as developing mutual interests with movements, civil society, academia. Those developments make unions today closer to cooperation with feminist movements, and more open to feminist ideas and agendas, than ever before.

Several authors mention chances of joint action of trade unions and feminist movements. The movements were somewhat NGOized, which dulled and bureaucratized their work. But in trade unions they can find not only allies who possess the necessary capacities to support the true equality and equity of women at work, but

[48] See: Neuman Stanivukovic et al. (2023), p. 5.

[49] Cullen (2021).

[50] Bhardwaj (2019-2020), p. 12; Elomäki and Kantola (2021), p. 40.

also to internationalize the problems faced by women in the world of work, and regarding their social status overall, in the age of neoliberalism. This unique symbiosis is not new, as the literature suggests, dating back to the 1970s and 1980s, but it is gaining importance once more now that the neoliberal system, reinforced by the patriarchal and conservative notions that are traditionally part of its core values, is positioned as a common obstacle to enjoyment even of basic labour rights. Both those rights who can be linked to the feminist agenda directly, as well as others who may not be part of that agenda but certainly influence the position of women in the world of work. For example, in many low-profit manufacturing industries, such as textiles, workers are forced to work hours significantly longer than the famous "3 times 8 hours" daily formula. This is a general problem, but if it is known that women workers are dominant in the textile industry, it certainly becomes a worthwhile problem for feminist considerations. The natural allies in fighting such trends are trade unions.

Feminism and trade unionism share the common value of uniting around basic values, joint and solidary action. If we analyse the way feminist movements operate, we will see that the methods are similar to the way trade unions make efforts to fight for their ideas and goals. In this sense, protests and strikes are visible on a micro level—above-described actions of feminists, supported to a greater or lesser extent by local trade unions, often resembled unionistic rebellious activities. Even the final results sometimes show remarkable similarities—some of the protests ended with the signing of agreements that closely resembled trade unions' collective agreements with employers. At the broader level, feminist movements and trade unions also have significant similarities in their methodologies of action. Advocacy of certain policies and changes in regulations is a common pattern of targeted action. In such situations, feminists can use not only the mobilization potential of trade unions, but primarily their institutionalized participation in social dialogue, and thus present their ideas to decision makers. On the other hand, conservative and pre-administered unions can learn a lot about the dissemination of ideas from feminist movements—continuous presence and campaign on social networks and in the general public, with the aim of a clearer view of political attitudes and goals, as well as proposing concrete solutions with clarification of their impact on workers and the realization of workers' rights—a recipe that in the past in feminist movements led to a wider mobilization of the public to support their aspirations, is something that unions could certainly use in their current tactics.

It is difficult to give a single assessment of the impact of neoliberalism on feminist movements in labour. While individualism as a target value of neoliberalism certainly weakened the sense of collectivity and solidarity, the predatory way of functioning of neoliberal mechanisms in the field of work and social protection certainly opened the way for feminist movements to shape and articulate very clearly their points of resistance to this way of thinking. The natural connection of feminists with trade unions has not come to the full extent. Although there are positive stories about the incorporation of feminist ideas and goals into trade unionism, and their implementation through collective bargaining, it seems that there is much greater potential that would have to be realized in the future, in order to create a stronger solidarity front against the devolution of workers' rights in general, as well as the more specific protection of women workers who are often the first to be impacted by the restrictive measures of neoliberal legislators or employers.

References

Aronson R (2016) The privatisation of hope. Boston Rev. https://www.bostonreview.net/articles/ronald-aronson-privatization-hope/

Backer A (2023) Exploring the "right to sit" movement in Kerala. In: Arora P, Raman U, König R (eds) Feminist futures of work – reimagining labour in the digital economy. Amsterdam University Press, Amsterdam, pp 231–239

Batliwala S (2012) ChaNGING their world – concepts and practices of women's movements. Association for Women's Rights in Development (AWID), Toronto

Bhardwaj M (2019-2020) Feminist social movement unionism from South to North. SOAS J Postgrad Res 14:7–30

Boyd GGD (2016) The girl effect: a neoliberal instrumentalization of gender equality. Consilience J Sustain Dev 15:146–180

Brenner J (1989) Feminism's revolutionary promise – finding hope in hard times. In: Miliband R, Panitch L, Saville J (eds) The socialist register. The Merlin Press, London, pp 245–263

Bryant M (2023) Iceland PM joins crowd of 100,000 for full-day women's strike. https://www.theguardian.com/world/2023/oct/24/iceland-prime-minister-joins-womens-strike-katrin-jakobsdottir#:~:text=The%20strike%20covered%20paid%20and,store%2C%20only%20men%20were%20working

Campbell B (2013) End of equality. Seagull Books, Calcuta

Castro N (2018) CUT-Brazil, a trade union centre at the forefront of the feminist struggle. In: Herberg M (ed) Trade unions in transformation – success stories from all over the world. Fridrich Ebert Stiftung, Berlin, pp 87–91

Committee for Economic, Social and Cultural Rights (2016) General comment No. 23 on the right to just and favourable conditions of work. E/C.12/GC/23 of 27 April 2016

Committee on the Elimination of Discrimination against Women (2010) General Recommendation No. 28 on the Core Obligations of States Parties under Article 2 of the Convention on the Elimination of All Forms of Discrimination against Women, CEDAW/C/GC/28 of 16 December 2010

Cullen P (2021) Trade union mobilization and female-dominated care work in Ireland: feminised and/or feminist? Polit Eur 74:136–163. https://doi.org/10.3917/poeu.074.0136

De Souza SP, Gupta S (2023) Why stories matter for representation, action, and collectivization. In: Arora P, Raman U, König R (eds) Feminist futures of work – reimagining labour in the digital economy. Amsterdam University Press, Amsterdam, pp 197–206

Elomäki A, Kantola J (2021) Gender, power and corporatism: complex relationships and analytical perspectives – an(other) introduction to the special issue. Polit Eur 74:38–52. https://doi.org/10.3917/poeu.074.0038

Franzway S (2004) 'We need to win …' Making feminist politics in trade unions and transnational labour activist networks. Refereed paper presented to the Australasian Political Studies Association Conference University of Adelaide 29 September–1 October 2004. University of South Australia

Helfert V (2024) Radical and utopian or partnership between men and women? Austrian Trade Union women, autonomous feminists and labour related concerns, 1970s–1980s. OeZG Aust J Hist Stud 35:96–116. https://doi.org/10.25365/oezg-2024-35-1-6

International Labour Organisation (2006) R198 – employment relationship recommendation. https://normlex.ilo.org/dyn/normlex/en/f?p=NORMLEXPUB:12100:0::NO::P12100_INSTRUMENT_ID:312535

Kauppert P, Kerner I (2016) Political feminism for a better future. Fridrich Ebert Stiftung. https://library.fes.de/pdf-files/iez/12693.pdf

Kenedy N (2023) Iceland's prime minister joins thousands of women on strike. https://edition.cnn.com/2023/10/23/europe/iceland-women-strike-scli-intl/index.html#:~:text=Prime%20Minister%20Katr%C3%ADn%20Jakobsd%C3%B3ttir%2C%20pictured,equality%20on%20October%2024%2C%202023

Korolczuk E (2016) Neoliberalism and feminist organizing: from "NGO-ization of resistance" to resistance against neoliberalism. In: Kováts E (ed) Solidarity in struggle – feminist perspectives on neoliberalism in East-Central Europe. Fridrich Ebert Stiftung, Budapest, pp 32–41

Kovačević L (2023) Gender perspective of development of labour law. In: Carapezza Figlia G, Kovačević L, Kristoffersson E (eds) Gender perspectives in private law. Springer, pp 105–127. https://doi.org/10.1007/978-3-031-14092-1

Liukkunen U (2019) The role of collective bargaining in labour law regimes: a global approach. In: Liukkunen U (ed) Collective bargaining in labour law regimes – a global perspective. Springer, pp 1–64. https://doi.org/10.1007/978-3-030-16977-0

Malehoko Tshoaedi C (2008) Roots of women's union activism: South Africa 1973–2003. Universiteit Leiden

Neuman Stanivukovic S, Robbe K, Thomas K (2023) Formations of feminist strike: connecting diverse practices, contexts, and geographies. Atlantis 44(2):1–13. https://doi.org/10.7202/1109368ar

Novitz T (2022) The legal framework established by the international labour organization. In: Paul S, McCrystal S, Ewan McGaughey E (eds) The Cambridge handbook of labor in competition law. Cambridge University Press, Cambridge, pp 11–26. https://doi.org/10.1017/9781108909570.003

Peels R, Mwamadzingo M (2022) Trade union revitalization: navigating uncertainty, change and resilience in the world of work. Int J Lab Res 11:1–17

Périvier H, Sénac R (2018) The new spirit of neoliberalism: equality and economic prosperity. Int Soc Sci J 67:1–12

Reljanović M (2022) Intersekcijska i višestruka diskriminacija devojčica i žena sa invaliditetom u obrazovanju i pri zapošljavanju: obaveze država potpisnica prema članu 6. Konvencije o pravima osoba sa invaliditetom. In: Kovačević Lj, Vujadinović D, Evola M (eds) Ukrštena diskriminacija žena i devojčica sa invaliditetom i instrumenti za njihovo osnaživanje = Intersectional discrimination of women and girls with disabilities and means of their empowerment. Pravni fakultet Univerziteta u Beogradu, Beograd, pp 51–72

Reljanović M (2023) Transition from work of seasonal workers to permanent labour immigration — the case of Serbia (Tranzicija od rada sezonskih radnika ka trajnoj radnoj imigraciji – sliučaj Srbije). Stanovništvo 61(2):129–144. https://doi.org/10.59954/stnv.528

Reljanović M, Rajić Ćalić J (2024) Menstrual leave and gender equality. Strani Pravni Život 68:1–14. https://doi.org/10.56461/SPZ_24101KJ

Reljanović M, Kovačević L, Krstić I, Petrović A (2023) Priručnik za primenu Međunarodnog pakta o ekonomskim, socijalnim i kulturnim pravima. Ministarstvo za ljudska i manjinska prava i društveni dijalog, Beograd

Seguino S (2005) Gender inequality in a globalizing world. Working paper no. 426, Levy Economics Institute of Bard College, Annandale-on-Hudson. https://www.econstor.eu/bitstream/10419/31496/1/505057905.pdf

UN General Assembly (1966) International Covenant on Economic, Social and Cultural Rights. Resolution 2200A (XXI) of 16 December 1966

Wånggren L (2018) Feminist trade unionism and post-work imaginaries. J Appl Soc Theory 1:102–124

Waterman P (1993) Social-movement unionism: a new union model for a new world order? Review (Fernand Braudel Center): 245–278

Zimmer R (2022) Solidarity as a central aim of collective labour law? In: López López J (ed) Inscribing solidarity: debates in labor law and beyond. Cambridge University Press, Cambridge, pp 43–62. https://doi.org/10.1017/9781009170260.003

Zimmermann A, Binswanger C (2021) Transitioning to gender equality. In: Binswanger C, Zimmermann A (eds) Transitioning to sustainability series, Volume 5: Transitioning to gender equality. MDPI, Basel, pp 1–13. https://doi.org/10.3390/books978-3-03897-867-1

Mario Reljanović is research fellow at the Institute of Comparative Law in Belgrade. He finished his PhD studies at the Law Faculty, Union University in Belgrade in 2011, in the fields of Labour Law and Human Rights Law. His areas of expertise are labour and social law, anti-discrimination law and human rights law about which has published over hundred research papers and conducted many studies. Mario Reljanović is director of the civil society organisation Center for Dignified Work. He served as the Head of Legal Clinic for Labour Law from 2009 to 2018 and taught Labour Law at Law Faculty, Union University in Belgrade.

Syrian Refugee Women Experiences of Work-Based Violence

Burcu Gumus and Jón Ingvar Kjaran

Abstract This article examines how the initial hospitality extended to asylum seekers by Turkey in response to the mass migration wave from the Middle East in the 2000s has gradually transformed into hostility. It also explores how restrictive asylum and migration regimes have contributed to the emergence of multi-dimensional precarity surrounding the lives of asylum seekers. The study focuses on the labor conditions of Syrian refugee women in Turkey, drawing on in-depth interviews conducted with 10 Syrian refugee women working in a textile workshop in Istanbul. The findings reveal that the prolonged stay of Syrian women workers in Turkey, moving beyond their guest status, has intensified their presence and precarity in economic and social contexts.

1 Introduction

By the end of 2023, approximately 117.3 million people worldwide were forcibly displaced due to persecution, conflict, violence, human rights violations and public disorder.[1] Turkey hosts one of the largest refugee populations worldwide. Approximately 3.2 million of the refugee population living in Turkey are Syrians under temporary protection.[2] Turkey's geographical location is among the main reasons for the migration movements it has experienced since its establishment. Economic, political and security problems in Turkey's neighboring countries have

[1] UNHCR (2023a), p. 2.

[2] UNHRC-Turkey, p. 1.

B. Gumus (✉)
Aarhus University, Aarhus, Denmark
e-mail: bgumus@ph.au.dk

J. I. Kjaran
University of Iceland, Reykjavik, Iceland
e-mail: jik@hi.is

F. Macioce et al. (eds.), *Feminist Legal and Political Practices*, Gender Perspectives in Law 6, https://doi.org/10.1007/978-3-032-02856-3_6

caused and continue to cause citizens of these countries to migrate to Turkey. As a result, Turkey has become a country where groups with different ethnic and religious backgrounds (transit migrants, irregular workers, professionals, retirees, asylum seekers and refugees) have migrated to for various reasons from past to present.[3] According to the data of the ministry of interior presidency of migration management,[4] the number of registered Syrians in Turkey in 2023 is 3,214,780. The number of unregistered Syrians in Turkey is unknown. A regulation enacted in 2016 granted the right to work to persons under temporary protection status in Turkey, the majority of whom are Syrians. However, according to data from the Turkish Ministry of Labor and Social Security, the number of Syrian asylum seekers with work permits in 2023 is 108,520. The remaining people work unregistered. It has been determined that employers prefer to employ unregistered workers who will work without insurance and who are unable to claim their legal rights, with salaries so low that Turks would not prefer to work.[5] Although unregistered work is against Turkish law, Syrians would have not been able to make a living if they had not worked, so the state would have to provide more assistance. To prevent this, the state turns a blind eye to the unregistered work of many of those who seek refuge in Turkey, especially Syrians.[6] The fact that Turkey is a country that makes contract with international companies to manufacture goods for global markets has constituted the economic system of being in constant need for cheap labor. The presence of asylum-seekers and refugees meets the need for cheap labor.[7]

Textile is one of the sectors with the highest female employment in Turkey. Many Syrian asylum-seeking women are employed in the textile sector, especially in contract manufacturing workshops which are called "merdiven altı tekstil atölyeleri (Informal/unregistered/ underground textile workshops)".[8] The suboptimal migration policies in Turkey and the lack of labor protection regulations[9] cause most migrants to be in a precarious working environment in Turkey and to be considered as unskilled workers regardless of their actual skills.[10] The shift from hospitality to hostility towards Syrian refugees in Turkey stems from a combination of social, political, and economic factors. The prolonged presence of millions of refugees has strained local economies, public services, and employment markets, particularly in economically vulnerable areas, leading to growing resentment. Initially, the Turkish government framed Syrians as "guests" deserving empathy and protection under an open-door policy. However, as the crisis persisted, political discourse shifted, with media and politicians portraying refugees as burdens, fostering societal animosity

---

[3] İçduyu (2009), p. 2.

[4] https://goc.gov.tr/gecici-koruma5638

[5] Akpamuk (2023).

[6] Erdoğan (2018), p. 55.

[7] Körükmez et al. (2022), p. 205.

[8] Öztürk (2023).

[9] Baykut et al. (2021), p. 162.

[10] Şenses (2016), p. 977.

and eroding public hospitality. This shift in public opinion has created a feedback loop between societal hostility and state policies, amplifying systemic discrimination and exclusion. Syrian women face heightened precarity due to their dual vulnerability as refugees and women in a patriarchal society, compounded by societal gender norms, limited language skills, and inadequate institutional solutions. This study aims to explore how the evolving perception of hospitality in Turkish society has shaped the precarity of Syrian women workers, with a particular focus on their experiences of workplace violence. Drawing on Derrida's concept of hospitality and Butler's notion of precarity, the research examines how societal and state-level shifts have deepened Syrian women's vulnerability in the workforce. At the same time, it highlights how these women exercise agency and navigate their precarious conditions, challenging the narrative that reduces them to passive victims. By providing a nuanced understanding of the interplay between policies, societal attitudes, and workplace violence, the study seeks to identify areas for meaningful intervention. Filling a gap in the existing literature, this research uniquely combines these theoretical frameworks to analyze the specific experiences of Syrian women workers in Turkey. In line with these explanations, the research questions within the scope of this study are as follows:

- How has the evolving perception of hospitality in Turkish society, shaped by state policies and EU refugee management strategies, contributed to the precarity and workplace violence experienced by Syrian women workers?
- How do Syrian women navigate and resist precarious working conditions, and how can these insights inform policies to address systemic causes of their marginalization?

As part of this study, in-depth interviews were conducted with 10 Syrian refugees living in Turkey using semi-structured questions, and the data obtained were analyzed through thematic analysis. During the thematic analysis process, the data were coded, key themes were identified, and the findings were interpreted within the framework of these themes. This process aimed to provide an in-depth understanding of the experiences of Syrian women refugees in line with the study's objectives.

The chapter is structured as follows: First, the policies of the EU countries and Turkey regarding refugees (migration) are evaluated by drawing on Derrida's notions of hospitality and Butler's precarity into account. In the second part, we focus on the experiences of women asylum-seekers working informally.

2 From Conditional Hospitality to Structural Precarity

The Syrian civil war, which began in 2011, triggered one of the largest refugee crises in modern history. By the end of 2023, over 117.3 million people worldwide had been forcibly displaced due to persecution, conflict, violence, and human rights violations.[11] Turkey hosts one of the largest refugee populations globally, with approximately 3.2 million Syrians living under temporary protection.[12] Initially, Turkey adopted an "open-door" policy, with President Erdoğan referring to Syrian refugees as "our brothers" and emphasizing religious and ethnic kinship.[13] This framing, rooted in temporary hospitality, was accompanied by policies that cast Syrians as "guests" expected to eventually return to their homeland. However, as the crisis became protracted, this discourse shifted, and the presence of millions of refugees began to strain Turkey's economy, public services, and social cohesion. Public sentiment, once rooted in empathy, eroded, giving way to hostility, particularly in economically vulnerable regions where competition for jobs and resources fueled resentment.

Turkey's approach to the refugee crisis also reveals a tension between its initial framing of hospitality and its political and economic realities. Temporary protection policies provided limited rights and no long-term solutions for integration, leaving Syrian refugees vulnerable to exploitation. Many refugees, particularly women, found themselves working in informal, low-wage jobs with no legal protections. This precarious existence reflects the limitations of hospitality as conceived by Jacques Derrida,[14] who criticize the conditional nature of hospitality in the modern nation-state. Derrida argues that while unconditional hospitality—welcoming the stranger without question—is an ethical ideal, sovereignty often transforms hospitality into an exclusionary and selective act. States prioritize the security and interests of their citizens, relegating refugees to the status of temporary guests who must rely on the goodwill of the host. This creates a dynamic where refugees are simultaneously included and excluded, welcomed yet marginalized, exposing the contradictions inherent in modern notions of hospitality.

This dynamic is not unique to Turkey but reflects broader patterns in global refugee governance. In the European Union, for instance, the refugee crisis intensified after the surge in Mediterranean crossings and high-profile tragedies such as the death of Syrian child Aylan Kurdi in 2015. While some European countries initially responded with solidarity, the growing influx of refugees revealed fractures within the EU's migration policies. States like Hungary and Slovakia opposed inclusive measures, framing migration as a security threat and adopting restrictive policies that contradicted the EU's commitments to liberal values. The result was a dual approach of offering hospitality while simultaneously reinforcing borders, imposing controls, and outsourcing migration management to countries like Turkey and Libya. These contradictions highlight the tension between hospitality and sovereignty, where efforts to protect refugees coexist with practices that perpetuate their exploitation and vulnerability. By imposing controls and outsourcing migration

---

[11] UNHCR (2023b), p. 3.

[12] UNHRC-Turkey, p. 2.

[13] Karaveli (2013).

[14] Derrida and Dufourmantelle (2020), p. 119.

management, states turn hospitality into a selective and conditional practice, leaving refugees vulnerable to exploitation in transit countries and informal economies.

Hannah Arendt's reflections on the refugee condition further illuminate the profound existential and material loss experienced by displaced individuals. In *We Refugees*, Arendt describes how refugees are stripped of their political belonging, social recognition, and dignity, reducing them to what she calls "the dregs of the world".[15] This existential loss extends beyond physical displacement, encompassing the deprivation of legal rights and social visibility. Without political recognition, refugees are rendered "superfluous," living in a state of isolation and precarity. Arendt's insights resonate with Judith Butler's concept of precarity,[16] which emphasizes how systemic inequalities make certain populations disproportionately vulnerable. While all human beings are inherently precarious due to their dependence on others, Butler argues that social categories such as gender, race, nationality, and class exacerbate this vulnerability for marginalized groups. For refugees, precarity is not limited to material insecurity but also includes existential threats to dignity and livability. The uncertainty of their legal status, lack of social recognition, and reliance on informal labor markets undermine their ability to build secure and meaningful lives.

In the context of Turkey, the dynamics of hospitality and hostility disproportionately impact Syrian refugee women, whose vulnerabilities are intensified by gender, legal invisibility, and economic precarity. Initially welcomed as *guests* under Turkey's temporary protection policies, Syrian women now face increasing hostility driven by economic pressures, rising xenophobia, and restrictive state policies. Their temporary legal status denies them access to stable protections and essential social services, pushing many into informal labor markets where they are subject to exploitation, abuse, and unsafe working conditions. This precarious existence is further compounded by societal marginalization and gender-based violence, which severely constrain their ability to live with dignity and stability.

Judith Butler's concept of precarity provides a framework for understanding how systemic inequalities produce and sustain this vulnerability. Syrian women are placed in a precarious position not only because of their refugee status but also due to their gendered roles, which expose them to additional risks, such as exploitation in care work, domestic labor, or other informal sectors. Moreover, Jacques Derrida's critique of conditional hospitality highlights the contradictions in Turkey's approach: while Syrian refugees are offered temporary shelter, their integration into society is systematically denied. This creates a state of exclusion, where Syrian women navigate cycles of instability, discrimination, and survival.

The intersection of conditional hospitality, structural precarity, and gendered exploitation leaves Syrian refugee women particularly vulnerable. Addressing these dynamics requires moving beyond temporary and exclusionary policies to implement sustainable solutions that prioritize their dignity, rights, and opportunities.

---

[15] Arendt (1998), p. 61.

[16] Butler (2004), p. 135.

Policies must focus on dismantling systemic barriers, ensuring that Syrian women have access to protections, resources, and the conditions necessary for a livable and dignified life.

3 Method

The critiques of feminist methodology toward mainstream research methods and its own internal interrogations are closely related to methodological and ethical debates in migration research that address disadvantaged and marginalized groups.[17] One of the main critiques of the feminist approach is the disregard for gender in knowledge production and the invisibility of women's experiences. This issue becomes particularly evident when the experiences of female migrants are examined in migration research without a gender perspective. Feminist methodology challenges the positivist claim of objectivity by emphasizing that knowledge cannot be considered apart from social power dynamics and that the researcher cannot be abstracted from their social reality.[18] This critique highlights that knowledge production is not independent of politics and that the research process is inherently political. In this regard, feminist methodology aims to problematize power relations at every stage of knowledge production, seeking not only to understand but also to transform.[19]

In migration studies, addressing research methodology and ethical principles within the framework of feminist methodology is crucial for making the experiences of migrants, particularly women, visible. Consequently, this study has been conducted in adherence to feminist research methods. This article draws on the experiences of immigrant women. The interviews were structured with an awareness of the significance of knowledge derived from the women's experiences and life narratives. In this research, as a feminist research principle, efforts were made to establish egalitarian relationships between the researcher and the participants. Particular care was taken to build close and sincere relationships based on mutual understanding, sharing of emotions, experiences, and ideas, avoiding hierarchical dynamics. The heterogeneity of social realities, the differentiation of female and male experiences even within the same cultural context, and the necessity of making inequalities, discrimination, contradictions, and conflicts experienced by women within these realities more visible, are the fundamental motivations behind conducting this research with women working in a sewing workshop. The fieldwork for this study was completed within four months from April to July 2024.

This article is based on data collected through in-depth, semi-structured interviews with 10 Syrian refugee women working in the same sewing workshop located in the Mehmet Akif neighborhood of Sultanbeyli district, Istanbul. Sultanbeyli, on

---

17 Coşkun (2022), p. 371.

18 Coşkun (2022), p. 372.

19 Hammersley (1992), p. 200.

the Asian side of Istanbul, is among the districts with the highest concentration of Syrian refugees. The Mehmet Akif neighborhood within this district is known for its relatively affordable housing by Istanbul standards and the prevalence of workshops engaged in subcontracted textile production. All participants live and work in the same neighborhood. The participants referred to as refugees in the study are individuals who fled their country and sought refuge in Turkey after the civil war broke out in Syria. Although they have the right to reside in Turkey, they do not have the right to work or obtain citizenship.

Due to the small number of participants, emphasis was placed on capturing their opinions, thoughts, perspectives, emotions and experiences. To better understand social reality, the data was meticulously extracted through these in-depth interviews.

The in-depth interviews were primarily conducted through personal connections. Two of the initial female participants facilitated access to other women in the workshop. During the interviews, news reports surfaced about an alleged incident in Kayseri, Turkey, where a Syrian man was accused of assaulting a Turkish girl. This incident led to attacks on Syrian-owned businesses and vehicles in Kayseri. The situation escalated as violence, fueled by hate speech spreading on social media, led to raids by local communities on areas with high concentrations of Syrian migrants across the country. As a result, five women who initially agreed to participate in the interviews later declined. Despite these challenges, three participants were reached through snowball sampling. Multiple visits to the workshop prior to the interviews helped ensure that participants felt comfortable during the sessions. During these visits, the relationships among the women working in the workshop and between the workers and their employer were also observed.

All interviews were conducted in the participants' homes at their request, with each session lasting three to three and a half hours. Participants were informed about the study's purpose, the voluntary nature of their participation, and assurances of confidentiality were provided. Due to the public sensitivity surrounding refugee protection in Turkey, all participants provided verbal consent only. Audio recordings were made only after explicit permission was obtained. The interviews were conducted with the assistance of an Arabic-Turkish translator who is a friend of the first author and works on humanitarian aid projects. The necessary ethical approval for the study was granted on May 31, 2024, by Istanbul Doğuş University under decision number E-42435178-050.04-62914.

The data collected from the in-depth, semi-structured interviews were analyzed using a feminist-informed thematic analysis, which involves identifying, analyzing, and interpreting patterns of meaning within the data.[20] This method was chosen because it allows for a systematic yet flexible approach to identifying, analyzing, and interpreting themes (patterns) within qualitative data while centering the lived experiences and voices of marginalized groups, consistent with feminist methodology. The transcripts were systematically coded line by line to identify meaningful units of data. Codes were developed inductively, meaning they emerged directly

[20] Braun and Clarke (2006), p. 79.

from the participants' words and experiences rather than being predefined. This ensured that the analysis remained grounded in the women's narratives. The initial codes were then grouped into broader themes that captured significant patterns across the data. MAXQDA 2020 software was used to analyze the data. To ensure the anonymity of the 10 Syrian refugee women in the study, the Syrian women have been designated as P1-P10. The socio-demographic data concerning the Syrian women are presented in Table 1.

All the women interviewed are Syrian and work as seamstresses. However, it was found that depending on the seasonal workload of the workshop or when they work overtime, they may also work in the ironing, quality control, or packaging departments. All 10 participants in the study indicated that they found their current jobs through an intermediary agency. The participants mentioned that there are intermediary agencies specifically focused on finding workers for Turkish companies in the

Table 1 Socio-demographic information of the Syrian participants

Participant pseudonym	Age	Marital Status	Education Level	Jobs in Syria	Duration of live in Istanbul	Working period in Istanbul	Previous jobs in Turkey
P1	38	Married with 4 children	High School	Housewife	12	11	Cleaning and housework
P2	35	Married with 3 children	High School	Housewife	12	12	Handcraft
P3	44	Married with 5 children	High School	Housewife	10	9	Worker in textile
P4	37	Widow with 2 children	Bachelor's degree	Architecture	11	10	Worker in textile
P5	32	Married with 4 children	High School	Housewife	12	12	Handcraft
P6	31	Married with 3 children	High School	Housewife	10	10	Cleaning and housework
P7	43	Married with 5 children	Primary school	Housewife	12	12	Handcraft
P8	31	Married with 2 children	Bachelor's degree	English Teacher	10	10	Worker in textile
P9	35	Widow with 4 children	Illiterate	Housewife	10	10	Cleaning and housework
P10	29	Married with 4 children	Primary school	Housewife	10	10	Handcraft

manufacturing sector that seek migrant labor. These agencies find jobs for them in exchange for a commission.

4 Findings

As shown in Table 2, all participants receive wages below the minimum wage and work 12 h a day in the workshop. The participants mentioned that they generally do not work on Saturdays but usually go to work on Sundays. It was also noted that if they choose to work overtime after their 12-h shifts, their pay may increase slightly. It was found that participants often work overtime to earn additional income. Aside from lunch, the participants do not receive any other benefits (such as private health insurance, transportation, performance bonuses, housing assistance, gift cards, etc.). We divide the findings into three sections to explore different aspect of how Syrian women experience their work and how it intersects with their refugee/migrant status. The focus is on how gender is constitutive in producing precarity and how they experience but also try to resist violence at work and in society.

4.1 Gendered Aspect of Work

Understanding the labor market situation of women in pre-war Syria is important for evaluating the employment decisions of Syrian women in Turkey. Before the war, women's participation in the labor force in Syria was constrained by legal barriers and sociocultural norms.[21] Urban women, especially in professional and technical fields, were more likely to be employed, with women filling 40% of white-collar

Table 2 Working Conditions of the participants

Participant pseudonym	Salary in Turkish lira	Insurance	Working time per day
P1	6500	No	12 Hours (8 A.M. to 8 P.M.)
P2	6500	No	12 Hours (8 A.M. to 8 P.M.)
P3	6500	No	12 Hours (8 A.M. to 8 P.M.)
P4	6500	No	12 Hours (8 A.M. to 8 P.M.)
P5	6500	No	12 Hours (8 A.M. to 8 P.M.)
P6	6500	No	12 Hours (8 A.M. to 8 P.M.)
P7	6500	No	12 Hours (8 A.M. to 8 P.M.)
P8	6500	No	12 Hours (8 A.M. to 8 P.M.)
P9	6500	No	12 Hours (8 A.M. to 8 P.M.)
P10	6500	No	12 Hours (8 A.M. to 8 P.M.)

[21] Buecher and Aniyamuzaala (2016).

jobs.[22] Employment levels were lower in cities like Raqqa and Daraa, but higher in coastal cities such as Latakia. Cultural norms determined socially acceptable jobs for women, and married women were generally expected to focus on household chores rather than paid work. However, these norms began to slowly change with the increasing participation of more educated women in the labor force.[23] There was a dual structure in female employment: women with lower education levels struggled to find work in cities, whereas university-educated women were employed in comparable rates to men, typically in the public sector and gender-based fields such as health and education.[24] Women preferred public sector jobs over private sector ones due to the stability and pride associated with state employment. Employment rates were highest among women living with family or siblings and lower among married women.[25]

In this study, nearly all the women interviewed expressed that they began working out of "necessity" after moving to Turkey to meet their basic needs and support their families. Initially, due to societal norms that did not view working outside the home as appropriate for women, they were limited to doing piecework within the home. Piecework, while labor-intensive and low-paying, allowed women to continue managing their household responsibilities. For instance, P3 mentioned that she did not object to her husband working if it did not interfere with her household duties. However, she noted that the piece rate of 35 TL (0.90 Euro) was insufficient to cover household expenses. Faced with the inadequacy of piecework to meet family needs, some of the women in our study often felt compelled to work outside the home. For that they had to engage in negotiation processes with their husbands, family members, or broader social networks to be. It was understood that, except for those who had worked in their home country, the women interviewed were not happy about working in Istanbul. Participants repeatedly emphasized that the responsibility of providing for the family should fall on men. They are constituted in the dominant cultural discourse as the "bread givers" and leaders of the household as some of our participants mentioned in the interviews:

> P10: The pillar of the house is the man who brings bread to the home. But living here is very hard. Everything is very expensive, and the salaries are very low. We all work, including the children, but we still barely make ends meet.
>
> P1: In the beginning, it was very difficult. My husband didn't want me to work at all. But we have no choice. It's not even a matter for discussion. In Syria, working wouldn't have been an option. Ultimately, bringing bread to the home is the man's job.

Butler's concept of precarity offers a valuable perspective from which to analyze the experiences these women who had to navigate gendered expectation of work and the necessity of providing for their family. Working outside their home in addition to their household duties contributed further to their precarity as we will discuss in

[22] Buecher and Aniyamuzaala (2016).

[23] Ertorer (2021), p. 2570.

[24] Øvensen and Sletten (2007), p. 13.

[25] Sparre (2008), p. 8.

the next section. Moreover, they experienced violence and oppression not only because of their migrant status but also because of their gender—being women in a patriarchal society. The pressure to participate in the labor force despite traditional gender roles is exacerbated by economic challenges such as low wages and high living costs, creating a dual oppression related to life and gender expectations. Participants' narratives also overlap with Kandiyoti's[26] concept of patriarchal bargaining. Accordingly, women make strategic choices to maximize their security or gains within patriarchal systems, not only within their own cultural context but also in the host community. In this case, Syrian women reluctantly accepted entering the labor force as a patriarchal bargain to ensure that their family would survive, despite adhering to traditional gender-based beliefs. In that respect, this illustrates how migration can partly disrupt the dominant discourse on gender roles as a response to economic and social pressures.

4.2 *Violence and Precarity at Work*

The influx of Syrian migrants into Turkey in large groups has intensified the informal and insecure employment regime in which the labor market precarity has become the norm. Specifically, the provision of low-wage, hazardous, and illegal jobs[27] and the perception of migrants as "disposable cheap labor" by employers[28] have contributed to the exploitation and reinforcement of precarity at work. In addition, if a Syrian migrant wants to be employed by a Turkish employer, the employer has to apply for the work permit. In other words, a migrant cannot apply for a work permit for themselves. Another important point is that the number of employees under temporary protection working in a workplace cannot exceed 10 percent of the total number of employees. To obtain a work permit for a Syrian with a temporary protection ID card, the employer must initiate the application process and apply to the Ministry of Labor, providing justification for hiring a Syrian instead of a Turkish citizen. Furthermore, the law states that employers are obliged to employ five Turkish citizens for each foreign employee.[29] The process is bureaucratically burdensome and imposes additional costs on employers, causing employers to be reluctant to employ Syrians, while creating and sustaining the exploitable labor force needed. In general, employers prefer asylum seekers (non-Syrians) who have no legal rights as they are not registered.[30]

These employment regimes, in the case of Syrian migrants, demonstrate that many of our participants were from the onset in a precarious situation at work. They

[26] Kandiyoti (1988), p. 280.

[27] Lee et al. (2020), p. 200.

[28] Wehrle et al. (2018), p. 93.

[29] Kutlu (2015), p. 14.

[30] Akpamuk (2023).

were for example totally dependent on the authority and good-will of their prospective employers, both in terms of gaining working permit but also to be hired in the first place as migrants with no legal rights might be preferred. In that respect, many Syrian women found work as domestic workers as those jobs were outside the contours of the employment regimes. Three of the participants mentioned that they worked as domestic workers before starting their jobs in the textile workshop.

> P6: We fled to Turkey 11 years ago because of the war. I have three children: two boys and one girl. In my home country, only my husband worked, and his salary was sufficient for all of us. Here, except for my daughter, we all work. I started working a year after we arrived. Before this job, I used to clean homes or apartments. One day, after finishing cleaning a house, the female homeowner accused me of theft to avoid paying me. When I tried to protest, she said she would report me to the police and have me deported. Since that day, I haven't worked in cleaning.
>
> P9: In one cleaning job, I was assaulted by the male homeowner and was not paid for my work.

The quotes reveal violence and exploitations experienced by some of our participants when employed as domestic workers. This kind of violence has been reported in other studies and reports and draws attention to the precarious situation of migrant workers and power imbalances between the homeowner and the migrant domestic worker.[31,32,33] It also demonstrates lack of job opportunities for Syrian migrant women and how the employment regime in Turkey constitutes them as "burden" for employers. Furthermore, many of them had little or no prior working experience and specific skills. Another significant issue identified was the lack of training provided for their job by their employers or fellow co-workers which caused them stress at work as P2 reveals in the following:

> P2: I had no prior work experience. They first put me in packaging. You might think it's very simple, just put the product in a bag and seal it, but there is a technique to it. Many Turkish workers here, especially, are reluctant to show the nuances of the job. Their hands move so fast that it takes time to understand what they are doing and how they are doing it.

Lack of training opportunities can be understood as epistemic violence[3435] as you are not given the skills and/or knowledge needed to perform the work. This could then lead to emotional stress and fear. Some of our participants reported that some employers had threatened them with deportation if they did not meet the expected standards of work. Training and developing skills were therefore crucial for our participants to avoid being accused of deliberate slow performance which could then either lead to being laid off or threats of deportation.

Participants reported being continuously subjected to verbal abuse from Turkish fellow workers who accused them of being "money-driven" in the sense of

---

[31] International Labor Organization (2016).

[32] Palalar et al. (2024), p. 192.

[33] Hellgren (2024), p. 7.

[34] Spivak (2010), p. 30.

[35] Ahmed (2012), p. 55.

attempting to earn more money through additional work despite receiving state aid. Additionally, they faced accusations of violating the rights of Turkish workers and "stealing" their jobs.

> P2: After all, we work at the same workplaces and live in neighboring neighborhoods. Despite working together and being neighbors, there is growing hatred. You can feel the accumulated anger. They fear we will take their husbands, that we will learn the job and take it from them, and that we will take their land. We are only trying to live and provide a better future for our children, just like they do.
>
> P4: Aside from learning the job and adapting to working conditions, the thing I struggle with the most is using the language. After all, I have been in Turkey for a long time. I understand everything said, but I can't express myself as well as I understand. The women here think I am doing it intentionally.

These two examples demonstrate well how migration regimes intersect with violence regimes at work. The labeling of newcomers as "guests" creates not only an environment of competition between the guest and the host[36] but also unequal power relations. As a matter of fact, it has led to the emergence of increasingly racist and xenophobic attitudes towards refugees and migrants in Turkey. Over time, these attitudes have turned into violent acts against Syrians, both at work and in society in general. For example, as our participants reported, they are often accused of "taking" jobs from Turkish citizen and met with suspicion by the co-workers who then are not willing to help them gaining the proper work training (see P2). These conditions then produce hierarchy of employment in which Syrian women find themselves at the bottom, being more susceptible for exploitation and violence. Furthermore, language also was a barrier for full acceptance at work and indicated by P4 and often used by Turkish employers to control migrant workers (see P9).

> P9: The Turks constantly tell us to speak Turkish so that we don't understand, they say we will do treacherous things behind our backs, we know. We already work 12 hours a day. We go home and deal with household issues. I can't understand why they are so worried about what we might do.

Speaking Turkish and adopting the norms related to Turkish culture are defining factors of belonging to the Turkish nation.[37] In order to be considered sufficiently Turkish, migrants must first overcome the language barrier. In other words, demanding that asylum-seekers speak Turkish is considered as an element that reinforces the dominance of Turkishness in the workplace. The fact that refugees cannot fully integrate into the society in terms of language limits their mobility in the labor market and increases their precarity. The experiences shared by P9 and P4 help us understand the difficulties migrants face with language, which not only makes them economically vulnerable, but also exposes them to social exclusion and discrimination.

These narratives of violence at work draw attention to the broader context of labor exploitation and precarious employment conditions faced by refugees and

[36] Carpi and Şenoğuz (2021), p. 133.

[37] Yıldız (2001), p. 35.

migrants. This is particularly true for migrant women because of the strict gender-based labor markets which offer them limited training or advancement opportunities, trapping them in low-skilled and precarious jobs. Furthermore, not being paid for their work, also demonstrate their lack of bargaining power in Turkey's informal labor market. Unable to negotiate fair working conditions or access legal remedies, Syrian migrant women are forced to accept exploitative working conditions as their only option. In other words, their precarious situation is exacerbated by both their migrant status and their gender. The precarious employment conditions faced by Syrian migrant women in Turkey must be understood through an intersectional lens that considers how gendered oppression operates across multiple dimensions. Patriarchal norms from their cultural legacy position women as dependent on male breadwinners, which limits their prior work experience and financial independence. Within family dynamics, this internalized subordination further exacerbates their vulnerability when they enter the labor market. At the same time, host-state structures and societal attitudes reinforce patriarchy through exclusionary practices, discriminatory policies, and limited job opportunities, particularly in informal, low-skilled sectors. Employers exploit this compounded vulnerability, creating a cycle of precarity where gender, migration status, and labor regimes intersect to deepen systemic inequality and expose women to violence, exploitation, and exclusion.

In the specific context of this study, Syrian migrant women working in Turkey are in precarious situation due to their lack of formal rights and being constantly reminded of their "otherness". The migration regime not only exposes them to economic exploitation but intersected with violence at work. Furthermore, employers often reminded our participants of their marginalized status as migrants in order to establish a social division between Turks (the hosts) and Syrians (the guests) as a means of control and manipulation. In fact, as Derrida demonstrates, the concept of hospitality, entails imbalance of power between the host (employer/Turkish society) and the guest (Syrian migrant). The host establishes power over the guest, creating an unequal relationship that manifests in multiple, intersecting forms of violence within Turkey's migration regime. Economic exploitation is evident as Syrian women are employed at lower wages than their Turkish counterparts, reflecting their vulnerability and lack of bargaining power. Their legal precarity intensifies this dynamic, as employers exploit their reliance on them for work permits, using the constant threat of dismissal to maintain control. At the same time, linguistic discrimination exacerbates their exclusion, as their inability to express themselves fluently in Turkish leads to their perception as "traitors" or untrustworthy by Turkish colleagues, fostering workplace hostility. Furthermore, institutional violence emerges through frequent raids by migration authorities and the looming threat of deportation, creating a tool of systemic control. Together, these elements intertwine to produce a context where labor exploitation, racism, and the threat of deportation intersect, sustaining and reinforcing regimes of violence.

4.3 *Fear and Insecurity*

Syrian women who participated in our study experienced uneasiness and fear which related to many aspects of their existence. In previous section we mentioned their fear of redundancy. Their precarious situation at work then as we will discuss in this section intersected with worries about being evicted from their homes and/or subjected to harassment or a racist attack. In other words, their existence could be compared to what Agamben[38] has termed as "state of exception" in the sense that due to their temporal migrant status they are not granted full legal protection. They become the constant guest who is then as previously discussed dependent on the hospitality of Turkish society which is offered to them conditionally. As Derrida[39] has argued hospitality can always be determined by control/dominance of the host over the guest. The workings of hospitality, as in the case of our participants, also demonstrates how it can reinforce the distinction between "us" (the host) and "the other" (the guest). As Sara Ahmed[40] points out, this distinction leads to suspicion and fear of the "other" and reminds us of that underneath hospitality there is hostility as many of our participants reported.

> P7: The anxiety is not only about the risk of physical attack. The state also contributes significantly to our insecurity. Even those with residence permits are being deported. We do not understand the criteria or the basis for these deportations. This situation is particularly distressing for women, as men are being deported, leaving us alone with our children.
>
> P1: I am anxious even at work, fearing someone might make a disparaging comment. For example, the Turkish public is sensitive to the conflict in Palestine, which is understandable and necessary. However, the same sensitivity is not extended to us. Didn't we also experience conflict? I do not believe we deserve this treatment.

P7 and P1 give account of how migration regimes in Turkey, intersecting with employment and violence regimes brings them into "state of exception" as migrants and guests. They experience on daily basis fear of violence and exclusion. Their temporal protection status as "special guests", while providing certain social benefits and services, is fraught with instability and uncertainty. For example there is no clear path to permanent residency or citizenship, and as both P7 and P1 mentioned, their existence is infused with instability and uncertainty. This creates a constant state of anxiety for many of our participants. In order to navigate their precarious existence and "state of exception" Syrian migrant women relied on informal migrant networks for information (WhatsApp groups) and refrained from interacting with governmental agencies. For example, many of them did not register into the official system which was often prerequisite for gaining some minimal social/economic benefits as revealed in the following excerpts:

> P8: To be insured means to be registered in the system, which makes it easier for the government to monitor us. Therefore, I believe not being insured is better.

---

[38] Agamben (2020), p. 41.

[39] Derrida and Dufourmantelle (2020), p. 97.

[40] Ahmed (2000), p. 22.

P4: To be honest, the arbitrariness in this country is very disturbing. We do not want to sign any official documents. We do not trust anyone in this country, including the government. You might think this is ingratitude since we are protecting our lives on this land. But the psychological battle we endure here is very severe.

By avoiding formal registration, refugees resist the state's attempt to fix them in place—geographically and socially. Registration often ties refugees to specific cities (or localities), determined by the Turkish government, which are frequently overcrowded and resource-strained. These areas experience significant competition for jobs, education, and social services, intensifying precarity and limiting opportunities for upward mobility. Not being registered, therefore, enables refugees to bypass these restrictions and maintain a degree of spatial autonomy. This freedom of movement allows them to explore alternative locations where they might find better employment opportunities, social networks, or access to informal support systems. In this way, invisibility becomes a tactic of survival and a rejection of the imposed boundaries that registration entails. Beyond resisting immediate restrictions, the choice not to register is also a strategic decision with long-term implications. If refugees are registered in Turkey, they risk being legally tied to the country. Under the EU-Turkey deal and international agreements, Turkey is officially considered a "safe third country," which means that registered refugees can be denied asylum in Europe and forcibly returned to Turkey. By remaining outside the system, they keep open the possibility of onward migration to Europe, where they hope to secure better living conditions and asylum opportunities. This form of invisibility, then, is not simply resistance but also an act of foresight and pragmatism, aimed at improving their future prospects. The refusal to register also reflects a profound lack of trust in official institutions that govern migration. From the perspective of refugees, the state's registration systems appear more concerned with control and containment than with protection or support. Refugees are often skeptical of whether registration will bring tangible benefits, such as access to housing, employment, or legal rights. Instead, they fear it may increase their vulnerability—through surveillance, deportation, or forced immobility. In sum, the decision to avoid registration should not be seen merely as an act of passivity or fear. Instead, it is a calculated act of resistance against biopolitical power structures. It is a way for refugees to reclaim agency over their lives by evading restrictive policies and seeking alternative routes to survival, freedom, and future mobility. Through invisibility, they challenge the state's attempts to surveil and control them while carving out spaces for autonomy within systems designed to constrain them.

Our participants also mentioned that they or their family members had experienced racist attacks, either at work or in other settings. P2 and P10 give examples of these physical and psychological attacks:

P2: The most frequent thing I hear, especially from the women at work, is "Go back to your country." Yes, we do not belong here. But we have no way of returning. We try to explain this both at work and on the street. We are already people who oppose Assad.

P10: My 16-year-old son was attacked after school. They beat him up, saying, "What are you doing here, Syrian?" He was stabbed in his leg and hip. He was bedridden for a year and then dropped out of school due to depression. Now, tell me, who can we sue? Even if

> we could, how would we afford a lawyer? And even if we paid, who would believe us here? Is there justice for us in this country?

These experiences shared by our participants are examples of psychological and physical violence. P2's frequent encounter with the discourse of "go back to your country" is an important explanation in terms of how language can be used to establish distinction between "us" (host) and "them" (the guests) to exclude and marginalize migrants. It further constituted the Syrian migrant as a stranger in Turkey as it is firmly indicated that they are "out of place" and not welcomed. P10's son being attacked reveal the extent of physical violence Syrian migrants are exposed to. The fact that attacks against Syrians take place in different cities of Turkey shows that racist discourse is not limited to verbal hostility, but also creates an environment that legitimizes aggression. The attack on P10's son is important in terms of revealing how this hostility translates into direct physical harm and how their presence becomes dangerous and unsafe. However, these narratives also reveal the institutional violence they face in terms of their lack of access to justice and protection. P10's despair about the cost of seeking legal recourse and justice helps us understand how systemic barriers contribute further to their precarious situation and violence experienced. The link between racist discourses and the different types of violence experienced is critical to understanding how the women interviewed and their families experience multi-layered dimensions of the violence—both at work and in society in general.

Participants in the study also found ways to adapt and find ways to live within the "liminal space of the new home".[41,42] Although each of the interviewed Syrian women has a unique story, it has been observed that their fears are largely similar. They attempt to cope with their fears by creating a community of care and a feeling of home for their family. Many of the women interviewed live with two or sometimes three families in one house due to their inability to pay rent. Consequently, it is understood that they work together on household chores, childcare, and caring for the elderly. P10 and P6 give some insight into these adaption strategies:

> P10: Living together in tiny houses is very challenging. However, it also makes our lives somewhat easier. We cry and laugh together. We have essentially become a family.
>
> P6: We are trying to adapt. For example, we now try to speak Turkish with our children instead of Arabic.

P6 narrates how she made the effort to speak Turkish with their children so their children might have a future in the host society. The effort to speak Turkish is not only a matter of cultural adaptation but also a strategy to seek inclusion into the Turkish society, as language can become barrier to full participation. In addition, the participants have learned to live together and cope despite challenging living conditions (P10). This adaptation shows how they reshaped their daily lives to survive within the limitations imposed by their migrant status. Participants emphasize the importance of community and collective support in their survival. Living together,

[41] Korac (2009), p. 67.

[42] Perez (2018), p. 1520.

speaking the same language and sharing problems is understood to create a micro community that provides emotional and practical solidarity for the women interviewed. Additionally, our participants mentioned that they take in and support newly arrived migrants.

5 Discussion and Summary

This study explored how the transition from conditional hospitality to hostility has shaped the work-based violence and precarity experienced by Syrian refugee women in Turkey. By employing Derrida's concept of conditional hospitality and Butler's notion of precarity, the analysis highlights the structural and gendered dynamics at play.

Turkey's initial framing of Syrian refugees as "guests" created temporary inclusion while masking systemic vulnerabilities. As economic and social pressures intensified, this conditional hospitality gave way to hostility, positioning refugees as scapegoats. This shift is particularly evident in the labor market, where Syrian women are exploited as unprotected, low-wage workers. The interviews illustrate that the label of "guest" reinforces unequal power relations, allowing employers and coworkers to justify exclusion and exploitation.

The findings show how gender intersects with precarious employment. Patriarchal norms, combined with legal restrictions and language barriers, push Syrian women into informal and hazardous work environments, such as textile workshops and domestic labor. Workplace precarity manifests through low wages, verbal abuse, and threats of deportation, exacerbating their vulnerability.

At the societal level, their marginalization is compounded by xenophobic attitudes and systemic exclusion. Butler's concept of *precarity* underscores how institutional frameworks produce conditions of heightened vulnerability, leaving these women in what Agamben terms a *state of exception*. They remain legally and socially excluded, navigating insecurity through avoidance of state systems and reliance on informal networks.

Despite these challenges, the findings highlight how Syrian women demonstrate agency and resilience. By creating micro-communities of care and mutual support, they resist complete marginalization and find ways to survive within hostile conditions. This challenges narratives that portray refugees as passive victims, emphasizing their strategic adaptations to systemic neglect.

In summary, the transition from hospitality to hostility reflects deeper structural failures to integrate Syrian refugees into Turkish society as rights-bearing individuals. Policies that perpetuate exclusion and precarity must be addressed through structural reforms, prioritizing legal protections, economic inclusion, and recognition of refugee agency.

References

Agamben G (2020) İstisna hali. Ayrıntı Yayınları, İstanbul
Ahmed S (2000) Strange encounters: embodied others in post-coloniality. Routledge
Ahmed S (2012) On being included racism and diversity in institutional life. Duke University Press
Akpamuk G (2023) Türkiye'deki Suriyelilerin çoğu neden kayıt dışı çalışıyor, hükümetin bu konuda politikası ne?. BBC News, May 25. https://www.bbc.com/turkce/articles/cz51zr816mlo
Arendt H (1998) Totalitarizmin kaynakları 2, Emperyalizm. İletişim Yayınları, İstanbul
Baykut S, Erbil C, Ozbilgin M, Kamasak R, Baglama SH (2021) The impact of hidden curriculum on international students in the context of a toxic triangle of diversity. Curric J 33(2):156–177. https://doi.org/10.1002/curj.135
Braun V, Clarke V (2006) Using thematic analysis in psychology. Qual Res Psychol 3(2):77–101. https://doi.org/10.1191/1478088706qp063oa
Buecher B, Aniyamuzaala JR (2016) Women, work & war: Syrian women and the struggle to survive five years of conflict. Care Research Study. https://library.alnap.org/help-library/women-work-war-syrian-women-and-the-struggle-to-survive-five-years-of-conflict
Butler J (2004) Precarious life: the powers of violence and mourning. Verso, London
Carpi E, Şenoğuz P (2021) Refugee hospitality in Lebanon and Turkey: on making the other. Int Migr 57(2):126–142
Coşkun F (2022) Sınırda karşılaşmalar: Göç eden bireylerin ben ve öteki olma durumlarına dair söylem analizi. MSGSÜ Sosyal Bilimler 2(26):368–379. https://doi.org/10.56074/msgsusbd.1175440
Derrida J, Dufourmantelle A (2020) Davet: Konukseverlik üstüne Dufourmantelle Derrida'yı konukseverliğin sorumluluğunu almaya davet ediyor. Metis Edebiyat, İstanbul
Erdoğan MM (2018) Türkiye'deki Suriyeliler: Toplumsal kabul ve uyum. İstanbul Bilgi Üniversitesi Yayınları, İstanbul
Ertorer SE (2021) Asylum regimes and refugee experiences of precarity: the case of syrian refugees in Turkey. J Refug Stud 34(3):2568–2592. https://doi.org/10.1093/jrs/feaa089
Hammersley M (1992) On feminist methodology. Sociology 26(2):187–206. https://doi.org/10.1177/0038038592026002002
Hellgren Z (2024) Struggle, exit, "resilience"or how precarious workers cope with late neoliberalism. Individual and collective agency of female migrant domestic workers in Spain. Int Polit Sociol 18(3):1–19. https://doi.org/10.1093/ips/olae029
İçduygu, A. (2009). International migration and human development in Turkey (HDRP-2009-52). United Nations Development Programme. https://hdr.undp.org/system/files/documents/hdrp200952.pdf
International Labor Organization (2016) A study of employers of migrant domestic workers in Lebanon – INTERTWINED. https://www.ilo.org/publications/study-employers-migrant-domestic-workers-lebanon-intertwined
Kandiyoti D (1988) Bargaining with patriarchy. Gender Soc 2(3):274–290. https://doi.org/10.1177/089124388002003004
Karaveli H (2013) Erdogan stokes the sectarian fires. New York Times, October 7. http://www.nytimes.com/2013/10/08/opinion/erdogan-stokes-the-sectarian-fires.html?_r=0
Korac M (2009) Remaking home: reconstructing life, place and identity in Rome and Amsterdam. Berghahn Books, New York
Körükmez L, Danış D, Karakılıç İZ (2022) Zorunlu göç bağlamında Suriyeli kadınların ücretli işgücüne katılımında toplumsal cinsiyet müzakeresi. Alternatif Politika 14(2):201–228. https://doi.org/10.53376/ap.2022.07
Kutlu Z (2015) Bekleme odasından oturma odasına, Suriyeli mültecilere yönelik çalışmalar yürüten sivil toplum kuruluşlarına dair kısa bir değerlendirme. Anadolu Kültür, Açık Toplum Vakfı, İstanbul. https://www.stgm.org.tr/sites/default/files/2020-09/bekleme-odasindan-oturma-odasina-suriyeli-multecilere-yonelik-calismalar-yuruten-sivil-toplum-kuruluslarina-dair-kisa-bir-degerlendirme.pdf

Lee ES, Szkudlarek B, Nguyen DC, Nardon L (2020) Unveiling the canvas ceiling: A multidisciplinary literature review of refugee employment and workforce integration. Int J Manag Rev 22(2):193–216

Øvensen G, Sletten P (2007) The Syrian labour market: Findings from the 2003 Unemployment Survey. Fafo, Oslo

Öztürk F (2023) Suriyeli kadın işçiler: '6 bin liraya kayıt dışı çalışmak zorundayız'. BBC News Türkçe, September 13. https://www.bbc.com/turkce/articles/cyd912v011lo

Palalar AD, Kamasak R, Sayin E, Vassilopoulou J (2024) Trapped in precarious work: the case of Syrian refugee workers in Turkey. In: Meliou E, Vassilopoulou J, Ozbilgin MF (eds) Diversity and precarious work during socio-economic upheaval: exploring the missing link. Cambridge University Press, Cambridge, pp 183–212

Perez MLE (2018) The sweet memories of home have gone': displaced people searching for home in a liminal space. J Ethn Migr Stud 45(9):1515–1531. https://doi.org/10.1080/1369183X.2018.1491299

Şenses N (2016) Rethinking migration in the context of precarity: The case of Turkey. Crit Sociol 7/8:975–987

Sparre SL (2008) Educated women in Syria: Servants of the state, or nurturers of the family? Crit Crit Middle East Stud 17(1):3–20

Spivak GC (2010) Can the subaltern speak? In: Morris RC (ed) Can the subaltern speak?: reflections on the history of an idea. Columbia University Press, pp 21–78

UNHCR (2023a) Countries Operations. Türkiye. https://reporting.unhcr.org/operational/operations/t%C3%BCrkiye#:~:text=T%C3%BCrkiye%20has%20been%20the%20largest,Refugee%20Convention%20and%20its%201967

UNHCR (2023b) Türkiye fact sheet September 2023. https://www.unhcr.org/sites/default/files/2023-10/bi-annual-fact-sheet-2023-09-turkiye.pdf

Wehrle K, Klehe UC, Kira M, Zikic J (2018) Can I come as I am? Refugees' vocational identity threats, coping, and growth. J Vocat Behav 105(1):83–101

Yıldız A (2001) Ne mutlu Türküm diyebilene: Türk ulusal kimliğinin etno-kültürel sınırları (1919–1938). İletişim Yayınları, İstanbul

Burcu Gumus is currently a postdoctoral researcher in the Department of Public Health - Sport Science at Aarhus University in Denmark. Her research primarily focuses on violence, examining the experiences of victims across diverse contexts. She has studied both refugees exposed to violence and individuals subjected to various forms of violence in online environments. More broadly, her work seeks to understand and theorize different experiences of victimization through a wide and interdisciplinary perspective.

Jón Ingvar Kjaran is Professor of sociology of education at the University of Iceland, School of Education, Faculty of Diversity and Education. Their research focus is on gender, sexuality, ethnicity, race, queer issues, migration, and violence. They are currently leading two research projects on gender violence funded by the Icelandic Research Fund. Their latest book is on queer activism in Indonesia and Malaysia, published in 2022 by Palgrave. Forthcoming in 2025 is a book about queer activism in Iceland.

Women on Boards: The Importance of Gender Equality at the Croatian National Level

Jelena Kasap, Višnja Lachner, and Ana Đanić Čeko

Abstract Discrimination against women on the national labour market is manifested in professional gender segregation, whereby employed women predominate in "female" sectors, such as the education, health and social welfare systems, and face a glass ceiling, which is why the share of women in managerial positions and in representative bodies is significantly lower than the proportion of men. Regardless of the normative framework in Croatia based on the Constitution of the Republic of Croatia, the Law on Gender Equality and the Labour Law, the underrepresentation of female presence in the boards of directors of the largest publicly listed companies as weal in the highest levels of administrative position is one of the most important indicators of the existence of hidden gender discrimination at the national level. According to its Gender Equality Strategy, the EU is committed to take concrete steps to promote gender equality in decision-making, including proposing legislation where relevant. On the way to achieving goals in the field of Gender Equality, the European Parliament and Council established the latest Directive on improving the gender balance among directors of listed companies and related measures. As the deadline for the implementation of the Directive into the national legislation is relatively short, it is important in this research to determine the current situation regarding this issue at the national level. Furthermore, the specific objective of the research is to determine and identify compatibility between the EU and national policies on gender equality and to emphasize challenges and barriers that prevent progress in this area on national level. Primarily, with the aim of determining the position of women in the political, business and administrative spheres, the historical-legal context will be analysed. Further short attention will be paid to EU public policies in this field, basic strategic documents, national politics and mechanisms emphasizing greater participation and involvement of women in public decision-making processes. In this regard, the research will include the analysis of the normative framework at the national level and beyond and the available data

---

J. Kasap · V. Lachner (✉) · A. Đ. Čeko
Faculty of Law, Josip Juraj Strossmayer University of Osijek, Osijek, Croatia
e-mail: jkasap@pravos.hr; vlachner@pravos.hr; adjanic@pravos.hr

F. Macioce et al. (eds.), *Feminist Legal and Political Practices*, Gender Perspectives in Law 6, https://doi.org/10.1007/978-3-032-02856-3_7

on the representation of women in the labour market. Finally, recommendations will be made to improve and enhance the system with proposals of good approaches and practice.

1 Introductory Consideration

Recognizing that the position of women in everyday life, especially on the labour market, in the legal sphere, and relevant bibliography, is often linked to a high degree of discrimination, this section of the research aims to summarize the most significant legal and social factors that contributed to the inferior status of women during the twentieth century[1]. The temporal determinants affecting this research are influenced by different characteristics of the legal systems that Croatia experienced during different historical periods: therefore, the research in the legal-historical context will also encompass the period of the late nineteenth century, as it was then that basic assumptions for women's inclusion in the labour market began to emerge, primarily through granting of educational rights to women.[2] In an attempt to summarize only the main circumstances that, within a legal context, defined the position of women during this period, the research will focus specifically on legal details related to the labour market and the employment of women, since many other relevant topics, such as feminist, gender-based issues and women's status in the context of the legal system (criminal, hereditary, family) have already been extensively discussed in legal historical literature. However, it is important to note that an examination of the legal status of women over the last century is impossible to separate from feminist ideas, and the position of women will be presented around periods that closely align with different phases of the feminist movement.[3]

---

[1] In the mid-nineteenth century, the "Women's Movement" developed as a result of women's efforts to improve their status and usefulness to society. The aims of the movement were to initiate measures of beneficence, temperance, and social welfare, and to initiate the struggle for civil rights, social liberties, higher education, paid occupations and the vote. Setting these goals is the result of women's growing awareness of the precariousness of their situation in the patriarchal society of the 1800s. Cruea (2005), p. 187, Goldin (2006), p. 3.

[2] During the twentieth century, Croatia was an integral part of various legal systems. Habsburg Monarchy (until 1918), SHS State, Kingdom of Serbs, Croats and Slovenes (1918–1921), Kingdom of Serbs, Croats and Slovenes (1921–1929), Kingdom of Yugoslavia and Banovina Croatia (1939–1941), Independent State of Croatia (1941–1945), the Federal People's Republic of Yugoslavia and the Socialist Federal Republic of Yugoslavia and since 1990 the Republic of Croatia. Čepulo (2012), pp. 257–282. Each period in the context of the research topic is marked by a different position of women in the private family and public life spheres, which is most often conditioned by the views of the prevailing political systems. Željko (2014), p. 25.

[3] Phase I started in the late nineteenth century and was characterized by a young, independent, unmarried female worker who generally never expected to have a career and left the workforce she 'married' into. Many women who were mainly engaged in agriculture left their previous jobs and started working in a factory during the onset of the Industrial Revolution. Phase 2, the transition period, lasted approximately from 1930 until 1950. This phase was marked by a significant

After a historical-legal context has been given, through a normative analysis of relevant legal sources, an overview of the basic Croatian legislative framework in this area is provided. Special emphasis is put on the political representation of women, equal participation of women and men in decision-making and occupying decision-making positions, and importance of balanced representation of women in economic sphere (women on boards, and the question of the glass ceiling). The data on the proportion of women in political representation and data of women in managerial (management) positions in the Republic of Croatia (hereinafter: RC) are being analysed (the highest positions (role) in public decision-making; female presence in the boards of directors of the largest publicly listed companies).

Despite continued efforts and some encouraging developments, men still significantly outnumber women in decision-making roles and leadership positions. In addition, various complex factors, including deeply ingrained gender stereotypes, significantly hinder women's professional choices and their access to equal opportunities for advancement to top management positions. The purpose of the paper is to give insight from Croatian perspective and to see how we have applied European politics and legislation to our legal framework and where Croatia stands in the field of political and economic decision-making, women on boards. Using and interpreting adequate normative basis and relevant and available data, we want to emphasize certain improvements and advancements, but also point out certain shortcomings, barriers and challenges. Short overview of the European main politics and legal sources and their reflection in the field of the importance of women in political and economic decision-making, have been pointed out. Special attention is put on the 2020–2025 the EU Gender Equality Strategy and Directive on improving the gender balance among directors of listed companies and related measures. The equal participation of women and men in decision-making and occupying decision-making positions is an issue that is not only related to respect for fundamental human rights, but also to the principle of good governance. Through final considerations, conclusions and recommendations are given in relation to the analysed scientific issues.

---

increase in the proportion of married women in the labour force, especially after the 1940s, when the marriage ban, which prevented married women from working in many professions, largely disappeared and part-time work opportunities became increasingly more prevalent. Women in stage 2, however, still did not intend to pursue a career but to work only according to the needs of their families. Phase 3 occurs from 1950 until the late 1970s, as the 'root of evolution'. During phase 3, the labour force participation rate of married women increases significantly. What distinguished women of this era from women in Stage 2 was the fact that they underestimated their future labour force participation when they were young, expecting to work only until they had a family, but generally exceeding those expectations, working outside the home for a significant portion of their life. Phase 4 dates back to the 'greater revolution', and continues to this day. During this phase, women began to more accurately predict their future participation in the labour force and anticipate combining work and family during the family formation and childbearing years. Stone and Hernandez (2012), pp. 35–36. Frederick et al. (2021).

2 Legal and Historical Presentation of the Position of Women in the Workplace and in the Labour Market Until the Beginning of the twenty-first Century

In an effort to improve the legal position of women in the second half of the nineteenth century and under the influence of Austrian legislation (in the context of the General Civil Code), the reform of education was undertaken in Croatia, and under the leadership of the Governor (Ban) Mažuranić, a significant shift was made compared to earlier legislation when it comes to women's education.[4] Unlike earlier reforms that related to children's education, this law made primary education mandatory for all male and female children, which was a significant shift in the organisation and modernisation of education.[5] In the period that followed the school reform, the education of women was characterized by significant changes in the context of acquiring a profession.

Since after finishing high school for girls, girls were still not allowed to enrol in grammar schools and could only continue their education at teacher training schools. It was not until 1892 that the school authorities founded a women's lyceum in Zagreb, as a kind of girls' grammar school.[6] Most of the participants chose the course in pedagogy and after their education were employed as teachers.[7]

The period at the turn of the 19th and 20th centuries was characterized by several important circumstances that contributed to the improvement of the position of women as well as their inclusion in the labour market. The right to education within the framework of Mažuranić's reforms was the first step towards the modernisation and liberalisation of the social position of women. However, the very fact that women were employed in low-skilled and low-paid jobs under the Austro-Hungarian Monarchy speaks for the fact that the lack of education opportunities prevailed in the real life of women at that time. Through higher education, women entered the social life of the community and had better opportunities when choosing a job.[8] Krešić in her research on the social and professional position of women at the turn of the 19th and 20th centuries points out that women could not be defence attorneys

[4] Raguž (2010), p. 88. More on issues of women's status within the Mažuranić's legislation in: Krešić (2019), p. 236.

[5] According to the rules, "every woman between the ages of 20 and 40 could attend it, regardless of her marital status, provided she could read and write". Additionally, she had to provide a "medical certificate confirming her physical and mental health and stating that she was not pregnant". Later on, it became possible for illiterate girls to enroll if they obtained a certificate from local authorities affirming they were "gifted", since every municipality aimed at training at least one girl for this profession, although many girls from rural areas remained illiterate. Krešić and Rakitičan, (2015), pp. 283–286. More details on establishment of schools in Croatia in the late nineteenth century in: Župan (2001), pp. 441–444, Franković (1958), p. 185.

[6] More details on establishment of the women's lyceum and the first school programme in: Ograšek Gorenjak (2006), pp. 160–162.

[7] Ograšek Gorenjak (2006), pp. 160–162.

[8] Krešić (2019), p. 243.

or judges in the proceedings, primarily because they could not even be educated for these professions.[9]

In the interwar period, educated women were mainly employed in grammar schools, libraries, hospitals, ministries, municipalities, agriculture stations, hygiene institutes, etc. The common element of all mentioned professions was the fact that these women were mostly "employed in state and municipal services, where they enjoyed the same rights as their male colleagues".[10]

In the interwar period, women were employed increasingly in all sectors due to industrial development, especially in jobs that were considered more suitable for women, such as clerks. Further features of the position of women in the labour sector was the inequality with male workers in terms of opportunities for advancement, positioning, and material rights.[11] It should be emphasized that in the literature dealing with women's labour rights, there is not a single woman in a managerial position either in industry or in state administration. For women in the interwar period, therefore, a career seemed attainable only if they were unmarried, while marriage still meant renouncing professional advancement.[12]

In the second contribution phase of the Croatian feminism, which covers the period between 1950 and 1970, women asserted themselves to the greatest extent by introducing the principle of gender equality between women and men.[13] Nevertheless, gender-specific legislation, typical of socialist countries, passed in the 60 s and 70 s of the last century, continued to limit women's opportunities in the labour market by concentrating their professional activity in "female" sectors with the continuing trend of lower wages and mostly without the possibility of professional advancement. Summarizing the bibliography that mostly dealt with the legal position of women in the socialist society, it can be concluded that the legislation of the time was still based on the traditional division of gender roles, a discriminatory policy that resulted in the violation of women's equality in the labour market by imposing

[9] For example, in the 1875 Act on Establishing the Jury Court Panels, women were expressly excluded from jury service, since one of the prerequisites for performing that service was that the person performing it be male. Krešić (2019), p. 243.

[10] The position of female lawyers was particularly discriminatory. As stated by Ograjšek-Goranjek: "Although the study of law offered them many administrative positions and they were employed as secretaries and clerks in various institutions, the problem arose when they showed ambition for advancement. The fact diminishing their credibility was that a married woman in the Yugoslav society had limited legal capacity. In addition, the legal and judicial circles were particularly reluctant to accept women into their ranks, usually justifying their choices by distrustful and patriarchal parties. Ograjšek Gorenjak (2019), pp. 242–243.

[11] More details on the wage inequality between men and women in the labor sector of the observed period in: Đuranović-Janda (1960), p. 114.

[12] This attitude is particularly represented in Professor Eisner's presentation of Yugoslav civil laws. "Performing an independent occupation will in many cases be incompatible with the tasks and duties of a married woman and family. If the purpose of marriage is to be achieved, the freedom of a married woman must be limited in this respect, although as a rule women were recognized as having full legal capacity." Eisner (1934), p. 84.

[13] HR-HDA 1234–12 (Društveni položaj), kut. 176, "Broj žena na fakultetima". Archival documents used in the content of the research are cited according to: Glazer (2022), p. 18.

on them the role of a mother and a housewife. Thus, in addition to paid work outside the home, women also had to bear the burden of family and household obligations. General characteristics of women's labour were low qualifications of employed women and the inadequate distribution of women in different sectors of the economy.[14]

An overview of women's position in management of the companies according to the available data of 1958 can be found in the archives of the Croatian Women's Conference. The archives contain a series of data on the final number of women in some of the company management positions. Data relevant for this research is the number of women in management positions. Out of 61 companies from the area of the People's Republic of Croatia (NRH) included in the research, only one was a woman director, i.e. acting woman director. It was the company "Domaća tvornica rublja", Zagreb.[15] According to the statistical bulletin Women in the Society and Economy of Yugoslavia, a comparison of data on women in managerial positions in 1961 and 1971 was made. The analysis shows that compared to 1961 when there were 0.4% of women in managerial positions in Croatia in 1971, a significant decline in the engagement of women in managerial positions was recorded i.e. only 0.2%.[16]

At the end of the seventies of the last century, i.e. in 1979, it was recorded that out of 7825 single management bodies, there were only 576 women. In 1983, out of 8339 women, 545 or 7% were in managerial positions.[17] Art. 160 of the Federal People's Republic of Yugoslavia (FNRY) Constitution stipulated that: "Each citizen, under equal conditions, has access to every workplace and every function in the society."[18] However, regardless of this, the analysis of the available data confirms the limited opportunities for women to achieve managerial positions in practice, even with the necessary qualifications.

---

[14] The aforementioned submissions on the employment of women are available within the archive fund of the Conference for the Social Activity of Croatian Women: HR-HDA 1234–12 (Social position), 178, Školovanje ženske omladine i njeno opredjeljenje za budući poziv". According to: Glazer (2022).

[15] HR-HDA 1234–12 (Društveni položaj), kut. 177, "Overview of the number of women who occupy one of the management positions in the company". Glazer, 36. Somewhat later data contained in the statistical yearbook of the year 1962 shows that there were 5758 business managers in the RC. Of that number, 415 were women, which is only 7%. In this research, managers are understood as directors, technical directors, directors of the economic and accounting sector, managers of the personnel department, commercial directors and company secretaries. Out of 1738 directors of commercial companies in the RC only 13 are women, which is 0.7%. The largest number of female directors were employed in trade and catering—a total of 7. There were no female directors in forestry, construction and transport. HR-HDA 1234–12 (Društveni položaj), kut. 177, "Žene rukovodioci". According to: Glazer (2022), p. 37.

[16] Savezni zavod za statistiku, (1973), p. 11. In 1971, most women were employed in the service sector, followed by administrative staff, experts and artists. Prpić (1976), p. 19.

[17] HD-HDA 1234-12 (Društveni položaj), kut. 180, "Some aspects of the implementation of the Resolution on the basic directions of social action to improve the socio-economic position and role of women in the socialist self-governing society". Glazer (2022), p. 32.

[18] Zečević (1975).

In the period of the 1980s, a small number of women were in positions enabling them to influence upbringing and education, such as the position of school principals and managers, managers of organizations for upbringing and education, university professors, heads of scientific and other research organizations, journalists, editors, etc. most of them were employed in public services, post offices, offices, etc.[19] In a very extensive study of women's education, Blagojević found that in 1981, the share of women in management positions was only 1.5%.[20] Earlier, Prpić warned about the problem of the complete presence of women in leadership positions of social organisations in the 1970s.[21] Furthermore, data on women's participation in workers' councils indicate women's activism in terms of enforcing workers' rights. Thus, in 1976, the share of women in the total number of members in workers' councils in Yugoslavia was 26.5%, in 1979 it amounted to 29.1%, and in 1981 it was 30.5%.[22]

Recent data on the gender distribution in managerial roles, pointed out by Jukić, shows that even in professions predominantly occupied by women, vertical gender segregation has persisted into the new century.[23] Thus, the number of women in teaching profession is significantly higher at lower levels of education but men still dominate among the teaching staff in higher education institutions.[24] The limited social and political progress for women during this period is reflected in the findings by Vuković and Šmaguc. They observe that "gender imbalance is evident in management roles within the vertical hierarchy of educational institutions (principals of primary and secondary schools), healthcare institutions and governmental entities, where women consistently comprise a minority."[25]

The transition processes in Croatia lasted simultaneously with the Homeland War, the process of independence and the creation of an independent state. In the transition period, the number of employed persons in Croatia decreased by 10%, with the number of employed women decreasing by 6% and the number of employed men by 13%.[26] When it comes to the period between 1991 and 2000, the literature

---

[19] Dijanić et al. (2002), pp. 320–321. See: Dujmović (2016), p. 46.

[20] See statistical data on the participation of women in the active population performing occupations listed by occupation, republics and provinces, 1981. Blagojević and Hjuson (2015), pp. 189–190. In addition, the author highlighted the educational structure of the population according to which women in 1989 made up almost half of specialists, more than a third of masters and only 28.2% of PhDs. In Croatia in 1989, there were 66.7% specialists, 34.1% masters and 30.04% PhDs. Blagojević (2015), p. 209.

[21] Prpić (1976), p. 55. See: Vuković and Šmaguc (2015), p. 305.

[22] Baranović (2000), p. 26.

[23] Jukić, (2013), pp. 541–558.

[24] Jukić (2013), pp. 541–558. See: Vuković and Šmaguc (2015), p. 305.

[25] Nikodem and Galić (2009), pp. 253–270.

[26] Leinert Novosel (1999), p. 31.

dealing with the position of women concerning work and employment lacks data on the participation of women in managerial positions.[27]

3 Political Participation of Women Until 1995

In addition to the right to education, the feminist movements that began at the end of the nineteenth century sought to achieve the political participation of women. In this context, women's right to vote and women's participation in political processes is an extremely important indicator of their social position. In the following section of the paper, the historical course of the struggle for women's suffrage and the political participation of women in the authorities of Socialist Yugoslavia, and then the RC, ending in 1995, will be briefly presented.

The fight for women's voting right has a long and complex history, and it began in Croatia at the time of the Austro-Hungarian Monarchy. However, from the end of the nineteenth century until the beginning of the First World War, women were excluded from political processes, and only men had the concrete right to vote in elections. The first significant step forward in the context of women's rights to vote was made before the adoption of the constitution itself when a series of regulations on local elections came into force, which gave women in Croatia and Slavonia the right to vote in municipal and city elections.[28] However, although several legal regulations in the interwar period regulated the right to vote in local elections, women's right to vote remained outside the normative framework until the end of the Second World War.[29]

During the Second Yugoslavia, a very small number of women were represented in the delegate system, trade unions, and the Communist Party of Yugoslavia/League of Communists of Yugoslavia (KPJ/SKJ), despite various campaigns that were carried out to increase the participation quotas of women and other socially inferior categories in political life.[30]

---

[27] Statistical data are available: Statistical Yearbooks of the RC, State Bureau of Statistics, Zagreb. From 2003 to 2024. Data are available on the website https://web.dzs.hr/Hrv/Archive/arh_stat_year.htm. The available research mainly deals with the unemployment of women and provides data on the number of employed women in certain industries or on the level of their education. Kerovec (2003).

[28] Decree on the Election of City Representatives for the Cities of Croatia and Slavonia and the Decree on the Election of Municipal Committees for the Administrative Municipalities of Croatia and Slavonia (November 1919). Ograjšek Gorenjak (2014), p. 95. Indicating the note 229.

[29] See: Constitution of the Federative People's Republic of Yugoslavia 1946, article 21, 23, 24.

[30] Žene u socijalizmu – od ubrzane emancipacije do ubrzane repatrijarhalizacije (2015). https://6yka.com/bih/zene-u-socijalizmu-od-ubrzane-emancipacije-do-ubrzane-repatrijarhalizacije/. "…In 1948, only 19.9% of women were members of the party, and only 9.7% of women participated in the Fifth Congress. At the Sixth Congress of the Communist Party of Yugoslavia, held in Zagreb in 1952, only six women were present in the Central Committee…In 1960, only 16% of women were members of the party. At the Eleventh Congress of the League of Communists in 1978, the partici-

The share of women in the total number of delegates in the assemblies of municipalities, the assemblies of the republics, and the assembly of the Socialist Federal Republic of Yugoslavia (SFRY) indicates a relatively low level of participation of women.[31] When it comes to the Socialist RC, the data is as follows. The share of women in the parliament in 1963 was 24.1%. By 1969, there was a sharp decline in the participation of women in the parliament, which the literature tried to justify with an economic stagnation. The share of women was 7.1%. In the period between 1974 and 1976 the share of women's participation varied between 16 and 18%, and in the Croatian Parliament in 1990, there were 16% women.[32]

The political participation of women after the political changes in 1991 was significantly reduced. After the multi-party elections in 1990, only 4.7% of women entered the Parliament (before 1990 there were from 16% to 18%), in 1993 it was 5.4%, and only after the 1995 elections did their number increase to 8%.[33] The representation of women in the first 10 years after the establishment of the independent Croatian democracy barely reached the worst percentage of women's representation in the Parliament of the Socialist RC.[34]

pation of women in politics increased to 23.3%." Data on the participation of women in municipal assemblies of the Socialist RC are available for the year 1958, when there were 6.5% women in municipal assemblies; there were 19.8% in 1963, 9.9% in 1967, 7.1% in 1969, there were 14.6% in 1974 and 16.6% of women in 1978. Tomšić (2024), p. 204.

[31] In 1974, it was 15.2% for the Municipal assemblies, 17.6% for the Republic assemblies, and 13.6% for the Federal Assembly. Analogous data for 1982 are 17.8% (Municipal assembly), 20.6% (Republic assembly), and for the Federal Assembly a little over 17%. The data on the representation of women in the Parliament show their share in the total number of representatives at the early 60 s reached 24%. In the period from 1965 to 1975, the share of women in the Parliament decreased to 8%, and in the period of the 80 s, it increased again and reached about 18% of the total number of representatives. Jugoslavenski pregled (1985), p. 189. Prema: Baranović (2000), p. 26. In the period from 1965 to 1975, the share of women in the Parliament decreased to 8%, and in the period of the 80s, it increased again and reached about 18% of the total number of representatives. Baranović (2000), p. 26.

[32] Leinert-Novosel (1994), p. 139.

[33] Leinert-Novosel (1994), p. 35. The proportion of women in the membership of political parties, as claimed by Baranović, has not changed significantly. In the two largest political parties: the Croatian Democratic Union and the Social Democratic Party, the share of women reached approximately 30%. Leinert-Novosel (1994), p. 139. Više o participaciji žena u političkom životu Republike Hrvatske: Belić and Bijelić (2000). Parliamentary representation of women in Croatia, 1990–2015, from which it follows that the number of women in Parliament was 9 in 1995, and 33 in 2000, available in the research: Ostroški (2016), pp. 68–69. In addition, this research allows an analysis of the data on representation of women in Croatian governments in the period from 1990 to 2016. More on the parliamentary representation of women in Croatia in: Šinko (2016), pp. 3–10.

[34] Šinko (2007), p. 74. See: Grafikon 1: Ženska zastupljenost u Saboru Socijalističke republike i Republike Hrvatske.

4 Legislative Framework

Gender equality implies the abolition of all dimensions of social stratification between women and men, irrespective of their mutual biological differences, and "based on belonging to the human community."[35] According to the document passed by the Council of Europe on 26 March 1998, titled "Gender Mainstreaming Conceptual Framework, Methodology and Presentation of Good Practices Policy", gender equality means, "equal visibility, empowerment, and participation of both sexes in all spheres of public and private life. Gender equality is the opposite of gender inequality, and not of gender difference; it aims to promote the full participation of women and men in a society."[36] The terms "equality" and "equity"are often used as synonyms, however, they convey different political connotations.[37] Thus, gender equity can be defined as "the equal position of men and women in private, social, and public life concerning all the rights they exercise in their positions or functions."[38] The fundamental purpose of gender equity is to ensure equal access to participation and use of resources, rights, and opportunities, regardless of gender, while eliminating discrimination arising from gender roles and stereotypes.[39] Moreover, besides gender equality, terms such as equity between gender,[40] equality between men and women, and equal representation of women and men are often used as synonyms for gender equity.[41]

Achieving equal gender representation at all societal levels is a key indicator of society's development. Recently, there has been an increasing discussion around gender-aware policies and promoting gender equality.[42] Thus, gender equality remains one of the key social goals in the RC. The first law[43] that included a definition

---

35 Kašić et al. (2005), p. 9; Galić, (2012), p. 157.

36 Rodin (2003), p. 75.

37 Human Rights Education Association (2014). http://www.ekvilib.org/wp-content/uploads/2017/06/01_Rodni-koncepti_Osvjezite-Znanje.pdf, p. 2.

38 Mateljak and Jurlina Alibegović (2023), p. 223.

39 In the document "Gender Equality Strategy", the European Commission considers guidelines and strategies for achieving gender equality in all EU member states, including recommendations for eliminating gender stereotypes and ensuring equal rights for women and men at all levels of society. (https://commission.europa.eu/strategy-and-policy/policies/justice-and-fundamental-rights/gender-equality/gender-equality-strategy_hr)

40 Galić (2023), pp. 21–36.

41 Mateljak and Jurlina Alibegović (2023), p. 223.

42 Mateljak and Jurlina Alibegović (2023), p. 224.

43 Until 2000, gender equality and the legal position of women were governed by the Constitution and ratified international treaties, according to Blagojević, et al. (2024), p. 82. The Constitution of 1990 did not explicitly mention gender equality, but it guaranteed the equality of all before the law and the prohibition of discrimination, including gender based discrimination (Constitution of the RC, Official Gazette, No. 56/90). The framers of the Constitution believed that gender equality was implicitly included in the principle of equality of all before the law, but later social development and pressure by women's organization's pointed to the inadequacy of these provisions, which led to the need for explicit guarantees of gender equality as stated by Smerdel (2013), p. 292.

of gender equality in the RC was the Gender Equality Law of 2003,[44] which besides the Constitution of the RC[45] laid the foundations for achieving gender equality at all social levels. Thus, at the constitutional level, with the introduction of an explicit guarantee of gender equality through the amendment of the Constitution in 2000,[46] Croatia ranked among the majority of countries in the world, 139 of which expressly recognize this right in their constitutional acts.[47] Since then, with this amendment to the Constitution, gender equality has become one of the fundamental values of the constitutional order, thus also being set as a basic criterion for the interpretation of constitutional provisions.[48]

The Gender Equality Act of 2003 was in force until 15 July 2008, when the new, currently valid, Act on Gender Equality[49] entered into force, the content of which is very similar to the first Act and "additionally harmonised with the provisions of international standards as well as with the EU law."[50] Art. 5 of this Act defines gender equality as women and men being equally present in all areas of public and private life, having equal status, equal opportunities to exercise all rights, as well as equal benefit from the achieved results. The definition of gender equality is important since it has not been defined in the Constitution of the RC. Moreover, the international treaties currently in force in the country, including the Convention on the Elimination of All Forms of Discrimination against Women (CEDAW) and the European Convention for the Protection of Human Rights and Fundamental

[44] Gender Equality Act, Official Gazette, 116/03. The aforementioned Act sets out the basic guidelines for the protection and promotion of gender equality as one of the fundamental values of the constitutional order of the Republic of Croatia. The Act also stipulates the method of protection against gender based discrimination to ensure equal opportunities for women and men in different social, political and economic spheres. Prema: Veštić (2017), p. 74.

[45] Constitution of the RC, Official Gazette, No. 56/90, 135/97, 08/98, 113/00, 124/00, 28/01, 41/01, 55/01, 76/10, 85/10, 05/14.

[46] Revision of the Constitution of the RC, Official Gazette, No. 113/00.

[47] MacKinnen (2014), p. 569.

[48] Pursuant to Art. 3 of the Constitution, the list of the highest values of the constitutional order of the RC includes freedom, equal rights, national equality, peace-making, social justice, respect for human rights, inviolability of ownership, conservation of nature and the environment, the rule of law and a democratic multiparty system, according to Blagojević et al. (2024), p. 84.

[49] Gender Equality Act, Official Gazette, No. 82/08. The short-term validity of the Gender Equality Act of 2003 is the result of the Decision of the Constitutional Court of the Republic of Croatia, which, deciding on the proposal for assessing the conformity of the Act with the Constitution, abolished the Gender Equality Act of 2003. Namely, the proposer considered that the Gender Equality Act of 2003 was an organic act because it elaborated human rights and fundamental freedoms established by the Constitution and that in accordance with Art. 82, para 2 of the Constitution, the majority of at least 76 members of the Croatian Parliament were required for its adoption. Given that 75 representatives voted for the adoption of the Gender Equality Act, the applicant considered that the Act was formally unconstitutional. The Constitutional Court accepted the proposal, determined that it was an organic law and, based on these facts it abolished the GEA of 2003, as under the Decision of the Constitutional Court of the Republic of Croatia No U-I-2696/2003 of 16 January 2008, Official Gazette, No. 14/08.

[50] Veštić (2017), p. 79.

Freedoms, do not provide a precise definition of the term. In addition to defining gender equality, the Act on Gender Equality of 2008 defines gender discrimination, including direct and indirect discrimination, as well as protections against less favourable treatment in connection with being pregnant or on maternity leave and in relation to sexual harassment. Consequently, the Act lays down the prohibition of discrimination in the field of employment and work in the private and public sectors (Art. 13), and prohibits discrimination based on marital and family status, sexual orientation, concerning the possibility of obtaining and purchasing goods, in the provision and access to services.[51]

In addition to the Act on Gender Equality of 2008, the constitutional provisions on gender equality were further elaborated through a series of laws and by-laws.[52]

The institutional mechanisms for the implementation of the Act on Gender Equality are the Office for Gender Equality,[53] which is an "expert service of the Government of the RC"(March 2004); Ombudsperson for Gender Equality[54] as an „independent body responsible for combating discrimination in the field of gender equality"(October 2003); coordinators in state administration bodies; commissions for gender equality as work-advisory bodies of the county assemblies, i.e. the Assembly of the City of Zagreb, and City and Municipal Commissions for Gender Equality.[55] In addition, one part of the institutional framework is represented by the competent working body of the Croatian Parliament, the Gender Equality Committee, which performs the rights and duties of the competent working body when it comes to areas related to the promotion and monitoring of the application of the principle of gender equality. The committee was established by the Standing Orders of the Croatian Parliament and has been operating since 2002.[56]

---

[51] The Bill on GEA of 2008.

[52] Anti-Discrimination Act, Official Gazette, No. 85/08, 112/12. Art. 7 para 4 and articles 30–37 and 91 of the Labour Act (Official Gazette, No. 93/14, 127/17, 98/19, 151/22, 46/23, 64/23) Also, the first Labour Act of the Republic of Croatia of 1995, Art. 2 expressly prohibits all forms of direct and indirect discrimination. See in Vasiljević and Valković, (2007), p. 21. For example: the Act on Protection against Domestic Violence (2017), Family Law (2015), Registered Partnership Act (2014), Health Care Act (2018), Social Welfare Act (2022), Law on Political Parties (1993), The Law on the Election of Representatives to the Croatian National Parliament (1999), according to: Blagojević et al. (2024), 85. More on legal framework see in: Ured za ravnopravnost spolova Vlade Republike Hrvatske (2023), Nacionalni plan za ravnopravnost spolova za razdoblje do 2027, pp. 7–8. https://ravnopravnost.gov.hr/nacionalni-plan-za-ravnopravnost-spolova-za-razdoblje-do-2027-godine/3442

[53] Decree on the Establishment of the Office for Gender Equality, Official Gazette, No. 18/04.

[54] Decision on Appointment of Ombudsperson for Gender Equality, Official Gazette, No. 157/03.

[55] Chapter IX, Art. 18–28 of the Act on Gender Equality of 2008. The Gender Equality Committee operating in all 20 counties and the City of Zagreb, as well as in around 90 municipalities and cities, is entrusted with the implementation of the Act on Gender Equality at the local level, according to the National Plan for Gender Equality for the Period until 2027, 8. https://ravnopravnost.gov.hr/UserDocsImages//dokumenti/NPRS%202027%20APRS%202024//Nacionalni%20plan%20za%20ravnopravnost%20spolova,%20za%20razdoblje%20do%202027.pdf

[56] Standing Orders of the Croatian Parliament, Official Gazette, No. 81/13, 113/16, 69/17, 29/18, 52/20, 119/20, 123/20.

of the key strategic documents is the National Plan for Gender Equality for the Period until 2027,[57] with the accompanying Action Plan, prepared by the Office for Gender Equality of the Government of the RC. The National Plan for Gender Equality for the Period until 2027 sets out and establishes specific goals to promote and achieve gender equality. The implementation of the goals of this mid-term strategy plan contributes to achieving greater social inclusion, and social cohesion, and improving the quality of life and the rule of law. The plan envisions a society free from gender inequalities, where gender does not affect income, free time, or roles within the family and society; it aims at eliminating gender-based violence in the society.[58] This document further identifies main developmental challenges and potentials within the following priority areas: 1. Promotion of women's human rights and gender equality; 2. Improvement of the position of women in the labour market; 3. Eliminating violence against women; 4. Implementing gender-sensitive education; 5. Improvement of the position of women in political and public decision-making; 6. Including gender equality principles in public policies; 7. Promotion of gender equality in international politics and cooperation.[59]

The equal participation of women and men in decision-making and occupying decision-making positions is an issue that is not only related to respect for fundamental human rights but also to the principle of good governance. Despite continued efforts and some encouraging developments, men still significantly outnumber women in decision-making roles and leadership positions. In addition, various complex factors, including deeply ingrained gender stereotypes, significantly hinder women's professional choices and their access to equal opportunities for advancement to top management positions.[60]

5 Analysis of the Political Representation of Women

The Act on Gender Equality (hereinafter: AGE) regulates the establishment and nomination of candidate lists for the election of members to the Croatian Parliament, for the members of the representative bodies of local and regional self-government units, and representatives of the European Parliament, according to which a significant imbalance in the representation of one gender on the lists must be avoided, i.e. gender imbalance is considered a representation of one gender lower than 40%,

[57] Ured za ravnopravnost spolova Vlade Republike Hrvatske (2023), Nacionalni plan za ravnopravnost spolova za razdoblje do 2027, https://ravnopravnost.gov.hr/nacionalni-plan-za-ravnopravnost-spolova-za-razdoblje-do-2027-godine/3442

[58] Ured za ravnopravnost spolova Vlade Republike Hrvatske (2023), Nacionalni plan za ravnopravnost spolova za razdoblje do 2027, pp. 4–5. https://ravnopravnost.gov.hr/nacionalni-plan-za-ravnopravnost-spolova-za-razdoblje-do-2027-godine/3442

[59] Ibid.

[60] Ibid.

commonly known as gender quota. Political parties and other authorized proposers who fail to adhere to this rule are also subject to financial penalties.[61]

There were 2302 candidates participating in the 2024 parliamentary elections, of which 57.9% were men (1333 M) and 42.1% were women (969 F). Unfortunately, the Ombudsperson for Gender Equality's recommendation to consider the gender balance in the positioning of male and female candidates on the lists was not heeded. As a result, women were underrepresented in the top three positions on the lists (first, second, and third), securing the smallest percentage in the first-place slots (17.8%) compared to 82.2% for men. Consequently, the positions to which women were most likely to be elected had the lowest representation. The situation from the last parliamentary elections (2020) was repeated with a significant share of the lists that were not drawn up by the provisions of the AGE—where the quota was not respected on 19.4% of the lists—even though women occupied 42.1% of the candidate lists. The aforementioned factors influenced the final results of the elections, showing that 24.5% of the representatives elected to the Croatan Parliament are women(37 F)[62] while 75.5% (114 M) are men, which is an increase in the share of women by 2% compared to the previous parliamentary elections, where only 22.5% of elected representatives were women.[63,64] However, the Ombudsperson for Gender Equality believes that the aforementioned projection reflects a critical issue and states that the "dynamics of achieving genuine gender equality in Croatia do not align with the rapidly evolving modern society,"[65] which has been changing much faster than the current trends in Croatia or the goals set by the international

[61] Act on the Financing of Political Activities, Election Campaigns, and Referendums, Official Gazettes, No. 29/19, 98/19.

[62] The proportion of female representatives in the European Parliament was 39.9% in February 2024, which is higher than the European average for national parliaments (31.6%). However, there are significant differences among member states in terms of their representation in Parliament: European Parliamentary Research Service – EPRS (2024), Women in politics in the 2024 election year. https://epthinktank.eu/2024/03/05/women-in-politics-in-the-2024-election-year/

[63] Pravobraniteljica za ravnopravnost spolova (2024b), Rodna analiza parlamentarnih izbora 2024. https://prs.hr/application/uploads/Rodna_analiza_parlamentarnih_izb.%20(prs)%20-%20 Copy%201.pdf, pp. 2–3.

[64] In the parliamentary elections held in July 2020, there was an increase in the representation of women in the Croatian parliament. For the first time, 34 women accounting for 22.5% of elected officials were elected. This marks an improvement compared to the previous ninth convocation where women made up only 12.5% of representatives. Additionally, in the HS convocation at that time, there were 48 (32%) women representatives, due to the introduction of substitute candidates for positions incompatible with their representative function. This represents a significant increase compared to the end of the ninth convocation, when the percentage of female representatives was 19.2%. In contrast, data from the European Parliament indicates that women constitute an average of 29% of the national parliaments of EU member states. Although this outcome represents a positive development, women are still significantly underrepresented in Croatia's highest representative body of parliamentary democracy, which is still inconsistent with the principle of gender equality, see in: Pravobraniteljica za ravnopravnost spolova (2021), Izvješće o radu Pravobraniteljice za ravnopravnost spolova za 2020, https://www.prs.hr/application/uploads/IZVJESCE_O_RADU_2020_Pravobranit.pdf, p. 159.

[65] Pravobraniteljica za ravnopravnost spolova (2024b), Rodna analiza parlamentarnih izbora 2024. https://www.prs.hr/application/uploads/Rodna_analiza_parlamentarnih_izb.%20(prs)%20-%20 Copy%201.pdf, p. 4.

community, such as the UN Sustainable Development Programme for the Period until 2030,[66] which identifies gender equality as one of the 17 global goals to be achieved by 2030. In our context, this indicates a potential 26-year delay.

In the elections for members of the European Parliament held in June 2024, the RC will be represented in the EU Parliament by 5 women and 7 men, making the proportion of women 41.6%.[67] Similarly, in the European Parliament elections held in 2019, the RC was represented by 5 women and 7 men,[68] and with the changes that followed the United Kingdom's withdrawal from the EU in 2020, the RC had 12 representatives, of which 4 were women and 8 men (33.3%).[69] This continued the trend of a relatively gender-balanced share of elected male and female members.

The composition of the Government of the RC does not reflect the achievement of gender equality to the same extent as the composition of the Croatian Parliament due to a relatively small sample of 19 members. The inclusion of only two women, representing just 11% of the 16th Government of the RC, underscores a troubling indicator of this disparity. Namely, this is the lowest percentage of women since 2000 and the composition of the seventh Government of the RC.[70]

Although the first quarter of the twenty-first century is almost over, women are still struggling to advance in decision-making and decision-making positions, which are still predominantly "male-occupied". Thus, the results of this year's parliamentary elections confirm that this (still primarily global) trend is very noticeable in the RC with little prospect for tangible and satisfactory progress under national laws and international legal standards within the framework of organisations of which Croatia is a member.

Despite obvious changes compared to the previous local elections held in 2017, the representation of women in executive and representative positions at the local level remains relatively low. A comparison of the results of the local elections held in 2017 and 2021 indicates a slight increase of women in these authorities. The results of the local elections in 2021 show that at the level of local and regional self-government, there were 27% of women in political bodies of local and regional

---

[66] United Nations (2015), The 2030 Agenda for Sustainable Development. https://sdgs.un.org/goals

[67] Members of the European Parliament (2024). https://www.europarl.europa.eu/meps/en/full-list

[68] Ured za ravnopravnost spolova (2019), Održani izbori za EU parlament. https://ravnopravnost.gov.hr/vijesti/odrzani-izbori-za-eu-parlament/3249. In the previous elections for the EU Parliament, held in 2014, 6 women and 5 men were elected to 11 seats from the Republic of Croatia, and the share of elected women was 54.5%.

[69] European Parliament (2024), Women in politics in the EU State of play in 2024, 3. https://www.europarl.europa.eu/RegData/etudes/BRIE/2024/760348/EPRS_BRI(2024)760348_EN.pdf

[70] Out of 18 members of the 15th Government of the RC, 4 were women and all of them held the positions of ministers (2020). Among the 48 deputies, 5 are presidents of representative clubs, six are vice-presidents of the Croatian Parliament, and out of a total of 5 vice-presidents of the Croatian Parliament, only one is a woman. With regard to the representation of women at the head of parliamentary committees, in the fourth quarter of 2022, there were 29 committees and commissions, 11 female deputies (37.9%) held the position of committee presidents, and another 11 female deputies (37.9%) held the position of vice president, see: Vlada Republike Hrvatske – Ured za ravnopravnost spolova (2020), Parlamentarni izbori 2020. https://ravnopravnost.gov.hr/istaknute-teme/zastupljenost-zena-u-politici/parlamentarni-izbori-2020/3447

self-government units (in representative bodies there were 29% of women, whereas in executive roles there were 11% women).[71,72]

It can be concluded that the participation of women at all levels of participation in public and political decision-making bodies in Croatia is below the EU average.[73] The results of the last local elections in 2021, where only 27% of women were elected, and the parliamentary elections of 2024, where only 24.5% of women were elected, are particularly worrying.[74,75] It is important to note that in terms of gender equality, these are the best results since the founding of the RC.

6 Analysis of the Representation of Women in Management Positions

In the continuation of the work, the data on the proportion of women in managerial (management[76]) positions in the RC will be analysed, showing that women are insufficiently represented in the highest positions (role) in public decision-making.

---

[71] Pravobraniteljica za ravnopravnost spolova (2024a), Izvješće o radu za 2023, 180. https://www.prs.hr/application/uploads/Izvje%C5%A1%C4%87e_o_radu_Pravobraniteljic.pdf

[72] According to data of the EIGE, women hold 34.1% of positions in representative bodies at the local level in the EU, 34.1% in representative bodies at the regional level. Only 17.2% of women are represented in executive bodies at the local level. (Statistical brief-Gender balance in politics 2020 (EIGE 2021, see: European Institute for Gender Equality (2021), Statistical brief: gender balance in politics 2020. https://eige.europa.eu/publications/statistical-brief-gender-balancepolitics-2020

[73] European Parliament (2024), Women in politics in the EU State of play in 2024. https://epthinktank.eu/2024/03/05/women-in-politics-in-the-2024-election-year/

[74] In contrast, women still make up the majority in the judiciary. Thus, the percentage of female judges has been increasing over the past decade to 60% of judges. According to data from 2023, more than 70% of judges in lower courts, such as municipal commercial and misdemeanour courts were women. On the other hand, the proportion of women decreases at higher instances in courts hierarchy. Namely, in 2023 the share of women in the Constitutional Court was 23.1%, and in the Supreme Court 27.3%. (Državni zavod za statistiku (2024), Žene i muškarci u Hrvatskoj, 58–74. https://podaci.dzs.hr/media/jcxp1r2c/women_and_man_2024.pdf

[75] There is a lack of publicly available data on the gender representation of employees in Croatian ministries and state administrative organisations. Data from the Ministry of Justice, Administration and Digital Transformation on the total number of employees in state bodies and public administration are available. (available at: Republika Hrvatska - Ministarstvo pravosuđa, uprave i digitalne transformacije (2024), Statistički prikaz Ministarstva pravosuđa, uprave i digitalne transformacije, 23–24. https://mpudt.gov.hr/UserDocsImages//dokumenti/Statisti%C4%8Dki%20prikaz//statisticki%20prikaz%20broj%2034_listopad%202024.pdf. But, according to data from the National Bureau of Statistics, it is evident that in 2023, the share of women in positions of officials and senior civil and public officials was 24.6%, while those with ambassador status were at 31% (Državni zavod za statistiku (2024), Žene i muškarci u Hrvatskoj, 81–82. https://podaci.dzs.hr/media/jcxp1r2c/women_and_man_2024.pdf

[76] The existing scientific and professional references examine women's representation in management positions: Davies (2011), pp. 1–39; Ružić and Perušić (2014), pp. 98–107; Mateljak (2024), pp. 453–465; Mateljak and Jurlina Alibegović (2023), pp. 223–243.

Thus, women make up only 20% of media company board members,[77] and only two women have been appointed presidents of media company boards.[78] Furthermore, there is currently not a single woman on the Board of the Croatian Academy of Sciences and Arts (HAZU), and only two women, out of 17 members, are in the presidency of the executive body of the HAZU Assembly.[79]

In this context, the Ministry of Tourism and Sports in the National Sports Programme 2019–2026 states that one of the shortcomings of the current sports management system is the incredibly low proportion of women in the highest decision-making positions in sports organisations, as well as in other sports-related positions.[80] Following the general and specific aims of the Action Plan, the primary goal is to approach the International Olympic Committee's requirement that 30% of women be in leadership positions in sports organisations.[81]

In 2020, 10% of women were members of the highest decision-making bodies in trade unions, and 29% of women were in the highest decision-making positions.[82] Likewise, the percentage of women in the management of the Croatian National Bank amounts to 28%. Since 2010, when the European Commission announced special measures to achieve balanced gender representation in companies, there has been a noticeable shift towards greater representation of women in decision-making positions in the EU economy. Data regarding the representation of men and women in decision-making positions across the EU was published by the European Institute for Gender Equality (hereinafter: EIGE, see Table 1). According to data relating to Croatia, for example, the share of women on the boards of the largest companies

[77] European Institute for Gender Equality (2024), Public broadcasters: presidents and members of the board/council (highest decision-making body). https://eige.europa.eu/gender-statistics/dgs/indicator/wmidm_med_pbrc__wmid_media_pbrc_bm

[78] https://dubrovacki.slobodnadalmacija.hr/dubrovnik/vijesti/hrvatska-i-svijet/ana-hanzekovic-krznaric-predsjednica-uprave-hanza-medije-a-zorica-vitez-sever-i-igor-cenic-clanovi-1222146. https://lidermedia.hr/tvrtke-i-trzista/stella-litou-u-rtl-u-prva-zena-na-celu-jedne-televizijske-kuce-u-hrvatskoj-147551

[79] Hrvatska akademija znanosti i umjetnosti (2022), Predsjedništvo Akademije izabrano na skupštini održanoj 24. studenoga 2022., mandat od 1. siječnja 2023–31. prosinca 2026. https://www.info.hazu.hr/predsjednistvo/

[80] Središnji državni ured za sport (2019), Nacionalni program športa, 45. https://mint.gov.hr/UserDocsImages//dokumentisdus/docs//Nacionalni%20program%20%C5%A1porta%202019.%20%E2%80%93%202026_.pdf

[81] Ibid. The Croatian Olympic Committee (hereinafter: HOO), as the highest non-governmental sports body, has 11.9% representation of women in its administrative structures. For more information on gender equality in sports in EU member states, see in: Europski parlament (2024), Rodna ravnopravnost u sportu. https://www.europarl.europa.eu/RegData/etudes/ATAG/2024/759597/EPRS_ATA(2024)759597_HR.pdf

[82] Europski institut za ravnopravnost spolova (2020), The proportion and number of women and men among members of the highest decision-making bodies of social partner organizations representing workers at national level. https://eige.europa.eu/gender-statistics/dgs/indicator/bpfa_g_offic_g14__wmid_socp_nat_empee_bm

Table 1 Data according to Gender Equality Index (2023), Power indicators in Croatia, Economic Domaine (women and men on corporate boards)[a]

	Share of members of boards in largest quoted companies, supervisory board or board of directors (%)		Share of board members of central bank (%)	
Country	Women	Men	Women	Men
HR	31	69	11	89
EU	33	67	28	72

[a]The sub-domain of gender-balance in economic decision-making is measured by the proportion of women and men on corporate boards of the largest nationally registered companies listed on stock exchanges and national Central banks. https://eige.europa.eu/gender-equality-index/2023/domain/power/HR

Source: https://eige.europa.eu/gender-equality-index/2023/domain/power/HR

increased from 17% in 2010 to 27% in 2020,[83] while in the largest companies in the EU, women held 31.6% of management positions in 2022.[84]

Thus, every year, to prepare the annual Report on their work, the Ombudsperson for Gender Equality researches the representation of women in management positions,[85] i.e. examines the share of women in economic decision-making positions, using data of the Croatian Financial Services Supervisory Agency (HANFA). According to the latest available data, the percentage of women on the boards of joint-stock companies whose shares or corporate bonds (as of 31 December 2023) were listed on the regulated market of the Zagreb Stock Exchange was 17.29%;[86] which represents a slight increase of 0.6% compared to the previous year.[87] On that day, the share of women in the supervisory boards of the listed joint-stock companies was 24.78%, which is a decrease of 1% compared to the previous year.[88,89]

Thus, there is a noticeable trend of a slight decrease in the share of women in issuer management, as stated by the Croatian Financial Services Supervisory

[83] See also data in Table 1.

[84] Europski institut za ravnopravnost spolova (2022a), Gender Equality Index – Power. https://eige.europa.eu/gender-equality-index/2022/domain/power

[85] More on previous research in the period of 2003 and further see at: https://www.prs.hr/cms/posts_all/1/36

[86] Hrvatska agencija za nadzor financijskih usluga (2023), Godišnji izvještaj o korporativnom upravljanju. https://www.hanfa.hr/media/ktjn5gt0/giku-2023.pdf, pp. 15–17.

[87] Pravobraniteljica za ravnopravnost spolova (2023), Izvješće o radu za 2022, 35. https://www.prs.hr/application/uploads/Izvje%C5%A1%C4%87e_o_radu_PRS_u_2022_cjelo.pdf

[88] Pravobraniteljica za ravnopravnost spolova (2023), Izvješće o radu za 2022, 41. https://www.prs.hr/application/uploads/Izvje%C5%A1%C4%87e_o_radu_PRS_u_2022_cjelo.pdf

[89] In 2002, among the largest companies listed on the stock exchange, 16.7% of women held the position of chief executive officer, 26.9% served as company board members and 12.5% were board presidents, see: Hrvatska agencija za nadzor financijskih usluga (2022), Godišnji izvještaj o korporativnom upravljanju, 16–18. https://www.hanfa.hr/media/rh5h4hae/izvjesce-giku.pdf; Europski institut za ravnopravnost spolova (2022b), Largest listed companies: CEOs, executives and non-executives. https://eige.europa.eu/gender-statistics/dgs/indicator/wmidm_bus_bus__wmid_comp_compex/bar/year:2022-B1/geo:HR/EGROUP:COMP/sex:M,W/UNIT:PC/POSITION:CEO/NACE:TOT

Agency in its Annual Report on Corporate Governance for 2021.[90] This trend began to improve in 2019, 2020, and 2021, and in the observed period of eleven years, the average percentage of that share was 16%. The proportion of women in share issuer management increased from 15% to 17% in 2020 and 2021, but the percentage of women on supervisory boards remained relatively stable between 2010 and 2021, with an average proportion of 21% over the observed period.[91]

Furthermore, in addition to HANFA data, data from the EIGE have also been analysed to monitor the gender structure in economic decision-making positions. Therefore, the latest statistical data on the proportion of men and women in non-executive positions in the 20 largest companies listed on the regulated market show that in the second half of 2024, the share of women was 27.9% and men 72.1%.[92] In the largest listed companies at the level of the EU, the average share of women was 37.2%, while the average share of men was 62.8%.[93] Compared to last year, the data for RC shows that there was a decrease in the proportion of women occupying non-executive positions. In the first half of 2023, the share of women stood at 31.8%, while men accounted for 68.2%.[94] At the EU level, there was an increase in the representation of women in these positions, with the average proportion of women amounting to 33.8% and men making up 66.2%).[95]

Therefore, it can be concluded based on the data of EIGE and HANFA that vertical segregation in management positions still exists, that is, the problem of the so-called "glass ceiling",[96] which the Ombudsperson for Gender Equality has been mentioning in her work reports for many years (for example in 2014, 2015, 2016, 2017, 2018 and 2019). Consequently, the above data indicates a great distance from

---

[90] Annual report on corporate governance in 2021: Hrvatska agencija za nadzor financijskih usluga (2021), Godišnji izvještaj o korporativnom upravljanju 2021. https://www.hanfa.hr/media/tyqjsegf/izvjesce-2021-hrv-verzija_final.pdf, 24–26.

[91] Hrvatska agencija za nadzor financijskih usluga (2021), Godišnji izvještaj o korporativnom upravljanju 2021, 76–78. https://www.hanfa.hr/media/tyqjsegf/izvjesce-2021-hrv-verzija_final.pdf

[92] Europski institut za ravnopravnost spolova (2024), Largest listed companies: CEOs, executives and non-executives. https://eige.europa.eu/gender-statistics/dgs/indicator/wmidm_bus_bus__wmid_comp_compex/bar/year:2024-B2/geo:HR/EGROUP:COMP/sex:M,W/UNIT:PC/POSITION:NON_EXEC/NACE:TOT

[93] Ibid.

[94] Europski institut za ravnopravnost spolova (2023), Largest listed companies: CEOs, executives and non-executives. https://eige.europa.eu/gender-statistics/dgs/indicator/wmidm_bus_bus__wmid_comp_compex/bar/year:2023-B1/geo:EU27_2020,HR/EGROUP:COMP/sex:M,W/UNIT:PC/POSITION:NON_EXEC/NACE:TOT

[95] Ibid.

[96] "The glass ceiling refers to the subtle and often invisible obstacles that hinder women's advancement at the workplace. Firstly, female managers are more likely to be assigned to auxiliary roles (such as personnel department, sales, administration) than their male counterparts are. It creates a much weaker basis for them to advance in their career. Secondly, the promotion selection processes may disadvantage women due to implicit criteria rather than formal discrimination. It is suggested that there are implicit criteria (rather than formal discrimination) that put women in a less favourable position", cited according to Abercrombie, et al. (2008), p. 206.

the goals set by the Directive on improving the gender balance among director positions of listed companies and related measures.[97]

Examples of good practices in this context, which RC should follow, are countries such as France, the Netherlands, Belgium, Italy, Denmark, the United Kingdom, Norway, and Iceland, which have more than 40% of women in non-executive decision-making positions in their largest corporations. In the analysed selection of companies, women held 19.7% of executive positions in the same period (2024) compared to 80.3% of men. In contrast, the average share of men in the EU is 76.7%, or 23.3% of women.[98]

7 Brief Insight into European Policies of the Gender Equality and Its Reflection: Importance of Women in Political and Economic Decision-Making (Management or Leadership Positions)

Achieving gender equality by requiring a balanced representation and participation of women and men in decision-making processes, management positions and labour market, represents foundation for respect and enjoyment of fundamental human rights. This contributes to the achievement of a responsible and democratic society, the ideals of the rule of law and the creation of an environment in which equal opportunities and equal rights for both genders are provided. It is unnecessary to specially highlight the scope of the gender equality politics within the legal framework of every democratic country. Gender equality is proclaimed as one of the most important European democratic principles, but also one of the values on which the EU is based. Apart from the main European legal treaties,[99] the foundation can be found in the Art. 23 of the Charter of Fundamental Rights of the European Union,[100] which prescribes the equality of women and men in all areas.

---

[97] *Directive (EU) 2022/2381 of the European Parliament and of the Council of 23 November 2022 on improving the gender balance among directors of listed companies and related measures.* https://eur-lex.europa.eu/legal-content/EN/TXT/?uri=CELEX%3A32022L2381

[98] Europski institut za ravnopravnost spolova (2024), Largest listed companies: CEOs, executives and non-executives. https://eige.europa.eu/gender-statistics/dgs/indicator/wmidm_bus_bus__wmid_comp_compex/bar/year:2024-B2/geo:EU27_2020,HR/EGROUP:COMP/sex:M,W/UNIT:PC/POSITION:EXEC/NACE:TOT

[99] "In all its activities, the Union shall aim to eliminate inequalities, and to promote equality, between men and women." https://eur-lex.europa.eu/legal-content/EN/TXT/HTML/?uri=CELEX:12016ME/TXT&from=hr#d1e302-13-1

[100] Art. 21, paragraph 1 of the chapter also refers to the prohibition of discrimination on any grounds (one of which is gender). Charter of Fundamental Rights of the European Union (2016/C 202/02). https://eur-lex.europa.eu/legal-content/HR/TXT/?uri=celex%3A12007P.

2020–2025[101] the EU Gender Equality Strategy presents the framework set by the European Commission in achieving full gender equality (gender-equal Europe until 2025).[102] The European Commission is basing the implementation of this Strategy by emphasizing gender aware politics and goal-oriented measures. Gender balance in political and economic decision-making is one of the Commission's priorities within the 2020–2025 Gender Equality Strategy. In the upcoming period, EU is trying to combine gender equality with issues and challenges regarding demographic movements, green and other technologies, AI, process of digitalization (digital technologies), effects of climate change. One of the five priority areas represents promoting gender equality in decision-making.

In the Report of the European Commission on the RC,[103] regarding gender equality and implementation of gender equality politics, it is stated that the RC along with many other European countries, is facing permanent challenges of quicker resolving issues regarding gender inequality, removing structural reasons of misbalance of power between men and women in different fields of society. When it comes to legal background, a significant normative expansion of Croatian anti-discrimination legislation has been laid down. But, what draws attention is the continuing problem of effective enforcement of the Croatian gender equality legislation.[104]

One of the indicators of unequal position is evident in underrepresentation of women in the processes of political and public decision-making, although certain progress is evident in this area. In addition, gender equality related issue that deserves further attention and improvement is the question of wage transparency. Under the influence of COVID, there has been no significant deterioration in the situation of women in the labour market, but certain pre-pandemic causes are still visible (labour market segregation, fixed-term work, and others).

The important Directive on improving the gender balance among directors of listed companies and related measures (Women on Boards Directive) (hereinafter: Directive) from 23rd November 2022[105] should also be specially highlighted. Negotiations at the European level took almost 12 years to adopt this Directive. This Directive represents an important segment of the 2020–2025 EU Gender Equality Strategy. Efforts have been made to achieve gender balance on corporate boards, to break glass ceiling, to improve gender balance among the directors of listed

---

[101] https://eur-lex.europa.eu/legal-content/HR/TXT/?uri=CELEX%3A52020DC0152

[102] https://commission.europa.eu/strategy-and-policy/policies/justice-and-fundamental-rights/gender-equality/equality-between-women-and-men-decision-making/eu-action-promote-gender-balance-decision-making_en

[103] In 2008, the Advisory Committee on Equal Opportunities for Women and Men was established to assist the Commission on Gender Equality. Available at: https://eur-lex.europa.eu/legal-content/HR/TXT/?uri=celex%3A32008D0590, https://eur-lex.europa.eu/summary/HR/c10919, https://eige.europa.eu/gender-mainstreaming/countries/croatia?language_content_entity=en

[104] Country report-Gender Equality, Croatia 2023, European Commission, 120. https://www.equalitylaw.eu/downloads/5932-croatia-country-report-gender-equality-2023

[105] Directive (EU) 2022/2381 of the European Parliament and of the Council of 23 November 2022 on improving the gender balance among directors of listed companies and related measures, OJ L 315, 7.12.2022, 44–59.

companies and to adopt adequate measures on European and national levels. Member states must transpose the Directive into their national legislation, until 28 December 2024. According to this Directive, it is required that listed companies have to have at least 40% of each gender amongst the members of non-executive boards, or 33% amongst all directors (by 30 June 2026). The expiry date of the Directive is also set at 31 December 2038. Member States are obliged to submit a report to the European Commission on the measures taken to achieve the objectives set by it. The purpose of this Directive is to ensure the application of the principle of equal opportunities and a more balanced representation of women and men among the directors of companies listed on the stock exchange. Considering the large share of highly educated and qualified women in the EU, it is expected that the application of appropriate measures and the Directive would contribute to better teamwork, more successful corporate management, better quality decisions, profitability, competitiveness, advancement towards such management positions in companies and others.

When talking about the under-represented gender and taking measures to ensure it, it is worth recalling Art. 23(1) of the EU Charter of Fundamental Rights, according to which the principle of equality shall not prevent the maintenance or adoption of measures providing for specific advantages in favour of the under-represented sex. When selecting candidates for appointment or election to a directorship, preference should be given to an equally qualified candidate of the underrepresented gender. However, this should not be unconditional, and should also be taken into account. It is important that the qualifications, experience and abilities of the candidate are considered when selecting candidates (objective assessment of each candidate in the context of the specific needs of each company and their expertise/experience/qualifications/results; clearly defined criteria, process transparency). Giving an unconditional advantage to a candidate solely because of gender can cause additional risks. The imposition of legal quotas (Member States with quota (38.2%), soft measures (31.4%) and no measures 17.6%)[106] and binding measures can accelerate progress towards gender balance in administrations, which has proven successful in certain European countries (France, Germany, Denmark, Belgium).

Unfortunately, women regarding their education, skills, knowledge and results, still remain under-represented in corporate decision-making. Progress in improving female representation on corporate boards and in business leadership positions, is very slow and uneven across the EU. According to available data, in 2022 around 32.2% of board members of the EU's largest publicly listed companies were women compared to 30% in 2021. More significant results and progress have been recorded in those Member States where binding measures have been introduced. "France, Italy, the Netherlands and Denmark are the countries where the largest listed companies have at least 40 % of each gender on their boards. Germany, Finland, Spain,

[106] See 2023 Report on Gender Equality in the EU, 45–46. https://commission.europa.eu/system/files/2023-04/annual_report_GE_2023_web_EN.pdf

Sweden, Ireland, Portugal and Austria have reached the 33 % target for all board members."[107] "Undoubtedly, it can be concluded that the countries that imposed quotas on themselves, even before the entry into force of the Directive, received a significant increase in women in management positions and thus strengthened corporate governance and the economy."[108]

The inclusion of a gender perspective in all EU policies and processes is essential for achieving the goal of gender equality. Gender equality perspective has to be integrated into every aspect of policy, planning, strategic documents, programmes and decision-making processes. Furthermore, in order to ensure the implementation of politics, measures and legal obligations within this area, it is important to indicate that the established institutional mechanisms are introduced in accordance with the legal instruments and politics on the European level, which, however, still needs to be further, updated and continuously harmonized. Throughout 2023, gender equality across different EU policy areas have been included in areas such as health, environmental and sustainable goals,[109] climate changes, energy and agriculture sector, artificial intelligence, digital sphere,[110] research and innovation, education, sport and many others.[111] In order to take additional measures, actions to achieve gender equality according to the EU Strategy, one of the four key areas is thriving in a gender-equal economy. According to the 2024 Report on Gender Equality in the EU, "significant gender gaps still exist in the labour market and in decision-making positions, including political representation".[112]

7.1 Short Overview to the Council of Europe-Gender Equality-Balance in Representation of Men and Women in Decision-Making in Political and Public Sector

This area is one of main and important policy goals of the Council of Europe. It has established an adequate framework, legal instruments, and standards[113] and has offered referral and guidelines regarding legal and administrative measures,[114]

[107] 2023 Report on Gender Equality in the EU, 43.

[108] Novaković (2024), p. 5.

[109] https://www.europarl.europa.eu/thinktank/en/events/details/an-inclusive-economy-for-women-in-the-gr/20211007EOT05922

[110] For example, see https://www.europarl.europa.eu/committees/en/hearing-on-securing-gender-equality-and-/product-details/20241129CAN74029

[111] For more see 2024 Report on Gender Equality in the EU, https://commission.europa.eu/document/download/965ed6c9-3983-4299-8581-046bf0735702_en

[112] Gender Equality Report from 2024, 2. https://commission.europa.eu/document/download/965ed6c9-3983-4299-8581-046bf0735702_en

[113] https://www.coe.int/en/web/genderequality/standards-and-mechanisms

[114] Special emphasis should be placed on the significance of particular administrative measures, especially with regard to referrals that public administration presents a good example of balanced

supporting measures including independent forms of oversight in monitoring the implementation of public politics in this area. The Council of Europe Gender Equality Strategy 2018–2023[115] (hereinafter: GES 2018–2023) and the Recommendation Rec (2003) 3 on balanced participation of women and men in both political and public decision-making of the Council of Europe[116] (hereinafter: Recommendation) are the two fundamental sources relevant to emphasize. Moreover, the Strategy is based on six priority areas, one of which refers to achieving balance in representation of men and women in decision-making in political and public sector. This segment of gender equality is important to build functional democracy. The Council of Europe will, therefore, thorough their referrals, recommendations, measures and activities insist on it being implemented in all the member states and achieve progress through purposefully oriented actions and overall approach.[117] In numerous member states, there is still resistance against changes, which prevents progress in achieving gender sensitivity of the bodies appointed for decision-making.

At the beginning of March 2024, the new Council of Europe Gender Equality Strategy 2024–2029[118] was adopted. During this period, the focus will be on the same six strategic goals. It should also be noted that this period is influenced by additional and new challenges in implementing and ensuring gender equality in general, and then in the area of achieving gender balance in decision-making and politics (management positions). This represents fourth strategic objective. It highlights the importance of further ensuring the equal participation of women and girls, men and boys in political and public decision-making; equal access to the labour market. This includes, among other things, full support for the implementation of the previously mentioned Recommendation Rec (2003)3, support for implementing parity measures and gender quotas and in creating policies that promote work–life balance in public services and in the private sector. Unfortunately, in most member states, the equal participation of women in political and public life,[119] in legislative and

---

distribution with the aim of creating a surrounding with equal opportunities for men and women regarding decision-making.

[115] Council of Europe Gender Equality Strategy 2018–2023, Committee of Ministers of the Council of Europe, March 2018, https://rm.coe.int/prems-093618-gbr-gender-equality-strategy-2023-web-a5/16808b47e1

[116] Recommendation Rec (2003) 3, Committee of Ministers of the Council of Europe, 12 March 2003, https://rm.coe.int/1680519084

[117] "65 to 70% of respondents indicated that they have taken legislative, policy and institutional measures." See Annual report 2023, Implementation of the Council of Europe Gender Equality Strategy 2018–2023, 38. For Croatia, see also 59 of the Annual report. https://rm.coe.int/gender-equality-strategy-annual-report-2023-en-2772-5949-9018-6/1680b15060

[118] https://search.coe.int/cm#_Toc155173006

[119] It is also worth mentioning the European Social Charter which proclaims equal opportunities and equal treatment, in matters of employment and occupation without discrimination on grounds of sex. Official Gazette No. 15/02–172, https://rm.coe.int/168047e017. See also Directive 2006/54/EC of the European Parliament and of the Council of 5 July 2006 on the implementation of the principle of equal opportunities and equal treatment of men and women in matters of employment

executive bodies of all levels, is still below the minimum of 40% standard agreed in the Council of Europe.[120]

8 Concluding Remarks

The results of the analysis of legal sources and literature in the field of protection of women's rights, speaks for the affirmation of the right to education, which women in our area began to exercise at the beginning of the last century, as well as the right of women to vote, which was finally affirmed in the period immediately after World War II. The summary of the literature that mostly dealt with the legal position of women in the socialist society, leads to the conclusion that the legislation of the time was still based on the traditional division of gender roles, a discriminatory policy that resulted in the violation of women's equality in the labour market by imposing on them the role of a mother and a housewife. For this reason, the period marked by the second phase of feminism, which also manifested itself in the territory of Federal Republic of Yugoslavia, was mainly marked by the greater inclusion of women in the labour market, who, despite their qualifications, continued to perform second-rate jobs without the possibility of advancement. There are only a small number of women in management positions in social enterprises, which until 1991 did not exceed the share of 1.5%.

When it comes to the participation of women in the political system, in the last 30 years, the political equality of women and men in European parliamentary democracies has recorded a gradual, linear growth. However, in Croatia, just like in other former socialist countries, as noted from the statistical data of the research, the practice of higher, "artificially" maintained percentages of women in parliaments already disappeared during the transition period. For this reason, the available data for the period until 2000 confirm a decrease in the share of women in parliamentary power, which began to increase slightly only in the late 1990s, and the same was true for the participation of women in ministerial positions within the executive branch. In conclusion, as already confirmed by the results of many pieces of research on an unequal position of women in a society, it can be stated that throughout history, men dominated politics while women primarily took on roles related to childcare and household. As a result, women tend to engage in lower levels of political activity, which was supported by the results of this research.

The results of the local, parliamentary, and European elections in 2024, as well as the representation of women in management positions, show that there is still a significant disparity and imbalance in the political and economic sphere of Croatia,

---

and occupation, OJ L 204, 26.7.2006, 23–36. Within the European Pillar of Social Rights, principles of ensuring equal opportunities and access to the labour market have been emphasized. https://hupt.hr/wp-content/uploads/Dokumenti/Europski_stup_socijalnih_prava.pdf

[120] See Europe Gender Equality Strategy 2024–2029, CM (2024)17-final. https://search.coe.int/cm#_Toc155173006

despite some progress achieved in terms of gender equality. Although the share of women in the political life of the RC has increased slightly compared to the last elections, they still make up a significantly smaller proportion in decision-making positions, both at the national level and at the level of local self-government and executive functions. Accordingly, the above data confirms that legal provisions such as gender quotas, although useful, are not sufficient to achieve real gender equality in political and economic decision-making.

Furthermore, women still make up a smaller percentage in high management positions, which is particularly noticeable in media and commercial companies. Compared to international standards and practices in some European countries, Croatia still lags in achieving balance in key decision-making positions. Although the share of women in managerial positions in the EU economy has increased, Croatia remains below these averages, which requires further legal and social changes. To achieve real gender equality, it is necessary to take additional steps that include faster and more consistent implementation of legislative measures, and intensifying changes in social norms that will allow women easier access to the highest positions in political, economic, and social structures.

Finally, we can conclude that the RC has made certain positive progress in the field of legislative and administrative measures in accordance with the Recommendation of the Council of Europe. In addition, appropriate institutional mechanisms for the implementation and monitoring of the principle of gender equality have been introduced. In this direction, mechanisms only need to be strengthened at the local and regional level, as well as at the level of state administration. With regard to the compatibility of the national policy with the European one, it is necessary to emphasize the adoption of a new National policy. In March of 2023, Croatia adopted National Gender Equality Plan for the period until 2027 and the corresponding action plan for the period until 2024.[121] As part of seven special goals, we highlight the improvement of the position of women on the labour market and the increase of the representation of women in the processes of public and of political decision-making. Eliminating gender-based discrimination in decision-making processes in public and private life, political activity and the economy, by creating conditions for the advancement of women (removing the so-called glass ceiling), the quality implementation of most of the strategic goals of the National Development Strategy is enabled.

Strengthen indicators to measure progress in decision-making and the establishment of consolidated databases. Should continuously work on the need for radical changes in rethinking the role of women in management positions (leading functions), as well as the elimination of societal and structural barriers that are the result of certain inherited traditions and values. Balanced participation of both genders in the public administration system can contribute to better work performance. Political

[121] https://ravnopravnost.gov.hr/UserDocsImages//dokumenti/NPRS%202027%20APRS%202024//Nacionalni%20plan%20za%20ravnopravnost%20spolova%202027.pdf

will and support certainly play a key role in ensuring the effective implementation of gender equality policies.

Furthermore, in order to ensure the implementation of politics, measures and legal obligations within this area, it is important to indicate that the established institutional mechanisms are introduced in accordance with the legal instruments and politics on the European level, which, however, still needs to be further, updated and continuously harmonized. In this context, it is crucial to include and connect larger representation and more frequent involvement of women in with the aim of achieving inclusive public administration, decision-making processes and management.

Women cover a smaller percentage (proportion) in this area and are deprived from equal participation opportunities, which are influenced by numerous limiting factors (economic, social, political and others). Nevertheless, certain positive examples and progress regarding gender equality are still visible. These positive trends were influenced by processes of Europeanisation, that is, the obligation for harmonising this area with the acquis of the EU, as well as other European policies for promoting gender equality, strengthening of the female role and necessity for greater female participation. There is visible progress with regard to higher women participation in spheres of decision-making and political power, as well as in finding employment and being appointed head (managerial) functions (workplaces), which is evident in analyses performed by different European and national bodies, whose duty is to monitor progress in gender equality.

References

Abercrombie N, Hill S, Turner SB (2008) Rječnik sociologije. Naklada Jesenski i Turk, Zagreb

Act on the Financing of Political Activities, Election Campaigns, and Referendums [Zakon o financiranju političkih aktivnosti izborne promidžbe i referenduma], Narodne novine [Official Gazette] Nos. 29/19 and 98/19

Anti-Discrimination Act [Zakon o suzbijanju diskriminacije], Narodne novine [Official Gazette] NoS. 85/2008 and 112/2012

Baranović B (2000) Slika žene u udžbenicima književnosti. Institut za društvena istraživanja u Zagrebu, Zagreb

Belić M, Bijelić B (2000) Žene u predizbornoj kampanji. B.a.B.e, Zagreb

Blagojević Hjuson M (2015) Sutra je bilo yesterday- Contribution to the social history of women in the second half of the 20th century. Institute for Gender Equality, Novi Sad. https://ravnopravnost.org.rs/wp-content/uploads/2017/02/4-Marina_Blagojevic_SUTRA_JE_BILO_JUCE.pdf

Blagojević A, Tucak I, Rešetar B (2024) Na putu prema rodnoj ravnopravnosti žena u hrvatskom društvu. J Pravni vjesnik 40:75–100

Božić A (1939) Položaj žene u privatnom pravu kroz historiju do danas (Doktorski rad). Pravni Fakultet Beograd, Beograd

Čepulo D (2002) Izborna reforma u Hrvatskoj 1875 – liberalizam, antidemokratizam i hrvatska autonomija. J Zbornik pravnog fakulteta u Zagrebu 52(3–4):665–692

Čepulo D (2012) Hrvatska pravna povijest u europskom kontekstu. Pravni fakultet Sveučilišta u Zagrebu, Zagreb

Charter of Fundamental Rights of the European Union (2016/C 202/02) https://eur-lex.europa.eu/legal-content/HR/TXT/?uri=celex%3A12007P

Constitution of the Federative People's Republic of Yugoslavia [Ustav Federativne Narodne Republike Jugoslavije], Službeni list FNRJ [Official Gazette of the FNRJ] 1946

Constitution of the Republic of Croatia [Ustav RH], Narodne novine [Official Gazette] Nos. 56/90, 135/97, 08/98, 113/00, 124/00, 28/01, 41/01, 55/01, 76/10, 85/10, 05/14

Cruea S (2005) Changing ideals of womanhood during the nineteenth-century woman movement. General Studies Writing Faculty Publications. https://scholarworks.bgsu.edu/cgi/viewcontent.cgi?article=1000&context=gsw_pub

Decision of the Constitutional Court of the Republic of Croatia No U-I-2696/2003 of 16 January 2008 [Odluka Ustavnog suda Republike Hrvatske], Narodne novine [Official Gazette] No. 14/08

Decision on Appointment of Ombudsperson for Gender Equality. [Odluka o imenovanju pravobraniteljice za ravnopravnost spolova], Narodne novine [Official Gazette] No. 157/03

Decree on the Establishment of the Office for Gender Equality. [Uredba o Uredu za ravnopravnost spolova], Narodne novine [Official Gazette] No. 18/04

Dijanić D, Merunka-Golubić M, Niemčić I, Stanić D (2002) Ženski biografski leksikon: Sjećanje žena na život u socijalizmu. Centar za ženske studije, Zagreb

Directive 2006/54/EC of the European Parliament and of the Council of 5 July 2006 on the implementation of the principle of equal opportunities and equal treatment of men and women in matters of employment and occupation, OJ L 204, 26.7.2006, 23–36

Directive 2022/2381 of the European Parliament and of the Council of 23 November 2022 on improving the gender balance among directors of listed companies and related measures. https://eur-lex.europa.eu/legal-content/EN/TXT/?uri=CELEX%3A32022L2381

Državni zavod za statistiku (2024) Žene i muškarci u Hrvatskoj. https://podaci.dzs.hr/media/jcxp1r2c/women_and_man_2024.pdf

Državno izborno povjerenstvo Republike Hrvatske (2021) Regionalna (područna) samouprava - rodna statistika izabranih kandidata lokalni izbori 2021. https://www.izbori.hr/site/UserDocsImages/2021/Lokalni%20izbori%202021/Rodna_statistika.pdf

Dujmović I (2016) Radnice u Jugoslaviji 1960-1980; Uloga i položaj u industriji i društvu i slučaj Rijeka (Diplomski rad). Sveučilište u Rijeci – Filozofski fakultet u Rijeci, Rijeka

Đuranović-Janda S (1960) Žena u radnom odnosu. Naprijed, Zagreb

Eisner B (1934) Privatnopravni položaj žene i njegovo uređenje u Jedinstvenom građanskom zakoniku za Jugoslaviju, Spomenica mauroviću u njegovoj šestogodišnjici. Globus, Beograd

Europe Gender Equality Strategy 2024-2029, CM (2024)17-final https://search.coe.int/cm#_Toc155173006

European Commission (2020) Gender equality strategy. https://commission.europa.eu/strategy-and-policy/policies/justice-and-fundamental-rights/gender-equality/equality-between-women-and-men-decision-making/eu-action-promote-gender-balance-decision-making_en#the-commissions-strategy

European Institute for Gender Equality (2021) Statistical brief: gender balance in politics 2020. https://eige.europa.eu/publications/statistical-brief-gender-balancepolitics-2020

European Institute for Gender Equality (2024) Public broadcasters: presidents and members of the board/council (highest decision-making body). https://eige.europa.eu/gender-statistics/dgs/indicator/wmidm_med_pbrc__wmid_media_pbrc_bm

European Parliament (2024) Women in politics in the EU State of play in 2024. https://www.europarl.europa.eu/RegData/etudes/BRIE/2024/760348/EPRS_BRI(2024)760348_EN.pdf

European Parliamentary Research Service (EPRS) (2024) Women in politics in the 2024 election year. https://epthinktank.eu/2024/03/05/women-in-politics-in-the-2024-election-year

Europski institut za ravnopravnost spolova (2020) The proportion and number of women and men among members of the highest decision-making bodies of social partner organisations representing workers at national level. https://eige.europa.eu/gender-statistics/dgs/indicator/bpfa_g_offic_g14__wmid_socp_nat_empee_bm

Europski institut za ravnopravnost spolova (2022a) Gender equality index-power. https://eige.europa.eu/gender-equality-index/2022/domain/power
Europski institut za ravnopravnost spolova (2022b) Largest listed companies: CEOs, executives and non-executives. https://eige.europa.eu/gender-statistics/dgs/indicator/wmidm_bus_bus__wmid_comp_compex/bar/year:2022-B1/geo:HR/EGROUP:COMP/sex:M,W/UNIT:PC/POSITION:CEO/NACE:TOT
Europski institut za ravnopravnost spolova (2023) Largest listed companies: CEOs, executives and non-executives. https://eige.europa.eu/gender-statistics/dgs/indicator/wmidm_bus_bus__wmid_comp_compex/bar/year:2023-B1/geo:EU27_2020,HR/EGROUP:COMP/sex:M,W/UNIT:PC/POSITION:NON_EXEC/NACE:TOT
Europski institut za ravnopravnost spolova (2024) Largest listed companies: CEOs, executives and non-executives. https://eige.europa.eu/gender-statistics/dgs/indicator/wmidm_bus_bus__wmid_comp_compex/bar/year:2024-B2/geo:EU27_2020,HR/EGROUP:COMP/sex:M,W/UNIT:PC/POSITION:NON_EXEC/NACE:TOT
Europski parlament (2024) Rodna ravnopravnost u sportu. https://www.europarl.europa.eu/RegData/etudes/ATAG/2024/759597/EPRS_ATA(2024)759597_HR.pdf
Franković D (1958) Povijest školstva i pedagogije u Hrvatskoj. Pedagoško-književni zbor, Zagreb
Frederick S, Lopez-Acevedo G, Robertson R, Bahena MAV (2021) From Jobs to Careers: Apparel Exports and Career Paths for Women in Developing Countries. Washington: World Bank Group
Galić B (2012) Promjena seksističkog diskursa u Hrvatskoj J Socijalna ekologija: journal for environmental thought and sociological research=Socijalna ekologija. Zeitschrift für Umweltgedanken und soziologische Forschun 21:155–178
Galić B (2023) Rodna ravnopravnost ili ravnopravnost spolova: sociološki prevladane dvojbe. In: Vasiljević S (ed) Rodna ravnopravnost: pravo i politike. Sveučilište u Zagrebu- Pravni fakultet, Zagreb, pp 21–36
Gender Equality Act [Zakon o ravnopravnosti spolova], Narodne novine [Official Gazette] Nos. 82/08, 116/03
Glazer T (2022) O položaju žene u Socijalističkoj Republici Hrvatskoj - djelovanje Konferencije za društvenu aktivnost žena Hrvatske (Diplomski rad). Sveučilište u Zagrebu, Zagreb
Goldin C (2006) The quiet revolution that transformed women's employment, education, and family. J Am Econ Rev 96(2):1–21
Government of the Republic of Croatia (2008) The bill on gender equality act with the final bill. http://edoc.sabor.hr/Views/AktView.aspx?type=HTML&id=20571
Hrvatska agencija za nadzor financijskih usluga (2021) Godišnji izvještaj o korporativnom upravljanju 2021. https://www.hanfa.hr/media/tyqjsegf/izvjesce-2021-hrv-verzija_final.pdf
Hrvatska agencija za nadzor financijskih usluga (2022) Godišnji izvještaj o korporativnom upravljanju. https://www.hanfa.hr/media/rh5h4hae/izvjesce-giku.pdf
Hrvatska agencija za nadzor financijskih usluga (2023) Godišnji izvještaj o korporativnom upravljanju. https://www.hanfa.hr/media/ktjn5gt0/giku-2023.pdf
Human Rights Education Association (2014) Manual for trainers: gender equality and gender mainstreaming. http://www.ekvilib.org/wp-content/uploads/2017/06/01_Rodni-koncepti_Osvjezite-Znanje.pdf
Jukić R (2013) "Ženska pedagogija" i feminizacija nastavničke struke kao čimbenici skrivenog kurikula. J Školski Vjesnik 62(4):541–558
Kašić B, Marijan J, Pešut J (2005) Vodič prema politici rodne jednakosti: izazovi i mogućnosti. Centar za ženske studije, Zagreb
Kerovec N (2003) (In-)equality of women in the labour market. J Soc Policy Rev 10(3):263–282
Krešić M (2019) Žensko pitanje u reformama bana Ivana Mažuranića. In: Čepulo D, Rogić Musa T, Roksandić D (eds) Intelektualac, kultura, reforma: Ivan Mažuranić i njegovo vrijeme - Zbornik radova znanstvenoga skupa održanoga u Zagrebu 5. studenoga 2014, Pravni fakultet Sveučilišta u Zagrebu. Leksikografski zavod Miroslav Krleža, Zagreb, pp 229–247
Krešić M, Rakitičan M (2015) Primaljstvo u Hrvatskoj i Slavoniji 1876-1918: zakonodavni okvir ustroja primaljske službe. J Hist Zbornik 68(2):277–295

Labour Act [Zakon o radu], Narodne novine [Official Gazette] Nos. 93/14, 127/17, 98/19, 151/22, 46/23, 64/23
Leinert Novosel S (1999) Žena na pragu 21. stoljeća – između majčinstva i profesije. TOD i EDAC, Zagreb
Leinert-Novosel S (1994) Žene u politici: je li intervencija potrebna. J Polit Misao 31(4):137–146
Lord Davies of Abersoch (2011) Women on boards. https://www.gov.uk/government/uploads/system/uploads/attachment_data/file/31480/11-745-women-on-boards.pdf
Luetić T (2006) Počeci visokoškolskog obrazovanja za žene u Hrvatskoj i usporedba sa stanjem u susjednim zemljama. J Hist Zbornik 59:61–68
MacKinnen AC (2014) Toward a renewed equal rights amendment: now more than ever. J Harv J Law Gender 37:569–580
Mateljak Ž (2024) Razina uključenosti žena u upravljačke procese u Republici Hrvatskoj. J Ekonomska misao i praksa 33:453–465
Mateljak Ž, Jurlina Alibegović D (2023) Međuzavisnost rodne zastupljenosti i postignutih rezultata u tijelima državne uprave u Republici Hrvatskoj. J Revija za socijalnu politiku 30:223–240. https://doi.org/10.3935/rsp.v30i2.1940
Members of the European Parliament (2024). https://www.europarl.europa.eu/meps/en/full-list
Miodrag Z (1975) Ustav Socijalističke Federativne Republike Jugoslavije, stručno objašnjenje. Institut za političke studije Fakulteta političkih nauka, Novinsko-izdavačko i grafičko preduzeće "Privredni pregled", Beograd
Nikodem K, Galić B (2009) Percepcija rodnih jednakosti i šansi pri zapošljavanju u hrvatskom društvu. Pogled nezaposlenih žena. J Revija za socijalnu politiku 16(3):253–270
Ograjšek Gorenjak I (2014) Opasne iluzije, rodni stereotipi u međuratnoj Jugoslaviji. Srednja Europa, Zagreb
Ograjšek Gorenjak I (2019) Ženska strana Zagrebačkog sveučilišta u međuraću. In: Roksandić D (ed) Zagreb 1924. – 1930. i 1945. – 1967. Društvo, kultura, svakodnevica: Znanstveni skup s međunarodnim sudjelovanjem. FF Press, Zagreb, pp 235–267
Ostroški LJ (2016) Žene i muškarci u Hrvatskoj. Državni zavod za statistiku, Zagreb
Pravobraniteljica za ravnopravnost spolova (2021) Izvješće o radu Pravobraniteljice za ravnopravnost spolova za 2020 godinu. https://www.prs.hr/application/uploads/IZVJESCE_O_RADU_2020_Pravobranit.pdf
Pravobraniteljica za ravnopravnost spolova (2023) Izvješće o radu za 2022. https://www.prs.hr/application/uploads/Izvje%C5%A1%C4%87e_o_radu_PRS_u_2022_cjelo.pdf
Pravobraniteljica za ravnopravnost spolova (2024a) Izvješće o radu za 2023. https://www.prs.hr/application/uploads/Izvje%C5%A1%C4%87e_o_radu_Pravobraniteljic.pdf
Pravobraniteljica za ravnopravnost spolova (2024b) Rodna analiza parlamentarnih izbora 2024. https://prs.hr/application/uploads/Rodna_analiza_parlamentarnih_izb.%20(prs)%20-%20Copy%201.pdf
Prpić K (1976) Zaposlenost i zapošljavanje žena u Hrvatskoj. J Žena- časopis za znanstvena, društvena i kulturna pitanja o mjestu i ulozi žene u porodici i društvu., br. 1
Raguž M (2010) Zakon od 14. listopada 1874. ob ustroju pučkih škola i preparandija za pučko učiteljstvo u kraljevinah Hrvatskoj i Slavoniji. J Senjski zbornik: prilozi za geografiju, etnologiju, gospodarstvo, povijest i kulturu 37(1):87–97
Recommendation Rec (2003) 3, Committee of Ministers of the Council of Europe, 12 March 2003, https://rm.coe.int/1680519084
Republika Hrvatska - Ministarstvo pravosuđa, uprave i digitalne transformacije (2024) Statistički prikaz Ministarstva pravosuđa, uprave i digitalne transformacije. https://mpudt.gov.hr/UserDocsImages//dokumenti/Statisti%C4%8Dki%20prikaz//statisticki%20prikaz%20broj%2034_listopad%202024.pdf
Republika Hrvatska - Središnji državni ured za sport (2019) Nacionalni program športa. https://mint.gov.hr/UserDocsImages//dokumentisdus/docs//Nacionalni%20program%20%C5%A1porta%202019.%20%E2%80%93%202026_.pdf

Revision of the Constitution of the Republic of Croatia [Promjena Ustava Republike Hrvatske], Narodne novine [Official Gazette] No. 113/2000
Rodin S (2003) Rodna jednakost – Temeljni pojmovi i uloga europskog konteksta: Hrvatska agenda jednakosti rodova za 21. stoljeće. In: Rodin S (ed) Jednakost muškarca i žene. Pravo i politika u EU i Hrvatskoj. Institut za međunarodne odnose, Zagreb, pp 210–211
Ružić V, Perušić M (2014) Položaj žena u menadžmentu – novi trendovi u fenomenu staklenog stropa. J Praktični menadžment 5:98–107
Savezni zavod za statistiku (1973) Žena u društvu i privredi Jugoslavije. Statistički bilten br. 788. Savezni zavod za statistiku, Beograd
Šinko M (2007) Žene u parlamentima – globalna perspektiva. J Polit Misao 44(2):71–92
Šinko M (2016) Parlamentarna predstavljenost žena u Hrvatskoj: nakon nevidljivosti i staklenog stropa – regresija. J Polit Anal 7(27):3–10
Smerdel B (2013) Ustavno uređenje europske Hrvatske. Narodne novine, Zagreb
Standing Orders of the Croatian Parliament [Poslovnik Hrvatskog sabora], Narodne novine [Official Gazette] Nos. 81/2013, 113/2016, 69/2017, 29/2018, 52/2020, 119/2020 and 123/2020
Stone P, Hernandez LA (2012) The rhetoric and reality of "opting out". Women who opt out. New York University Press, New York
Tomšič V (2024) Žena u razvoju socijalističke samoupravne Jugoslavije. AFŽ Arhiv. http://afzarhiv.org/items/show/382.pdf
United Nations (2015) The 2030 Agenda for Sustainable Development. https://sdgs.un.org/goals
Ured za ravnopravnost spolova Vlade Republike Hrvatske (2023) Nacionalni plan za ravnopravnost spolova za razdoblje do 2027. https://ravnopravnost.gov.hr/nacionalni-plan-za-ravnopravnost-spolova-za-razdoblje-do-2027-godine/3442
Vasiljević S, Valković I (2007) Vodič za promicanje politike jednakih mogućnosti na radnom mjestu. CESI, Zagreb
Veštić S (2017) Zakon o ravnopravnosti spolova – razlozi donošenja i institucionalni mehanizmi osiguranja provedbe. J Zbornik radova Veleučilišta u Šibeniku 11:73–94
Vlada Republike Hrvatske – Ured za ravnopravnost spolova (2019) Održani izbori za EU parlament. https://ravnopravnost.gov.hr/vijesti/odrzani-izbori-za-eu-parlament/3249
Vlada Republike Hrvatske – Ured za ravnopravnost spolova (2020) Parlamentarni izbori 2020. https://ravnopravnost.gov.hr/istaknute-teme/zastupljenost-zena-u-politici/parlamentarni-izbori-2020/3447
Vuković K, Šmaguc T (2015) Društveni kontekst izbora zanimanja žena u Hrvatskoj u razdoblju od kraja 19. do početka 21. Stoljeća. J Ekonomska misao i praksa 24(1):297–310
Željko D (2014) Obiteljskopravni položaj žena u Hrvatskoj u razdoblju od 1914. do 2014. godine. J Pravnik 48(96):21–48
Žene u socijalizmu. – od ubrzane emancipacije do ubrzane repatrijarhalizacije. https://6yka.com/bih/zene-u-socijalizmu-od-ubrzane-emancipacije-do-ubrzane-repatrijarhalizacije/
Župan D (2001) "Uzor djevojke": obrazovanje žena u Banskoj Hrvatskoj tijekom druge polovine 19. st. J Časopis za suvremenu povijest 33(2):435–452

Jelena Kasap is an Associate Professor at the Faculty of Law Osijek at the Chair of Legal History and Roman law. After completing study of Law at the Faculty of Law in Osijek, she was employed as an assistant at the same institution, Department of Legal History and Roman Law. She defended her doctoral dissertation entitled "Loan for use in the European legal tradition" on June 16, 2016 at the Faculty of Law in Zagreb. At the Faculty of Law in Osijek, she participates in teaching General History of Law and the State in the Integrated University Study of Law and in the subject History of Administration and Archival Studies at the Professional Administrative Study. She has been a researcher on several international projects, an active participant in several conferences held in the Republic of Croatia and abroad.

Višnja Lachner is an Associate Professor at the Faculty of Law Osijek at the Chair of Legal History and Roman law. After graduation, in December 2008 she started working as young teaching and research assistant at the Faculty of Law Osijek, at the Chair of Legal History. Professional orientation towards Croatian History of Law and State derives from Postgraduate (doctoral) study of Public law and Public Administration at the Faculty of Law in Zagreb. In 2015, she defended her doctoral thesis "Legal status and organization of the Royal Borough of Osijek from 1881 to 1934". She has been a researcher on several international projects, an active participant in several conferences held in the Republic of Croatia and abroad. Her areas of scientific and professional interest are the history of local administration and self-government, the history of the legal position of women, and the history of social work.

Ana Đanić Čeko is an Associate Professor at the Chair of Administrative Law and Science at the Faculty of Law J. J. Strossmayer University of Osijek and a Head of the Green Legal Clinic. She obtained here Ph.D. at Faculty of Law, University of Zagreb with a doctoral dissertation "Appeal in Administrative Dispute in Croatian and Comparative Law". She has been a researcher on several international projects, teaches in several study programs at the Faculty of Law in Osijek. She is a member of the Secretariat within in the Institute of Public Administration, an external associate of the Croatian Academy of Legal Science and member of the Scientific Council for Public Administration, Judiciary and the Rule of Law of the Croatian Academy of Sciences and Arts. She is a member of two university boards and several faculty committees. She is an associate of the State School of Public Administration and the Judicial Academy. She is the winner of the 'Eugen Pusić' award for the best paper in the young scientist category in 2020 and the award for excellence in teaching and work with students 2022/2023, as well as the Green Charter of the Osijek-Baranja County for 2021. Her areas of scientific and professional interest are (national and European) general and special administrative procedures and disputes, legal remedies, environmental protection and law, social care.

Feminist Intersectionality: Practices of Care, Work, Bodies and Identities

The European Court of Human Rights and the Regulation of the Headscarf: Shifting Narratives

Naoual El Yattouti and Benjamin Nurkić

Abstract This chapter seeks to present a critical analysis focusing on the European Court of Human Rights' (ECtHR) case law on religious symbols, specifically exploring the treatment of headscarves compared to other religious signs or expressions. The central question revolves around how Muslim women's voices are either considered or silenced within the ECtHR's case law. The Court has been criticised for not considering the arguments of female Muslim applicants regarding the headscarf, and solely relying on governments' arguments that are often unfounded or ideologically influenced. In Europe, restrictions on religious symbols primarily impact Muslim women, evident from the significant number of cases they bring forward, the vast majority of which are unsuccessful. By not receiving adequate protection of their religious rights, Muslim women who seek to wear the headscarf are increasingly being excluded from many areas of social life such as employment and education, inadvertently limiting their participation. This chapter sheds light on the aspects the ECtHR overlooks, but are crucial for a proper balancing test, namely the lived reality of Muslim women that are impacted by religious dress prohibitions. Various empirical studies have illustrated that there are socio-economical and psychological effects related to religious dress prohibitions, and that the impact of such prohibitions goes beyond the freedom to manifest one's religion. In this light, considering the applicant's lived reality, allows to safeguard fundamental rights and freedoms in a more holistic manner.

N. El Yattouti
Law Faculty, University of Antwerp, Antwerp, Belgium
e-mail: naoual.elyattouti@uantwerpen.be

B. Nurkić (✉)
Faculty of Law, University of Tuzla, Tuzla, Bosnia and Herzegovina
e-mail: bnurkic@bih.net.ba

F. Macioce et al. (eds.), *Feminist Legal and Political Practices*, Gender Perspectives in Law 6, https://doi.org/10.1007/978-3-032-02856-3_8

1 Introduction

The headscarf worn by a large number of Muslim women, regularly sparks ongoing debates in multiple European countries about the increasing presence of religion in public spaces and how religious diversity is managed. Restrictions of religious symbols or dresses can be found in numerous European countries in many different areas such as employment or education, and in various forms. While some European States have not introduced restrictions on religious dress,[1] some have restrictions applicable in select areas. Take for example Bosnia and Herzegovina, Denmark, Finland, the Netherlands and Norway that prohibit religious dress only for certain State functions such as the police, military officers and the judiciary.[2] On the other hand, France and Belgium are known to have introduced the most stringent restrictions on religious symbols, such as blanket bans on full-face veils in public spaces and prohibitions on religious dress for teachers and students in public schools, with an increasing number of prohibitions in public and private employment.[3] These restrictions have led to many legal disputes, including before the European Courts. Although the vast majority of European countries has not introduced religious dress prohibitions, the European Court of Human Rights (ECtHR) and the European Court of Justice (CJEU) have repeatedly allowed employers and states a wide margin to introduce restrictions to the wearing of religious symbols.

This chapter seeks to present a critical analysis of prohibitions on the headscarf, and the jurisprudence surrounding it, focusing on the ECtHR. There is a vast amount of literature on the topic, with many criticizing the Court's rulings. This chapter seeks to contribute to the existing literature by exploring how the Court considers and engages with the argumentation put forth by Muslim women as applicants.

In this light, it will explore if and how the cases on the headscarf may be treated differently compared to other religious symbols or depending on the applicant's identity.[4] Given that the headscarf debate is not only gendered, but also oftentimes involves women from vulnerable ethnic or socio-economic groups, intersectional sensitivity is necessary to accurately measure the proportionality of prohibitions. Continuing, this contribution will shed light on the arguments the Court misses. In its jurisprudence so far, the Court does not seem to consider the concrete impact of the prohibitions on visible Muslim women beyond their religious freedom. By not receiving adequate protection of their religious rights, visible Muslim women are increasingly being excluded from many areas of social life in some European

---

[1] Countries such as Greece, Cyprus, Croatia, Poland and Portugal do not have any legislation prohibiting the wearing of religious symbols in public or private employment. Also, Armenia, Azerbaijan, Belarus, Estonia, Georgia, Hungary, Iceland, Ireland, Latvia, Lithuania, Malta, Moldova, Montenegro, North Macedonia, Romania, Serbia, Spain, Sweden, Turkey, Ukraine, and the United Kingdom do not stipulate headscarf or full-face veil bans. There are States such as Bulgaria, Slovenia, Switzerland (some cantons), and Denmark that prohibit full-face veils, while allowing headscarves. On these headscarf regulations see: Alibašić and Akgonul (2024).

[2] Alibašić and Akgonul (2024).

[3] Howard (2017); Hutten and Mustafa (2022), pp. 7–8.

[4] See Castillo-Ortiz, Ali and Samanta (2019).

countries, inadvertently limiting their participation in society, which may possibly perpetuate oppressive cultural or gender norms. These effects deserve attention and must be adequately weighed in any proportionality test relating to religious rights.

The first part of the chapter aims to offer a rough overview of the basic concepts, and to refer to literature for the reader who wishes to expand their knowledge. The second part analyzes some of the ECtHR's jurisprudence regarding cases on the headscarf and other religious dress, focusing on the arguments that are convincing to the Courts, and to the way the viewpoints of the applicants are considered. The third and final part focuses on the overlooked aspects, such as the social and psychological impact on some visible Muslim women, the potential overspill of these prohibitions on other fundamental rights, and how this may or should affect the proportionality test.

2 Setting the Scene: The Headscarf and Religious Freedom

2.1 The Role of Islamophobic and Orientalist Discourse

Among many others, Amnesty International reported in 2022 how Islamophobia in Europe is presented in various aspects, among which are the headscarf and full-face veil prohibitions.[5] With a reported increase of Islamophobia in Europe in recent years, it should not surprise that discussions on the acceptability of and tolerance towards Islamic religious manifestations continue to stir.[6] An important part of this discussion surrounds the visibility of religious symbols. With compulsory dress codes and prohibitions dress in employment, education and public spaces on the headscarf and full-face veil, various European States interfere with many women and girls' fundamental rights to freedom of expression and freedom to manifest their religion or belief, and arguably their bodily autonomy.[7]

While prohibitions on religious dress are usually formed in a neutral manner, they often target the headscarf.[8] In this light, a few words on Orientalism and the history of 'unveiling' might be relevant. The concept of *Orientalism*, coined by Palestinian-American intellectual and activist Edward Said refers to the ways the West has come to understand and represent 'the Orient' and people from 'the Orient'.[9] Orientalist writings and ideologies actively shape the world they describe,

---

[5] Amnesty International (2022); Bayrakli and Hafez (2024); European Union (2024).

[6] Howard (2017); Howard (2020).

[7] Velthuis, Verkuyten, Noll and Smeekes (2022); Howard (2017).

[8] Ghumman and Ryan (2013).

[9] Said (1978).

and perpetuate views of people from 'the Orient' as inferior, subservient, and in need of saving, to justify Western colonialism and imperialism, and contemporary foreign and domestic policies.[10] Some authors such as Ahmed, Fanon and Abu-Lughod have described the practice of unveiling Muslim women under colonial rule as a method of subordination and domination. By portraying the collective of Muslim women as oppressed and in need of saving, the rhetoric of colonialism was rendered morally justifiable.[11] These ideas can still be found in contemporary discussions on the headscarf.[12]

It is undeniable that there have been and still are many issues surrounding national politics on the headscarf. As illustrated by the current protests and acts of defiance in Iran against the compulsory wearing of the headscarf, the fundamental rights and bodily autonomy of women are far from safeguarded.[13] It is not surprising that the image of 'the Muslim woman in need of saving' remains active, as currently there are still far too many women that are left without a choice. This is not only the case on the level of the nation-state's oppressive measures, but also on an individual and community level.[14] Think of girls and women who are forced to wear the headscarf by family members, or who would be ostracized from their communities if they would unveil. Yet the greatest pitfall in these discussions is the usage of the argument of protecting women's rights *against* women's *own* will to wear the headscarf. When the same weight is not given to wearing or not wearing the headscarf, and the woman's own arguments are ignored, women's fundamental rights and freedoms, including their autonomy, are failed. To link back to the colonial roots of the issue, France used to instrumentalize feminist ideas of freedom and gender equality to coerce the colonised Algerian women to unveil. French feminist groups lead campaigns to aid this project and, 'N'êtes-vous donc pas jolie? Dévoilez-vous!', or translated 'So are you not beautiful? Unveil yourselves!', was to be read on colonialist propaganda posters spread in Algeria.[15] While there seems to be more nuance added to the debates, to present day the sentiment that Muslim women wearing the headscarf should unveil themselves in order to be free still exists. It prompts the question, should it not be up to the women involved to decide the conditions to their freedom?

2.2 *Religious Freedom and the Convention*

The right to freedom of private thought, conscience, and religion is enshrined in Article 9 of the Convention. Classically the right to religious freedom is divided in two categories: the *forum internum,* or the actual belief, and the *forum externum,* the

[10] Hibri (2023).

[11] Ahmed (1992), p. 151; Haq (2022); Fanon (1965), pp. 38–39. Abu-Lughod (2002).

[12] Kılıç, Saharso and Sauer (2008).

[13] Ali and Kayyal (2023); Qazi Zada and Qazi Zada (2024).

[14] Abu-Lughod (2002).

[15] Bouattia (2019).

manifestations of the belief such as dietary rules or the wearing of religious symbols or dress.[16] Some religious signs and clothing are generally accepted by the Court as falling within the scope of Article 9, such as the headscarf or the turban.[17] Whereas the *forum internum* enjoys absolute protection under Article 9 (1), the *forum externum* can be subjected to limitations.[18] These limitations must be prescribed by law, have a legitimate aim, and be considered proportionate and necessary in a democratic society.

In the balancing exercise of Article 9, the margin of appreciation (MoA) has come to play a crucial role.[19] The MoA is based on the idea that each society is entitled to a certain degree of flexibility when it comes to resolving inherent conflicts between individual rights and national interests or when navigating different moral beliefs.[20] When ruling on the right to freedom of religion the ECtHR is known to apply a wide MoA.[21] In the case of *Kokkinakis* the ECtHR emphasises that with regard to Article 9 '[...] a certain MoA is to be left to the Contracting States in assessing the existence and extent of the necessity of an interference.'[22] A judiciously applied MoA can be both justified and welcomed, as it recognises that domestic courts may possess a better understanding of the nuanced aspects of a particular dispute.[23] However, criticism has been directed at the ECtHR for its application of the MoA in cases involving religious neutrality.[24] A display of restraint by the ECtHR has been noted in these cases that does not correspond to a measured MoA, but is more akin to an absolute judicial retreat.[25]

---

[16] Howard (2017), p. 6.

[17] For more on what is considered as a religious manifestation: El Yattouti (2024).

[18] Griffiths (2016).

[19] Cumper and Lewis (2018); also, for example: *Karhuvaara and Iltalehti v. Finland,* ECtHR, App. No. 53678/00, Judgement 16 February 2005, para. 42; *Palomo Sánchez and Others v. Spain*, ECtHR, App. Nos. 28,955/06, 28,957/06, 28,959/06, and 28,964/06, Judgement 12 September 2011, para. 62.

[20] Benvenisti (1998); Velaers and Foblets (CitationRef CitationID="CR65">2019</CitationRef>), pp. 762–763.

[21] Monica Lugato (2013); Berry (2019).

[22] *Kokkinakis v. Greece*, ECtHR, App. No. 14307/88, Judgement 25 May 1993, para. 47.

[23] Hunter-Henin (2022).

[24] Both the ECtHR and the CJEU have been criticised for the way they have dealt with cases concerning religious neutrality, often described as an attitude of deference: Jolly (2024), Masmaliyeva (2020); Hunter-Henin (2022); Benvenisti (1998). While the MoA is typically associated with the ECtHR, the CJEU has granted a wide MoA to a public employer in its most recent religious freedom case of *OP v. Commune d'Ans.*

[25] Hunter-Henin (2022).

2.3 An Unneutral Neutrality?

Religious secularism or neutrality is an argument that is usually invoked in cases surrounding the headscarf. Initially, the idea behind secularism is the protection of religious freedom and equal treatment for all. In this regard, it is important to point out the distinction between inclusive and exclusive neutrality. Inclusive neutrality seeks to ensure equal treatment by avoiding discriminatory acts, thus in essence allowing for the wearing of religious symbols and only scrutinising behaviour. Examples of States that adhere to an inclusive form of neutrality are the United Kingdom, the Netherlands and Germany.[26] Exclusive neutrality on the other hand, pursues a form of equality that addresses impressions and perceptions beyond acts and their consequences. It seeks to eliminate any appearance of bias, including religious symbols.[27] Examples of States that adhere to an exclusive form of neutrality are Belgium, and France.[28] Specifically France is an interesting example with its strict unique understanding of State secularism, known as *laïcité,* that has led to many far-reaching prohibitions on religious manifestations.[29]

According to some, cases about religious symbols reflect and reinforce certain assumptions about religion and secularism in Europe.[30] Many authors have analysed the case law of the ECtHR regarding religious dress worn by Muslim women and have pointed out issues with the interpretation of religious neutrality and secularism, which have been found to negatively depict Islam and its customs. Medda-Windischer named the type of secularism often accepted by the ECtHR an 'intolerant secularism' or 'enlightenment fundamentalism', in the way it prohibits the wearing of religious symbols.[31] Evolvi and Gatti argued a notion of Christian secularism is more fitting, because the ECtHR appears to only apply 'intolerant secularism' or 'enlightenment fundamentalism' to non-Christian symbols.[32] To illustrate, cases involving Islam often consider Muslim dress as a threat to European identities while the Christian crucifix was considered as a mark of national tradition and a passive symbol in the *Lautsi* case.[33] Other authors such as Smet and Hunter-Henin pointed out how the ECtHR assumes an attitude of deference when it comes to religious neutrality, by consistently granting a wide MoA to States that invoke the argument.[34] This leads to the pattern that when cases concern States that abide by an exclusive form of religious neutrality, such as France, the applicant seeking to wear religious

---

26 Hennette-Vauchez (2020).

27 Smet (2020).

28 Hennette-Vauchez (2020).

29 Hennette-Vauchez (2017).

30 Hutten Mustafa (2022).

31 Medda-Windischer (2017).

32 Evolvi and Gatti (2021).

33 *Lautsi v. Italy*, ECtHR, App. No. 30814/06, Judgement 3 November 2009.

34 Hunter-Henin (2022); Smet (2022).

dress is almost certain to lose their case.[35] The disparate impact of this interpretation of neutrality on certain religious groups, prompts the question if neutrality can always be considered neutral.

2.4 *Intersectionality and Intersectional Discrimination*

Although intersectionality has gained exponential popularity recently, protection against intersectional discrimination seems to remain limited.[36] There is a vast amount of literature that defines the concept of intersectionality and intersectional discrimination.[37] We speak of intersectional discrimination when an individual or group is discriminated against based on criteria that are so closely related that they create a unique and new form of discrimination. The protected criteria influence each other and simultaneously interact with existing power relations within a given socioeconomic context.[38] Intersectionality was popularized by Crenshaw's application of the concept to black women who tried to challenge discrimination in the United States but kept running into legal walls.[39] Sometimes courts recognized the plaintiff's difference from the "dominant norm" within the discriminated category to override the black woman's appeal. In other cases, the court looked over the plaintiff's experience of discrimination precisely because it was perceived to be different from other members of the discriminated category.[40] In this way, the plaintiff's intersectional identity was ignored or used as a shield, depending on the circumstances of the case.

While the concept of intersectionality has been around for decades, there are still many unclarities regarding the concrete workings and consequences of intersectional discrimination in legal judgements. There is a vast amount of literature available with theories on intersectional methodology and discrimination law, and criticisms towards the current lack of intersectional approaches in the case law of the ECtHR and the CJEU.[41] While this contribution will not delve into the ins and outs of intersectional discrimination, it is a highly relevant topic for the case of religious discrimination of Muslim women. Muslim women in the Western European context often find themselves at the intersection of discrimination based on gender, religion, ethnicity, class and age,[42] in various combinations. Intersectional analyses

---

[35] Evolvi and Gatti (2021).

[36] Solanke (2016).

[37] Atrey (2019).

[38] Ajele and McGill (2020); Solanke (2011).

[39] Crenshaw (1991).

[40] Skeet (2019).

[41] Howard (2024).

[42] When it comes to minors being prohibited from wearing religious signs, usually in educational contexts.

can help to better understand the complex ways in which Muslim women experience the structural curtailment of their human rights, which in turn *should* influence proportionality analyses.[43]

3 The ECtHR and Muslim Women as Applicants

Over the past two decades, numerous cases related to religious dress have been brought before the ECtHR, most of which involve female Muslim applicants challenging restrictions on wearing the headscarf.[44] It is important to note that to date, only in one of those cases a violation of religious freedom was found.[45] This is a remarkably low success rate, especially in comparison to cases on religious dress where the applicants are non-Muslim women or Muslim men.[46] However, not only the outcomes of the cases are relevant, but also are the argumentations that lead to the Court's conclusion. In what follows, a few cases will be discussed, with a focus on what arguments were decisive for the Courts, and how much weight was given to the arguments of the applicants. For this contribution, the main analysis will be limited to the cases of *Dahlab v. Switzerland, Leyla Şahin v. Turkey*, and *Eweida and others v. the UK*, and will incorporate references to additional jurisprudence to foster a more comprehensive understanding, and to allow comparison.

In the ECtHR's first case involving the headscarf, *Dahlab v. Switzerland,* a Muslim elementary schoolteacher was prohibited from wearing a headscarf while teaching.[47] Invoking the MoA doctrine, the Court concluded that the school's dress code policy was necessary and proportionate, rejecting her claim of a violation of Article 9. The Court acknowledged the challenges in assessing the impact of a 'powerful external symbol' such as a headscarf on the religious freedom of very young children. However, it expressed concerns about its potential proselytising effect, particularly considering the teacher's role as a representative of the State. Additionally, the Court found that the headscarf 'appear[ed] to be imposed on women by a precept which is laid down in the Koran and which, as the Federal Court noted, is hard to square with the principle of gender equality.' It was 'therefore […] difficult to reconcile the wearing of an Islamic headscarf with the message of tolerance, respect for others and, above all, equality and non-discrimination that all teachers in a democratic society must convey to their pupils.'[48]

The Court found that depending on the age of the pupils and the hierarchical nature of the teacher-student relationship, pupils can be particularly receptive to

[43] Costello and Ahmed (2023).

[44] More than two thirds of the cases.

[45] *Lachiri v. Belgium*, ECtHR, App. No. 3413/09, Judgement 18 September 2018.

[46] Evolvi and Gatti (2021).

[47] *Dahlab v. Switzerland*, ECtHR, App. No. 42393/98, Judgement 15 February 2001.

[48] *Dahlab v. Switzerland*, para. 1 under 'The Law'.

outward symbols, which can justify the expectation that teachers, as representatives of the State, must embody the State's neutrality.[49] Dahlab argued that her wearing of the headscarf had gone unnoticed for 4 years and had never caused any disturbance within the school, which proved that the religious beliefs of others had been respected. Further, she had always shown tolerance towards her students, who encompassed a wide range of nationalities and were therefore particularly accustomed to diversity and tolerance.[50] This, however, seemed to be of no significance to the Court's reasoning. The young age of the students and their vulnerability due to the hierarchical nature of the student-teacher relationship, justified the restriction on outward religious symbols without necessitating empirical evidence that there were students influenced or negatively impacted by the religious symbol. This reasoning, however, would mean that schools and teachers displaying outward religious symbols, by default threaten the religious freedom of (young) students.

The opposite was ruled in the case of *Lautsi v. Italy*, where it was found that crucifixes in secondary school classrooms do not violate the rights to education and religious freedom of the students and their parents.[51] To establish that there was no indoctrination, the Court held that the greater visibility of the crucifix was offset by three factors. First, the presence of crucifixes was not associated with compulsory teaching about Christianity. Second, there was no evidence of intolerance towards other religions or those without any religion. Third, the children's parents could influence and educate them in the way of their own convictions.[52] According to Dahlab's arguments the same should be believed about her headscarf, as it did not interfere with her teaching and there had not been any disturbances, however, this 'indoctrination test', was not applied or developed in the case of Dahlab, and even further, her arguments were not given any weight in the balancing test. This prompts the question whether young students' religious rights are only infringed upon by non-Christian symbols. It may also be problematic to generalise the needs of young students. There might also be minoritized students that could benefit from seeing their religion, or another minoritized religion, represented by their teacher. If anything, it normalizes the presence of minoritized religions and diversity in important layers of society at a young age, which should be considered in the proportionality test.[53] Evidently, in these cases teachers should always refrain from any acts that could be considered proselytising.

Being the first of its kind in a series of decisions concerning the headscarf, *Dahlab* has directly influenced the ECtHR's following cases,[54] such as the case of *Leyla Şahin v. Turkey*. In this case a medical student at Istanbul University faced restrictions on taking certain courses and exams due to her wearing of a headscarf,

---

[49] *Dahlab v. Switzerland*, para. 1 under 'The Law'.

[50] *Dahlab v. Switzerland.*

[51] *Lautsi v. Italy* App No 30814/06 (ECtHR, 3 November 2009).

[52] *Lautsi v. Italy*, para. 78.

[53] Spiro (1989).

[54] For an overview see: Witte and Pin (2021); Skeet (2019).

which violated State regulations.[55] In response to disciplinary measures taken by the university, she filed an Article 9 claim. The Court sided with Turkey, granting a wide MoA to the country's constitutional and cultural values concerning gender equality and State secularism, deeming the headscarf worn by the student a potent symbol capable of infringing on the rights and freedoms of fellow students. This case has faced substantial criticism from scholars, who argued that it reflects insufficient scrutiny of the government's arguments, lacks proportionality, extends a questionably wide MoA and perpetuates harmful ideas by endorsing the government's interpretation of the headscarf as a symbol of political, extremist Islam, and women's subjugation which may be considered Orientalist.[56] These ideas are particularly evident when the Court reiterated its reasoning from the case of *Dahlab*, suggesting that the headscarf is 'imposed on women by a religious precept (…) hard to reconcile with the principle of gender equality,' and that it 'might have some kind of proselytising effect.'[57] In absence of supporting evidence, however, this position seems to be a product of fear rather than judgement.[58]

In Judge Tulkens dissenting opinion on the case, she pointed out numerous flaws in the judgment, such as the striking lack of attention paid to the applicant's autonomy, and the Court's reasonings surrounding the headscarf stating, 'wearing the headscarf has no single meaning; it is a practice that is engaged in for a variety of reasons. It does not necessarily symbolise the submission of women to men and there are those who maintain that, in certain cases, it can even be a means of emancipating women. What is lacking in this debate is the opinion of women, both those who wear the headscarf and those who choose not to.'[59] While it cannot be denied that there are many women who are made to wear the headscarf, this can in no way justify that women who choose to wear the headscarf and even legally fight for this right, are not heard or believed. Women protesting for the right to unveil in Iran, do not delegitimize the protests in France that fight for the right to wear the veil. As Tulkens argues, both should be heard, both should have their fundamental rights and freedoms supported and safeguarded, and one does not invalidate the other.

The case of *Eweida et al. v. the United Kingdom* is not a 'headscarf case', but a case where the applicants are Christian women, which illustrates the contrast in approach. It addresses four combined complaints concerning religious freedom at work, two of which are on religious dress. Eweida, a check-in assistant for British Airways, and Chaplin, a nurse, faced restrictions on wearing the crucifix necklace

---

[55] *Leyla Şahin v. Turkey*, ECtHR, App. No. 44774/98, Judgement 10 November 2005. Some other cases on students being prohibited to wear religious symbols: *Köse and Others v. Turkey*, ECtHR, App. No. 26625/02, Judgement 24 January 2006; Karaduman v. Turkey, ECtHR, App. No. 16278/90, Judgement 3 April 2007; *Dogru v. France*, ECtHR, App. No. 27058/05, Judgement 4 December 2008.

[56] Among many others: Gibson (2007); Bleiberg (2005); Marshall (2006).

[57] *Leyla Şahin v. Turkey*, ECtHR, App. No. 44774/98, Judgement 10 November 2005, para. 111.

[58] Gibson (2007).

[59] *Leyla Şahin v. Turkey*, ECtHR, App. No. 44774/98, Judgement 10 November 2005. Dissenting Opinion of Judge Tulkens, paras. 11–12.

by their employers.[60] When deciding whether these were manifestations of religion the Court stated about Eweida, 'It was not disputed in the proceedings before the domestic tribunals and this Court that Ms. Eweida's insistence on wearing a cross visibly at work was motivated by her desire to bear witness to her Christian faith.',[61] and about Mrs. Chaplin that '[her] determination to wear the cross and chain at work was a manifestation of her religious belief (...).'[62] Interestingly, the wording of the Court is quite different from the wording in the two previous cases regarding the headscarf. To repeat, in the case of *Dahlab* the Court stated: '[the headscarf] appears to be imposed on women by a precept which is laid down in the Koran (…).'[63] In the case of *Şahin* the Court argued that, 'The applicant said that, by wearing the headscarf, she was obeying a religious precept and thereby manifesting her desire to comply strictly with the duties imposed by the Islamic faith', and further that, 'it must be borne in mind the impact which wearing such a symbol, which is presented or perceived as a compulsory religious duty (…).'[64] On the contrary, in the case of *Eweida* the emphasis was put on the choice of the applicants which is reflected in the wordings used by the Court such as 'her desire to bear witness', 'her determination', 'her' Christian faith—as opposed to 'the' Christian faith.[65] This difference is quite significant. In the case of *Eweida,* the religious beliefs are presented in a 'specificised' and 'individualised' manner, through the use of possessive pronouns. This presentation underlines the personal and specific nature of the beliefs. In *Dahlab's* and *Şahin's* cases on the other hand, the religious belief remains 'genericised', meaning the belief is presented in a more general manner without specific details or personalisation. This creates further distance and detachment from the belief, treating it as a more abstract and foreign concept. This difference in presentation then has a discursive impact on the construction of identity and the concept of 'Otherness'.[66] To combat the danger of genericizing religious practices, the applicant's viewpoints should be given priority over the State's, the Court's or the 'general public's' opinions on the religious practice at hand.[67]

These three cases point out a difference in approach of the ECtHR when it comes to Muslim women when compared to Christian women. However, these are not

[60] *Eweida and Others v. United Kingdom*, ECtHR, App. Nos. 48,420/10, 59,842/10, 51,671/10, and 36,516/10, Judgement 15 January 2013, paras. 10–11, 13, 20. The two other cases concerned two Christians who refused to provide services to same-sex couples for religious reasons. These cases will not be discussed further in this contribution.

[61] *Eweida and Others v. United Kingdom*, ECtHR, App. Nos. 48,420/10, 59,842/10, 51,671/10, and 36,516/10, Judgement 15 January 2013, para. 89.

[62] Ibid, para. 97.

[63] *Dahlab v. Switzerland*, ECtHR, App. No. 42393/98, Judgement 15 February 2001. Note also that the Federal Court's interpretation of the headscarf is given more weight than the lived experience of Dahlab.

[64] *Leyla Şahin v. Turkey*, ECtHR, App. No. 44774/98, Judgement 10 November 2005, para. 78, 115.

[65] Peroni (2014).

[66] Benfquih (2020).

[67] El Yattouti (2024).

isolated cases. An elaborate analysis conducted by Evolvi and Gatti revealed that the ECtHR discourses are largely consistent when it comes to the Muslim headscarf.[68] Another example is the case of *Köse v. Turkey*, concerning students wishing to wear the headscarf in a Turkish school. In this case the Court referred to *Şahin* and the case law of Turkish courts, according to which, '[A]llowing pupils to wear the Islamic headscarf is incompatible with the principle of secularism since the headscarf is in the process of becoming the symbol of a vision that is contrary to women's freedom and the fundamental principles.'[69] In another case, *Kurtulmuş v. Turkey*, regarding a university professor seeking to wear the headscarf, the ECtHR referred to *Dahlab* and ruled against the applicant to protect religious neutrality and secularism.[70] Evolvi and Gatti draw attention to how comparisons between discourses about Christian and Muslim symbols show how the ECtHR seems to consider Islam as the 'Other' to European culture. While the Muslim veil is portrayed in a monolithic way, and is attributed a set of meanings, the Christian cross is allowed a nuanced set of meanings, and is not deemed as inherently incompatible with secularism.[71] This way, applicants who wear the headscarf are hardly subjects of the narratives, and their needs and motivations are overlooked to prioritise an alleged protection of society and national identities.[72] In contrast, the applicants seeking to wear the crucifix were heard when they explained their reasons and their needs.

The same applies to the cases involving religious symbols worn by Muslim men.[73] In the case of *Hamidović v. Bosnia & Herzegovina* for example, in which a Muslim man refused to remove his skullcap while at a tribunal, there is no mention of gender or public order. The Court stated it saw, '(…) no reason to doubt that the applicant's act was inspired by his sincere religious belief that he must wear a skullcap at all times, without any hidden agenda to make a mockery of the trial, incite others to reject secular and democratic values or cause a disturbance.'[74] The Court continued that the applicant had a respectful attitude and was willing to comply, while the female Muslim applicants' attitudes and behaviours were not considered in the previous cases. The religious viewpoints of Dahlab or Şahin were not fully acknowledged by the Court either, while the beliefs of Hamidović were described as 'importan[t] to an individual' and 'sincere'.[75] The way the Court handled *Hamidović* was comparable to the case of *Eweida*, and seemed to be inspired by a

---

[68] Evolvi and Gatti (2021).

[69] *Köse and Others v. Turkey*, ECtHR, App. No. 26625/02, Judgement 24 January 2006.

[70] *Kurtulmuş v. Turkey*, ECtHR, App. No. 65500/01, Judgement 24 January 2006; Skeet (2019).

[71] *Lautsi v. Italy*, ECtHR, App. No. 30814/06, Judgement 3 November 2009.

[72] Evolvi and Gatti (2021).

[73] *Arslan and Others v. Turkey*, ECtHR, App. No. 41135/98, Judgement 23 February 2010; *Hamidović v. Bosnia and Herzegovina*, ECtHR, App. No. 57792/15, Judgement 5 December 2017.

[74] *Hamidović v. Bosnia and Herzegovina*, ECtHR, App. No. 57792/15, Judgement 5 December 2017.

[75] *Hamidović v. Bosnia and Herzegovina*.

concern for religious pluralism.[76] This illustrates that Muslim women may be granted less agency to determine the meanings of their religious attire, not only compared to non-Muslim women, but also compared to Muslim men, which highlights the importance of applying an intersectional approach when analysing the case law of the ECtHR. In the Court's precedents at the intersection of gender and religion, it has not yet engaged with the gender dimension of the claims of female religious applicants.[77] However, scholarly analysis has shown that in the ECtHR's case law under Article 9, neither the religion nor the gender of the applicant serves as an outcome predictor. Yet when these factors are combined, it leads to conclusions that strongly hint towards intersectional discrimination.[78] While the Court does not explicitly tackle the intersection of gender and religion, it arguably plays a role in the assessment of Muslim women's cases.

4 Overlooking the Applicant's Lived Experience: A Minor Detail?

It has been two decades, yet Evans's critique remains relevant, as she argued that the ECtHR fell into 'the error of refusing to engage with the reality of Muslim women's lives.' She further highlighted how these judgments reflect two contradictory stereotypes of Muslim women prevalent in political discourse. The first portrays Muslim women as victims—oppressed by a gendered religion, requiring protection from abusive male relatives, and passive in the face of male-dominated cultural norms. The second depicts them as aggressors—fundamentalists imposing their values on unwilling and vulnerable others.[79] It leaves to wonder about the lived experiences of the women who seek to wear the headscarf, and how headscarf prohibitions affect them in their daily lives. These are aspects that do not receive the appropriate attention in the ECtHR's proportionality test. Another aspect that deserves more attention is the potential spillover effect that the headscarf prohibitions have on other (fundamental) rights besides the right to religious freedom.

---

[76] Evolvi and Gatti (2021); *Hamidović v. Bosnia and Herzegovina*, ECtHR, App. No. 57792/15, Judgement 5 December 2017.

[77] Brems (2021).

[78] *Mikyas and Others v. Belgium*, ECtHR, App. No. 50681/20, Judgement 9 April 2024. Third Party Intervention by the Human Rights Centre at Ghent University and the Equality Law Clinic at Université Libre de Bruxelles.

[79] Evans (2006), pp. 52, 66, 67.

4.1 Psychological Impact and Social Exclusion

It seems that in the ECtHR's case law, empirical studies on the concrete impacts of headscarf restrictions are rarely consulted, focusing exclusively on the issue through a legal lense.[80] This contribution, however, argues that measuring and including the concrete outcomes produced by legal decisions is crucial, especially in the context of religious dress prohibitions, given the significant impact on the lives of many Muslim women and girls.[81] Including the concrete impact of religious dress prohibitions on the lives of Muslim women, offers a more holistic analysis of legal measures and decisions. Considering how Muslim women wearing the headscarf respond to these regulations, and how it impacts their social positions in society, can and should serve as valuable input for weighing the proportionality of legal measures. Another argument it may serve, is that religious dress prohibitions' outcomes can go beyond religious rights in some cases, and may also impact the rights to education, freedom of expression, labour rights, and the right to private life.

This contribution will examine the data found in empirical research on Muslim women's response to headscarf and full-face veil prohibitions in three countries that are reported to have strict prohibitions: France, Belgium and Turkey.[82] *The Open Society Justice Initiative* conducted a survey in 2013 that aimed to examine Muslim women's response regarding France's ban the full-face veil in public. The survey aimed to measure whether the respondents would continue wearing a full-face veil or take it off in response to the ban. According to the survey, eight participants removed their full-face veil, while 27 continued to wear it despite the ban. One respondent started wearing the niqab after the law was passed in December 2010, and three others adopted it following the law's enforcement.[83] They stated that their decision to keep wearing the niqab stems from a belief that removing it would mean renouncing their faith or giving up an integral part of their religious identity.[84] A similar survey was conducted in Turkey following the implementation of a headscarf ban for women in educational institutions and in public employment in 1989. The survey indicated that the largest percentage of women in the sample did not unveil after facing the ban (43%). The second largest group in the sample took off their headscarves in places where the ban was enforced (33.7%). Some of them started wearing a wig or hat to go around the ban (19%), and just a small minority of them unveiled completely (1.2%). Women who decided to unveil did so for vari-

---

[80] See for example Hennette-Vauchez (2020). This article argues that "colorblindness might have entrenched rather than corrected racial inequality in the United States, some versions of the contemporary elevation of 'religious neutrality' in Europe may be producing similarly inegalitarian outcomes, p. 593.

[81] See Freedman (2007).

[82] While focal point of this contribution is the headscarf and not the full-face veil, nonetheless, it is an interesting case study with empirical research available. For example: Bouteldja (2013).

[83] Bouteldja (2013), p. 2.

[84] Bouteldja (2013).

ous reasons, which were mentioned as the primary motivations for their decision, namely completing their education (73%); keeping their jobs (22.5%); because of their prospects (19.7%); and because of an academic career (11.1%).[85] In Belgium, research on the impact of the headscarf ban on adolescent Muslim girls in Flanders, emphasized the effects on psychological well-being and professional development. The study revealed that 54.3% of the surveyed girls considered the headscarf essential to their identity development, while 33.3% viewed it as an integral part of their identity. The bans lead to negative emotions: 97.1% feel insecure without their headscarf, and 57% experience feelings of humiliation. This daily confrontation contributes to a negative state of mind for 15.2% of the girls, affecting their school experience. On a professional level, 84.8% of students considered their choice of higher education based on the ability to wear a headscarf during classes and internships. Additionally, 41% feel demotivated to attend school because of the ban. The study concluded that the headscarf ban in schools negatively impacts the identity development and psychological well-being of adolescent Muslim girls, with potential consequences for their professional futures.[86]

Although these studies covered only their own national context, they indicate that for many Muslim women and girls wearing the headscarf, the prohibitions may negatively affect their emotional well-being and influences their career and education choices or opportunities. It must be recognized, however, that it is a complex, sensitive debate, and the data might possibly leave blind spots. It might be difficult to reach the women who do not wear the headscarf out of free will, or perhaps they do not always feel comfortable participating in such studies, or for coming out as 'not wanting to wear it', for many different reasons. Therefore, it is difficult to assess whether for some women and girls, these prohibitions have had any emancipating effect, or contrarily, if these prohibitions further pushed them into social isolation. This contribution will focus on the empirical evidence at hand, but acknowledges the knowledge gap, and aims to be mindful of potential blind spots in its assessment.

Shahzad and Fatima argue that women may decide to wear the headscarf due to personal reasons influenced by cultural and traditional factors, closely tied to multiple aspects of one's identity, including gender, race, and ethnicity.[87] The decision to either resist or comply with prohibitions thus has significant implications not only in terms of education, employment, social integration, and other opportunities, but also for one's physical and mental well-being. The severity of the impact may vary based on the type of religious dress. Wearing the full-face veil for example, can result in total exclusion from public life, as seen in France and Belgium. Women who refused to take off their full-face veils after the ban came into effect in France reported engaging in fewer outdoor activities, including routine tasks like taking their children to school, going on family outings, shopping, or visiting the post

[85] Guveli (2011), pp. 177–178.

[86] Kawtar Bakir (2018).

[87] Shahzad and Fatima (2024), p. 2.

office.[88] Many respondents described their post-ban experience as akin to 'living in a jail'.[89] Even those who removed their full-face veils felt restricted in their mobility, expressing discomfort in public spaces without them. Furthermore, most respondents experienced reduced social interaction after the ban, with many facing verbal abuse, and some even encountering physical violence.[90]

While the wearing of the headscarf does not result in total exclusion, it can lead to restricted access to education, employment, sports, and other areas, depending on a State's specific regulations. A Stanford survey provides compelling data on the impact of the 2004 French law banning religious symbols in primary and secondary public schools.[91] The findings reveal that Muslim students are more likely to drop out of secondary education compared to their non-Muslim peers. Additionally, Muslim students tend to take longer to complete their secondary education. One other particularly noteworthy finding is that the veiling law has widened disparities between Muslims and non-Muslims. The employment gap has widened by over a third (from an initial gap of 10.9%), and the gap in labour force participation has more than doubled (from an initial gap of 5.3%). Similarly, the gap in cohabitation with parents has increased by more than a third from the initial gap of 6.9%.[92] Moreover, the ban has reinforced the religious identities of young Muslim women and girls, who have been the most affected by these restrictions.[93] The intersectional discrimination faced by visible Muslim women in France, strengthened by religious dress prohibitions, is what Hopkins refers to as 'sexist Islamophobia'.[94] Eight out of ten women who wear the veil in France have reported experiencing acts of Islamophobia.[95] Examples include the exclusion of mothers from school trips because of their headscarves and the violent attempt to terminate a Muslim woman's pregnancy, highlighting the harsh realities in France's current socio-political landscape.[96] Due to prohibitions targeting Muslim women's religious dress, there are higher rates of unemployment and precarious unemployment for visible Muslim women compared to other groups of women, further increasing already existing labour market discrimination.[97]

The empirical study from Turkey showed similar results. In the area of education, women who continued to wear the headscarf were less educated and more

---

[88] 26 out of 35 of the respondents see Bouteldja (2013), p. 8.

[89] Bouteldja (2013), p. 8.

[90] 27 out of 35 of the respondents. See Bouteldja (2013), p. 9.

[91] Abdelgadir and Fouka (2020), p. 9.

[92] Abdelgadir and Fouka (2020), p. 10. About this topic also see Hopkins (2015), p. 158.

[93] Freedman (2007), pp. 42–43.

[94] Hopkins (2015), p. 156.

[95] Hajjat and Mohammed (2013), p. 27, according to Hopkins (2015), p. 156.

[96] See Hopkins (2015), pp. 160–161.

[97] Hopkins (2015), p. 161.

likely to drop out of school.[98] Regarding employment, veiled women have a smaller share in the labour market compared to unveiled women.[99] Corekcioglu found that female employment was higher in Islamist municipalities in Turkey than in secular ones after the repeal of the headscarf ban, countering the idea that only secular policies may empower women.[100] This again highlights the complexity of the debate, and the different factors that need to be taken into account. In some cases, secular policies will be empowering, in others, they will be disempowering. The same may be said about more liberal policies, or even anti-secular policies. This is why it is crucial for policymakers and courts to consider the voices and experiences of the affected women and girls, instead of relying on their own (perhaps ideologically influenced) conceptions on the matter. As Guveli argued, the headscarf bans in Turkey also played a role in excluding lower-class women from accessing resources and privileged positions, which proves that the intersection with economic class may also be relevant to the discussion.[101]

In conclusion, empirical research shows that many Muslim women and girls are unlikely to remove their headscarves in the face of religious dress bans, even at the cost of educational and employment opportunities, or certain aspects of social life. These prohibitions further increase existing forms of discrimination. Second, religious dress prohibitions not only infringe upon religious rights and expressions, but may also lead to social exclusion, and may have negative psychological effects. These factors should be considered in the proportionality test when assessing religious dress restrictions, in order to safeguard the fundamental rights and freedoms of an already highly stigmatized group.[102]

4.2 *Beyond Religious Rights: Potential Impact on Other Rights*

Based on the empirical studies that showed the far-reaching impacts of prohibitions, the question arises whether it suffices to scrutinise headscarf restrictions solely in the light of the right to religious freedom. So far, the ECtHR has regarded headscarf prohibitions solely as a violation of the right to religious freedom, however, one could argue that the headscarf could be considered as an integral part of many Muslim women's identities.[103] In this light, wearing a headscarf may be viewed as a

[98] For example, 63% of women who wear a wig or hat, instead of a headscarf, have a university education, and 52% of the unveiled women have a university education. At the same time, 40% of veiled women have a university education. In general, for the both observations, see Guveli (2011), pp. 180–181.

[99] 73% of unveiled women are active in the labour market and 55% of veiled women are active in the labour market. See Guveli (2011), p. 181.

[100] Corekcioglu (2021), p. 403.

[101] Guveli (2011), p. 184.

[102] Solanke (2016).

[103] See Davies (2024), p. 6; Idriss (2005), p. 294.

public manifestation of one's private identity. In the European context, where Muslims are a minority and often belong to marginalised ethnicities, the headscarf may allow women to express their private identities publicly, advocating for equality and other fundamental rights.[104] In that sense, in some cases the headscarf may represent Muslim women's agency in protecting and establishing their rights.[105] However, as mentioned prior, it is quite a sensitive and complex debate, with a great part of the discussion surrounding the meaning of the headscarf and why women choose to wear it. For example, many assume that wearing the headscarf is not a decision at all but is forced upon women and girls, while others believe it is a decision solely based on religion and is inherently oppressive. Yet, in this discussion too little attention is paid to the arguments of Muslim women themselves. Not taking away from the validity of the concerns surrounding gender oppression, the various other reasons for wearing religious dress cited by many Muslim women themselves should be considered in an equal manner. These reasons include but are not limited to, reasons of cultural identity, personal freedom in public, emancipation, and rebellion against Islamophobia and Western society's impositions.[106] Further, the resistance of Muslim women to comply with the prohibitions may affect their lives in a broader sense than their religious freedom, such as their right to education or employment, depending on the specificities of the prohibitions. Therefore, viewing the headscarf as solely a form of religious expression, and prohibitions thereof as only an infringement to religious freedom, might not fully encompass the complexities of the issue.

According to the established ECtHR's jurisprudence and the wide interpretation of the right to private life as protected by Article 8, extending its protection well beyond the private to the public sphere, the wearing of the headscarf could fall within its scope.[107] While some applicants have raised Article 8 violations, the Court has consistently addressed these cases solely through the lens of Article 9, arguing that there is no need to examine Article 8 separately, as the issues overlap.[108] However, the current approach may be insufficient, as it overlooks the complex meaning and significance of the headscarf for many women, which, as argued, cannot always be reduced to the mere following of religious precepts. Further, in the many cases where Muslim girls and women resist to comply with religious dress prohibitions, it leads to their *de facto* exclusion from full access or enjoyment of other rights relating to education and employment. Arguably, these considerations are highly relevant for the proportionality assessment of the ECtHR, where more weight should be granted to the actual lived experience of Muslim women. Especially considering the far-reaching impacts of prohibitions of religious dress.

104 Kulenović (2006), p. 717; Loxston and Jachens (2023), p. 318; Brown (2006), p. 428.

105 As Mizel argues "[t]he hijab constitutes one of the psychological and social needs, and it is a cultural expression that distinguishes between men and women in the Muslim society. It changes according to the changing social, cultural and economic conditions." Mizel (2019), p. 215.

106 See Bouteldja (2013); Guveli (2011).

107 Costello and Ahmed (2023), p. 104; Marshall (2008).

108 For example: *Leyla Şahin v. Turkey*, ECtHR, App. No. 44774/98, Judgement 10 November 2005.

Evaluating the headscarf beyond its religious meaning and including empirical research instead of restricting evaluation to the balancing of legal principles, are necessary steps towards a more holistic protection of fundamental rights and freedoms.

5 Conclusion

This chapter aimed to present a critical analysis of prohibitions of the headscarf and its impact on the affected women and girls, as well as the ECtHR jurisprudence surrounding it. It examined how the Court considers the arguments of Muslim women as applicants and found that remarkably little attention is given to their perspectives. In comparison to non-Muslim women and Muslim men who seek to wear religious dress, Muslim women's arguments are given the least weight. This was seen in cases like *Dahlab v. Switzerland* and *Leyla Şahin v. Turkey*, compared to cases in which the Court addressed Christian symbols, such as the crucifix in *Eweida et al. v. the United Kingdom*, or even to religious dress worn by Muslim men in the case of *Hamidović v. Bosnia Herzegovina*. In these cases, the ECtHR applied a more individualised and nuanced approach to religious dress, whereas the headscarf was seen as a broad imposition linked to gender inequality and religious subjugation. Most probably not unrelated, the success rate of headscarf cases was significantly lower than cases regarding other types of religious dress.[109]

Continuing, this contribution shed light on the perspective the Court consistently missed, namely that of the lived experiences of visible Muslim women. In its jurisprudence so far, the Court does not seem to consider the concrete impact of the prohibitions, that can go far beyond the applicant's religious freedom. Various empirical studies have indicated that for many Muslim women, the headscarf is not merely an expression of religious belief, but may also carry different meanings related to cultural identity, personal freedom, or resistance against Islamophobia. The ECtHR's reliance on the State's arguments, that are often influenced by ideology and stereotypes, has led to rulings that disregard the perceptions and lived experiences of the applicants. Further, studies have shown that because many Muslim women resist to comply with prohibitions, they are increasingly being excluded from many areas of social life, inadvertently limiting their participation in society, which can negatively affect their mental health, and which in some cases may perpetuate oppressive cultural or gender norms. These effects require attention and must be adequately weighed in any proportionality test relating to religious rights, especially considering the heightened vulnerability to intersectional discrimination that visibly Muslim women face.

[109] Excluding the cases on the full-face veil, which again has Muslim women as applicants.

References

Abdelgadir A, Fouka V (2020) Political secularism and Muslim integration in the West: assessing the effects of the French headscarf ban. Am Polit Sci Rev 114(3):707–723

Abu-Lughod L (2002) Do Muslim women really need saving? Anthropological reflections on cultural relativism and its others. Am Anthropol 104(3):783–790

Ahmed L (1992) Social and intellectual change and the discourse of the veil. In: Woman and gender in Islam: historical roots of a modern debate. Yale University Press, New Haven, pp 127–143

Ajele G, McGill J (2020) Intersectionality in law and legal contexts. LEAF's Femin Strateg Litigat Proj 4:1–80

Ali S, Kayyal M (2023) The impact of mandatory Hijab Laws on women's rights in Iran: A human rights perspective. Glob Campus Hum Rights J 7:22–39

Alibašić A, Akgonul S (2024) Yearbook of Muslims in Europe, vol 15. Brill, Leiden

Amnesty International (2022) Regional overview of Islamophobia in Europe

Atrey S (2019) Intersectional discrimination. Oxford University Press, Oxford

Bakir K (2018) The influence on adolescent Muslim girls as a result of the headscarf ban. Thesis, Vives Katholieke Hogeschool

Bayrakli E, Hafez F (2024) European Islamophobia report 2023. Leopold Weiss Institute, Istanbul

Benfquih Y (2020) Reasonable accommodation in education: An integrated human rights approach on the basis of the right to equality, inclusive education and freedom of religion. PhD Thesis, University of Antwerp

Benvenisti E (1998) Margin of appreciation, consensus, and universal standards. New York Univ J Int Law Polit 31(4):843–854

Berry SE (2019) Chapter 5: Avoiding scrutiny? The margin of appreciation and religious freedom. In: The European Court of Human Rights and the Freedom of Religion or Belief. Brill, Leiden, pp 103–127

Bleiberg B (2005) Unveiling the real issue: evaluating the European Court of Human Rights' decision to enforce the Turkish headscarf ban in Leyla Şahin v. Turkey. Cornell Law Rev 91:129–170

Bouattia M (2019) Du colonialisme à la laïcité: La France continue de faire la guerre aux musulmanes. https://www.middleeasteye.net/fr/opinion-fr/du-colonialisme-la-laicite-la-france-continue-de-faire-la-guerre-aux-femmes-musulmanes

Bouteldja N (2013) After the ban: The experiences of 35 women of the full-face veil in France. Open Society Foundations, New York

Brems E (2021) Hidden under headscarves? Women and religion in the case law of the European Court of Human Rights. Relig Hum Rights 16(2–3):173–200

Brown K (2006) Realising Muslim women's rights: the role of Islamic identity among British Muslim women. Women's Stud Int Forum 29(4):417–430

Castilo-Ortiz P, Ali A, Samanta N (2019) Gender, intersectionality, and religious manifestation before the European Court of Human Rights. J Hum Rights 18(1):76–91

Corekcioglu G (2021) Unveiling the effects of a headscarf ban: evidence from municipal jobs in Turkey. J Comp Econ 49(2):382–404

Costello RÁ, Ahmed S (2023) Citizenship, identity, and veiling: interrogating the limits of Article 8 of the European Convention on Human Rights in cases involving the religious dress of Muslim women. J Law Relig 38(1):81–107

Crenshaw K (1991) Mapping the margins: intersectionality, identity politics, and violence against women of color. Stanford Law Rev 43(6):1241–1299

Cumper P, Lewis T (2018) Empathy and human rights: the case of religious dress. Hum Rights Law Rev 18(1):61–87

Davies G (2024) OP v Commune d'Ans: The entirely neutral exclusion of Muslim women from state employment. ELB Blogpost 55/2023

El Yattouti N (2024) On turbans, abayas, and colanders: the scope of religious dress in a pluralistic society. Oxford J Law Relig
European Union Agency for Fundamental Rights (2024) Being Muslim in the EU: experiences of Muslims. Vienna
Evans C (2006) The islamic scarf in the European Court of Human Rights. Melb J Int Law 7:52–74
Evolvi G, Gatti M (2021) Proselytism and ostentation: a critical discourse analysis of the European Court of Human Rights' case law on religious symbols. J Relig Eur 14(1–2, 162):–188
Freedman J (2007) Women, Islam and rights in Europe: beyond a universalist/culturalist dichotomy. Rev Int Stud 33(1):29–44
Ghumman S, Ryan AM (2013) Not welcome here: discrimination towards women who wear the Muslim headscarf. Hum Relat 66(5):671–698
Gibson N (2007) An unwelcome trend: Religious dress and human rights following Leyla Şahin v. Turkey. Neth Q Hum Rights 25(4):599–640
Griffiths E (2016) The 'reasonable accommodation' of religion: Is this a better way of advancing equality in cases of religious discrimination? Int J Discrim Law 16(2–3):161–176
Guveli A (2011) Social and economic impact of the headscarf ban on women in Turkey. Eur Soc 13(2):171–189
Haq M (2022) The war on Muslim women's bodies: a critique of Western feminism. https://www.law.georgetown.edu/immigration-law-journal/blog/the-war-on-muslim-womens-bodies-a-critique-of-western-feminism/
Hennette-Vauchez S (2017) Is French laïcité still liberal? The republican project under pressure (2004–15). Hum Rights Law Rev 17(2):285–312
Hennette-Vauchez S (2020) Religious neutrality, laïcité and colorblindness: a comparative analysis. Cardozo Law Rev 42:539–595
Hibri C (2023) Orientalism: Edward Said's groundbreaking book explained. https://theconversation.com/orientalism-edward-saids-groundbreaking-book-explained-197429
Hopkins CT (2015) Social reproduction in France: religious dress laws and laïcité. Women's Stud Int Forum 48:154–164
Howard E (2017) Religious clothing and symbols in employment: a legal analysis of the situation in the EU Member States. European Commission, European network of legal experts in gender equality and non-discrimination
Howard E (2020) Law and the wearing of religious symbols in Europe. Routledge, London
Howard E (2024) Intersectional discrimination and EU law: time to revisit Parris. Int J Discrim Law 24(4):292–312
Hunter-Henin M (2022) Religious neutrality at Europe's highest courts: shifting strategies. Oxford J Law Relig 11(1):23–46
Hutten W, Mustafa N (2022) Contesting neutrality dress codes in Europe. Open Society Institute, New York
Idriss MM (2005) Laïcité and the banning of the 'hijab' in France. Leg Stud 25(2):260–295
Jolly S (2024) Achbita & Bougnaoui: a strange kind of equality. https://www.cloisters.com/insights/achbita-bougnaoui-a-strange-kind-of-equality-XrZyJ
Kılıç S, Saharso S, Sauer B (2008) Introduction: the veil: debating citizenship, gender and religious diversity. Soc Polit 15(4):397–410
Loxston R, Jachens L (2023) "Liberty can be for you one thing, and for me something different": Muslim women's experiences of identity and belonging in Switzerland. Eur J Psychol 19(4):308–323
Lugato M (2013) The margin of appreciation and freedom of religion: between treaty interpretation and subsidiarity. J Catholic Leg Stud 52:49–70
Marshall J (2006) Freedom of religious expression and gender equality: Sahin v Turkey. Mod Law Rev 69:452–461
Marshall J (2008) Conditions for freedom of religious expression: a case study of the headscarf in France and Turkey. Int J Constit Law 6(4):682–712
Qazi Zada S, Qazi Zada MZ (2024) The Taliban and women's human rights in Afghanistan: the way forward. Int J Hum Rights 28(10):1687–1722

Skeet CH (2019) Intersectionality as theory and method: human rights adjudication by the European Court of Human Rights. In: Creutzfeldt N et al (eds) Routledge handbook of socio-legal theory and methods. Routledge, London

Skenderovic D (2020) Headscarf bans in Europe: a comparative analysis. Comp Eur Polit 18(1):30–54

Solanke I (2011) Infusing the silos in the Equality Act 2010 with synergy. Ind Law J 40(4):336–358

Solanke I (2016) Chapter 18: a method for intersectional discrimination in EU labour law. In: Bogg A et al (eds) Research handbook on EU labour law. Edward Elgar Publishing, Cheltenham

Spiro DA (1989) Public schools and the road to religious neutrality. Phi Delta Kappan 70(10):759–763

Velaers J, Foblets M-C (2019) Religious diversity in Europe: a shared responsibility of courts, parliament and society. In: Lemmens K et al (eds) Human rights with a human touch: liber amicorum Paul Lemmens. Intersentia, Cambridge, pp 755–774

Velthuis E, Verkuyten M, Noll JV, Smeekes A (2022) Tolerance of the Muslim headscarf: perceived reasons for wearing a headscarf matter. Int J Intercult Relat 90:86–96

Cases

Arslan and Others v. Turkey, ECtHR, App. No. 41135/98, Judgement 23 February 2010

Dahlab v. Switzerland, ECtHR, App. No. 42393/98, Judgement 15 February 2001

Eweida and Others v. United Kingdom, ECtHR, App. Nos. 48420/10, 59842/10, 51671/10, and 36516/10, Judgement 15 January 2013

Hamidović v. Bosnia and Herzegovina, ECtHR, App. No. 57792/15, Judgement 5 December 2017

Karhuvaara and Iltalehti v. Finland, ECtHR, App. No. 53678/00, Judgement 16 February 2005

Köse and Others v. Turkey, ECtHR, App. No. 26625/02, Judgement 24 January 2006

Kurtulmuş v. Turkey, ECtHR, App. No. 65500/01, Judgement 24 January 2006

Lautsi v. Italy, ECtHR, App. No. 30814/06, Judgement 3 November 2009

Leyla Şahin v. Turkey, ECtHR, App. No. 44774/98, Judgement 10 November 2005

Mikyas and Others v. Belgium, ECtHR, App. No. 50681/20, Judgement 9 April 2024

Palomo Sánchez and Others v. Spain, ECtHR, App. Nos. 28955/06, 28957/06, 28959/06, and 28964/06, Judgement 12 September 2011

Naoual El Yattouti is a PhD Researcher and FWO-fellow at the Law Faculty of the University of Antwerp. Her research concerns the intersection between healthcare and human rights law, focusing specifically on the rights to freedom of religion and non-discrimination of healthcare providers and patients. She has received the First Laureate Prize for her Master Thesis on ‘Concordant Care: a Patient’s Right or Discrimination?’ awarded by the Belgian Journal of Health Law in 2021, and the Young Scientist Award for Best Poster Presentation awarded by the World Association for Medical Law in 2022.

Benjamin Nurkić is a PhD Researcher at the Faculty of Law at the University of Tuzla and a member of the Constitutional Committee of the House of Representatives of the Parliament of the Federation of Bosnia and Herzegovina. He is also a fellow of the I·CONnect Blog of the International Journal of Constitutional Law. The main focus of his research is the protection of human rights and establishing the rule of law in post-conflict societies.

Gender Justice and Social Justice: Reproduction and Difference

Angela Condello

Abstract In the present chapter I argue that gender justice is not only a matter of; social justice, but also it could be conceived as an approach that connects the idea of justice with the way in which the relations among genders are conceived, articulated, and categorized beyond material conditions. In essence, gender is not only central matter of social justice but also intertwind with the construction of collective imagination and symbolic order of society. I specifically refer to radical feminist approaches and difference feminism, bridging them to design a fruitful approach towards present social problems, such as the incompatibility between full-time careers and the needs related to care work.

1 Gender Justice and Social Justice

The complex interplay between law and feminism addresses a vast array of topics, among which are sexuality and reproduction, vulnerability, labour, family, and health. Since before the first-wave of feminism in the West, questions of equality and discrimination, as well as of social justice, have been debated across these and similar themes in the fields of law concerned with feminist legal practices (private and constitutional law, criminal law, legal theory).[1] Nothing can seem to stop the fertile exchange between law and feminism as evidenced by the increasing interest in these studies, following both analytic approaches stemming from the philosophy of language and critical approaches influenced by post-colonial and intersectional studies on sexed and gendered forms of domination.[2] Among the domains of femi-

[1] Young (1990); Simone et al. (2022); Rigo and Alessandrini (2023); Condello and Bottici (2024).
[2] Crenshaw (1991); Alviar and Jaramillo (2012); Mercat-Bruns (2016).

A. Condello (✉)
University of Messina, Messina, Italy
e-mail: acondello@unime.it

F. Macioce et al. (eds.), *Feminist Legal and Political Practices*, Gender Perspectives in Law 6, https://doi.org/10.1007/978-3-032-02856-3_9

nist scholarship, law is particularly significant: as a normative order, it shapes and regulates our life and often produces wrongful forms of oppression, domination and privileges. Therefore, underlying social structures such as race, gender or class can be fruitfuly examined through the lens of the law. Conversely, legal studies, can explore the connection between law and justice, particularly through critical and radical approaches.

Despite the longstanding relationship between law and feminist theory and the enduring relevance of the methodologies developed within this dialogue, various social problems keep being rooted precisely in the interconnection between legal orders and gender relations, both via the symbolic order and imagination defining the female subject, on the one hand, and the legislations and public policies aimed at fostering a fair social order, on the other hand. On top of this, apparently contradictory phenomena characterize the present era: the labour market is formally becoming increasingly egalitarian and the number of women in leading positions is rising (although the growth has had many setbacks), while at the same time full-time parenting often seems to be the model to achieve, as a (quasi-)deliberate choice. Such parenting styles involving, for example, 24/7 breastfeeding, are popular not only in rural areas but also in metropolitan areas, where families are typically nuclear (constituted by parents and children), and care work is often concentrated within the nuclear family, either primarily on parents or delegated to paid workers, while cohabitation by closer kins is viewed more as an experimental phenomenon than a real opportunity.[3]

Against such a contradictory and complex background, the European Institute for Gender Equality[4] keeps confirming that gender inequalities are increasing: it has recently announced that Europe is one of the major geographic regions expected to decline in population in the next years (nearly 70 million people by 2050), and it denounced that the fertility rate is currently below the replacement rate. The decrease in childbirth is a serious issue also outside of Europe, in other areas of the Global North: in the United States, for example, an inglorious comment made by J. D. Vance recently resurfaced. He said that America is run by a "bunch of childless cat ladies" (referring to Kamala Harris in particular). This sad meme expresses a more profound remark on how women in industrialized countries are having fewer and fewer children: both in Europe and in the United States schools and universities are progressively facing issues in filling their classes.[5] The wider fact is that our societies are organized on a pyramid scheme, with the young supporting the old: yet the bottom of the pyramid is eroding fast.

Furthermore, not coincidentally, in January 2024, *The Economist* cross-referenced various data on how motherhood hurts careers.[6] Despite typical

---

[3] Profeta (2020); Saraceno and Naldini (2007).

[4] EIGE:https://eige.europa.eu

[5] EIGE: https://eige.europa.eu

[6] https://www.economist.com/interactive/graphic-detail/2024/01/30/how-motherhood-hurts-careers

post-Covid 19 tools like the Italian "PNRR" Mission (Plan for recovery and resilience: National Strategy for Gender Equality) of the *Dipartimento Pari Opportunità*, aimed at promoting the use of performance indicators to measure gender justice in institutions, companies, and Offices, all recovery plans seem to be weak (when they are not failing) on the side of gender equality policies.[7]

Taken together, these facts suggest that something is fundamentally amiss. There must be underlying dynamics that persist and that cause persistent effects on the societal structure, thereby perpetuating issues such as those mentioned above. Why does the situation continue to worsen, with a clear-cut birth dearth in industrialized countries, labour issues in developing countries, and the fall of female careers virtually everywhere? This vicious circularity in my opinion needs to be addressed starting from a comparative analysis of theoretical approaches in feminist legal practices. In this chapter I focus on the socio-reproductive problem, paying tribute to Marxian feminism for some insights that are still central today. I shall continue to parallel this perspective with some crucial intuitions related to the philosophical concept of difference, and finally I will emphasize the relationship between difference and constant demands for justice, concluding that gender justice implies social justice and vice versa.

The streams within legal feminism considered in this chapter share some core premises, starting from the need for a sharp critique of the modern legal system and of modern universalism, a system which is built around a dominant subject (male, white, middle-class). I take into consideration radical feminist approaches focusing on the material conditions affecting gender relations (class-gender) and other approaches focusing on how male and femal subjects are imagined (mainly difference feminism or "feminism of the symbolic"). Indeed, legal feminism, across these and other streams, shares the logical premises of feminism—i.e., that the social structure is patriarchal and that the law merely maintains, if not even establishes purposefully, the conditions of domination of men over women. The common trait of the various streams within legal feminism is the recognition of the structural subordination of women within society, and the consequent criticism against the alleged neutrality of law.[8] Legal feminism has in its core the quest for justice, considered from the point of view of the actual role played by law in current injustices and of its potential value as an instrument to fight injustices, to eliminate discriminations, and to consider the different life conditions of female and male subjects. Thus, I argue that to fight injustices and contradictions, it is necessary to have a perspective that includes both aspects of radical feminism and aspects of difference feminism: in other words, the material and concrete conditions as well as the imaginary should be analyzed together.

---

[7] Cfr. the studies published by the *Review of Economics of the Household*, for instance after Covid-19: https://link.springer.com/journal/11150

[8] Bartlett (1990); Minda (1995); Olsen (1995a, b); Cornell (1999).

From a feminist point of view, the main critique of the law is that it is sexist by definition,[9] because the first building blocks of the modern legal systems (e.g., 1789 Declaration of the Rights of Man and the Citizen) assume legal subjects as always gender-neutral and thus all subsumed into manhood, and they privilege one sexed body over others (the masculine). Hence, the fundamental problem with modern legal systems is that their neutrality does not recognize the subjectivity of women because it presupposes a universal subject, and such neutrality does not reflect the presence of different subjectivities. That is to say, by pretending to be neutral, the law has turned into a tool of domination.

The attempt to subvert this balance of harmful neutrality has been made in different directions. First by imagining strategies to achieve justice that do not necessarily pass through the positive norm, and second by using law as a tool for the struggle. In different ways, these accounts of legal normativity build a critique of the abstract equality of treatment between sexes in terms of subjective rights and invite us to think instead through the substantial differences hidden in the folds of society, at various levels, both in the private spheres (e.g. in the family) and in public relations (e.g. in the workplace).[10] In my view, radical feminism (particularly stemming from Marxist positions) and difference feminism share a common drive towards a vision of gender relations that presupposes a theory of justice and more specifically of *social* justice. This is achieved through the struggle to change the material life and working conditions of women, the fair sharing of care and domestic obligations, and social welfare policies (Marxist feminism), or it is pursued through a revolution in the symbolic order (difference feminism),[11] as well as the uses of language or imagination and myth (especially via thinkers like Cornell, Kristeva, Irigaray and Cixous). Radical feminist practices in law, especially the most radical in political terms (i.e., Marxist feminism) and in theoretical terms (i.e., European difference feminism, such as the Italian "feminism of the symbolic" inspired by the Milan Women's Bookstore), share the need to root the law *beyond* or *before* the law, in values, transcending the singular legal tool, the singular case, or the singular policy.[12] To put it differently, they share a deconstructive drive to settle legal orders in what is *not yet there*, between what there is and what there should be.[13] For this reason, I read them in their interrelations as such practices that are first and foremost revolutionary because they reposition our way of understanding the function of law within society.

If we consider the short circuits typical of today's world—for instance, the abovementioned work/life contradictions—it becomes clear that new approaches are necessary to achieve gender justice: a form of justice understood in radical terms, encompassing both symbolic and social dimensions. By linking these two

[9] Smart (1992).
[10] Cornell (1990a).
[11] Muraro (2018).
[12] Arruzza (2013).
[13] Cornell (1990b).

aspects—one focused on material conditions and the other on the imaginary—gender justice gains depth and can encompass its various facets: redistributive justice to overcome disadvantages, women's empowerment through education, reproductive justice, and, more broadly, a vision of justice aimed at recognizing and permanently overcoming stigmas, stereotypes, and forms of symbolic violence. In the following paragraphs, I will explain why and how such a methodological perspective could be conceived to integrate insights from radical feminism and philosophy, as well as from the standpoint of difference feminism.

2 Production and Reproduction

March 8, 1911. International Women's Rights Day is celebrated for the first time at the initiative of the German socialist thinker and activist Clara Zetkin. The occasion, officially, is a major protest for the unfair working conditions of women along with their minimum wages and wrongful treatment. For Zetkin and other socialist feminists, however, celebration serves to emphasize the deep and mutual relationship between social justice and gender justice. As contributors to *Die Gleichheit*, the militancy journal of the party (towards the end of the nineteenth century), these feminists argue that the struggle for women's rights is first and foremost a battle for social equality, since there can be no liberation of women without revolution and no revolution without a complete and lasting liberation of women. They argue that no woman will be free until the world becomes "just" in several ways and at several levels—within the imaginary, in everyday practices, and public policies. Following Engels,[14] they maintain that a social revolution begins in the family, and they anticipate in some ways the famous feminist motto "the personal is political", later popularized by the publication of feminist activist Carol Hanisch's 1970 essay.[15] In other words, already at the beginning of twentieth century, social-democratic thinkers such as Clara Zetkin, Rosa Luxemburg or Aleksandra Kollontai identified a nexus of reciprocal causality bridging gender justice with social justice.[16] There can be no just relations between men and women if society as a whole—shaped by labour relations and class dominations—is itself unjust; conversely, society in its entirety cannot be truly just if gender relations remain profoundly unequal.

About three decades later, in 1938, Virginia Woolf's *The Three Guineas* exposes the intrinsic connections between global injustice, war, patriarchy, and capitalism, emphasizing the need to deal with gender relations by starting from

[14] Engels (1884).

[15] http://www.carolhanisch.org/CHwritings/PersonalIsPol.pdf. Hanisch (1970).

[16] Zetkin (1957-1960) and Zetkin (1984).

social relations and from the material life conditions of the exploited social groups.[17] The achievements in terms of equality and the emancipatory processes of first-wave feminism were, in her view, not sufficient, since a deeper structure continued to anchor gender domination—: one reflected this, for example, in labor relations as well as in the unequal wages. Similar observations were made, in the second half of the twentieth century, by Marxist feminists, who denounced the sexual domination underlying social domination and drawing parallels between the seemingly egalitarian relations of the market and those between man and woman, both of which are, in fact, fundamentally non-egalitarian.[18] From this perspective, the gap between the personal and the political dimension diminishes: a critical reflection on how facts are interpreted and how this gap is negotiated becomes crucial to women's actual capability to achieve a free, fulfilled and just existence.

Years before Carol Hanisch claimed that the personal is political.[19] Engels wrote that in the world of workers, it is basically a general rule that after marriage women abandon paid work or they must limit it significantly, because their function becomes above all the management of the home.[20] Such intuitions were developed by socialist feminists like Zetkin, Luxemburg, and Kollontaj. Following this line, as early as the 1970s, radical feminism, using a Marxist methodology, described care as an invisible work, relating it to capitalist development as well as to market interests and balances.[21] This stream invites us to conceive reproduction as labor (either wage-based or not) because it is closely connected to and interdependent with processes of value production. Indeed, the reproductive labor constitutes the material basis of the current neoliberal form of production. The interconnections between reproduction and production have progressively changed-both socially and individually, while care work has also evolved in response to the transformations of capitalism.[22]

The question, today, is still that formulated by Engels: how can reproductive work be recognized in a world that values production over reproduction? In other terms: if the symbolic order, the imaginary, and our contemporary mythology, are all divided between production and care, which is understood as vocation/affection, how can things get substantially better? As a matter of fact, capitalism, as recently confirmed by US presidential elections, appears to be harmoniously integrated within global politics. This form of capitalism tends to lower wages and erode workers' rights, thereby forcing families to work longer hours, and to outsource care work. The personal and domestic dimensions continue to be rendered invisible,

---

[17] 1929: in *A room of one's own*, Woolf had already shown that patriarchy can only be dismantled by rethinking the female subject as autonomous and independent. The real revolution must start at a symbolic level—a theme that will be focal in twentieth century difference feminism. By no chance Woolf becomes of the main literary references for difference feminists.

[18] Marella (2000); Dal Re and Perini (2014) and Dal Re (2020).

[19] Hanisch (1970).

[20] Engels (1884).

[21] Dal Re and Perini (2014).

[22] Dal Re and Perini (2014).

functioning merely to sustain what is considered to "*really count*". For thinkers such as Iris Marion Young, and for critical theorists more generally, neither formal nor substantive justice can be achieved solely through the distributive paradigm or a principle of equality focused on labour.[23] It is not enough to enshrine social rights on paper: genuine transformation can occur only by breaking away from the power dynamics that dominate and oppress all categories deriving from the models deemed "normal". Not by chance, philosopher Chiara Bottici suggests to think in terms of a plurality of "second sexes" (following de Beauvoir's intuition), claiming that all vulnerable categories (not only women) are somehow "second" in comparison to a "main" model considered normal, be it in terms of class, ethnicity, religious belonging, or gender.[24]

As argued by Nancy Fraser, it is crucial to keep the focus on the economic variables at stake in theories and political practices within feminism: struggles for the recognition of differences should proceed parallel with a quest for equality and redistribution of resources.[25] Subjects should be understood in their multi-dimensionality, since gender must always be considered in relation to the material conditions of life (economic positioning, capabilities, etc.). Starting from an idea that society is ordered according to various hierarchies, this perspective on legal feminism thus suggests using the law as a tool to subvert masculine domination within society, also starting from variables other than gender/sex. Radical feminists in the 1960s and 1970s, however, had already underlined the importance of considering the social conditions interacting with gender relations, although some of them had considered Marxism to tarnish feminism;[26] as a matter of fact, Marxist and feminist approaches have in common the critique against patriarchy and all forms of domination also in the domestic realm of the family.

In the *German Ideology* (1846) Marx and Engels had already shown how capitalism rests upon the bourgeois model of the family because the family is what allows the bourgeois to be himself. The bourgeois family enables the bourgeois subject to exist as such. The bourgeois family, in fact, possesses a strong patrimonial structure based on capital and profit—one that historically relegated women to the private sphere of the nuclear, isolated household by excluding them from productive relations. This configuration results from the penetration of market logic into the structure of the family: in the relationship between exchange and production, the apparently egalitarian form of exchange between private individuals both conceals and presupposes the unequal relations of production. A similar dynamic can be observed in the relationship between the public and the domestic spheres. In both, the right of equals—characteristic of the market—conceals a system of hierarchically ordered legal relations grounded in gender inequality, just as the liberal legal regime of the family does.

---

[23] Young (1990).

[24] Condello and Bottici (2024).

[25] Fraser (1997).

[26] Hartmann (1979).

From the point of view of feminism, Marxism is sometimes considered as misleading, since it perceives gender and sexuality as pre-social categories—as if what women share was only the physiological condition of menstruating, giving birth or breastfeeding: the limit between the social and the pre-social dimension is very complex from the perspective of gender.[27] The interactions between Marxism and feminism are clearly complex in that they both aim at overturning structural and organized social domination;[28] and yet, attitudes of reciprocal skepticism and diffidence have emerged through the decades.

Radical feminism does not conceive gender and sexuality as mere limits to the freedom of female subjects, but as the index of a larger system of power, of social facts and dynamics lying in sexual differences. As claimed by Catherine MacKinnon, sexuality is for radical feminism what labour is for Marxism: they are both social processes that create gender relations—the aspiration of such stream is to combine the analysis of the social construction of the female sexuality with the possibility to overturn systematic subordinations. Typically situated within critical legal studies, this perspective does not reject the law as such but rather invites a reconsideration of its use: to employ it in ways that favor women and to cultivate a feminist consciousness, with the aim of dismantling the harmful dualism between male and female that produces various forms of injustice.

Socialist feminists like Clara Zetkin, and later Raya Dunayevskaya emphasized the correlation between international-institutional and economic structures, the class struggles, and the conditions of women, both at home and at work.[29] No social justice can be achieved without gender justice, and vice versa. The question is, then as now, how these two dimensions should interact. The condition of women, like that of other subjects who deviate from "normality"—that is, from the model around which modern legal systems are constructed (male, middle-class, etc.)—should be examined in terms of the social ties and obligations imposed upon them. These ties and obligations are not necessarily linked to biological characteristics, such as menstruation or childbirth, but may instead relate to factors such as ethnicity or social class.

To recapitulate, given the strict interconnection between issues of social justice and issues of gender justice, different views have developed, suggesting different approaches—some are more radical, some more liberal. The short circuits between these different approaches are reflected in policies that alternate and often conflict with each other. Perhaps another perspective could help grasping the reasons why the female condition remains so incredibly problematic.[30] To add a different theoretical level in the discourse, I will briefly sketch how the concept of difference,

---

27 Arruzza (2013).

28 MacKinnon (1983).

29 Condello (2025).

30 It is by no chance that the Nobel prize for economics, in 2023, was awarded to Claudia Golding for her works on labour policies for women understood as a cultural and moral issue.

widely used in other approaches to legal feminism, might also help interpreting the complexity of the present times.

3 Justice as Difference[31]

Simone de Beauvoir's famous adage—"one is not born, but becomes a woman"[32]—means that female identity is the product of social constructions rooted in patriarchy. The sentence might be misleading if interpreted as an obliteration of sexual difference, and of the physiologically divergent characteristics of men and women. De Beauvoir is also one of the main references of the so-called difference feminism, which claims the importance of re-imagining our symbolic world, our imaginary and our language according to the duplicity of the world (in which male and female subjects coexist). As the title of her work suggests, she invites us to think in terms of the feminine not as a shadow or merely sexual dimension, in which the masculine is considered primary (the principal).

Broadly speaking, difference constitutes a path to liberate women from both domination rooted in physiologically divergent characteristics and domination embedded in culture and society.[33] Such an approach adds value to the unique character of each individual experience, in contrast to frameworks that pursue abstraction and universality by erasing particularities such as sexual differences between men and women. The distinctiveness of each life resides in its absolute diversity. Understood philosophically within a tradition traceable to Nietzsche, difference is primarily an ontological feature of all beings and things: it is not, as has often been suggested, merely the divergence between two aspects of two beings (or categories of beings) differing because of factor A or factor B; rather, it is the very possibility of divergence. Drucilla Cornell describes it as a "not yet"—that which is not yet present but could emerge. It is this hypothetical dimension that renders difference a logic of possibility, a space in which singularities can assert themselves in the world.[34]

As a core concept of feminist legal practice, difference provides a critical gaze over the world and attributes a specific force to the unique nature of each life and each experience before the law. Thus understood, difference is therefore also a key concept to relate the universality of legal provisions with the specificity of the needs of each person, where justice means the possibility of finding each person's justice. Difference is hence not only a way to find the right balance between the generality

[31] I want to thank Alberto Andronico, Ann Genovese, Maria Drakopoulou and Karin Van Marle for the conversations about the concept of difference and its theoretical relevance to build a critique of society and for the clarifications on how difference is first and foremost a quest for other possible worlds.

[32] De Beauvoir (1949).

[33] Cavarero and Guaraldo (2024).

[34] Andronico (2002).

of the norms and the particularity of the facts, the events, the singular lives—but it corresponds, following its theoretical roots, to the very possibility of achieving justice.

Apparently inconsistent and divergent, the perspective of radical feminism (focused on economic and material conditions) and the perspective of difference feminism (focused on the ontologically divergent attributes) are often contradictory. The contradiction might be explained since often radical feminism has been identified with Marxist approaches to class condition, and only sometimes with what was called radical liberal feminism (second wave feminism), a stream that understands patriarchy as the roots of women's subordination. The short circuit described in the first section of this chapter (women's careers and the decrease of childbirth) suggests bridging the two points of view to grasp the most meaningful aspects of both. Radical feminism risks to obliterate the ontological and constitutive difference man/woman to focus on the social conditions, while difference feminism risks to insist excessively on sexual difference and to obliterate the concrete life conditions of the subjects. Radical positions can be misleading in both cases; as we have seen, even radical liberal feminism has been criticized because it pushes the equality between man and woman to an extent where the female subject re-lives in the shadow of a "main" subject and reproduces a model where oppressors lead over oppressed human beings.[35]

Similar contradictory phenomena have been central to many debates within legal feminism, particularly regarding the tension between work and care:[36] what should women choose—career or family—and, more importantly, why should they have to choose at all? I argue that in order to provide the right balance and allow women to pursue the most meaningful process of individuation within their own experience, it is crucial to bridge the socio-economic critique developed by Marxist perspectives with the theoretical insights offered by difference feminism. The latter, in fact, invites us to consider the concrete aspects of struggles for gender justice within a different theoretical approach, through a reconsideration of the positions of women[37] in all forms of narrative, in myth and the imaginary, and the so-called symbolic order.[38]

To avoid short circuits between more concrete and more symbolic struggles, I find it crucial to focus on the problems that are timely in a specific moment in history. Nowadays, for instance, some of the most worrying data concern the difficulties in managing the balance between work and family, as well as the increasing need for a reconceptualization of care, an issue often pressed between women's demand for achievements and success in the public sphere, on the one hand, and societal expectations for over-participating forms of parenting, on the other. To provide equal chances for care and for work without seeing care as an alternative to

[35] Arruzza et al. (2019).

[36] Stewart et al. (2011).

[37] Brogi (2022).

[38] Muraro (2018).

career, new solutions must be discussed that leave the choice and individuation up to each woman. Each one for herself: when the focus on care becomes excessive, some aspects are sacrificed; on the contrary, when work (and just that) is the criterion to measure a fulfilled life, and the expectations become high either on one aspect or on the other, serious problems can arise.

I argue that a possible way out of the short circuits produced by conflicting streams would be to focus on practices of care such as those described by authors like Lynn Segal[39] or Catherine Rottenberg.[40] These are practices that start from theoretical approaches but constantly lean on the concrete problems—from intimate care to childcare, healthcare and elderly care. Broadly, the care for the world surrounding us. A similar approach cuts across dimensions like the social and the economic and considers the symbolic importance of actions in a time where carelessness reign—by recognizing that things do not need to go this way. By embracing the concreteness and revolutionary attitude of radical approaches, as well as the importance of conceiving subjects in their independence and relationality. Texts like *The Care Manifesto*[41] show how to reconceptualize the different positions of subjects in view of transformations based on cooperative work, on the structure of families in the urban areas and outside of them, in the industrialized countries and in the poorer areas.

A new potential framework of reflections in feminist legal studies could profit from similar practices: how? For example, by expanding our understanding of kinship—thereby reexamining certain entrenched and often overly rigid legal categories—or by imagining forms of "promiscuous" care, provided both by relatives and friends within new communitarian arrangement. In Elena Pulcini's terms, feminist legal practices should aim to reconceptualize a new care for the world.[42] From this perspective, female—and more generally, vulnerable or oppressed—subjects might hope for liberation from profit-driven chains of power, which are often deeply symbolic and generate expectations across multiple levels, such as the gendered division of labor. Such chains can produce social short-circuits, fostering heightened concern, anxiety, and grief, even in industrialized countries where equal rights are ostensibly guaranteed.

To conceive justice as difference means to think in feminist terms without being trapped in this or that stream, or model, or discourse or sets of codes and vocabularies.[43] It also means to embrace a way of conceptualizing law, politics, and society in terms of a plurality of subjects who are all equally dignified and powerful. Bridging feminist traditions by focusing on the material and the symbolic dimensions can lead to more fruitful approaches towards the present problems and the short circuits described in the first section. In conclusion, let me briefly restate the argument

[39] Segal (2023).

[40] Gordon and Rottenberg (2023).

[41] The Care Collective (2020).

[42] Pulcini (2009).

[43] Gilligan (1982).

developed in this chapter. I started by underlining some contradictions in our present society, such as those related to work-life balance. Against this background, I have sought to critically examine approaches to gender relations that can help us understand the present and imagine ways to overcome its contradictions. Among the various feminist perspectives on law, I consider radical feminism and difference feminism to be particularly powerful today, as each, in its own terms, contributes to rethinking gender relations with a shared goal: a more just society in which no one is dominated or oppressed—either in their concrete and material conditions or in the ways their subjectivity is imagined and narrated.

References

Alviar H, Jaramillo I (2012) Feminismo y crítica jurídica. El análisis distributivo como alternativa crítica al legalismo liberal. Universidad de los Andes, Bogotá
Andronico A (2002) La decostruzione come metodo. Riflessi di Derrida nella teoria del diritto. Giuffrè, Milano
Arruzza C (2013) Dangerous Liasons. The marriages and divorces of marxism and feminism. Merlin Press, London
Arruzza C, Bhattacharya T, Fraser N (2019) Feminism for the 99%: a manifesto. Verso Books, New York
Bartlett KT (1990) Feminist legal methods. Harv Law Rev 103:829–888
Brogi D (2022) Lo spazio delle donne. Einaudi, Torino
Cavarero A, Guaraldo O (2024) Donna si nasce (e qualche volta lo si diventa). Mondadori, Milano
Condello A (2025) Clara Zetkin. In: Kirste S, Albrecht K (eds) Rechtsphilosophinnen. Surkhamp, Frankfurt
Condello A, Bottici C (2024) Difference feminism and anarchafeminism. Perspectives on gender justice, Teoria e critica della regolazione sociale, pp 145–156
Cornell D (1990a) The doubly-prized world: myth, allegory and the feminine. Cornell Law Rev 75:644–699
Cornell D (1990b) From the lighthouse: the promise of redemption and the possibility of legal interpretation. Cardozo Law Rev 11:1690
Cornell D (1999) Beyond accommodation: ethical feminism, deconstruction, and the law. Rowman & Littlefield Publishers, Lanham
Crenshaw K (1991) Mapping the margins: intersectionality, identity politics, and violence against women of color. Stanford Law Rev 43(6):1241–1299
Dal Re A (2020) Il lavoro di riproduzione e le macchine. Alcune considerazioni in tempi di pandemia. Scienza e Filosofia 23:30–43
Dal Re A, Perini L (eds) (2014) Gender Politics in Italia e in Europa. Percorsi di studi di genere per le lauree triennali e magistrali. Padova University Press, Padova
De Beauvoir S (1949) Le deuxième sexe. Gallimard, Paris
Engels F (1884) Der Ursprung der Familie, des Privateigenthums und des Staats. Im Anschluss an Lewis. Morgan's Forschungen. Hottingen, Zurich
Fraser N (1997) Justice interruptus. Critical reflections on the "postsocialist" condition. Routledge, London
Gilligan C (1982) In a different voice. Psychological theory and women's development. Harvard University Press, Cambridge
Gordon N, Rottenberg C (2023) From human rights to a politics of care. Hum Int J Hum Rights Hum Dev 14(3):327–346
Hanisch C (1970) The personal is political. In notes from the second year. Women's Liberation

Hartmann H (1979) The unhappy marriage of marxism and feminism: towards a more progressive union. Cap Class 3(2):1–33
MacKinnon C (1983) Feminism, marxism, method, and the state: toward feminist jurisprudence. Signs J Women Cult Soc 8(4):635–658
Marella MR (2000) Break on through to the other side: appunti sull'influenza di Marx nel femminismo giuridico. Rivista critica del diritto privato VIII-4:741–766
Mercat-Bruns M (2016) Discrimination at work: comparing European, French, and American law. University of California Press, Berkeley
Minda G (1995) Postmodern legal movements. Law and jurisprudence at the century's end. New York University Press, New York
Muraro L (2018) The symbolic order of the mother. Suny Press, Albany
Olsen F (1995a) Feminist legal theory I. Foundations and outlooks. New York University Press, New York
Olsen F (1995b) Feminist legal theory II. Positioning feminist theory within the law. New York University Press, New York
Profeta P (2020) Gender equality and public policy: measuring progress in Europe. Cambridge University Press, Cambridge
Pulcini E (2009) La cura del mondo: paura e responsabilità nell'età globale. Bollati Boringhieri, Torino
Rigo E, Alessandrini D (2023) Social reproduction and the challenge to legal studies. Spec Iss Feminists@Law 12(2)
Saraceno C, Naldini E (2007) Sociologia della famiglia. Il Mulino, Bologna
Segal L (2023) Lean on me. A politics of radical care. Verso Books, New York
Simone A, Boiano I, Condello A (2022) Legal feminism. Italian theories and perspectives. Routledge, Abingdon
Smart C (1992) The woman of the legal discourse. Soc Leg Stud 1:29–44
Stewart A, Niccolai S, Hoskyns C (2011) Disability discrimination by association: a case of the double yes? Soc Leg Stud 20(2):173–190
The Care Collective (2020) The care manifesto. The politics of interdependence. Verso Books, New York
Young IM (1990) Justice and the politics of difference. Princeton University Press, Princeton
Zetkin C (1957-1960) Ausgewählte Reden und Schriften (Band I bis III). Dietz Verlag, Berlin
Zetkin C (1984) Zur Geschichte der proletarischen Frauenbewegung Deutschlands. Verlag Marxistische Blätter, Frankfurt

Angela Condello (1984) is Associate Professor of Philosophy of Law at the University of Messina. She is a legal philosopher and directs LabOnt Law at the University of Torino. She held Jean Monnet Module on human rights and critical legal thinking (2017–2020) and Jean Monnet Project on labour and social identity (2016–2017). She has published 5 monographs (e.g., *Analogica. Il doppio legame tra diritto e analogia*, 2018 and *Il diritto come metodo e la scienza algoritmica. Una critica a partire da Bobbio e Scarpelli*, 2022) and edited numerous journal issues (Law and Literature, Law Text Culture, Rivista di Estetica, International Journal for the Semiotics of Law), on top of volumes—e.g. *Sensing the Nation's Law* (2018), *Il denaro e i suoi inganni* (2018, Spanish ed. 2020), *Money, Social Ontology and Law* (with J. R. Searle and M. Ferraris, 2019), *Femminismo giuridico. Teorie e problemi* (2019, English ed. 2022), *Post-Truth, Philosophy and Law* (2019), *Law, Labour and the Humanities* (2019), *New Rhetorics for Contemporary Legal Discourse* (2020). A book on female freedom and social justice is forthcoming for Einaudi (2026). *Pensiero umano e intelligenza artificiale* (J. R. Searle), translated by A. Condello, was published in 2023. *Vita e parole. La violenza e la discesa nell'ordinario* (V. Das), translated by A. Condello, came out in summer 2024. She co-directs the series *Sotto Sopra la Legge* (Mimesis) and *Gender, Justice and Legal Feminism* (Springer) and collaborates with the Forum Disuguaglianze Diversità on issues related to care, gender justice, and social justice.

The Hague Child Abduction Convention Through the Lenses of Gender and Vulnerability: A Road Less Travelled in Strasbourg

Sanja Djajić

Abstract Cases before the European Court of Human Rights involving the Hague Convention on the Civil Aspects of International Child Abduction (1980) are numerous and reveal recurring factual and legal patterns that often remain unaddressed. Statistics indicate that the majority of so-called 'abductors' are mothers. This analysis, based on approximately 80 cases from the European Court of Human Rights, examines several key factors: the profile of the taking parent ('abductor'), including primary caregiver status, nationality, and gender; the custody rights at the time of the abduction and any subsequent changes; the availability of options for the taking parent to return with the child; and the vulnerability of the foreign mother, both as an individual and as a parent.

The findings show that foreign national mothers, often primary caregivers, face precarious situations abroad. When they leave a foreign country with their child, authorities frequently interpret this as a violation of the Hague Convention. In Strasbourg, such cases are typically framed as breaches of the left-behind parent's Article 8 rights under the European Convention on Human Rights. While the Court generally upholds these claims, it offers limited consideration of the vulnerable position of the mothers involved.

The aim of this contribution is to demonstrate that adopting a gender-sensitive approach, combined with the concept of vulnerability, is both justified and essential in Hague Convention cases before the Court. The Court is well-positioned to implement these frameworks, having developed them in other contexts. Such a shift would address existing blind spots regarding gender and vulnerability, ensure equitable human rights protection, harmonize the application of the Hague Convention with human rights standards, and adequately reflect evolving social and family dynamics in an increasingly globalized world.

I would like to thank Professor Maja Stanivuković for her insightful comments and helpful discussions on earlier drafts, and Marija Srećkov for her dedicated research assistance.

S. Djajić (✉)
University of Novi Sad School of Law, Novi Sad, Serbia
e-mail: sdjajic@pf.uns.ac.rs

F. Macioce et al. (eds.), *Feminist Legal and Political Practices*, Gender Perspectives in Law 6, https://doi.org/10.1007/978-3-032-02856-3_10

1 Introduction

The Hague Convention on the Civil Aspects of International Child Abduction (Hague Convention or HC) has been well-known as an efficient and widely accepted instrument for returning children to the country of their habitual residence following their abduction to a foreign country. Its strengths have mainly been the expediency and efficiency of its procedures that have become known and accepted by national authorities, which makes the Hague Convention one of the most successful international agreements. On the other hand, there have been certain concerns regarding its interpretation and implementation, mostly directed against the mechanical and formalistic approach to its enforcement, which on more than one occasion neglected the welfare of all persons involved, even when national authorities played by the book. Given the sensitivity of issues involving child welfare, the right to private and family life, and the vulnerability of different categories of individuals often involved in abduction cases, it is essential to assess the impact of the Hague Convention from multiple perspectives.

The perspective that lends itself to assessment is the one taken by the European Court of Human Rights (ECtHR or the Court) when applying human rights standards to the Hague Convention cases. The number of cases that reached Strasbourg in relation to the application of the Hague Convention by national authorities is significant and seems to reveal recurring factual and legal patterns. Statistics on international child abduction show that in majority of cases taking parents are mothers. These women are foreign nationals, primary caregivers with custody rights, who find themselves in precarious situations in a foreign country. Their decision to leave the foreign country with their child is generally perceived by the authorities as a violation of the Hague Convention. When such cases reach the ECtHR, the issue is typically framed as a violation of the left-behind parent's rights under Article 8 of the European Convention on Human Rights. The Court usually rules in favor of the Hague Convention return claims offering surprisingly little consideration to the vulnerable position of the mother, faced with the demand to return with her child to a foreign country.

The ECtHR has introduced the concept of vulnerability for specific categories[1] and recognized the importance of adopting a gender-sensitive perspective.[2] Alexandra Timmer defines vulnerability in the ECtHR's case law as a framework addressing heightened risks faced by certain individuals or groups due to structural inequalities or specific circumstances.[3] The Court uses this concept to impose enhanced state obligations, ensuring substantive equality and protection against marginalization or discrimination. A gender-sensitive approach by the ECtHR involves interpreting and applying the ECHR in ways that recognize and address the specific experiences, needs, and vulnerabilities of individuals based on their gender.

[1] Boutier (2024).

[2] Fredman (2016), Jelić (2023).

[3] Timmer (2013).

However, in cases related to the Hague Convention, the Court appears less inclined to apply these concepts to foreign mothers. When considered collectively, especially given their frequency, these cases reveal a significant gap—or perhaps an urgent need—to address core issues through the frameworks of vulnerability and gender. To echo the words of Marie-Bénédicte Dembour in reading ECtHR cases involving mothers as applicants: "I shall read them in a woman's voice and a feminist light."[4]

This contribution will begin with an overview of the background of the Hague Convention, highlighting its key benefits and shortcomings. It will then provide a review of ECtHR case law related to Hague Convention cases, followed by an examination of the Court's treatment of vulnerability and gender in other cases. This comparison will help illustrate the difference in approach, leading to suggestions on how to extend the concepts from the latter group of cases to the Hague Convention jurisprudence.

2 The Hague Convention on the Civil Aspects of International Child Abduction: Its Origins, Benefits and Weaknesses

The Hague Convention on the Civil Aspects of International Child Abduction has been hailed as one of the most successful conventions of the Hague Conference on Private International Law.[5] The Hague Convention's main objective is to protect children from international parental abduction, i.e. from a wrongful removal or retention across international borders in violation of the custody rights of another parent by ensuring the child's prompt return to the country of its habitual residence.[6] The Hague Convention works on the assumption that custody decisions should be made by the courts in the country of the child's habitual residence. The Hague Convention is thus seen as procedural or simply an instrument for bringing the child home where all parental and custody disputes are to be resolved by national courts. Pursuant to the Hague Convention, international abduction will exist only if the removal or retention is conducted in violation of custody rights which are guaranteed and vested by national law—violation of other parental rights, such as visitation rights, are not covered by the definition of abduction and in turn such violation will not trigger the application of the Hague Convention.[7] Once international abduction has taken place the mechanism of the Convention is put into operation involving Central Authorities and national courts of the country where the child has been taken to, which will decide whether the abduction has indeed taken place and decide

[4] Dembour (2006), p. 197.

[5] Schuz (2013), p. 4; Freeman and Taylor (2023), p. 2.

[6] Article 1 of the Hague Convention.

[7] Ibid, Article 3.

on the child's return.[8] There are exceptions to the obligation to return the child: grave risk that its return would expose the child to physical or psychological harm or otherwise place the child in an intolerable situation,[9] the holder of the custody right has not exercised the right or consented to the removal,[10] expiration of 1 year period following which the child has settled in its new environment or the child's objection to return if the child's age and maturity are appropriate to take into account its views.[11] As a general exception, Article 20 provides that the return of the child "may be refused if this would not be permitted by the fundamental principles of the requested State relating to the protection of human rights and fundamental freedoms."

The Hague Convention has been seen as a procedural tool providing only for the prompt return of the child[12] to the place of its habitual residence on the assumption that such return is in the best interest of the child[13] thereby establishing the so-called 'remedy of return'.[14] It does not set any rules regarding the allocation of custody or parental rights, which is the matter left to national laws and national courts. Custody rights established in national law are protected insofar as they provide the basis for triggering the international return procedure. Therefore, arguably, only the custody rights of the left-behind parent are recognized and enforceable under the Hague Convention.

It should be noted that the context and timing of the Hague Convention are important for understanding its relatively simple and formalistic structure, as well as the interpretation of its provisions. The Hague Convention was adopted in 1980, at a time when the issue of international child abduction by parents was becoming more prominent due to factors such as the rise in international marriages and increased cross-border movement.[15] While the human rights framework was already in place during the 1980s, it was not as developed as it would later become. This may explain why the Hague Convention contains very few references to human rights, although *lato sensu* it belongs to the human rights framework, with its primary aim being the protection of the best interests of the child.

At the time of the Hague Convention's adoption, the typical pattern of parental abduction was perceived as the forceful removal of a child by a foreign parent—usually the father—who either lacked custody rights or was not the primary caregiver, from the parent, typically the mother, who had custody rights and with whom

---

[8] Ibid, Articles 6–11.

[9] Ibid, Article 13.

[10] Ibid, Article 13.

[11] Ibid, Article 12.

[12] Article 11 of the Hague Convention requires national courts to act expeditiously and reach a decision on return within 6 weeks from the date of the commencement of the proceedings.

[13] Schuz (2013), p. 301.

[14] Weiner (2002), p. 279.

[15] Pérez-Vera Report (1982); Elrod (2023), pp. 51–52.

the child resided.[16] The abducted child was perceived as victim "who suffers from the sudden upsetting of his stability, the traumatic loss of contact with the parent who has been in charge of his upbringing, the uncertainty and frustration which come with the necessity to adapt to a strange language, unfamiliar cultural conditions and unknown teachers and relatives."[17]

However, the world has changed significantly since the early 1980s, and so have the patterns of child abduction. One major shift is that, in the majority of cases, it is women—often foreign nationals—who are the primary caregivers and who find themselves in the role of "abductors".[18] According to the 2017 official statistics from the Hague Conference on Private International Law: "73% of taking persons were mothers, a higher proportion than the 69% recorded in 2008, 68% in 2003 and 69% in 1999. In 2015, 24% of the taking persons were fathers and the remaining 3% comprised grandparents, institutions or other relatives. Where the information was available, the large majority (80%) of taking persons were the 'primary carer' or 'joint-primary carer' of the child. Where the taking person was the mother, this figure was 91% but only 61% where the taking person was the father."[19] This shift appears to be at odds with the underlying assumptions of the Hague Convention and the societal paradigms of the 1970s and 1980s. These statistics also reveal "a gender aspect to this new paradigm which was not there before".[20]

This paradigm shift and the development of human rights have put the Hague Convention assumptions on the back foot. While the original intention was to protect domestic primary caregivers from child abduction by a foreign parent without custody rights, the new context reveals a different pattern: protection is now provided to the domestic parent, who is not the primary caregiver, against abduction by a foreign parent who is the primary caregiver and has sole or shared custody rights. Single mothers raising their children can find themselves in a precarious situation in a foreign country—as both a single parent and a foreigner. Their plans to return to their country of origin may face numerous obstacles despite their custody rights, and the Hague Convention can sometimes serve as an impediment.[21] Additionally, custody decisions may change after the custodial parent leaves the country, and new custody arrangements can even be accompanied by criminal charges for abduction.

---

[16] "Indeed, it has been recognised by Adair Dyer, former Deputy Secretary General of the Hague Conference, that in the 1970's when the Convention was being prepared the paradigm case was that of the father who became so frustrated with being denied access to his child or children after the court had granted sole custody to the mother, that he stole the child, went abroad, and then underground."—Beaumont and McEleavy (1999), p. 9.

[17] Dyer Report (1978), p. 21.

[18] Salter (2014), pp. 19–23; Lamont (2011), pp. 369–370; Elrod (2023), p. 60.

[19] Prel. Doc. No 11 A of September 2017 - Part I—A statistical analysis of applications made in 2015 under the *Hague Convention of 25 October 1980 on the Civil Aspects of International Child Abduction*—Global report, p. 3, available at https://assets.hcch.net/docs/d0b285f1-5f59-41a6-ad83-8b5cf7a784ce.pdf

[20] Hale (2013), p. xi.

[21] Stanivuković and Djajić (2022), pp. 123–156.

In these new circumstances, the so-called "abductor" faces a difficult dilemma: either to get separated from the child although she is the primary caregiver or to accompany the child and return, facing not only the precarious situation they sought to escape from but also the potential consequences of the new custody arrangements, loss of custody rights, or even criminal charges. Although the Hague Convention includes provisions aimed at protecting the child's best interests, along with exceptions for return under Articles 12, 13, and 20, these exceptions seem limited in scope due to the standard of narrow interpretation,[22] especially considering the contemporary landscape of human rights protection. The Hague Convention assumes that the child's best interest is to be returned to the country of habitual residence, thereby safeguarding the custody rights of the left-behind parent. However, this approach leaves blind spots for the broader human rights protection of all persons involved, including the taking parent.

The 2020 HCCH Guide to Good Practice acknowledges that protecting a child from the trauma of being separated from the taking parent could potentially justify an exception under Article 13(1)(b). In such cases, the protection of the taking parent can be achieved indirectly through the protection of the child, particularly when the taking parent is unable or unwilling to return to the child's habitual residence. However, it is noted that domestic courts rarely uphold such claims. The reasons put forward before domestic courts under Article 13(1)b include: criminal prosecution against the taking parent in the child's habitual residence due to wrongful removal or retention, immigration issues faced by the taking parent, lack of effective access to justice in the child's habitual residence, medical or family reasons concerning the taking parent, and unequivocal refusal to return.[23]

Therefore, it has seemed not only natural but also necessary to complement the Hague Convention with human rights standards. A common reference point has been the UN Convention on the Rights of the Child due to the shared focus of both conventions on the welfare and best interest of the child.[24] The European Convention on Human Rights has also been a regular companion to the application of the Hague Convention—particularly when the responsibility of an ECHR member state is at stake, as the European Convention offers a range of protection options, primarily for children but also for other individuals affected by its implementation. The following section will discuss how the ECtHR has approached the application of the Hague Convention.

[22] Schuz (2013), p. 302; Baruffi and Holliday (2022), p. 492.

[23] HCCH Guide (2020), pp. 43–48.

[24] McEleavy (2015), pp. 365–405.

3 European Court of Human Rights Case Law on the Hague Convention: Continuities and Disruptions

Case law addressing alleged violations of the European Convention in relation to Hague Convention cases can illustrate the evolution of the ECtHR's application of human rights standards to issues arising from the enforcement of the Hague Convention in national legal settings. This research is based on an evaluation of all publicly available cases in which the ECtHR considered the merits of claims based on or related to the Hague Convention (78 cases from 2000–2023),[25] with the aim of assessing how this convention fits within the broader framework of protections guaranteed by the ECHR. The analysis of these cases focuses on several key aspects central to this research: the profile of the taking parent ("abductor"), including primary caregiver status, nationality, and gender; the status of custody rights at the time of the abduction and any subsequent changes; the availability of options for the taking parent to return with the child; and the vulnerability of the taking foreign mother, both as an individual and in relation to her parenthood status.

The factual patterns in these cases are in line with the general statistics of the application of the Hague Convention discussed above. An overview of cases in which the ECtHR assessed the application of the Hague Convention in relation to rights under the ECHR, most frequently Article 8, shows that in five out of six cases (83%) the alleged abductors were mothers of foreign nationality, and in all but two cases, they held either sole or shared custody rights. Therefore, in the majority of cases, mothers of foreign nationality with custody rights decided to leave the child's country of habitual residence and return to their home country. In twelve cases, mothers faced criminal charges for abduction in the countries they left behind. In another twelve cases, alleged domestic violence was among the reasons for leaving the original country of residence.

The chronology of cases highlights both continuities and disruptions in the evolving interplay between the Hague and Strasbourg Conventions. Early cases before the ECtHR reveal a common pattern: allegations of violations under the Hague Convention, stemming from the non-return of a child, were framed as breaches of Article 8 of the ECHR, which protects the rights of the left-behind parent. In such cases, the left-behind parent—typically asserting his rights under the Hague Convention—argued that the state where the other parent had taken the child failed to ensure the child's return. Consequently, the European Convention functioned as an international enforcement mechanism for the Hague Convention, which

[25] During this period, 102 cases referencing the Hague Convention were declared admissible and decided on their merits, as documented in the HUDOC database. This research focuses on 78 of those cases where the ECtHR determined that the Hague Convention was applicable. The Hague Convention may not apply for various reasons, the most common being the absence of abduction as defined by Article 3, due to custody arrangements, non-violation of custody rights, or the consent of the left-behind parent. The first case to address the merits of a Hague Convention claim under the ECHR was *Ignaccolo-Zenide v. Romania* (no. 31679/96, 25 January 2000). The most recent case included in this analysis is *Ghazaryan v. Armenia* (no. 30129/21, 28 November 2023).

otherwise depends solely on national authorities. A typical and frequently successful claim by a left-behind parent was that the respondent state either failed to issue an order for the child's return or failed to enforce such an order, thereby violating the parent's rights under the European Convention.

The ECtHR appeared to show considerable deference to the Hague Convention's return mechanism, despite defenses and critiques that its application risked being overly formalistic or mechanical, without sufficient regard for the specific circumstances of each case or careful evaluation of the custody decisions made by national authorities. In other words, the Hague Convention was protected by a generous margin of appreciation provided to the states, and the ECtHR was ready to accept its underlying premise—that returning the children to their habitual residence was in their best interest,[26] regardless of other circumstances of the case.

However, this trend was altered by the landmark case *Neulinger and Shuruk v. Switzerland*.[27] In this case, the ECtHR determined that Switzerland violated Article 8 of the ECHR by ordering the return of a child under the Hague Convention. It was the first case in which the ECtHR found a violation of Article 8 in favor of the taking parent.[28] The mother had alleged domestic violence, including physical and verbal abuse by the father.

The ECtHR noted that the Hague Convention requires the swift return of an abducted child unless there is a serious risk, emphasizing that the child's best interests are a key principle of the HC. For the first time, the ECtHR stated that a child's return cannot be automatically or mechanically enforced under the HC and that courts must take the child's best interests into account to ensure compliance with Article 8 of the ECHR. This requires domestic courts to conduct "an in-depth examination of the entire family situation and of a whole series of factors, in particular of a factual, emotional, psychological, material and medical nature" and to make "a balanced and reasonable assessment of the respective interests of each person, with a constant concern for determining what the best solution would be for the abducted child in the context of an application for his return to his country of origin."[29]

Also for the first time, the Court engaged with the return procedure under the Hague Convention, even though it had been conducted "by the book". From a human rights perspective, the procedure was found to suffer from significant deficiencies that could breach the rights of both the child and the taking parent. In other words, proper administration of the Hague Convention was not necessarily sufficient to protect human rights, and the underlying assumption—that return is always in the best interest of the child—was now being questioned.

Additionally, the position of the taking parent became a significant factor for the first time: "As to the mother, she would sustain a disproportionate interference with

[26] *Carlson v. Switzerland*, no. 49492/06 (6 November 2008), para. 80.

[27] *Neulinger and Shuruk v. Switzerland*, no. 41615/07 (Chamber Judgment 8 January 2009) (Grand Chamber Judgment 6 July 2010).

[28] Kruger and Lembrechts (2023), p. 152.

[29] *Neulinger and Shuruk v. Switzerland*, no. 41615/07 (Grand Chamber Judgment 6 July 2010), para. 139.

her right to respect for her family life if she were forced to return with her son to Israel. Consequently, there would be a violation of Article 8 of the Convention in respect of both applicants if the decision ordering the second applicant's return to Israel were to be enforced."[30] Thus, enforcing the return order would not only be contrary to the best interests of a very young child who was too dependent and attached to his primary caregiver, but the mother's reasons for not returning were also found to be justifiable. Moreover, the return order, if enforced, would also violate her right to family life.

This case emphasized that a return order could infringe upon the rights of a mother fleeing with her child, emphasizing her role as a parent. The exceptions outlined in the Hague Convention gained greater prominence, requiring national authorities to examine these exceptions more closely through a human rights lens, particularly considering the vulnerabilities of both children and fleeing parents.

This approach was followed in *Šneersone and Kampanella v. Italy* where the ECtHR found that the return of the child without his mother, who was a primary caregiver since his birth, would be contrary to the child's best interest, but also that Latvia's courts conducted an adequate analysis and found that mother "did not have sufficient financial means to reside there and was essentially unemployable, since she did not know any Italian."[31] The final result was that returning the child would be in breach of rights to family life of both mother and the child.

In *X v. Latvia*, the circumstances were dramatic and exposed deficiencies in the HC return procedure. A single mother and primary caregiver left Australia for her native Latvia with her 3-year-old daughter, as the sole holder of custody rights. It was only later that the father succeeded in obtaining both paternal and sole custody rights through Australian courts, and in securing a return order under the HC through Latvian courts. The mechanical application of the HC, without an effective analysis of the overall situation, the best interests of the child, or a reasonable assessment of the respective interests of each party, resulted in the return order. The ECtHR found that the failure of Latvian courts to assess "[t]he issue of whether it was possible for the mother to follow her daughter to Australia and to maintain contact with her"[32] *inter alia* led to violation of the right to family life of the mother who submitted the application only on her behalf.

Following criticism of the *Neulinger and Shuruk* judgment by various actors, including the Hague Conference on Private International Law,[33] the ECtHR appeared to lower the threshold from "an in-depth examination of the entire family situation and of a whole series of factors, in particular of a factual, emotional, psychological, material, and medical nature"[34] established in *Neulinger* to "an effective examination

---

[30] *Ibid*, para. 151.

[31] *Šneersone and Kampanella v. Italy,* no. 14737/09 (12 July 2011), para. 94.

[32] *X v. Latvia*, no. 27853/09 (Grand Chamber Judgment 26 November 2013), para. 117.

[33] Vajić (2015), p. 288.

[34] *Neulinger and Shuruk v. Switzerland*, no. 41615/07 (Grand Chamber Judgment 6 July 2010), para. 139.

of allegations made by a party on the basis of one of the exceptions expressly provided for."[35] The ECtHR explicitly overruled the *Neulinger* standard[36] and returned to granting states a wider margin of appreciation when deciding on Hague Convention claims. This shift was arguably made to preserve the urgency of HC procedures. However, the Court still emphasized the need for procedural discipline, asserting that decisions should not be automatic or stereotyped, and that exceptions must be interpreted strictly.[37] Despite this clarification and the lowering of the standard, a violation of the mother's rights under Article 8 was found in the *X v. Latvia* case.

After this interlude, beginning with *Neulinger and Shuruk v. Switzerland* and concluding with *X v. Latvia*, where the ECtHR intervened to address human rights deficiencies in the Hague Convention's formalistic procedures—considering the vulnerable positions of both the child and the mother and humanizing the HC through exceptions outlined in Articles 13 and 20 of the HC—the Court subsequently shifted back to a more deferential approach in HC return decisions. In later cases, the ECtHR largely ceased considering how the return of a child without its primary caregiver, or the return of the taking parent, might affect either party. Additionally, the Court reinstated its earlier decision-making patterns: if it is in the best interest of the child not to be separated from the mother, the expectation is that the mother must return to the country she left, unless very compelling arguments are presented against her return. The overwhelming statistics and patterns involving foreign women and their dire prospects in the countries they fled were once again obscured in judicial reasoning. This return to the Court's original stance effectively resulted in a loss of focus on the gender and vulnerability aspects of these cases.

For example, in *Voica v Romania*,[38] the ECtHR did not uphold the mother's claim against the return order. She had left France for Romania with her children, for whom she was the primary caregiver, following the collapse of her marriage, her former husband's criminal conviction for domestic violence, and her finding employment in Romania. After she left, the French courts changed the custody arrangements in favor of the father, leaving the mother with only visitation rights to be exercised in France. The Court did not assess the implications of her position. This case also highlights the problematic nature of the HC's promise that it deals solely with return procedures, leaving final custody decisions to the courts of the child's habitual residence after the return. This promise seems misleading, as it is unlikely that courts will reinstate custody rights to parents—usually mothers—who had custody before leaving with their children. In 18 out of 78 cases discussed

---

[35] *X v. Latvia*, no. 27853/09 (Grand Chamber Judgment 26 November 2013), para. 118.

[36] *Ibid*, para. 105.

[37] *Ibid*, paras. 92–119.

[38] *Voica v. Romania*, no. 9256/19 (7 July 2020).

herein mothers were stripped off their custody rights immediately after leaving the country.[39]

In *Michnea v. Romania*, the ECtHR ruled that the child's return to Italy was required under the HC and the ECHR. The child was 5 months old, while the mother did not speak Italian, had no job prospects in Italy, and her marriage was clearly over. Yet, the Court did not assess the circumstances of her potential return to Italy or the impact of separating the child from her mother.[40] In *Thomson v. Russia*, the ECtHR ruled for the return of a 4-year-old girl to Spain, despite the mother's argument that she could not join her daughter because she lacked residence, a place to live, and income in Spain. The Court acknowledged that in some cases, limitations on a mother's return could justify her decision not to return. However, it held that only limitations like criminal sanctions or lack of access to the foreign country's territory could justify non-return, and these factors were not present in this case.[41] As a result, the mother's position was marginalized, both individually and in relation to the child. The Court did not explore the possible effects of separating the child from her primary caregiver but seemed to imply that the mother was expected to return. Similar reasoning can be found in *Velasco Ayra v. Russia*, where the ECtHR ordered the return of a 6-month-old baby from Russia to Spain.[42]

In *X v. The Czech Republic*,[43] a mother left the U.S. with her 2-year-old daughter for whom she was the primary caregiver. After the Czech courts ordered the child's return, the mother also returned to the U.S. with the child to avoid separation. However, the U.S. courts then stripped her off her custody rights, and she faced criminal proceedings. She then approached the ECtHR claiming that the return violated both her and her daughter's right to family life. The ECtHR rejected her claim on both the merits and in the revision. The Court found that the limitations on her rights were attributable to her own decisions, without considering her circumstances, either past or present.

The Court has occasionally referred to potential obstacles to a parent's return in its more recent decisions, but it remains unclear how much weight these considerations carry when assessing the position of a foreign parent. For example, in

---

[39] These statistics include only custody arrangements made prior to the ECtHR decision, so it is likely that the actual number is higher.

[40] In order to confirm that the habitual residence of the five-month girl was in Italy the Court stated that she had lived *all her life* prior to her removal from Italy, that Italy was the only home *the child had known at that time, the child had been, at least to a certain degree, integrated in a social and family environment in that country. - Michnea v. Romania*, no. 10395/19 (7 July 2020), para. 47 (emphasis added). For an opposing perspective on the interpretation of habitual residence for babies, see: "At times, its application has become highly technical particularly with regard to habitual residence, a concept which, it has to be said, does not work well with regard to babies (though these form a tiny minority of abductions under the Convention)." (Lowe 2023, p. 402) Also, the CJEU took a different position regarding the habitual residence of infants in *Mercredi* (C-497/10, paras. 52–56).

[41] *Thompson v. Russia*, no. 36048/17 (30 March 2021), paras. 66–69.

[42] *Velasco Ayra v. Russia*, no. 54628/19 (11 January 2022).

[43] *X v. The Czech Republic*, no. 64886/19 (Judgment 12 May 2022) (Revision 30 March 2023).

Campanelli v. Russia, the ECtHR laid out certain standards only to conclude that these did not objectively rule out the possibility of the mother's return together with the child: "It was not implied that M.L. did not have access to Italian territory, that the criminal proceedings pending against her in Italy would necessarily lead to her separation with the child in the event of return, or that the applicant might actively prevent her from seeing the child in Italy or deprive her of parental rights or custody."[44] The mother had objected to the return on the grounds that she was the primary caregiver of a small child, had no knowledge of the Italian language, and was facing criminal charges for child abduction in Italy. Nevertheless, the ECtHR ruled that the mere existence of criminal proceedings did not "objectively rule out the possibility of the mother's return." This contradicts the Court's earlier interpretation of the same criteria and demonstrates a lowering of the defenses available to mothers facing return orders. In other words, the threshold was raised again and the burden shifted onto the taking parent.

A similar line of reasoning, with the expectation that the mother, who held custody rights, would return due to the breach of the father's custody rights despite ongoing criminal proceedings, was repeated in *Osso v. Bulgaria*[45] (regarding return to Switzerland), and *Kukavica v. Bulgaria*[46] (regarding return to Germany), without considering the real possibilities and prospects of such returns. The ECtHR even contemplated alternative arrangements for mothers' lives in foreign countries, without adequately addressing the real-life circumstances that had compelled them to leave those countries in the first place.

These cases illustrate patterns in both facts and paradigm shifts, including the Court's recent distancing from cases where the vulnerable position and rights of taking parents were considered—either alone or alongside the best interests of the child—but without providing effective protection to them. The overall case statistics further reflect this shift, this time in large numbers. In only four cases did the ECtHR find that returning the child would be against the child's best interests due to separation from the mother, where the mother also had valid reasons not to return.[47] In three of these cases, the mother's right to family life was found to have been breached.[48] In five cases, the Court was silent on the position of the taking parent, assuming instead that the mother would not return, but concluded it was in the child's best interests to remain in the new country with the mother.[49] In 14 cases, the ECtHR acknowledged that separation from the mother would be contrary to the

---

[44] *Campanelli v. Russia*, no. 35474/20 (4 October 2022), para. 29.

[45] *Osso v. Bulgaria*, no. 51056/21 (13 June 2023).

[46] *Kukavica v. Bulgaria*, no. 57202/21 (13 June 2023).

[47] *Neulinger and Shuruk v. Switzerland*, no. 41615/07 (Grand Chamber Judgment 6 July 2010); *Šneersone and Kampanella v. Italy*, no. 14737/09 (12 July 2011); *X v. Latvia*, no. 27853/09 (Grand Chamber Judgment 26 November 2013); *Satanovska and Rodgers v. Ukraine*, no. 12354/19 (28 January 2021).

[48] *Neulinger and Shuruk v. Switzerland, X v. Latvia, Satanovska and Rodgers v. Ukraine*.

[49] *Koons v. Italy*, no. 68183/01 (30 September 2008); *Macready v. The Czech Republic*, no(s). 4824/06 and 15,512/08 (22 April 2010); *B. v. Belgium*, no. 4320/11 (10 July 2012); *Phostira*

child's best interests but argued that the mother should follow her child despite challenges[50] such as visa and visitation rights restrictions,[51] another disabled child that she had to take care of in her native country,[52] health issues,[53] or having no job or place to stay,[54] as well as ongoing criminal proceedings in the destination country.[55] In two cases, the Court ruled that the mother was at fault for the situation, thus justifying coercive measures against both her and the child, even though she was the primary caregiver. In all other cases, which make up two-thirds of the total, the human rights of the taking parent were not taken into consideration, regardless of the case outcome.

The question here is why the ECtHR fails to consider statistics demonstrating that, in the overwhelming majority of cases, it is women with custody rights who are effectively prevented by the Hague Convention from relocating to their country of origin. The ECtHR has shown a tendency to defer to the Hague Convention, despite the complex and vulnerable positions of both the child and the foreign mother. One could argue that the "best interest of the child" standard is always present to mitigate the harsh formalism produced by the Hague Convention. Indeed, this standard is prominently featured in the text of the Convention on the Rights of the Child, the preamble to the Hague Convention, and the case law of the ECtHR.

However, what undermines this optimism is the ECtHR's assumption that the return ordered under the Hague Convention by itself ensures the protection of the child's best interests—an assumption that is nearly unrebuttable. With only a few exceptions, as discussed above, the ECtHR readily accepts that returning the child to the place of habitual residence is almost always better for the child than allowing the child to stay with its primary caregiver. The ECtHR's failure to recognize the changed landscape of the Hague Convention leads to the conclusion that in the Court's perspective, separating the child from its primary caregiver is almost always in the child's best interest.

In most cases, the pattern shows that single mothers or women in abusive relationships are in vulnerable positions in foreign countries, hampered by the operation of the Hague Convention. Their vulnerability stems from several factors,

---

Efthymiou and Ribeiro Fernandes v. Portugal, no. 66775/11 (05 February 2015); *Vilenchik v. Ukraine*, no. 21267/14 (3 October 2017).

[50] *Maumousseau and Washington v. France*, no. 39388/05 (6 December 2007); *V.P. v. Russia*, no. 61362/12 (23 October 2014); *Blaga v. Romania*, no. 54443/10 (1 July 2014); *Adžić c. Croatia* (no. 1), no. 22643/14 (12 March 2015); *K.J. v. Poland*, no. 30813/14 (1 March 2016); *Vladimir Ushakov v. Russia*, no. 15122/17, (18 June 2019); *Rinau v. Lithuania*, no. 10926/09 (14 January 2020); *Thompson v. Russia*, no. 36048/17 (30 March 2021); *Velasco Ayra v. Russia*, no. 54628/19 (11 January 2022); *C.-A.D. and L.-C.D. v. Russia*, no. 29601/20 (7 June 2022); *Campanelli v. Russia*, no. 35474/20 (4 October 2022); *G.K. v. Cyprus*, no. 16205/21 (21 February 2023); *Osso v. Bulgaria*, no. 51056/21 (13 June 2023); *Kukavica v. Bulgaria*, no. 57202/21 (13 June 2023).

[51] *Maumousseau and Washington v. France*, no. 39388/05 (6 December 2007).

[52] *Rinau v. Lithuania*, no. 10926/09 (14 January 2020).

[53] *Vladimir Ushakov v. Russia*, no. 15122/17, (18 June 2019).

[54] *Thompson v. Russia*, no. 36048/17 (30 March 2021).

[55] *G.K. v. Cyprus*, no. 16205/21 (21 February 2023); *Osso v. Bulgaria*, no. 51056/21 (13 June 2023).

including gender, foreign nationality, difficulties related to residence and employment, domestic violence, health issues, potential criminal charges, and, at times, the abuse of the return mechanism by the other parent.[56] The Court remains blind to these evident patterns and individual hardships. In fact, vulnerability has been addressed, but only in a very limited number of cases. The question arises as to why the ECtHR has not mainstreamed the concepts it has addressed in few HC cases—such as gender and vulnerability—as they are known to its broader jurisprudence. These concepts are present in the ECtHR's case law and will be discussed in the next section.

4 The European Court of Human Rights and the Development of Vulnerability and Gender-Sensitive Approaches

The concept of vulnerability has gained increasing importance in human rights discourse and beyond, over the past few decades. It has emerged as an interdisciplinary term, central to various settings and debates.[57] This "vulnerability turn"[58] has sparked considerable academic discussion, highlighting both its benefits and risks. While vulnerability can enhance protection, it also raises concerns about vagueness, ambiguity, exclusion, stigmatization and stereotypes.[59] scholars argue that the concept of 'vulnerabilisation' serves various purposes but also carries certain risks of exclusion and excessive overreach.[60]

Despite these concerns and the lack of a precise definition—although it is omnipresent in international documents and case law[61]—there is consensus that vulnerability is integral to international human rights law and holds significant potential for providing effective protection. The concept acknowledges human interdependence and structural inequality, offering a framework for advancing human rights discourse in terms of substantive equality and social justice. It serves as an alternative or enhancement to the traditional liberal paradigm, which centers on the autonomous, omnipotent, rational, and invulnerable individual.[62]

Vulnerability serves multiple functions. As Macioce explains, "[v]ulnerability—irrespective of its qualification in individualistic or universalistic terms, and the reference to individuals or (also) to groups—has been interpreted as a reason for the

[56] Bucher (2009), p. 492.

[57] Nungesser and Schirgi (2024), pp. 251–260.

[58] Bernardini (2023), p. 1415.

[59] Timmer et al. (2021), pp. 194–196.

[60] Engström et al. (2022), pp. 118–136.

[61] Heri (2021), pp. 151–152.

[62] Heri (2021), p. 145; Peroni and Timmer (2013), p. 1061.

recognition of rights, for the attribution of obligations, and for the implementation of specific procedures and mechanisms of protection".[63]

The concept of vulnerability has also gained recognition in the case law of the ECtHR. It was first introduced in the 2001 case of *Chapman v. UK*, where the Roma minority was identified as a vulnerable group.[64] This recognition of a vulnerable group marked a significant development and arguably became central to discussions on vulnerability. Since then, both the Court and academic discourse have expanded and refined the concept, broadening the list of vulnerable groups and redefining the characteristics of vulnerability associated with them.[65]

The development of this concept has taken several directions, including shifting from identity-based group vulnerability to a more positional understanding of vulnerability,[66] as well as identifying individual factors of vulnerability within groups. Timmer highlights that the ECtHR's approach to conceptualizing vulnerability is not always entirely consistent, but that it nevertheless extends beyond groups to encompass a broader range of contexts and individuals.[67] This broader consideration of positional group vulnerability and individual factors provides a useful framework for theorizing the vulnerability of women within the context of the Hague Convention. For example, women who are primary caregivers with custody rights may face difficult choices: staying in a foreign country and confronting numerous obstacles, leaving with the imminent risk of being declared an abductor with serious consequences, or separating from their child as the primary caregiver. These limited and difficult options place such women in a vulnerable position.

Nearly all commentators of the condition of vulnerability in human rights law and the jurisprudence of the ECtHR advance the Martha Fineman's concept of vulnerability as universal and inherent to the human condition. According to Fineman, vulnerability is shaped by an individual's lived experiences, inevitable dependency

---

[63] Macioce (2022), p. 76.

[64] Peroni and Timmer (2013), p. 1063.

[65] Peroni and Timmer (2013), pp. 1064–65.

[66] "Group membership, in this case, does not depend on what the individual subjects are, but on their position within a context of risk or uncertainty, and the possibilities of action that these subjects are given or precluded.(…) Vulnerability is here, more simply, a positioning—with respect to certain vulnerability factors—that is common among subjects who are unrelated in every other respect, and who are therefore included in the group only as long as, and to the extent that, those factors persist."—Macioce (2022), p. 73.

[67] Timmer identifies several situations, many of which extend beyond the vulnerability typically associated with minority groups: inherent vulnerability of children and persons with mental disabilities, vulnerability due to state control (persons in detention), vulnerability due to gender (women in domestic violence or precarious reproductive health situations), vulnerability due to a legal power imbalance (persons who are accused and persons who lack legal capacity), vulnerability due to espousal of unpopular views (demonstrators and journalists), vulnerability in the context of migration (detention and expulsion of asylum seekers), vulnerability due to group-membership (Roma, people with impaired health, and (to some extent) asylum seekers), compounded vulnerability. Timmer (2013), pp. 152–162.

on others, and resilience to institutions and the environment.[68] While her theory transcends the scope of this research, it has some relevant, albeit general implications. It suggests that individuals can still find themselves in precarious positions despite the protection of human rights or legal mechanisms, and that formalism should not obscure the vulnerability of (liberal) subjects.

Formalism can sometimes lead to anomalies, masking the unequal distribution of privileges and disadvantages. For instance, the Hague Convention offers no specific mechanism to protect the custody rights of the taking parent, while the left-behind parent can trigger the HC's proceedings. The assumption that national courts in the child's habitual residence will resolve parental and custody disputes on equal footing for both parents is misleading. In reality, this exacerbates the vulnerability of taking parents. Their access to a foreign country and its courts, the risk of criminal charges, and the potential reputation as an abductor place them in a much more precarious position—one not immediately visible within the formal structure of the HC. After all, it was the ECtHR which took a stand that the Hague Convention is "essentially an instrument of a procedural nature and not a human rights treaty protecting individuals on an objective basis."[69]

The ECtHR has expanded its discussion of vulnerability beyond group identity, developing and relying on a more comprehensive concept of vulnerability. The point being made here is that, although the ECtHR has recognized and promoted this broader understanding of vulnerability, it has been underutilized in cases involving the Hague Convention. Even the rare references to the specific situation of a taking mother highlight the need for and justification of attributing vulnerability to women in such circumstances. The absence of this approach effectively excludes certain categories of women from the protection of human rights. The concept of vulnerability is meant to address such gaps, and to shed light on the forgotten victims of the Hague Convention's application.

The ECtHR's focus on gender has been versatile, ranging from anti-discrimination provisions to gender-sensitive approaches and gender mainstreaming, all aimed at achieving gender equality. As Jelić notes, "[t]he Court's acknowledgement of the applicability of Article 14 in cases of indirect discrimination is important from the perspective of feminist justice. By using this method, the Court adopts a more gender-sensitive approach to adjudication, recognizing the systemic discriminatory effects on women, even when the law appears gender-neutral, rather than merely acknowledging that a particular female applicant suffered a violation of a substantive article".[70] Notions such as gender mainstreaming and feminist justice have become part of human rights discourse. However, critics argue that gender perspective still requires judicial proactivity, with calls for greater efforts to integrate

---

[68] Fineman (2008), pp. 1–23.

[69] *Neulinger and Shuruk v. Switzerland*, no. 41615/07 (Grand Chamber Judgment 6 July 2010), para. 145. Also, *Šneersone and Kampanella v. Italy*, no. 14737/09 (12 July 2011), para. 92.

[70] Jelić (2023), p. 44.

gender perspectives and mainstreaming into cases brought before the ECtHR[71] and that there is "a need to reconsider the strategies in place to ensure a gender-sensitive, inclusive practice of human rights adjudication".[72] Additionally, some argue that gender equality has yet to be fully conceptualized.[73] Nevertheless, a gender-sensitive approach is far from unfamiliar to the ECtHR especially in circumstances which demonstrate the gender bias in application of legal norms.

5 Extending the Concepts of Vulnerability and Gender-Sensitive Approaches to the Hague Convention Jurisprudence Before the European Court of Human Rights

This section will explore how the concepts of vulnerability and gender can be extended to Hague Convention cases before the ECtHR. In the 78 cases analyzed herein, the ECtHR has never referenced the overwhelming paradigm shift and general trends in child abduction cases that could serve well for introducing the vulnerability of women in such situations. In fact, the ECtHR has only rarely addressed the application of the Hague Convention from the perspective of the taking parent.[74] On several occasions, it acknowledged that certain factors may indeed provide justifiable obstacles for women to return, though this has not resulted in favorable outcomes for taking parents.[75]

Addressing the Hague Convention through the concept of vulnerability could provide the key for balancing human rights. This would allow the Court to conduct human rights mainstreaming of the HC, redefine its underlying premises (such as the best interests of the child), and challenge the options purportedly available to foreign mothers under the HC. Human rights mainstreaming seems particularly relevant here, especially considering the ECtHR acknowledged that the Hague Convention is not a human rights treaty.[76] Such human rights mainstreaming could be achieved through a gender-sensitive and a vulnerability-focused approach to the HC cases, given the broader context and the well-known asymmetry resulting from the formalistic and mechanical application of the Hague Convention. However, the

---

[71] Evans (2023), pp. 21–34.

[72] Van Leeuwen (2024), p. 173.

[73] Alkiviadou and Manoli (2021), p. 206.

[74] Only in three cases (*Neulinger and Shuruk v. Switzerland*, *X v. Latvia*, *Satanovska and Rodgers v. Ukraine*) it was found that the right of the mother was breached due to the return order. In all other cases it seems that taking parents are deprived of agency and protection under the ECtHR.

[75] As the statistics above demonstrate, in 14 cases the Court implicitly required mothers to return, reasoning that separation from the child would be contrary to the child's best interests.

[76] *Neulinger and Shuruk v. Switzerland*, no. 41615/07 (Grand Chamber Judgment 6 July 2010), para. 145; *Šneersone and Kampanella v. Italy*, no. 14737/09 (12 July 2011), para. 92.

overall background and outcomes of the HC system, as well as the ECtHR's procedural approach to it, have been noted in dissenting opinions and commentaries. In their joint dissenting opinion in the case of *R.S. v. Poland*, where the ECtHR found a violation of the left-behind father's right to family life, Judges Nicolaou, Wojtyczek, and Vehabović pointed to a crucial missing element in the Court's analysis:

> Context is all-important. It is therefore necessary to add a few important points to the presentation of the factual circumstances. The spouses were Polish nationals who got married in Poland and subsequently moved to Switzerland, where they had their children. That was apparently on the understanding that married life would continue unimpeded. Unfortunately it did not and, as confirmed by the Polish courts in the divorce proceedings, the marital split was entirely due to the conduct of the applicant. He formed a relationship with an employee, with whom he set up home very close to where his wife also had to live. She found herself completely isolated but did not abandon hope that her husband might return to her. Matters reached a crisis point when the applicant's partner became pregnant. As established in the divorce proceedings, the applicant placed his wife in a very vulnerable position. He closed his own bank account and deactivated his wife's credit card. He announced to his wife that their savings amounting to 80,000 Swiss francs (CHF) would be divided into two parts but that she would receive only CHF 9000–10,000. Then the applicant ordered his wife to quit their flat and move into a two-bedroom apartment. The applicant also took most of the documents belonging to his wife, such as her employment certificates and her letters. The health of the applicant's wife deteriorated: she developed anaemia, lost weight and started to suffer from severe depression.
>
> These events, coupled with what was accepted by the domestic court as the applicant's harsh attitude towards her, put her in an intolerable position. She then informed the applicant in April 2008 that she would be petitioning for divorce in Poland. There was nothing untoward in pursuing such a course. She was registered as being domiciled in Poland. She was therefore not forum shopping. The way things had turned out, she could no longer expect a decent life in Switzerland and had no alternative but to seek a new beginning in her home country.[77]

This dissenting opinion highlights the typical paradigm in Hague Convention cases, exposing the blind spots of the ECtHR. More importantly, it shows that the vulnerable position of the mother is evident and well-known to the Court but deliberately omitted from consideration. Such insights are not isolated. For instance, Judge Dedov observed: "All these deficiencies, in my view, should lead to a different perception of the interplay between the Convention for the Protection of Human Rights and Fundamental Freedoms and the Hague Convention. Today the Hague Convention predominates entirely over Article 8 of the Convention because no comprehensive analysis of the best interests of the child is possible for either the national courts or for the European Court of Human Rights. The Court, in my humble view, is therefore placed in a position that runs counter to its role to protect vulnerable persons and to fight against discrimination."[78]

---

[77] *R.S. v. Poland*, no. 63777/09 (12 July 2015), joint dissenting opinion of Judges Nicolaou, Wojtyczek and Vehabović, para. 2.

[78] *Vladimir Ushakov v. Russia*, no. 15122/17 (18 June 2019), dissenting opinion of the Judge Dedov. Similar observations can also be found in dissenting opinions in cases *Adžić c. Croatia* (no. 1), no. 22643/14 (12 March 2015) and *Thompson v. Russia*, no. 36048/17 (30 March 2021).

The vulnerability of taking parents, who are usually mothers with foreign nationality, has also been noted in commentaries,[79] as well as in policy papers and projects such as the *Protection of Abducting Mothers in Return Proceedings: Intersection between Domestic Violence and Parental Child Abduction*.[80] Statistics show that in most cases, the pattern reveals that single mothers, or women in abusive or dysfunctional relationships, are in a vulnerable position in a foreign country and are hampered by the operation of the Hague Convention. While their vulnerability is evident, the Court seems blind to these obvious patterns and individual hardships. Incorporating a vulnerability approach would not necessitate the automatic dismissal of the Hague Convention claims of left-behind parents, but rather careful consideration and balancing of both parents' positions, along with the best interests of the child.

There is no reason why gender should not be part of the discussion when applying the Hague Convention, especially when so many other factors underpinning its application have been subtly yet radically changed. Statistics show that in over 80% of cases, the abductors are mothers with custody rights and foreign nationality. However, the Court fails to recognize the gender implications of these cases and misses the opportunity to apply the gender-sensitive approach it has used in cases where gender was central, particularly when certain rules or practices placed a disproportionate burden on women.[81] In fact, the ECtHR has already adopted this approach in cases of domestic violence,[82] which figures as a prominent reason of taking mothers in the HC cases.[83] It should be natural to apply the same gender-sensitive approach to cases under the Hague Convention. The mechanical application of the Hague Convention can thus imply gender bias and inequality.[84]

A feminist reading of the outcomes of these cases reveals that men usually prevail, suggesting that the Hague Convention often protects the dominant position of fathers.[85] Keyes criticizes the existing approach to the HC, arguing that it "obscures the scope, and the need, for analysis of gender in private international law".[86] Given that the majority of abductors are mothers, often the primary caregivers, concerns arise over the automatic return of children in situations where the HC fails to account for the motivations behind leaving the country. Courts often prioritize strict rules

[79] Bucher (2009), pp. 490–493; Trimmings and Momoh (2021), pp. 3–4.

[80] POAM Project (2020), p. 7.

[81] Jelić (2023), p. 35.

[82] In finding violation of Article 3 in conjunction with Article 14, in relation to domestic violence, the Court found: "Substantive gender equality can only be achieved with a gender-sensitive interpretation and application of the Convention provisions that considers the factual inequalities between women and men and the way they impact women's lives."—*Volodina v. Russia*, no. 41261/17 (9 July 2019), para. 111.

[83] Trimmings and Momoh (2021), p. 4.

[84] Similarly to the finding that, in Article 9 cases, it is usually men who prevail over women in vindicating their religious rights. See Castillo-Ortiz (2019).

[85] Bucher (2009), p. 492.

[86] Keyes (2019), p. 104.

over the safety of mothers and children. Such a rigid approach perpetuates harmful stereotypes about women and neglects the needs of vulnerable families, even though the Hague Convention is often regarded as effective.[87]

Salter argues that Hague Convention proceedings often target women as the primary focus of punitive action, reinforcing legal and cultural stereotypes of women as deceitful or false accusers. Instead of facilitating neutral adjudication in custody matters, the Hague Convention can serve as a medium through which the gender biases of domestic legal regimes are extended internationally.[88] From a feminist perspective, "[t]here are serious unresolved issues with the impact of this Convention on women," as its strict and mechanical application fails to adequately consider "caring relationships between mothers and children, the circumstances of an individual mother's case, and the mother's specific interests".[89]

A gender-sensitive approach requires the recognition that the mechanical application of the Hague Convention inadvertently affects foreign women and mothers, much as the ECtHR has recognized that domestic violence predominantly affects women and constitutes a form of gender discrimination. This approach mandates a shift in focus to the position of women, calling for an in-depth analysis of the human rights of all parties involved and an inclusive human rights adjudication. Such an approach could have altered the outcome in cases like *Voica v. Romania*,[90] by considering that the mother left due to domestic violence and new prospects in her home country, thereby accounting for the risks she faced and the unequal burden-sharing regarding the right to family life. A feminist interpretation of the facts in *Michnea v. Romania*,[91] viewed from the perspective of a mother of a 5-month-old baby, would not force her to choose between leaving her home country or abandoning her child. This reading would necessarily shift the focus to the causes and consequences of these impossible choices.

Given that the gender status of the primary caregiver is intertwined with her status as a foreign national, along with the potential risks related to residence permits, this pattern could give rise to intersectional discrimination [92] or compounded vulnerability.[93] Similar issues have been discussed in relation to the ECtHR's case law, notably concerning refugee women,[94] migrant women,[95] and minority women.[96] Admittedly, the longstanding critique that the Court has been insensitive to

[87] Keyes (2019), pp. 108–111.

[88] Salter (2014), p. 13.

[89] Keyes (2024), p. 275.

[90] *Voica v. Romania*, no. 9256/19 (7 July 2020).

[91] *Michnea v. Romania*, no. 10395/19 (7 July 2020).

[92] "Foreignness is an intersectional category, which is to say that it implicates identity at the intersection of many different social structures: nationality, national origin, race, religion, class, ethnicity, gender, and others." – Achiume (2021), p. 48–49.

[93] Timmer (2013), pp. 161–162.

[94] Krstić (2023), pp. 113–132; Pittaway and Bartolomei (2002), pp. 21–32.

[95] Peroni (2018), pp. 93–110.

[96] Jelić (2024), pp. 355–381.

intersectional gender discrimination[97] remains valid. The failure to recognize multiple discriminatory factors reinforces harm and perpetuates inequality.

6 Conclusion

Cases involving the Hague Child Abduction Convention before the ECtHR highlight recurring factual and legal patterns that often remain unaddressed. Statistics show that mothers, typically foreign nationals and primary caregivers, face precarious situations when they leave with their child. These actions are often deemed violations of the Hague Convention. In most cases, the ECtHR has upheld the rights of left-behind parents, usually fathers, under Article 8 of the European Convention. Although in a few cases the ECtHR objected to the mechanical application of the Hague Convention and the rigid enforcement of child return at the expense of guarantees under Article 8, the assumption that return is in the child's best interest remained the primary principle. This principle was sometimes tempered by procedural requirements, such as the obligation of national courts to effectively examine the overall family situation. However, what generally remains unaddressed is the position of the mother who has taken the child. As a result, the ECtHR can be seen as equally guilty as national courts, in adopting a mechanical, formalistic, and overly deferential approach to the Hague Convention.

Given that the Hague Convention contains no provisions for the protection of primary caregivers and is considered by the ECtHR as a procedural rather than a human rights treaty, the European Convention should not be applied solely to enforce return orders. While a gendered perspective on abduction cases may not have been explicitly recognized when the Hague Convention was adopted, the disproportionate impact it has on women today should be addressed through the lens of gender equality to ensure equitable human rights protection.

Incorporating a vulnerability and gender-sensitive approach would not require the automatic dismissal of the Hague Convention claims by left-behind parents. Instead, it would encourage a careful consideration and balancing of both parents' positions, alongside the best interests of the child.

References

Achiume T (2021) Race and refugees in international law. In: Costello C (ed) The Oxford handbook on international refugee law. Oxford University Press, Oxford, pp 43–59

Alkiviadou N, Manoli A (2021) The European Court of Human Rights through the looking glass of gender: an evaluation. Goettingen J Int Law 11(1):191–211. https://doi.org/10.3249/1868-1581-11-1-alkiviadou-manoli

[97] Radačić (2008), pp. 841–857.

Baruffi MC, Holliday J (2022) Child abduction. In: Beaumont P, Holliday J (eds) A guide to global private international law. Hart Publishing, Oxford, pp 481–495
Beaumont PR, McEleavy PE (1999) The Hague Convention on International Child Abduction. Oxford University Press, Oxford
Bernardini MG (2023) Vulnerable capacity. Notes on a quiet legal revolution. Int J Semiot Law 36:1415–1442. https://doi.org/10.1007/s11196-022-09950-1
Boutier I (2024) Understanding vulnerability through the eyes of the European Court of Human Rights' jurisprudence: challenges and responses. Peace Human Rights Govern 8(1):27–52. https://doi.org/10.14658/PUPJ-PHRG-2024-aof-6
Bucher A (2009) La dimension sociale du droit international privé. Recueil des cours 341:9–535
Castillo-Ortiz P, Ali A, Samanta N (2019) Gender, intersectionality and religious manifestation before the European Court of Human Rights. J Hum Rights 18(1):76–91. https://doi.org/10.1080/14754835.2019.1581054
Dembour MB (2006) Who believes in human rights? Reflections on the European Convention. Cambridge University Press, Cambridge
Dyer Report (1978) Adair Dyer, 1978 report on international child abduction by one parent ('legal kidnapping'). In: Hague conference on private international law, Tome III - Actes et documents de la quatorizame session 6 au 25 octobre 1980, La Haye 1982
Elrod L (2023) The global effort to deter parental kidnapping: a history of the Hague Child Abduction Convention. In: Freeman M, Taylor N (eds) Research handbook on international child abduction. Edward Elgar Publishing, Cheltenham, pp 47–62
Engström V, Heikkilä M, Mustaniemi-Laakso M (2022) Vulnerabilisation: between mainstreaming and human rights overreach. Neth Q Hum Rights 40(2):118–136. https://doi.org/10.1177/09240519221092599
Evans J (2023) Gender mainstreaming at the European Court of Human Rights: the need for a coherent strategy in approaching cases of violence against women and domestic violence. Univ Miami Inter-Am Law Rev 54(1):1–38
Fineman MA (2008) The vulnerable subject: anchoring equality in the human condition. Yale J Law Fem 20(1):1–23
Fredman S (2016) Emerging from the shadows: substantive equality and article 14 of the European Convention on Human Rights. Hum Rights Law Rev 16(2):273–302
Freeman M, Taylor N (2023) Nurturing the 1980 Hague Abduction Convention. Laws 12(4):1–12
Hale B (2013) Foreword. In: Schuz R (ed) The child abduction convention: a critical analysis. Hart Publishing, Oxford
HCCH Guide to Good Practice (2020) Hague Conference on Private International Law: Guide to Good Practice Child Abduction Convention: Part VI - Article 13(1)(b). https://assets.hcch.net/docs/225b44d3-5c6b-4a14-8f5b-57cb370c497f.pdf
Heri C (2021) Responsive human rights: vulnerability, ill-treatment and the ECtHR. Hart Publishing, Oxford
Jelić I (2023) Feminist justice and the European Court of Human Rights. In: Krstić I et al (eds) Legal issues of international law from a gender perspective - gender perspectives in law, vol 3. Springer, Cham. https://doi.org/10.1007/978-3-031-13459-3_2
Jelić I (2024) The rights of minority women before the European Court of Human Rights: critical review in light of the practice of the UN Human Rights Committee and other international human rights bodies. Annals 72(3):355–381. https://doi.org/10.51204/Anali_PFBU_24301A
Keyes M (2019) Women in private international law. In: Rimmer SH, Ogg K (eds) Research handbook on feminist engagement with international law. Edward Elgar Publishing, Cheltenham, pp 103–117
Keyes M (2024) Feminist approaches to private international law. In: Kramer X, Piñeiro LC (eds) Research methods in private international law: a handbook on regulation, research and teaching. Edward Elgar Publishing, Cheltenham, pp 265–285

Krstić I (2023) The recognition of refugee women in international law. In: Krstić I et al (eds) Legal issues of international law from a gender perspective - gender perspectives in law, vol 3. Springer, Cham, pp 113–132. https://doi.org/10.1007/978-3-031-13459-3_6

Kruger T, Lembrechts S (2023) Case law of the European Court of Human Rights on international child abduction. In: Freeman M, Taylor N (eds) Research Handbook on International Child Abduction. Edward Elgar Publishing, Cheltenham, pp 149–162. https://doi.org/10.4337/9781800372511.00023

Lamont R (2011) Mainstreaming gender into european family law? The case of international child abduction and Brussels II revised. Eur Law J 17(3):366–384

Lowe N (2023) Whither the 1980 Hague Abduction Convention? In: Freeman M, Taylor N (eds) Research handbook on international child abduction. Edward Elgar Publishing, Cheltenham, pp 387–402

Macioce F (2022) The politics of vulnerable groups. Implications for philosophy, law, and political theory. Palgrave Macmillan, Springer, London. https://doi.org/10.1007/978-3-031-07547-6

McEleavy P (2015) The European Court of Human Rights and the Hague Child Abduction Convention: prioritising return or reflection? Neth Int Law Rev 62:365–405

Nungesser F, Schirgi A (2024) Debating the vulnerability zeitgeist: introduction to an interdisciplinary trialogue. Hum Stud 47:251–260. https://doi.org/10.1007/s10746-024-09742-5

Pérez-Vera Report (1982) Explanatory report by Elisa Pérez-Vera on the Convention on the Civil Aspects of International Child Abduction. Acts and documents of the fourteenth session (1980), tome III, child abduction. https://assets.hcch.net/docs/a5fb103c-2ceb-4d17-87e3-a7528a0d368c.pdf

Peroni L (2018) The borders that disadvantage migrant women in enjoying human rights. Neth Q Hum Rights 36(2):93–110. https://doi.org/10.1177/0924051918771229

Peroni L, Timmer A (2013) Vulnerable groups: the promise of an emerging concept in European Human Rights Convention law. Int J Const Law 11(4):1056–1085. https://doi.org/10.1093/icon/mot042

Pittaway E, Bartolomei L (2002) Refugees, race and gender: the multiple discrimination against refugee women. Refuge Canada J Refugees 19(6):21–32. https://doi.org/10.25071/1920-7336.21236

POAM Project (2020) Protection of abducting mothers in return proceedings: intersection between domestic violence and parental child abduction. Research project funded under the European Union's Rights, Equality and Citizenship Programme 2014–2020. https://research.abdn.ac.uk/wp-content/uploads/sites/15/2022/05/Best-Practice-Guide_POAM.pdf

Radačić I (2008) Gender equality jurisprudence of the European Court of Human Rights. Eur J Int Law 19(4):841–857. https://doi.org/10.1093/ejil/chn044

Salter M (2014) Getting Hagued – the impact of international law on child abduction by protective mothers. Altern Law J 39(1):19–23

Schuz R (2013) The child abduction convention: a critical analysis. Hart Publishing, Oxford

Stanivuković M, Djajić S (2022) The right of the parent to return to its country of origin in the light of the Hague Convention on the Civil Aspects of International Child Abduction and the European Convention on the Protection of Human Rights. Annals 70(1):123–156. https://doi.org/10.51204/Anali_PFBU_22105A

Timmer A (2013) A quiet revolution: vulnerability in the European Court of Human Rights. In: Fineman M, Grear A (eds) Vulnerability: reflections on a new ethical foundation for law and politics. Ashgate, Burlington

Timmer A, Baumgärtel M, Kotzé L, Slingenberg L (2021) The potential and pitfalls of the vulnerability concept for human rights. Neth Q Hum Rights 39(3):190–197. https://doi.org/10.1177/09240519211048009

Trimmings K, Momoh O (2021) Intersection between domestic violence and international parental child abduction: protection of abducting mothers in return proceedings. Int J Law Policy Family 35(1):1–19. https://doi.org/10.1093/lawfam/ebab001

Vajić N (2015) The Interaction between the European Court of Human Rights and the Hague Child Abduction Convention. In: Župan M (ed) Private international law in the jurisprudence of European Courts - family at focus. Faculty of Law Osijek Josip Juraj Strossmayer University of Osijek, Osijek, pp 285–293

Van Leeuwen F (2024) Epistemic blind spots, misconceptions and stereotypes: the home birth jurisprudence of the European Court of Human Rights. Eur J Int Law 35(1):153–174. https://doi.org/10.1093/ejil/chae002

Weiner MH (2002) Navigating the road between uniformity and progress: the need for a purposive analysis of the Hague Convention on the Civil Aspects of International Child Abduction. Colum Hum Rights Law Rev 33(2):275–362

Thalia, Kruger Sara, Lembrechts Marilyn, Freeman Nicola, Taylor Research Handbook on International Child Abduction The 1980 Hague Convention Case law of the European Court of Human Rights on international child abduction Edward Elgar Publishing 149-162

Sanja Djajić is a tenured Professor of Public International Law at the University of Novi Sad School of Law. She has studied at law schools in Serbia (Belgrade, Novi Sad), the United States (UCONN School of Law), and the United Kingdom (LSE), and has been a visiting fellow at several universities, including LSE, K.U. Leuven, and Vienna. She is a recipient of the Ron Brown and Chevening scholarships. While her primary professional focus is public international law, she has also integrated various legal disciplines both academically and in practice, including human rights, international investment law, and the application of international law within national legal systems.

Bodies in Context: Strengthening Intersectionality's Potential for Addressing Structural Inequalities

Lorena Sosa

Abstract Intersectionality, while powerful in identifying overlapping systems of oppression, remains challenging to use in judicial decisions and legal frameworks, particularly regarding its potential to capture structural inequality and discrimination. This chapter explores how a focus on human bodies can enhance legal and social understandings of intersectional discrimination and strengthen the structural dimensions of intersectionality. It critically examines how intersectionality in legal practice is constrained by three primary limitations: (1) the tendency to analyse single or additive categories of discrimination rather than exploring how they are created, interconnected, and mutually reinforcing; (2) a focus on identities more than on systems of oppression; and (3) an emphasis on vulnerable groups rather than the structural forces that place them in positions of vulnerability. To address these issues, this paper proposes a body-centred approach, positioning bodies as the material embodiment of intersecting inequalities, which can help reveal structural dynamics. The approach highlights four dimensions. Firstly, looking at bodies as a whole reveals the artificial nature of single-axis examinations of equality. Secondly, it views sexuality and reproduction as socially and culturally defined practices that shape the perceived function of bodies, offering insights into the socioeconomic, political, and interpersonal factors that shape discrimination and exclusion. Thirdly, it underscores the symbolic dimension of bodies, arguing that inclusive representation and meaningful participation can challenge stereotypes and reshape the social construction of difference. Finally, the framework explores how human bodies are situated within material contexts of place and space, unveiling larger structural dynamics. Through case studies from the Inter-American Court of Human Rights on violence against trans women, this four-layered approach highlights how an inter-

L. Sosa (✉)
Utrecht University, Utrecht, The Netherlands
e-mail: L.P.A.Sosa@uu.nl

F. Macioce et al. (eds.), *Feminist Legal and Political Practices*, Gender Perspectives in Law 6, https://doi.org/10.1007/978-3-032-02856-3_11

sectional perspective rooted in corporeal experience can reveal the structural and systemic forces that perpetuate inequality beyond individual cases, providing legal and theoretical tools to challenge entrenched biases within law and policy.

1 Introduction: Intersectionality Troubles

For the past four decades, intersectionality's usefulness to critically inquire into situations of inequality and improve legal responses has inspired generations of legal scholars.[1] Its potential to explore how categories used to distinguish and differentiate between individuals and groups (such as gender, race, or class) are created, how they interact, and how they connect to different systems of oppression, helps reveal inequality in its full complexity. By focusing on the categories of distinction ('migrant status', 'ethnicity', 'sexual orientation', 'gender identity', 'disability') and how these sustain systems of inequality ('nationalism', 'racism', 'heteronormativism', 'cisnormativism', 'ableism'), intersectionality can look beyond groups ('migrant women', 'Roma women', 'lesbian', 'transgender women', 'disabled women') towards transformative responses that combat discrimination. Moreover, intersectionality highlights both the individual and the structural: it provides a basic explanation of the social system that is expressed and experienced individually.[2] This structural approach to intersectionality, examining the dynamics and processes that make and give meaning to categories of difference leading to subordination,[3] holds great transformative potential.

Looking at gender-based violence (GBV) through an intersectional lens can help illustrate these notions. Since intersectionality suggests that social categories of distinction are manifested at the level of personal experience, at the group level, and the systemic level through their configuration within social institutions, social practices, organizations, and the law, it posits that legal responses to GBV should not only look into the individual case presuming its incidental nature, but also address the structural aspects of intersectional inequality in the social and institutional dimensions that impact on cases of violence. Moreover, it suggests that categories determining individuals' and groups' social positioning intersect at different levels (such as norms, policies, and their implementation), and attests that violence can occur in multiple domains (family, workplace, educational institutions, and so on). In this sense, intersectionality can provide 'volume' to the analysis of violence cases because it requires to examine them at those different levels and within each

[1] Fredman (2016a); Askin and Stoll (2024); Atrey (2019); Burri and Schiek (2009); Yuval-Davis (2011); Carbado et al. (2013); Salem (2016); Davis and Zarkov (2017).

[2] Montoya and Agustín (2013).

[3] Crenshaw (1991).

domain.[4] However, several institutional barriers and legal practices restrain intersectionality's overarching transformative potential.[5]

A first constraint for intersectionality's potential in analysing inequality-related issues comes from the general emphasis on antidiscrimination law to address inequality, which has limited transformative power and difficulties in the realization of social justice. Even more problematic is the general tendency to reduce nondiscrimination to the categorical approach. Antidiscrimination law largely continues to rely on single categories of discrimination, despite improved approaches that discuss single grounds 'capaciously' or 'contextually'.[6] While there are approaches that explore multiple (single) grounds of discrimination or attempt to embed intersectionality as an additional new ground, they continue to fall short of a 'strict' intersectional approach, missing its full potential.[7]

A second limitation derives from characterizing intersectionality as a tool capturing 'identities', particularly in judicial cases, norms and public policies. Yuval-Davis has pointed out that insufficient understanding of intersectionality has led to analytical confusion in UN bodies recommending the use of intersectionality in terms of 'identity'.[8] Indeed, intersectionality, as a concept discussed in the early 90 s, provided a useful articulation for the discontent with essentializing views of 'women' and the erasure of the experiences of those who are not white, heterosexual, middle class, national, abled-bodied, young, etc. Black, Chicana, and postcolonial feminists referred to 'multiple' and 'contradicting' identities to show their unequal position among women and argued that the full experience of a person cannot be reduced to "womanhood" or "blackness".[9] Yet, the way laws and legal studies responded to those claims attracted criticism[10] since it reduced law as a medium for performing identities instead of exploring law's potential to overcome structural disadvantages.[11]

This emphasis on intersectionality primarily as a tool to theorize individual and social identities can be misleading, since intersectionality has been concerned with power relations and disadvantaged positioning from its outset.[12] Intersectionality suggests that attention to identities should be coupled with the confrontation of power in ways that uncover how power works through creating and deploying overlapping identity categories.[13] Identities manifest the intersection of multiple hierarchies *and* the ways such hierarchies are maintained. Intersectionality reveals that

[4] Sosa and Ruth (2023).

[5] Burri and Schiek (2009); Schiek (2011); Fredman (2016b); Sosa (2017); Atrey (2019).

[6] Fredman (2016b); Atrey (2019).

[7] Atrey (2019).

[8] Yuval-Davis (2006), p. 196.

[9] Lorde (1984).

[10] Crooms (1997); Prins (2006).

[11] Verloo (2006); Schiek and Lawson (2011).

[12] Cho et al. (2013)

[13] Cho et al. (2013), p. 797.

what matters 'is not (victims') identity but how they are socially identified and hence treated'.[14]

Similarly, the excessive attention to 'groups' also offers a restrictive view of intersectionality, often resulting in the incorporation of *vulnerable groups* in many legal documents and case law. On the positive side, group-centred approaches to intersectionality can make marginalized groups visible, including them in policies and institutional arrangements. Moreover, allowing them to voice their intersectional experiences and desires can strengthen democratic processes.[15] Although this can be considered an improvement in terms of recognizing diversity and overcoming the limitations of a formal equal-treatment approach, this approach has several shortcomings. For instance, it often lacks attention to the social and institutional context that creates vulnerability, can trigger stigma, promote stereotypes,[16] or encourage the adoption of paternalistic measures.[17]

Intersectionality reminds us that it is the intersection of social categories of difference that *makes* people vulnerable or limits their rights. It encourages the examination of how such vulnerability comes to exist and adopting measures that can tackle the underlying factors. Vulnerability relates to social positioning, and thus can be identified and changed through institutional action. Moreover, intersectionality seeks to counter essentializing and stereotyped views of any group by recognising that *within the groups*, there is always diversity. This anti-essentialising effect of intersectionality is strengthened by challenging the idea that it can be determined a priori that one category (i.e. gender) is the primary source of discrimination affecting a group (i.e. women) and calling for a comprehensive examination of the relation and importance between categories.[18] In this way, intersectionality could reveal the multiple systems of oppression relevant in a case and context.

Yet, the promises of intersectionality, particularly the potential to address structural inequality, remain challenged by these limitations. Could the attention on bodies promoted in feminist legal theories 'support' the structural approach to intersectionality in such a way as to challenge these legal/practical constraints? Bodies emerge in feminist theories as constructed entities, regulated through social

[14] Mackinnon (2015).

[15] Crenshaw (1991).

[16] Yet, states have an obligation to counter gender stereotypes in international human rights law. See for instance, CEDAW Article 5. The European Court of Human Rights has addressed gender stereotyping in multiple cases, i.e. *Konstantin Markin v. Russia*. See also: Cusack and Timmer (2011); Timmer (2011); Cusack (2013); Brems and Timmer (2016).

[17] Approaches focussing on 'vulnerable groups' often use a victimizing language that ignores structural inequality and/or agency. For instance, different institutions have recently included "women in prostitution" (rather than prostitutes) as a vulnerable group, pointing at gender as the main source for inequality, thus presenting prostitution as a form of GBV *per se* that requires state intervention, regardless of a woman's position vis à vis prostitution, the gendered labour market, or her migrant status.

[18] Hancock (2007).

practices, institutions, and discourses.[19] They appear deeply intertwined with social, cultural, and political power relations. This chapter explores to what extent bodies can contribute to capture intersectional inequalities and counter the legal emphasis on (single) categorical approaches to inequality, identities and vulnerable groups that currently constrain intersectionality.

2 Looking Through the Body to Capture Intersectional Inequality

Human bodies have been largely neglected in law, influenced by the Cartesian mind/body dichotomy underlying the ethical foundation of law. Even in human rights law, the materiality of human bodies is often rejected, preferring a moral conceptualisation of humans that relies on their dignity and rationality.[20] Moreover, the human body envisioned in law is *male, white, autonomous, adult and heterosexual.*[21] This body becomes the norm, pushing deviant bodies to the margins[22] and subjecting them to sexism,[23] racism,[24] binarism,[25] ableism,[26] ageism,[27] 'weightism'[28] and other forms of oppression. Bodies can unveil the power hierarchies and social inequalities, showing the tensions between human rights claims of universality and human diversity.[29]

Bodies can help reveal intersectional and structural inequalities in four ways, each suggesting specific areas of inquiry. These four dimensions shape the analytical lens deployed in the analysis of case law below. Firstly, bodies, marked by age, sex, size, colour, ability, class, culture, etc., constitute a complete and harmonious whole. Since isolating one of these aspects can only be done theoretically, the *wholeness of bodies* challenges traditional single-axis non-discrimination approaches and helps capturing intersecting categories. This first dimension thus raises the question of which social categories of distinction are highlighted by the

---

[19] Spelman (1982); Smart (1990); Butler (1993); Grosz (1994a); Grosz (1994b); Grear (2013); Lorber and Martin (2013); Elizabeth Wicks (2016); Fineman (2022).

[20] See: Mooney (2014); Neal (2014); Addis (2019); Yahyaoui Krivenko (2020); Tigchelaar and Breuil (2024).

[21] Charlesworth (1995); Charlesworth and Chinkin (2000); Kapur (2006); Orford (2006); Wilde et al. (2007).

[22] Otto (2006); Grear (2009); Mignolo (2013); de Beco (2021).

[23] De Beauvoir (1953); Davis (1983); Hooks (1984); MacKinnon (1989); Butler (1990); Young (1990); MacKinnon (1993); Fraser (1997).

[24] hooks (2013); Davis (1983); Hill Collins (1998); Kapur (2005).

[25] Butler (1993); Fausto-Sterling (2000).

[26] Charlton (1998); Nario-Redmond (2019).

[27] Cuddy and Fiske (2002); Macnicol (2006).

[28] Mason (2012); van Amsterdam (2013).

[29] Brems (2001); Brems (2004); Brems (2015).

wholeness and materiality of bodies, and how these interact and determine individuals' positioning.

The second dimension of examination draws from feminist legal theories highlighting how (female) bodies are a focal site of state regulation and control, particularly in relation to sexuality and reproduction. Sexuality has functioned as a tool of social control of women and female bodies through the regulation of sexual behaviour,[30] violence,[31] the objectification and commodification of bodies,[32] and reproduction.[33] In addition, the desirability of certain bodies bearing offspring (or not),[34] very often relates to their material characteristics, such as race or ethnicity,[35] physical or mental disabilities,[36] or gender identity.[37] Sexuality and reproduction emerge as social, cultural, and political practices, with socially and culturally prescribed meanings and experiences beyond the biological phenomenon.[38] Socioeconomic, cultural, political, personal, and interpersonal factors are implicated, including individuals' place in society, since the role and function of bodies are inevitable connected (and sometimes reduced) to their sexual and reproductive dimensions. This approach helps to highlight how sexuality and reproduction as corporal aspects can be affected by inequality and discrimination (which bodies are sexualised and reproduced) and at the same time can lead to it by limiting their function to or excluding them from reproduction or sexuality.

The representation of bodies constitutes the third dimension. Mainstream portrayals of bodies replicate the norm and relegate bodies not fitting that ideal to a subordinated position. Moreover, bodies are often fully depicted through a single aspect of their embodiment, enforcing stereotypes. The symbolic construction of a 'normal' body determines which bodies are 'acceptable' and which require intervention, influencing how people experience and shape their bodies.[39] Representation includes the material or *constitutive representation*, asking how certain subjects are represented, and the *political representation,* questioning who speaks for those depicted,[40] since giving voice and participation are essential concepts connected to equality. Exploring how bodies are depicted and whether they are given meaningful participation can challenge stereotypes by representing bodies in a comprehensive and empowering manner, thus impacting the social construction of categories of difference. This third dimension also looks into symbolic violence, understood as a

---

[30] Smart (1990); Smart (1992).

[31] Lorde (1984); Crenshaw (1991); Merry (2009).

[32] MacKinnon (1989); MacKinnon (1993).

[33] Spelman (1982); Ussher (2006); Thomson (2002).

[34] Siegel (1992).

[35] Hill Collins (1998); Teicher (2020); Murray (2021); Murray (2022).

[36] Kamrat-Lang (1995); Spektorowski (2004); Herzog (2018); McConnell and Shanon (2022).

[37] Radi (2020).

[38] Ussher (2006).

[39] Foucault (1982); Wacquant (2005).

[40] Spivak (1999).

form of domination that naturalizes dichotomies and asymmetries (male/female, white/black, etc.) embedded in different forms of communication.[41]

Lastly, human bodies are embedded in the material context of place and space, revealing larger structures. Looking at the connections between bodies and place/space can illuminate their material dependency and limitations and provide richer accounts of context beyond the historical dimension. Also, bodies can be restricted to specific spaces, either by physically restraining them to specific places or institutions (such as prisons or hospitals), segregating them (neighbourhoods, schools, or economic activities), or by their formal and informal exclusion/inclusion (i.e. prohibiting entry and participation, or simply not removing barriers). While the impact of detention and other forms of institutionalisation on bodily autonomy and bodily integrity have been largely studied and regulated,[42] segregation and other forms of territorial dynamics resulting in the exclusion of bodies, particularly informal ones, such as class distinctions between neighbourhoods or schools, are less commonly addressed.

This four-dimensional body-centred lens can strengthen *structural* approaches to intersectionality. Firstly, by emphasising the wholeness of bodies as the canvas where all these intersecting categories inevitably materialize. Secondly, attention to sexuality and reproduction can highlight people's function and position in society, reinforced in third place by examining how their bodies are represented, who can speak for them, and lastly, exploring where bodies are embedded. This analytical approach is applied below in two cases of gender-based violence against trans persons before the Inter-American Court. *Azul Rojas Marin v. Peru*, and *Vicky Hernandez v. Honduras*.

3 Applying the Body-Centred Lens: Violence Against Trans Women

The cases of *Azul Rojas Marin v. Peru*[43] and *Vicky Hernandez v. Honduras*[44] of the Inter-American Court of Human Rights are particularly suitable for testing to what extent a 'body-centred' lens can strengthen an intersectional analysis. In both decisions, decided favourably, the Court investigated the interaction between gender and other categories (sexual orientation and gender identity), adopting an intersectional approach to a certain extent, and incorporating a structural dimension.

---

[41] Bourdieu (1977).

[42] See for instance, Davis (2003); Davis (2007); Anderson (2010); Stanley et al. (2012); Davis (2014); Bachmann (2016); Russell (2020).

[43] Inter-American Court of Human Rights, *Case of Azul Rojas Marín et al. v. Peru*, Judgment of March 12, 2020, hereinafter: *Azul Rojas*.

[44] Inter-American Court of Human Rights, *Vicky Hernández et al. v. Honduras*, Judgment of March 26, 2021, hereinafter: *Vicky Hernández*.

At the time of the incident, Azul Rojas Marín was 27 years old and identified as a gay man. By the time the Inter-American Court heard the case, she identified as a woman. The Court confirmed that sexual orientation and gender identity or gender expression are categories protected by the American Convention of Human Rights. It found that Azul was unlawfully detained 'owing to her sexual orientation or gender identity',[45] raped and tortured by state agents, and that the authorities' lack of investigation and prosecution violated her right to judicial guarantees and protection. The Court also emphasized that the LGBTQI community in the region had historically been a victim of structural discrimination, stigmatization, different forms of violence, and violations of fundamental rights. In *Vicky Hernandez*, concerning the murder of a trans woman sex-worker living with HIV and human rights defender, the Court considered that she was in "a particularly vulnerable situation where numerous factors of discrimination converged *intersectionally*".[46] The Court applied the Inter-American Convention on the Prevention, Punishment, and Eradication of Violence against Women (Belem do Pará Convention) for the first time in a case of a trans woman. It also referred to the case as a (trans)femicide and a crime based on prejudice. In both cases, the Court examined the specific context of discrimination against LGBTI people and ordered a comprehensive set of reparations, ranging from compensation to the setting up of scholarships, training of professionals and other awareness raising activities, in addition to amendments to laws and regulations, including the elimination of the intention to "eradicate of homosexuals and transvestites" from Peru's district and regional Public Security Plans (*Azul Rojas*) and the adoption of a law on gender identity (*Vicky Hernandez*).

The Court approached categories of distinction differently in each case. In *Azul*, sexual orientation becomes a necessary category of analysis for the events, when she identified as a gay man. This was certainly the approach of the Inter-American Commission.[47] The Representatives, on the other hand, argued that both Azul's sexual orientation and her 'non-normative gender expression' triggered the discriminatory violence. The Court saw the relation between Azul's gender expression and sexual orientation as a gay man as key. It found that Azul was pulled over, detained, verbally abused, raped and tortured 'due to her sexual orientation or gender expression'. It explained that:

> At times, it may be difficult to distinguish between discrimination due to sexual orientation and discrimination due to gender expression. Discrimination due to sexual orientation may be based on a real or perceived sexual orientation, so that it includes cases in which a person is discriminated against owing to the perception that others have of their sexual orientation. This perception may be influenced, for example, by clothing, hairstyle, mannerisms or behaviour that do not correspond to traditional or stereotypical gender standards or that constitute a non-normative gender expression. In this case, third parties could have associated the presumed victim's gender expression with a specific sexual orientation.[48]

[45] *Azul Rojas*, para 81.

[46] *Vicky Hernández*, para. 135.

[47] *Azul Rojas*, para 83.

[48] *Azul Rojas*, para 94.

This reasoning seems strengthened by an expert testimony in the case indicating that rape was carried out using "an instrument that symbolically represents authority [such as] the police baton, [...] sends the symbolic message [...] of restoring a masculinity that is threatened by the perception of the victim as not complying with the established order of masculinity".[49] This connection of gender expression and sexual orientation breaks with the usual merger "gender identity and expression" present in so many documents. Yet, the Court did not explore how the dynamic between these categories' changes throughout Azul's gender transition. How did the connection of gender expression, sexual orientation and gender identity change? Her gender transition process, and thus her changing body, remained invisible in the case despite it appearing as the canvas on which the underlying discrimination materialises. Bringing Azul's body as a comprehensive whole could help understand these categorical dynamics, and how they apply to the case.

In the case of *Vicky Hernández*, while gender expression was also key, the Court took a clearer intersectional approach. It considered that the fact that Vicky was a trans woman sex-worker, who lived with HIV, and carried out an activity in defence of the rights of trans women, was very relevant. These characteristics, the Court held, put her in a position of vulnerability where *multiple factors of discrimination converged in an intersectional way*.[50] Based on this, the Court carried an intersectional reading of article 9 of the Belem do Pará Convention, finding that it was applicable to the case, and the State was responsible for non-compliance with the obligations established therein. The Court argued that "trans women are women," broadening the category of gender and proposing a comprehensive view of female bodies and identities.

However, this approach was contented in partially dissenting opinions. Judge Odio Benito brought an interesting critique of the use of categories of distinction in the case. She argued that there is a "necessary distinction between sex (biological) and gender (hierarchical social construct), and…serious confusion that the erroneous equalizing of "gender identity" with sex has introduced into the academic and political debate".[51] "Everything tends towards the concept that only "gender identity" exists",[52] she continued. There is ample need for clearer analysis of the categories of distinction at play in this case, and the relation between them, if structural inequality is to be challenged. Yet, the closer we look at bodies as a complete whole, the more evident the spectrum of sex becomes.[53] Considering bodies as a non-fixed wholeness can help to move beyond the established divide 'sex as biology/gender construct' and explore the interactions between sex, gender, gender identity, gender expression and sexual orientation, without any *a priori* hierarchy.

[49] *Azul Rojas*, para 163.

[50] *Vicky Hernandez*, para 135.

[51] *Vicky Hernandez*, dissenting opinion Judge Odio Benito, para 4.

[52] *Vicky Hernandez*, para 12.

[53] Fausto-Sterling (2000); Fausto-Sterling (1992).

Sexuality was also key to both cases, perceived as deviant behaviour. Azul's sexuality triggered the violence and the response of the authorities, impacting her credibility, putting her physical integrity at risk and subjecting her to humiliating treatment. The police agents taking Azul's report, far from taking her seriously, told her "they should have put you in a cell so that everyone could fuck you."[54] Even the prosecutor allegedly said to the presumed victim: "but if you're a homosexual, how am I going to believe you."[55] The forensic report referred to "un-natural sex relations" and included unnecessary information on the frequency with which the victim had sexual relations and the age at which she became sexually active. Similarly, during the psychiatric assessment, Azul was asked whether she masturbated, the frequency with which she had sexual relations, at what age she had become sexually active, the number of sexual partners she had had, whether she practiced oral sex, whether she watched pornography, whether she had frequented brothels, whether she had had sexual contact with animals, and whether she had had sexual relations with minors."[56] The Court considered that the anal rape and the comments relating to sexual orientation revealed a discriminatory purpose, constituting violence based on prejudice.

Sexuality is deeply engrained in the structural elements determining the social positioning of trans women in Honduras, and Vicky Hernandez' individual positioning by largely limiting them to prostitution as their primarily function. This reduction to one function helps to outline the oppressive nature of the social and institutional context, and it also allows to depict Vicky's agency. On the one hand, prostitution emerged as the most likely economic activity of trans women, exposing them to structural (police) violence. On the other hand, Vicky was a sex-worker and an activist in that regard. Although the Court recognised their unequal position in society, it failed to discuss the economic dimension of sex-work and the livelihood implications of a curfew on those workers. A clearer focus on sexuality and reproduction as determinants of the attributed function of bodies could have highlighted the structural dynamics in place and go beyond the specific cases of these victims, transforming those structures for all.

In relation to *representation,* gender expression dominated the Court's analysis. In the case of Azul, there was a contrast between Azul's depiction during the domestic proceedings (as a male) and during the trial before the Court (as a woman), in line with her gender transition. It also remained clear that she suffered violence due to her perceived homosexuality and she identified openly as a gay man when events happened. The authorities' actions clearly manifested stereotypes around homosexuality, as discussed above. The Court recalled that "stereotyping based on sexual orientation refers to a preconception of attributes, conducts or characteristics possessed by a person based on their sexual orientation, in this case in particular, by

[54] *Azul Rojas*, para 164.

[55] *Azul Rojas,* para 200.

[56] *Azul Rojas,* para 201.

homosexual men or men perceived as such".[57] These prejudices and gender stereotypes affected the objectivity of State officials responsible for investigating complaints, influencing their perceptions when determining whether or not an act of violence occurred, and their evaluation of the credibility of witnesses and of the victims themselves.[58] Azul's representation was reduced to her sexuality, presented as deviant and in a stereotypical way, making her unworthy of justice.

In the case of *Vicky Hernandez*, the Court focused on the legal recognition of her self-determination. It recalled that the right of each person to define their sexual and gender identity autonomously is protected by the American Convention. The Court found that Vicky's right to gender identity was infringed in three different moments: a) as a consequence of her homicide; b) within the framework of the investigations proceedings, and c) within the general legal framework of Honduras which did not recognize her female gender identity. Indeed, Vicky was murdered because she was a trans-woman sex-worker. The negative depiction of trans-gender sex workers was evident in the testimonies corroborating police violence, claiming that "they gave the city a bad image" and that "they were men and had no reason to dress as women."[59] The Court has indicated that violence against the LGBTI community has a symbolic purpose; the victim is chosen to communicate a message of exclusion or subordination, irrespective of whether that person self-identifies with a specific category. This symbolic violence, argued the Court, may result in hate crimes.[60]

In addition, since Vicky's self-perceived gender identity was not legally registered, the investigation following her death addressed her as male ("John Doe") and possible crime of passion, making it impossible to recognise the case as gender violence and discrimination due to its trans feminine identity, despite being endemic in the region and thus calling for "enhanced" due diligence.[61] The impossibility to reflect her self-perceived gender and name in her identity document, impacted significant on the investigations. In the same way, the Court considered that the lack of recognition of self-perceived gender identity could, more generally, foster discrimination and social exclusion, and thus call to pass a gender identity law.

Lastly, the analysis looks at the spatial situation of bodies. Three dimensions shed light on the structural embedding of bodies: (1) the general social and political context, (2) the physical restrictions formally derived from law, and (3) informal physical restrictions like their undesirability in certain spaces.

In both cases, the social positioning of LGBTI people was illustrated by reference to the structural context. The Court drew from different reports to outline the context of structural discrimination against LGBTI people and their unequal social positioning in the region. In *Vicky,* the Court took a step further focusing on how the social context of discrimination impacted trans women, and sex workers

[57] *Azul Rojas*, para 198.

[58] *Azul Rojas,* para 199.

[59] *Vicky Hernandez,* para 35.

[60] *Vicky Hernandez,* para 70.

[61] *Vicky Hernandez,* para 134.

specifically. The risk of violence in this context, also by state agents, was high for both victims, enhancing the obligations of the states to investigate these cases.

In both cases, there were also physical restrictions sanctioned by law. *Azul* was in (arbitrary) detention when she suffered the abuse, triggering concrete state responsibilities. Regardless of whether it is imposed legitimately or arbitrarily, the corporeal aspects implicated in detention are many, and therefore enjoy detailed regulation.[62] Consequently, the Court paid detailed attention to this situation, and the extra surveillance and due diligence of the state regarding persons in detention was easily justified. *Vicky*'s murder occurred while a curfew from 9 p.m. to 6 a.m. was in force, declared following the coup d'état on June 28, 2009. Everyone should have remained in their homes and only the police patrols and armed forces were present on the streets. This state of emergency allows for the limitation of freedoms if established by law, pursuing a legitimate aim and are proportional. The banning of gathering in public places impacts disproportionally on deviant bodies, particularly sex-workers, in two ways. Firstly, the curfew prevented sex workers from their only income generating income, which in the case of *Vicky*, this was coupled with her responsibilities as breadwinner towards her mother and niece. This social-class implications of the curfew were not considered by the Court, as it did not recognise the economic dimension of *Vicky's* sexuality, since prostitution was her only source of livelihood.[63] Secondly, the State's absolute control of the public spaces and the movements of everyone in them posed excessive risk on trans sex-workers given the proven the context of frequent raids, arbitrary detentions, ill-treatment, rape, extortion and also killings by the police, they suffered.

The informal physical restrictions affecting both victims were also similar, suggesting the existence of a centre and a periphery where deviants bodies belong (or do not belong), and where violence seems justified. Bodies are marked by their spatial placement, hinting to their structural positioning. *Azul* was detained "undocumented, in suspicious circumstances, and in a place frequented by miscreants."[64] This sufficiently justified her detention. The boundaries that deviant bodies cannot cross were explicit in Peruvian Public Safety plans seeking the "eradication of homosexuals and transvestites." The Court considered this as "a highly discriminatory element that exacerbates the prejudices against the LGBTI population and, therefore, promoted the possibility of violence based on prejudice occurring" and ordered the State to eliminate it.[65] Similarly, the night Vicky disappeared, she was walking with two friends in the red-light district where they worked, when a police patrol that tried to arrest them. They fled in different directions and lost contact with

[62] See for instance, UN General Assembly, United Nations Standard Minimum Rules for the Treatment of Prisoners (the Nelson Mandela Rules): resolution / adopted by the General Assembly, 8 January 2016, A/RES/70/175, and directly applicable to OAS states, Advisory Opinion Oc-29/22 of May 30, 2022, on Differentiated Approaches with Respect to Certain Groups of Persons Deprived of Liberty.

[63] Tigchelaar and Breuil (2024).

[64] *Azul Rojas,* paras 102 and 118.

[65] *Azul Rojas*, para 255.

Vicky, who appeared dead the following day. In this case, several reports indicated that the bodies of the 15 trans women were found on the street, each one with significant signs of violence; eight with bullet wounds, two with their heads having been beaten, one stoned, one stabbed, one run over, one burned and one dismembered, castrated and beheaded (para 34). The "street", thus, becomes a pointer of the structural vulnerability affecting trans women, sex workers, and other non-conforming bodies.

4 Final Observations

This chapter explored whether attention to the body can contribute to capture structural intersectional inequalities and overcome some of the current constraints that intersectionality faces: the pre-eminence of single-categorical analysis, and the emphasis on identities and vulnerable groups over structural elements of inequality.

The "body-centred" approach proposed in this chapter considers the wholeness of bodies as a way of stressing the interaction between categories of social distinction, such gender, gender expression, age, health, disability, colour, size, etc. This can expand anti-discrimination approaches by preventing single category analysis and moving beyond additive categories to examine the interaction between categories as they "play" and materialise in bodies. The first dimension of the approach suggests that while the Court does a good job looking into interconnected categories in both cases, looking at the bodies of Azul and Vicky as a complete whole could have contributed to explore more fully how the categories of sexual orientation, gender expression and gender identity interact in *Azul,* and discuss the construction of sex, gender and gender identity and their interrelation in *Vicky*, helping to address the arguments in the dissenting opinions to the majority judgment. The relation between "material" aspects such as "sex" and more clearly socially constructed ones, such as sexual orientation or gender identity was brought to the fore by these trans bodies, forcing the Court to examine the connections, despite limitedly in scope and depth and excluding other aspects such as age, class, etc.

The approach also explores the role of sexuality and reproduction as a social, cultural, and political practice prescribing meanings and functions to bodies, in which also socioeconomic, personal, and interpersonal factors are implicated. In both cases, sexuality appeared as deviant and revealed the subordinated position of gay men and sex-workers, the biases and stereotypes affecting their credibility and the investigation of the cases, and their belonging/not belonging to certain places. In the case of *Vicky,* besides the vulnerability it created, it also showed the economic dimension of prostitution, bringing a more comprehensive look on the adoption of curfew by the state. This element of the analysis can provide concrete examples about how the social beliefs and institutional arrangements around sexuality, reproduction and production shape individuals and groups and determines their social positioning.

The attention to the representation of bodies proposed by the analytical lens seeks to challenge stereotypes by representing bodies in a comprehensive and empowering manner, thus impacting the social construction of categories of difference, and strengthening intersectionality's aim of giving voice to marginalized groups. In the case of *Azul,* questions of representation indicated the relevance of gender expression to fully understand the events. It also highlighted the concrete impact of stereotypes in access to justice and impunity. In *Vicky*, representation highlighted the relevance of recognizing legal gender identity, impacting on the investigation of the facts, and more generally, contributing to her marginalization. Recognising the symbolic dimension of the violence helps delineate its implications and the obligations of states.

Lastly, the proposed framework highlights the spatial situation of bodies and their embeddedness in larger structures. In both cases, the social context of inequality and discrimination against LGBTI persons was emphasised. Three dimensions are discussed, denoting the larger structures that place the victims in situations of vulnerability and inequality. Firstly, the general socio-political context of discrimination against LGBT people in the region, with the particularities of each case. Secondly, physical restrictions formally imposed in regulations that impact disproportionally on the victims, such as detention in the case of *Azul* and a curfew banning people from public spaces in the case of *Vicky.* Lastly, both cases showed that there are informal physical restrictions that reduced or banned victims to/from specific areas with increased personal risks due to police abuses: red districts or areas where LGBT persons often visit.

The application of the proposed body-centred analytical lens focusing on sexuality, bodies' representation and their spatial situation helped moving the discussion beyond identities and vulnerable groups, while the notion of bodies as embodiment of multiple inequalities contributed to the exploration of the dynamics between categories of distinction. In this sense, the initial intersectional analysis of the Court was strengthened, revealing the structural inequalities affecting the victims more comprehensively.

References

Addis A (2019) Dignity, integrity, and the concept of a person. ICL J 13:323–372. https://doi.org/10.1515/ICL-2019-0015

Anderson L (2010) Punishing the innocent: how the classification of male-to-female transgender individuals in immigration detention constitutes illegal punishment under the fifth amendment. Berkeley J Gender Law Just 1:1–31

Askin E, Stoll H (2024) Contested equality: international and comparative legal perspectives. Edward Elgar Publishing

Atrey S (2019) Intersectional discrimination. Oxford University Press. https://doi.org/10.1093/oso/9780198848950.001.0001

Bachmann CL (2016) No safe refuge: experiences of LGBT asylum seekers in detention. UK Lesbian & Gay Immigration Group and Stonewall
Bourdieu P (1977) Outline of a theory of practice. Cambridge University Press
Brems E (2001) Human rights: universality and diversity. Brill Nijhoff, The Hague
Brems E (2004) Reconciling universality and diversity in international human rights: A theoretical and methodological framework and its application in the context of Islam. Hum Rights Rev 5:5–21. https://doi.org/10.1007/s12142-004-1005-5
Brems E (2015) Diversity and European human rights: rewriting judgments of the ECHR. Cambridge University Press
Brems E and Timmer A (2016) Stereotyping and human rights law. Intersentia
Burri S, Schiek D (2009) Multiple discrimination in EU law. Opportunities for legal responses to intersectional gender discrimination. European Network of Legal Experts in the Field of Gender Equality
Butler J (1990) Gender trouble: feminism and the subversion of identity. Routledge, New York
Butler J (1993) Bodies that matter, vol 36. Routledge, pp 809–813. https://doi.org/10.1177/0306312706056409
Carbado D, Crenshaw KW, Mays VM, Tomlinson B (2013) Intersectionality: mapping the movements of a theory. Du Bois Rev 10:303–312. https://doi.org/10.1017/S1742058X13000349. INTERSECTIONALITY
Charlesworth H (1995) Human rights as men's rights. In: Peters J, Wolper A (eds) Women's rights human rights. Routledge, pp 103–113
Charlesworth H, Chinkin C (2000) The boundaries of international law: a feminist analysis. Manchester University Press
Charlton JI (1998) Nothing about us without us: disability oppression and empowerment. University of California Press, Berkley
Cho S, Crenshaw KW, McCall L (2013) Toward a field of intersectionality studies: theory, applications, and praxis. Signs J Women Cult Soc 38:785–810. https://doi.org/10.1017/CBO9781107415324.004
Crenshaw KW (1991) Mapping the margins: intersectionality, identity politics, and violence against women of color. Stanford Law Rev 43:1241–1299. https://doi.org/10.2307/1229039
Crooms L (1997) Indivisible rights and intersectional identities or, "what do women's human rights have to do with the race convention?". Howard Law J 40:619–640
Cuddy AJC, Fiske ST (2002) Ageism: stereotyping and prejudice against older persons. Ageism stereotyping and prejudice against older persons. MIT Press, Cambridge
Cusack S (2013) The CEDAW as a legal framework for transnational discourses on gender stereotyping. In: Hellum A, Aasen HS (eds) Women's human rights: CEDAW in international, regional and national law. Cambridge University Press. https://doi.org/10.1017/CBO9781139540841.007
Cusack S, Timmer A (2011) Gender stereotyping in rape cases: the CEDAW Committee's decision in Vertido v. The Philippines. Hum Rights Law Rev 11:329–342
Davis A (1983) Women, race & class. Vintage Books
Davis A (2003) Are prisons obsolete? Seven Stories Press
Davis A (2007) Racialized punishment and prison abolition. In: Lott TL, Pittman JP (eds) A companion to African-American philosophy. Blackwell Publishing Ltd. https://doi.org/10.1002/9780470751640.ch23
Davis A (2014) Deepening the debate over mass incarceration. Social Democr 28:15–23. https://doi.org/10.1080/08854300.2014.963945
Davis K, Zarkov D (2017) EJWS retrospective on intersectionality. Eur J Women's Stud 24:313–320. https://doi.org/10.1177/1350506817719393
de Beauvoir S (1953) The second sex. Alfred A. Knopf, New York
de Beco G (2021) Disability in international human rights law. Oxford University Press. https://doi.org/10.1093/oso/9780198824503.003.0005
Fausto-Sterling A (1992) Myths of gender: biological theories about women and men. Basic Books

Fausto-Sterling A (2000) Sexing the body. Basic Books, New York. https://doi.org/10.1007/s13398-014-0173-7.2
Fineman MA (2022) Reasoning from the body: universal vulnerability and social justice. In: A Jurisprudence of the Body. Springer, pp 22–40
Foucault M (1982) The subject and power. Crit Inq 8:777–795
Fraser N (1997) Justice interruptus: critical reflections on the "postsocialist" condition. Routledge, New York
Fredman S (2016a) Intersectional discrimination in EU gender equality and non-discrimination law. European network of legal experts in gender equality and non-discrimination. https://doi.org/10.2838/241520
Fredman S (2016b) Substantive equality revisited. Int J Const Law 14:712–738. https://doi.org/10.1093/icon/mow043
Grear A (2009) Redirecting human rights: facing the challenge of corporate legal humanity. Palgrave Macmillan. https://doi.org/10.1057/9780230274631
Grear A (2013) Human bodies in material space: lived realities, eco-crisis and the search for transformation. J Hum Rights Environ 4:111–115
Grosz E (1994a) Volatile bodies: toward a corporeal feminism. Indiana University Press
Grosz E (1994b) Lived bodies: phenomenology and the flesh. Routledge
Hancock AM (2007) When multiplication doesn't equal quick addition: examining intersectionality as a research paradigm. Perspect Polit 5:63–79. https://doi.org/10.1017/Si537592707070065
Herzog D (2018) Unlearning eugenics: sexuality, reproduction, and disability in post-Nazi Europe. University of Wisconsin Press
Hill Collins P (1998) It's all in the family: intersections of gender, race, and nation. Hypatia 3:62–82
Hooks B (1984) Feminist theory: from margin to center. South End Press
Hooks B (2013) Writing beyond race. Routledge
Kamrat-Lang D (1995) Healing society: medical language in American eugenics. Sci Context 8:175–196. https://doi.org/10.1017/S0269889700001940
Kapur R (2005) Erotic justice: law and the new politics of postcolonialism. Glass House Press
Kapur R (2006) Human rights in the 21st century: take a walk on the dark side. Sydney Law Rev 28
Lorber J, Martin PY (2013) The socially constructed body: Insights from feminist theory. In: Kivisto P (ed) Illuminating social life: classical and contemporary theory revisited. Sage, Thousand Oaks, pp 249–274. https://doi.org/10.4135/9781446215470
Lorde A (1984) Sister outsider: essays and speeches. Crossing Press. https://doi.org/10.1300/J155v11n03_01
MacKinnon CA (1989) Toward a feminist theory of the state. Harvard University Press
MacKinnon CA (1993) Only words. Harvard University Press
Mackinnon CA (2015) Intersectionality as method: a note. Signs J Women Cult Soc 38:1019–1030
Macnicol J (2006) Age discrimination: an historical and contemporary analysis. Cambridge University Press, Cambridge
Mason K (2012) The unequal weight of discrimination: gender, body size, and income inequality. Soc Probl 59:411–435. https://doi.org/10.1525/SP.2012.59.3.411
McConnell D, Shanon P (2022) The devolution of eugenic practices: sexual and reproductive health and oppression of people with intellectual disability. Soc Sci Med 298:114877. https://doi.org/10.1016/J.SOCSCIMED.2022.114877
Merry SE (2009) Gender violence: a cultural perspective. Blackwell
Mignolo W (2013) Who speaks for the "human" in human rights? In: Barreto JM (ed) Human rights from a third world perspective: critique, history and international law. Cambridge Scholars Publisher, pp 140–172
Montoya C, Agustín LR (2013) The othering of domestic violence: the EU and cultural framings of violence against women. Soc Polit 20:534–557. https://doi.org/10.1093/sp/jxt020
Mooney A (2014) Human rights and the body. Routledge
Murray M (2021) Race-ing Roe- reproductive justice, racial justice, and the battle for Roe v. Wade. Harv Law Rev 134:2025–2102

Murray M (2022) Abortion, sterilization, and the universe of reproductive rights. William & Mary Law Rev 63:1599–1638
Nario-Redmond M (2019) Ableism. Wiley-Blackwell
Neal M (2014) Respect for human dignity as substantive basic norm. Int J Law Context 10:26–46
Orford A (2006) International law and its others. Cambridge University Press
Otto D (2006) Lost in translation: re-scripting the sexed subjects of international human rights law. In: Orford A (ed) International law and its others. Cambridge University Press, pp 318–356
Prins B (2006) Narrative accounts of origins: a blind spot in the intersectional approach? Eur J Women's Stud 13:277–290. https://doi.org/10.1177/1350506806065757
Radi B (2020) Reproductive injustice, trans rights, and eugenics. Sex Reprod Health Matters 28:1824318. https://doi.org/10.1080/26410397.2020.1824318
Russell BC (2020) Analysis of the effects of legal sex markers in detention: Single-sex detention facilities, conversion therapy, and violations of human rights. Int J Gender Sex Law 1:347–376
Salem S (2016) Intersectionality and its discontents: Intersectionality as traveling theory. Eur J Women's Stud 25:403–418. https://doi.org/10.1177/1350506816643999
Schiek D (2011) Organizing EU equality law around the nodes of 'race', gender and disability. In: Schiek D, Lawson A (eds) European Union non-discrimination law and intersectionality. Ashgate Publishing, pp 11–27
Schiek D, Lawson A (eds) (2011) European Union non-discrimination law and intersectionality. Ashgate Publishing
Siegel R (1992) Reasoning from the body: a historical perspective on abortion regulation and questions of equal protection. Stanford Law Rev 44:261–381
Smart C (1990) Law's power, the sexed body, and feminist discourse. J Law Soc 17:194–210
Smart C (1992) Regulating womanhood. Routledge
Sosa L (2017) Intersectionality in the human rights legal framework on violence against women: at the centre or the margins? Cambridge University Press. https://doi.org/10.1017/9781316771525
Sosa L, Ruth MM (2023) The Istanbul Convention from an intersectional perspective. In: De Vido S, Frulli M (eds) Preventing and combating violence against women and domestic violence: a commentary on the Istanbul Convention. Edward Elgar Publishing, pp 5–21
Spektorowski A (2004) The eugenic temptation in socialism: Sweden, Germany, and the Soviet Union. Comp Stud Soc History 46:84–106. https://doi.org/10.1017/S0010417504000052
Spelman EV (1982) Woman as body: ancient and contemporary views, Feminist theory and the body: a reader. Edinburgh University Press, pp 32–41
Spivak GC (1999) A critique of postcolonial reason: toward a history of the vanishing present. Harvard University Press, Cambridge
Stanley EA, Spade D, Queer (In)Justice (2012) Queering prison abolition, now? Am Q 64:115–127. https://doi.org/10.1353/aq.2012.0003
Teicher A (2020) Social mendelism: genetics and the politics of race in Germany, 1900–1948, Social mendelism. Cambridge University Press. https://doi.org/10.1017/9781108583190
Thomson M (2002) Reproductivity, the workplace and the gendering of the body (politic). Law Lit 14:565–594. https://doi.org/10.1525/lal.2002.14.3.565
Tigchelaar J, Breuil BO (2024) No-bodies human rights. an interdisciplinary exploration of bodies in human rights. Utrecht Law Rev 20:6–23. https://doi.org/10.36633/ULR.943
Timmer A (2011) Toward an anti-stereotyping approach for the European Court of Human Rights. Hum Rights Law Rev 11:707–738. https://doi.org/10.1093/hrlr/ngr036
Ussher JM (2006) Managing the monstrous feminine: regulating the reproductive body. Routledge, London
van Amsterdam N (2013) Big fat inequalities, thin privilege: An intersectional perspective on "body size". Eur J Women's Stud 20:155–169. https://doi.org/10.1177/1350506812456461/FORMAT/EPUB
Verloo M (2006) Multiple inequalities, intersectionality and the European Union. Eur J Women's Stud 13:211–228. https://doi.org/10.1177/1350506806065753

Wacquant L (2005) Carnal connections: on embodiment, apprenticeship, and membership. Qual Sociol 28:445–474. https://doi.org/10.1007/s11133-005-8367-0
Wicks E (2016) The state and the body: legal regulation of bodily autonomy. Hart Publishing
Wilde R, Otto D, Buss DE, Shalakany A, Gross A (2007) Queering international law. Am Soc Int Law:119–132
Yahyaoui Krivenko E (2020) Gender and human rights: expanding concepts. Edward Elgar Publishing
Young IM (1990) Justice and the politics of difference. Princeton University Press
Yuval-Davis N (2006) Intersectionality and feminist politics. Eur J Women's Stud 13:193–209. https://doi.org/10.1177/1350506806065752
Yuval-Davis N (2011) Beyond the recognition and re-distribution dichotomy: intersectionality and stratification. In: Lutz H, Herrera Vivar MT, Supik L (eds) Framing intersectionality - debates on a multi-faceted concept in gender studies. Routledge

Cases

Inter-American Court of Human Rights, *Case of Azul Rojas Marín et al. v. Peru*, Judgment of March 12, 2020
Inter-American Court of Human Rights, *Vicky Hernández et al. v. Honduras*, Judgment of March 26, 2021

Lorena Sosa is Associate Professor in International law and Human Rights at Utrecht University, affiliated with the Netherlands Institute of Human Rights (SIM) and the Utrecht Center of European Research into Family and Law (UCERF). Her research explores the inclusiveness of international human rights law concerning gender, sexual orientation, gender identity/expression, and sex characteristics (SOGIESC). She has published extensively on gender-based violence and intersectionality, and conducted several studies on gender-based violence for the European Commission, the Council of Europe and the United Nations. Lorena has received prestigious grants by the Dutch Scientific Organization and the European Commission for her research on violence against transgender persons. She is co-founder and coordinator of the research platform EQUALS, within the law school, an the UU IOS (In)Equality Platform since 2023. Her current research focuses on corporality, structural inequality and human rights.

Normalizing Queer and the Loss of Critical Potential? Same-Sex Marriage: To Equality or Liberation?

Damir Banović

Abstract This article begins with methodological perspectives on the relationship between law and queer, drawing from the rich history of the Critical Legal Studies Movement. This is important for analyzing and establishing a dialectic between queer and law. The article continues with a critical examination of the institution of marriage from a radical feminist perspective, focusing on various intimate, economic, sexual, and other aspects. It then explores the idea of "queering" marriage, incorporating certain feminist critical viewpoints and translating them into a specific queer perspective to analyze the institution of marriage from both social and legal viewpoints. The article concludes with the possibility of reconciling two seemingly opposing concepts: law and queer.

1 Introduction

In this chapter, I explore the conflict between two concepts: (1) queer and (2) the law, as well as the possibility of reconciling the tension between them. I define queer as a both a movement and a theory that redefines the concept of identity, shifting from stability and essentialism toward an understanding of identity as fluctuation and constant (re)construction. Queer method, can be understood as a continuous process and a conversation on many levels that includes intersectionality, multidisciplinary approaches, and diversity. Queer questions normalcy, while law has usually been associated with (1) formal structure, (2) institutionalized procedures, (3) the idea of normativity, (4) normatively fixed identities, and (5) the

D. Banović (✉)
Faculty of Law, University of Sarajevo, Sarajevo, Bosnia and Herzegovina
e-mail: d.banovic@pfsa.unsa.ba

F. Macioce et al. (eds.), *Feminist Legal and Political Practices*, Gender Perspectives in Law 6, https://doi.org/10.1007/978-3-032-02856-3_12

background idea of what is "normal" and conventionally accepted, usually supporting the heteronormative idea of morality.

In concrete, this paper will focus on the concept of marriage, its critique in feminism and queer theory as fundamentally unjust and hetero-patriarchal. But, in recent years, we have seen the normalizing of same-sex relationships through (1) wider social acceptance and (2) the introduction of the concept of same-sex marriage or equivalents into the legal sphere. Moreover, to be legally recognized, we need a stable social concept with some idea of what it constitutes. In some sense, we need to give up the idea of queer to enter the normative sphere.

2 Some Methodological Observations and Critical Viewpoints

One possible understanding of queer theory and the relationship between queer and law is provided by Romero.[1] Regardless of the impossibility of defining the concept "queer", it tends to be associated with opposition to or transgression of sexual, gender or intimacy norms.[2] This could be understood as queer theory criticizing essentialist conceptions of sexuality and gender and opening space for their reconceptualization. Moreover, queer theory scrutinizes, criticizes and deconstructs dominant discourses present in various areas of social life and human creation, such as literature, social sciences and humanities, politics, etc.[3] This would imply a critique of the dominant discourses in law, the legal and social discourse of the concept of marriage and the way in which law "stabilizes" the heteronormative concept. Thus, queer theory analyzes, criticizes and deconstructs ideologies, ideals, values, principles, a that support those dominant discourses and[4] whether and how they influence or justify those discourses.[5] In addition, queer theory criticizes certain liberal assumptions about human subjectivity.[6] This especially refers to liberal assumptions concerning gender and sexuality.[7] As queer theory that is framed within critical legal studies takes over some of the basic methodological assumptions that are part of critical legal movement.[8] This concerns uncertainty towards law as science, questioning whether a text has one correct

[1] Romero (2009).

[2] Romero (2009), p. 190.

[3] Romero (2009), p. 190.

[4] Romero (2009), p. 190.

[5] Romero (2009), p. 190.

[6] Romero (2009), p. 190. Certainly, one should not forget that liberal feminist and gay and lesbian movements exist that have liberal ideas as their starting point.

[7] Romero (2009), p. 190.

[8] See more in Delgado (1993), p. 744.

interpretation, doubting the law's supposed neutrality and objectivity.[9] Similarly, as Delgado follows the track of other authors within the critical legal movement, "feminist legal scholars challenged law's deeply inscribed patriarchy, showed that gender and sex roles are constructed, not natural".[10] Additionally, feminist critical race (and I would add queer legal) theorists have questioned the idea of law as being impartial, offering different approaches that are "based on narrative and experience".[11] Critical race theorists argue that the dominant group usually has antecedently created "group of 'truths', myths, and received wisdoms" about race.[12] This can also be applied to feminist and queer discourse. "Intersectionality" is another characteristic and methodological approach of post-modern critical race, feminist and queer legal theories taking positions and insights from each other. As Delgado argues, "gays and lesbians of color are demanding recognition of their unique needs and experiences".[13] Intersectionality means that we should examine how different identities, such as race, class, and sexual orientation combine.[14] To this list we could add other some other identities such as gender identity, sex characteristics, etc. Moreover, some authors have criticized this position, challenging whether these categorizes are stable and if there is "a characteristic black, straight or female point of view".[15] *Specific identity position* presupposes a level of identity essentialization to which critical feminist, race or queer theories are deeply opposed. However, without this *identity position*, it is not even possible to contextualize a discriminatory position that includes different identity elements of, for instance, a gay man of African American descent. Contrary to *contextualization*, as Delgado argues, are the views of Martha Fineman.[16] Focusing on differences can weaken the group's voices.[17] As Martha Fineman argues, "the competition should not be with each other in the margins of society but with the powerful, dominant main structures whose visions and versions of reality are reflected in society's institutions.[18] In that sense, our common goal, "for feminists of all races, classes, characteristics, and orientation" but also for all "men who seek significant change in our social and cultural institutions".[19]

---

[9] Delgado (1993), p. 744.

[10] Delgado (1993), p. 744.

[11] Delgado (1993), p. 745.

[12] Delgado (1993), p. 746.

[13] Delgado (1993), p. 753.

[14] See Delgado (1993), p. 753 for more. Delgado notes how Angela Harris and Kimberlé Crenshaw have criticized the essentialist position within the broader feminist movement (Delgado 1993, p. 754). The problem behind this criticism is that women's experiences can easily be framed within general terms without taking into account features like race or class (Delgado 1993, p. 754).

[15] Delgado (1993), p. 753.

[16] Delgado (1993), p. 755; Fineman (1990).

[17] Fineman (1990), p. 40; Delgado (1993), p. 755.

[18] Fineman (1990), p. 40.

[19] Fineman (1990), p. 40; see also Delgado (1993), pp. 755–756.

In my understanding, the critical legal movement takes the position that the foundational idea is that law embodies hetero-patriarchal ideals, establishing social constructs of male and female identities supported by the concept of heterosexual marriage. Law and legal systems inherently function within established essential categories, institutional processes, and stability. Law and legal institutions function within *essentialized categories* because they need stability and stable categories for at least some reasonable time. This is in contradiction to the critical (race, feminist, or queer) legal movement ideas on identities as constructs and in constant flux. Moreover, as Martha Fineman argues, "shared beliefs, social and cultural 'metanarratives, shaped in accordance with dominant ideology, influence what is chosen from among competing and contradictory facts and conclusions".[20] Law, as a normative system, has been built around such choices.[21] Law is not only an articulation of specific social interests but "operates as a potentially coercive or punitive force in the lives of people whose circumstances of preferences do not conform to the norms".[22] The way in which sexual family (and, if I may add, factual relationship) is presented in law can be a distortion or fragmentation of social reality.[23] But precisely that legal image creates "the legal reality and forms the basis for state regulation".[24] Legal image is an expression of what is seen as "appropriately constituted family" and consequently it defines what is normal and what is deviant.[25]

In this chapter, I explore queer legal theory from three perspectives: as critique, as theory, and as a movement within outsider jurisprudence, which can be defined as follows:

> As a theory and movement, queer legal theory is a postmodern discipline (or a group of disciplines) that applies the methodological path established within critical legal studies guided by specific queer experiences. Understood in this way, queer legal theory starts from non-essentialized sexual and gender identities, viewing them as temporary, fluid and indeterminate, criticizing law, practices and policies that seek to exclude, categorize, subordinate or eliminate anything that does not fit into binary concepts of sexuality and gender. This approach could be named as outsider queer legal theory.[26]

From this perspective and the perspective of critical feminism, I will try to critically address issues of same-sex marriages. Moreover, I will examine if there is the possibility of reconciling legal recognition with the concept of queer.

---

[20] Fineman (1990), p. 46.
[21] Fineman (1990), p. 46.
[22] Fineman (1990), p. 46.
[23] Fineman (1990), p. 46.
[24] Fineman (1990), p. 46.
[25] Fineman (1990), p. 46.
[26] Banović (2023), p. 74.

3 Critiques of Marriage from a Feminist Perspective

The concept of marriage holds legal, traditional, religious, and political significance. It embodies our views on what defines a family. Still, "formal, legal, heterosexual marriage continues to dominate our imagination when we confront the possibilities of intimacy and family".[27] Politicians and religious leaders praise the marriage relationship as sacred and the alternative as "threatening and dangerous to society, destructive to cherished values".[28] But history has shown us how marriage played "its role in oppressing women, gays and lesbians, and racial and religious minorities".[29] Feminist critique has pointed out that "the institution of marriage is the location of a lot of abuse and violence".[30] For Chambers, the institution of marriage "(…) has been a fundamental site of women's oppression (…)".[31] Moreover, critics usually argue that marriage is: (1) essentially patriarchal, (2) heteronormative, (3) harmful, (4) a relation of ownership, and (5) reform cannot change "its oppressive nature".[32] Since it is heteronormative and normative, it essentializes human nature and limits our sexuality and gender identity. Not only does the law promote and support discrimination, but marriage as a social construct is essentially unjust. However, some theorists argue that marriage and family laws protect women[33] and that significant progress has been made. On the other hand, some theorists argue that same-sex marriage should be introduced and that it "will empower gays and lesbians and counteract social stigma against same-sex relationships".[34] Two crucial questions or theses are: (1) Can we reform marriage? And (2) Is the institution of marriage essentially unjust, and if it should be abolished as such.[35] Put another way, the question is whether marriage can "be liberated from its history of oppression".[36] If we see marriage as essentially unjust, then it is impossible to reform it.[37] Feminists like Sheila Cronan and Claudia Card have argued for abolishing the institution of marriage to reduce social pressures to marry and meet gender roles.[38] Some critics argue that marriage law has sustained "unjust systematic discrimination," and its unjust nature is only contingent.[39] If this is true, then (legal)

[27] Fineman (2009), p. 45.
[28] Fineman (2009), p. 47.
[29] Brake (2012), p. 111.
[30] Fineman (2001), p. 262.
[31] Chambers (2017), p. 11.
[32] Brake (2012), p. 111.
[33] Brake (2012), p. 111.
[34] Brake (2012), p. 111.
[35] See more in Brake (2012), p. 111.
[36] Brake (2012), p. 112.
[37] See more in Brake (2012), p. 112.
[38] Brake (2012), p. 118.
[39] Brake (2012), p. 112.

reform is possible, and it "becomes a matter of equal opportunity and rectification".[40] Ann Ferguson contends that recognizing same-sex marriage can help weaken the belief in gender differences.[41] Similarly, Elisabeth Brake argues that we should remove gender from marriage and remove "the amatonormative structure of marriage".[42] To conclude, what would this reform look like if we could implement it? One way is to promote equality for both heterosexual and homosexual couples and to address social and legal discrimination of the unmarried.[43] But this is choosing the path of equality rather than liberation. Another approach is to eliminate marriage and state "jurisdiction" in regulating intimate relationships while simultaneously introducing and recognizing various relationships, including friendships and networks.[44]

History teaches us that women have been discriminated against and oppressed in the institution of marriage, often depicted as a mechanism of systematic oppression.[45] In the United States, for example, into the 1970s, "marriage deprived wives of full human rights".[46] In the U.S. and English law, husbands were allowed to discipline their wives, meaning that the authorities legally permitted or ignored physical abuse.[47] Wives have been seen as husbands' property, including "rights to sexual access and their bodies," and "marital rape was deemed legally impossible (…)".[48] In modern and contemporary legal systems, the wives' legal status has changed significantly, and mainly for the better.[49] This also includes comprehensive legal protection within the United Nations,[50] the Council of Europe,[51] and the European Union.[52] Even with legal reforms, marriage remains a source of oppression for women due to limited life opportunities shaped by legal, social, and economic influences.[53] There are specific issues linked to violence and economic dependency stemming from gender roles.[54] This is a particular kind of "intimate violence"[55] that appears in marriage against women, but also in same-sex partnerships

---

[40] Brake (2012), p. 112.

[41] Brake (2012), p. 118.

[42] Brake (2012), p. 118.

[43] See more in Brake (2012), p. 111.

[44] Brake (2012), p. 115.

[45] Brake (2012), p. 112.

[46] Brake (2012), p. 112.

[47] Brake (2012), p. 112–113.

[48] Brake (2012), p. 113.

[49] Brake (2012), p. 114.

[50] See more, Banović (2019), pp. 73–91.

[51] See more, Kulenović (2019), pp. 93–104.

[52] See more, Bećirović Hanušić (2019), pp. 105–119.

[53] Brake (2012), p. 114.

[54] Brake (2012), p. 114.

[55] "Feminist theory diverges on explanations of male violence" (Brake 2012, p. 115). For example, it can include (1) violent pornography, (2) "innate male aggressiveness", (3) a culture that promotes and tolerates war and violence, (4) a culture of misogyny, (5) different social and economic factors, etc. (Brake 2012, p. 115).

and sometimes against men by women.[56] According to Brake, "intimate violence" occurs in specific conditions of intimate and "exclusive relationships that provide conditions for abuse by hiding the couple in a materially and socially private sphere".[57] Existing legal frameworks and marriage laws offer varying legal and financial motivations for women to engage in and remain in these types of relationships.[58] Simultaneously, economic dependence reinforces and perpetuates the oppression of women.[59] It is precisely because marriage has reinforced the gender-based division of labor, which leads to economic dependency.[60] However, this also includes psychological and physical costs, in addition to economic dependency.[61] Additionally, social pressure and marital expectations further reinforce gender roles in marriage.[62]

4 More on Marriage, Family, Critique, and Compulsory Heterosexuality

We can argue that a shared assumption remains "that the appropriate family is founded on the heterosexual couples – a reproductive, biological pairing that is designated as divinely ordained in religion, crucial in social policy, and a normative imperative in ideology".[63] Marriage is undeniably a legal relationship, significant for both individuals and society.[64] It is defined by law that establishes criteria and rules: (1) who can marry; (2) what are the consequences and advantages of a marriage; (3) what are economic and other consequences that follow when the marriage ends, etc.[65] Nevertheless, laws on marriage leave the married couples daily implementation in which they fill the content and meaning.[66] This is expressed through the principle of "marital privacy".[67] For individuals, marriage can mean different things like: (1) a legal tie, (2) symbolic commitment, (3) a privileged sexual relationship and reproductive unit, (4) "a relationship of hierarchy and subordination,"

[56] Brake (2012), p. 115.
[57] Brake (2012), p. 115.
[58] Brake (2012), p. 115.
[59] Brake (2012), p. 116.
[60] Brake (2012), p. 116.
[61] Brake (2012), p. 116.
[62] Brake (2012), p. 118.
[63] Fineman (2009), p. 46.
[64] Fineman (2001), p. 240.
[65] See more in Fineman (2001), p. 240.
[66] Fineman (2001), p. 241.
[67] Fineman (2001), p. 241.

(5) a sense of fulfillment, (6) fulfilling a religious obligation, (7) economic relationship, etc.[68] From the perspective of the state and the society, it can mean (1) imposition of order in different contexts (e.g., "preferred method of containing and harnessing (male) sexuality in the interests of the larger society"), (2) reflection of moral or religious conventions and rules, (3) the way through which the society reproduces itself (reproductive tasks of making children, raising them, educating them to become workers, citizens, etc.[69] There exist even more diverse individual and personal understandings, as well as state and societal understandings, of what marriage means, along with its functions and purposes. Following the above, "marriage is expected to do a lot of work in our society".[70] However, the question is whether or not marriage is "essential to accomplishing any of the societal goals or objectives we assign to it".[71] As Fineman continues, marriage does not have the same meaning and relevance as an institution as it did 50 years ago.[72] It has changed, but "marriage, as the preferred societal solution, has become the problem".[73] Some of our ideas about "why marriage?" and "what is marriage" constitute problems, and they still pertain. To expose some: "women in and outside of the family, were primarily defined by their roles of wife, mother, and daughter".[74] Being placed in a specific gender role "assumes economic dependency, self-sacrifice, and subservience".[75] Some authors even advocate for abolishing marriage as a legal category and transitioning it to the realm of private contracts.[76] If marriage would not have been state-regulated and controlled, this may have affected "the state interest in controlling and regulating sexual affiliations".[77] This could open the space for same-sex partners and other different versions of sexual arrangements to be an equal and "privately preferred sexual connection".[78] If there is no institution of marriage, there are no economic and other social benefits for heterosexual couples.[79] At the same time, we would not have punishable "deviant" sexual behaviors among consenting adults.[80] Logically, this would introduce other forms of the family not only interpreted through heterosexual lenses, erasing terms like "single mother" or "married mother".[81] Even if we are still to accept the existence of the institution of marriage regulated by the state, we cannot overlook the advancements

[68] Fineman (2001), p. 242.

[69] Fineman (2001), p. 242.

[70] Fineman (2001), p. 244.

[71] Fineman (2001), p. 245.

[72] Fineman (2001), p. 245.

[73] Fineman (2001), pp. 245–246.

[74] Fineman (2001), pp. 248–249.

[75] Fineman (2001), p. 249.

[76] Fineman (2001), p. 261.

[77] Fineman (2001), p. 263.

[78] Fineman (2001), p. 263.

[79] Fineman (2001), p. 263.

[80] Fineman (2001), p. 263.

[81] Fineman (2001), pp. 263–264.

achieved by theorists and activists regarding gender violence, reproductive rights, the legal dynamics between wife and husband, etc.[82] But still, societies mandate "the traditional, role-defined, marital family form".[83] Somehow, even with the best intentions to implement the egalitarian principle, "marriages tend to slip into traditional and gendered patterns".[84]

Nevertheless, marriage almost always includes a heterosexual couple.[85] Heterosexual marriage has been perceived as essential not only as a fundamental "relationship of the nuclear family but to the very basis of society itself".[86] Throughout history, governments have enforced laws against various forms of extramarital sexual relationships, including cohabitation, fornication, and adultery.[87] To this list, we can include criminalization of same-sex sexual consenting acts. Nowadays, states have decriminalized different forms of non-marital sexual acts and behaviors, allowing for "alternative" families and relationships to gain some protection.[88] According to Fineman, norms that define family from a male perspective and as "male-headed" that position heterosexual union as its foundation, have faced threats from the changes that have occurred. Ideas about family and marriage have changed with the influence and evolution of the legal thought that takes individuals and not entities as the focus of attention, introduced by legal principles such are equality and freedom.[89] Reforms have occurred by legally recognizing informal heterosexual unions and same-sex relationships.[90] According to Fineman, precisely the feminist critiques of the family (and of the marriage) have impacted these legal reforms.[91] But still, non-traditional unions (e.g., informal heterosexual relationships, same-sex relationships) are required to be equated with the standard model of heterosexual marriage.[92] Legalizing same-sex relationships usually entails complying with the heterosexual idea of marriage.[93] Consequently, with the concept of family. This is a standard liberal position by which rights and freedoms should be expanded in the same way or as a modified version to other forms of relationships. This also means that any form of multiparty marriage should never be socially accepted and legalized.[94] This radically challenges our conception of two

[82] Fineman (2001), pp. 250–252.

[83] Fineman (2001), p. 270.

[84] Fineman (2001), p. 270.

[85] Some religious leaders and politicians will oppose including same-sex couples in the definition of marriage since it has been understood as a "natural, divinely ordained relationship (…) to heterosexual couples" (Fineman 2001, p. 243). See also Waaldijk (2024).

[86] Fineman (2009), p. 47.

[87] Fineman (2009), p. 47.

[88] Fineman (2009), p. 47.

[89] Fineman (2009), p. 54.

[90] Fineman (2009), p. 45.

[91] Fineman (2009), p. 55.

[92] Fineman (2009), p. 45.

[93] See also Emens (2009).

[94] Emens 2009, p. 259.

parties and a monogamous relationship. True liberation should encompass a variety of choices, from being single to being able to embrace the "traditional" image of marriage or to engage in a multiparty relationship based on polyamorous foundations.

Nevertheless, the fight for equality in marriage and in the family has had severe limitations, both in theory and in practice.[95] It did not bring the necessary sharing between partners in all fields of marital and family life.[96] Moreover, marriage and family are social institutions that are deeply defined by our system of beliefs and knowledge more strongly and significantly than the coercive potential of law.[97] As a result, these critiques indicate that liberal values of equality and freedom, along with legal reforms targeting narrow aspects of family relationships, are insufficient and require more comprehensive and radical analysis. Unfortunately, society has not evolved in line with the law's egalitarian principles introduced throughout the legal system.[98] According to Fineman: "the family continues to operate as the most gendered or role-defined of our institutions, allowing for and justifying pervasive, ingrained, and persistent patterns of gender inequality in the larger society".[99]

Some authors have criticized the institution of marriage from the perspective of "compulsory heterosexuality" and highlighted the possibilities presented by recent legal changes concerning same-sex marriage of "decoupling heterosexuality and marriage".[100] Additionally, "some theorists argue that same-sex marriage has the potential to eradicate compulsory heterosexuality".[101] According to these ideas, legally recognizing same-sex marriage creates opportunities to "reform traditional marriage." At least in some aspects. However, this does not mean that the institution of marriage should be perceived only from the perspective of "compulsory heterosexuality" but as a political institution as well,[102] and not only a political institution but also a legal one, enforced by the state and prevailing ideology. Marriage, whether heterosexual or same-sex, has been "primarily located in our legal and political institutions such as courts and legislatures, involving the interpretation of regulations, statutes, and constitutions".[103] Different forces, including the state, "impose, manage, organize, propagandize and forcefully maintain the political institution of marriage".[104] They include (1) different and preferential economic arrangements for married persons and economic disadvantages against the unmarried,[105] (2) laws that

[95] Fineman (2009), p. 57.

[96] Fineman (2009), p. 57.

[97] Fineman (2009), p. 58.

[98] Fineman (2009), p. 61.

[99] Fineman (2009), p. 61.

[100] Robson (2009), p. 313.

[101] Robson (2009), p. 313.

[102] Robson (2009), p. 313.

[103] Robson (2009), p. 313.

[104] Robson (2009), p. 314.

[105] It is often stated that marriage benefits individuals and that married people tend to be healthier, happier, and wealthier (Robson 2009, p. 314). But "it is important to remember that the state itself creates the conditions that allow the married to be wealthier and healthier, and (…) perhaps happier (…)" (Robson 2009, p. 314).

discriminate against the unmarried, (3) special attention to the promotion of marriage, especially for women, (4) social pressure to marry, etc.[106] In the case law of the U.S. courts that involve marriage, the judiciary will usually directly or indirectly stress "the importance of marriage by invoking human civilization and the sacred".[107] Not only economic benefits, laws, and legal regulations are strategies to enforce marriage and to maintain "a system of compulsory matrimony," but there is also a permanent social pressure to marry.[108] As Robson writes, "heterosexual feminists have long criticized the social pressure exerted on women to marry".[109] The need for marriage has been depicted in television shows, magazines, and self-help books about finding a husband and organizing a wedding.[110] This idea of universalization of marriage, matrimony (also for same-sex couples), and heterosexuality leaves no place for questioning these institutions and practices.[111] Dissenters are usually portrayed as "immature, uncommitted, unfaithful, disloyal, undevoted, and overly sexual".[112] The picture is even more radical if we are talking about unmarried women that are portrayed as "unacceptable and illegitimate" and, if they are sexually active, "somehow dishonest and disreputable".[113] Contemporary psychology elaborated extensively our individual choices which are actually "rarely neutral, unbiased, or individualistic".[114] With this in mind, our life choices are often the result of various stated or unstated influences.[115] Marriage, in particular, is "a decision with an elaborate social context".[116] That is why the personal choice of homosexuals to pursue marriage is similar to that of heterosexuals, shaped by different social choices.[117] That, of course, does not mean that there is no genuine personal choice to enter marriage, regardless of whether it is heterosexual or homosexual.[118] However, this does not mean that we should not question and critically examine "our choices" to enter marriage, particularly as the hetero-patriarchal paradigm shapes them.[119] It is important to be critical of the institution of marriage even if there are calls for equality for same-sex marriages. Extending the concept of hetero-patriarchal marriage to same-sex couples will not necessarily bring freedom.[120]

[106] Robson (2009), pp. 314–325.

[107] Robson (2009), p. 322.

[108] Robson (2009), p. 323.

[109] Robson (2009), p. 323.

[110] Robson (2009), p. 323–324.

[111] Robson (2009), p. 324.

[112] Robson (2009), p. 324.

[113] Robson (2009), p. 324.

[114] Robson (2009), p. 324.

[115] Robson (2009), p. 324.

[116] Robson (2009), p. 324.

[117] Robson (2009), p. 324.

[118] See also Robson (2009), p. 324.

[119] See also Robson (2009), p. 324.

[120] See more in Robson (2009), p. 328.

5 Queering Marriage?

Under the significant influence of poststructuralism, the theoretical directions began to develop, questioning binary positions as fixed, solid and permanent categories.[121] In other words, we can talk about the third wave of feminism, which manifests itself through different approaches of critical feminist studies but also represents the basis of critical queer (and legal) studies. They embed positions on the fluidity and diversity of individual identities. If we accept this point of view as correct, then any position that starts from the identity "we" is in itself problematic.[122] Consequently, identity is freed from essentialization and an *a priori* nature, as are gender identities.[123] The third wave of feminism and views on identity instability and fluidity are precisely the place where feminism and queer theory intersect.[124,125] It is the queer theory and queer movement that try to erase the essentialized categories of homosexual and heterosexual, introducing the concept of "person" and his/hers understanding of an intimate relationship with one or more individuals. Therefore, I argue that intersectionality between feminism and queer theory, comes together in the:[126]

(1) Critique of hetero-patriarchal values and norms;
(2) Critique of law, especially family and marital law that supports hetero-patriarchal values and principles;
(3) Critique of marriage as fundamentally unjust, abusive, and oppressive towards women and same-sex couples;
(4) Critique of marriage as an institution that fosters and maintains binary and gendered roles;
(5) Arguing for identity and multi-faceted, fluid, constructive, and ever-changing perspectives;
(6) Arguing for individuality in interpersonal relationships.

Moreover, intersectionality could be applied theoretically and methodologically. Both streams of critical thinking are inspired by each other and take a position to support their arguments.

However, developments in law have shown a different direction, mainly in applying egalitarian principles and introducing various forms of legally recognized same-sex partnerships such as registered partnerships, civil unions, and/or same-sex marriages. According to Kees, legally speaking, marriage has always been

[121] Ždralović (2019), p. 40.

[122] Ždralović (2019), p. 40.

[123] Ždralović (2019), p. 40.

[124] Perhaps the most significant scholar in feminism and queer studies of this direction is Judith Butler, particularly her "Gender Trouble: Feminism and the Subversion of Identity", first published in 1990 (see more in Ždralović 2019, p. 40). See also: Spiers (2007).

[125] Ždralović (2019), p. 40.

[126] See more on queer critique of marriage: LaSala (2007); Maine (2022).

heterosexual.[127] From 1948, the right to marry for different sex couples has been recognized in international human rights law and from the 1970s, same-sex couples have started claiming that right and freedom.[128] We have seen some progress at the national level where the growing number of countries have made it possible for some transgender persons to marry a person of different gender.[129] On the other hand, more countries have granted some or more benefits for same-sex couples through (1) cohabitation recognition or (2) different forms of registered partnerships.[130] Since 2001, 34 countries have legalized marriage for same-sex couples.[131] At the same time, some other countries have defined marriage as exclusively heterosexual.[132] As for the international human rights law, the right to marry has some relevance for same-sex couples and transgender persons.[133] Human rights law has taken the equality principle, extending the benefits of heterosexuals to same-sex couples without major structural and legal reforms following the principle of liberty. It remains to be seen if and how (international) human rights law will develop following specific request of intersex, non-binary, third-sex, bisexual, polyamorous or asexual individuals.[134]

6 Are There Alternatives?

Conceptually, some theorists defended the idea of same-sex marriage, focusing "on the value of chaste, exclusive, sexual dyads".[135] For example, Stephen Macedo defended the concept of same-sex marriage on the grounds that it would discourage promiscuity and support gay and lesbian individuals in leading better lives.[136] This is a fairly conservative argument that pushes same-sex marriages into the social and legal framework of a heterosexual-patriarchal marriage. Some others argue that excluding same-sex partnerships from benefits like health care, inheritance, and social rights is also unjust.[137] This is only because marital law gives this kind of beneficial treatment to married individual.[138] There is an important question about whether providing benefits through marriage for the LGBT community will liberate

[127] Waaldijk (2024), Chap. 1.
[128] Waaldijk (2024), Chap. 1.
[129] Waaldijk (2024), Chap. 1.
[130] Waaldijk (2024), Chap. 1.
[131] Waaldijk (2024), Chap. 1.
[132] Waaldijk (2024), Chap. 1.
[133] Waaldijk (2024), Chap. 1.
[134] Waaldijk (2024), Chap. 1.
[135] Brake (2012), p. 120.
[136] Brake (2012), p. 120.
[137] See more in Brake (2012), p. 121.
[138] See more in Brake (2012), p. 121.

or assimilate them into the heteronormative paradigm?[139] That is why some gay and lesbian theorists have rejected the idea of same-sex marriage.[140] The LGBT community often chooses more flexible, open, and less possessive relationships.[141] Marriage could hinder LGBT liberation and diversity, and it will distinguish legitimate relationships from those that are not, encouraging only one acceptable version of same-sex relationships.[142] For some scholars like Card, same-sex marriage will enable negative characteristics typically associated with heterosexual marriage, such as abuse and violence.[143] This is only if we accept the argument that marriage is inherently unjust. According to Brake, if we adequately reform the heterosexual version of marriage, there is no danger that the same adverse effects will appear in same-sex marriages.[144] Additionally, excluding gays and lesbians from the institution of marriage is seeing them as inferior, tending to "displace them from the center of political life and from status as full and equal citizens".[145] To her, same-sex marriage is the way to gay and lesbian liberation.[146] This argument is problematic because it assumes that all unmarried individuals—whether single, in a relationship, divorced or in another situation—will fail to realize their potential as citizens.[147] A citizen's status cannot rely upon the marital.[148] Additionally, some feminists argue that same-sex marriage can help combat gender roles, as it has traditionally been viewed as binary and hetero-patriarchal.[149] Same-sex marriage undermines its symbolic value and changes its social conception and imagination. As Chambers argues, the most significant change in reforming the institution of marriage has been the introduction of same-sex marriages and civil unions in some European countries (e.g., the Netherlands, the U.K., Spain, France), and in Canada and the U.S.[150] If marriage remains regulated by the state, the principle of equality demands recognition of same-sex relationships.[151]

But, moving from the heterosexual paradigm for same-sex unions or marriages, there is an additional model called "polyamory".[152] This concept avoids hierarchy and "encompasses various models of intimate relationships of more than two

[139] Brake (2012), p. 121.
[140] Brake (2012), p. 120.
[141] Brake (2012), p. 120.
[142] See more in Brake (2012), p. 120.
[143] Brake (2012), p. 121.
[144] Brake (2012), p. 121.
[145] Brake (2012), p. 122.
[146] Brake (2012), p. 122.
[147] Brake (2012), p. 122.
[148] Brake (2012), p. 122.
[149] Brake (2012), p. 123.
[150] Chambers (2017), p. 11.
[151] Chambers (2017), p. 11.
[152] See more in Emens (2009), p. 259.

people".[153] According to Emens, polyamorous individuals follow an ethical vision that includes five main principles: (1) self-knowledge, (2) radical honesty, (3) informed consent among partners, (4) self-possession, and (5) privileging love and sex over other emotions and activities (for example, jealousy).[154] There are strong arguments for the idea of monogamy as a choice and for "thinking critically about its margins".[155] This does not mean that an individual must change his/her sexual preferences or practices, but broaden the perspective for well-founded alternatives.[156] However, monogamy (one partner at a time) and supermonogamy (one partner ever) are forms of relationships that are socially accepted, ideals of true love, and are generally supported by policy and law.[157] In general, "polyamory refers to *emotionally* connected relationships openly involving three or more people".[158] Also, "it was intended to differentiate *emotionally connected* relationships from simple coupling, casual dating around, or recreational sex; it literally means "many loves".[159] It starts from the premise that love, as well as sexuality, is fluid and changing.[160] Among polyamorous individuals, non-sexual intimate relationships are also considered to be part of the concept.[161] Additionally, this concept, similar to queer and queer theory, opposes exclusion, hierarchy, and strict definitions.[162] Polyamory is, in that sense, identical to queer, and "the models of poly relationships are also theoretically limitless".[163] For some, polyamory does not mean only practicing multi-party relationships and other forms of intimacy, but it is also "a conscious theory of relationships".[164] From a queer perspective, individual liberation should be the primary goal. Being able to question your sexuality, sexual relations, and gender identity are foundational principles. In my understanding, queer theory and practice mean liberation from the oppressive elements of marriage so elaborately represented in feminist critiques. Nevertheless, some other movements like "Marriage Boycott" call on "couples to abstain from marriage until all couples can marry",[165] which is more compromising and evolutionary in changing some conceptual elements of marriage (paradigm of marriage as heterosexual). The other way has been promoted by "The Alternatives to Marriage Project," which fights against discrimination of the

153 Emens (2009), p. 259.
154 Emens (2009), p. 259, 274–276.
155 Emens (2009), p. 260.
156 Emens (2009), p. 260.
157 Emens (2009), p. 264.
158 Loving More (2025).
159 Loving More (2025).
160 Loving More (2025).
161 Emens (2009), p. 265.
162 Emens (2009), p. 265.
163 Emens (2009), p. 266.
164 Emens (2009), p. 274.
165 Brake (2012), p. 111.

unmarried.[166] Some others, like Stephen Pearl Andrew, who argues against marriage and for free love, have imagined "a society based on free love principles" that would allow "a variety of amorous relations: monogamy, serial monogamy, polygamy".[167]

There are two potential ways to reconcile queer and law: (1) eliminating state regulation in marriage and substituting it with private contracting, or (2) encompassing a broad range of intimate and sexual relationships, from the freedom to be single to being married or involved in a polyamorous marriage. If we embrace the notion of legally recognizing various relationships, whether monogamous or polyamorous, and by avoiding amatonormativity and heteronormativity,[168] reconciliation could be possible. A complete abolition of marriage will empower other organizations, such as churches, cultural groups, social services, and others, to take control.[169] As Brake puts it: "rejecting amatonormativity does not mean prohibiting or discouraging sexual and romantic relationships"; instead, it involves limiting its pressure and promoting relationship diversity in both the social and legal realms.[170]

7 Conclusion

Feminism has criticized the institution of marriage from different perspectives. Those perspectives focuse either on the unequal position of women in marriage, seeking the recognition of equal rights and privileges granted to men, or on the abolishment of the regulation of marriage by the state. As we have seen, queer legal theory accepts certain feminist positions by criticizing the egalitarian aspirations of the LGBT community. The premise from which it starts is whether or not marriage is essentially unfair and why would LGBT people seek the same institution for themselves? The second line of criticisms address the necessary essentialization of identity pursued by law, which queer legal theory substantively disagrees with. Legal recognition would lead to certain "queer behaviors" being defined as socially acceptable, while other practices and behaviors would be considered "deviant". As the text shows, the LGBT movement primarily went through the process of legal recognition either through registered partnership, civil union, but also the introduction of the institution of same-sex marriage in 34 countries around the world. Does this, however, abolish the critical potential of queer legal theory (and radical feminism)? Probably yes. In addition, a wide range of other forms of intimate private relationships that the law does not recognize are being excluded. Nevertheless, it may be possible to move towards a compromise and retain both the critical potential and some form of legal protection. If it were to exist, it should have been manifested

[166] Brake (2012), p. 111.

[167] Brake (2012), p. 125.

[168] See more in Brake (2012), p. 123.

[169] Brake (2012), p. 123.

[170] Brake (2012), p. 125.

in (1) the abolition of state interference in legal regulation of marriage (but also forms of intimate relationships) and its transfer to the sphere of private regulation, or allowing minimal influence; (2) the abolition of discrimination between the married and the non-married in terms of privileges and special rights if some form of state regulation or support is accepted. The legal regulation should encompass a wide range—from being alone to different forms of intimate relationships involving either two or more adults in polyamorous relationships. In this way, the principle of egalitarianism and liberalism could be reconciled in a dialectical relationship.

References

Banović D (2019) Ujedinjene nacije: pravni okvir i mehanizmi za rodnu ravnopravnost. In: Gavrić S, Ždralović A (eds) Rodna ravnopravnost. Teorija, pravo, politike. Uvod u rodne studije za studentice i studente društvenih nauka u BiH. University of Sarajevo – Faculty of Law and Sarajevo Open Centre, Sarajevo, pp 73–91

Banović D (2023) Queer Legal Theory. In: Vujadinović D, Álvarez del Cuvillo A, Strand S (eds) Feminist Approaches to Law. Gender Perspectives in Law, vol 1. Springer, Cham. https://doi.org/10.1007/978-3-031-14781-4_4 (page 74)

Bećirović Hanušić A (2019) Evropska unija: pravni okvir i mehanizmi za rodnu ravnopravnost. In: Gavrić S, Ždralović A (eds) Rodna ravnopravnost. Teorija, pravo, politike. Uvod u rodne studije za studentice i studente društvenih nauka u BiH. University of Sarajevo – Faculty of Law and Sarajevo Open Centre, Sarajevo, pp 105–119

Brake E (2012) Minimizing marriage: marriage, morality, and the law. Studies in Feminist Philosophy. https://doi.org/10.1093/acprof:oso/9780199774142.003.0006

Chambers C (2017) Against marriage. An egalitarian defence of the marriage-free state. Oxford University Press

Delgado R (1993) The inward turn in outsider jurisprudence. William Mary Law Rev 34:741–768. https://scholarship.law.wm.edu/wmlr/vol34/iss3/6

Emens FE (2009) Compulsory monogamy and polyamorous existence. In: Fineman MA, Jackson JE, Romero AP (eds) Feminist and queer legal theory. Intimate encounters, uncomfortable conversations. Ashgate, pp 259–285

Fineman M (1990) Challenging law, establishing differences: the future of feminist legal scholarship. Fla Law Rev 42(1):25–43. https://scholarship.law.ufl.edu/flr/vol42/iss1/2

Fineman MA (2001) Why marriage. Va J Soc Policy Law 9(1):239–271

Fineman MA (2009) The sexual family. In: Fineman MA, Jackson JE, Romero AP (eds) Feminist and queer legal theory. Intimate encounters, uncomfortable conversations. Ashgate, pp 45–63

Kulenović N (2019) Vijeće Evrope: pravni okvir i mehanizmi za rodnu ravnopravnost. In: Gavrić S, Ždralović A (eds) Rodna ravnopravnost. Teorija, pravo, politike. Uvod u rodne studije za studentice i studente društvenih nauka u BiH. University of Sarajevo – Faculty of Law and Sarajevo Open Centre, Sarajevo, pp 93–104

LaSala MC (2007) Too many eggs in the wrong basket: a queer critique of the same-sex marriage movement. Soc Work 52(2):181–183. https://doi.org/10.1093/sw/52.2.181

Loving More (2025). https://www.lovingmorenonprofit.org/home/new-what-is-polyamory/

Maine A (2022) Queering marriage: the homoradical and anti-normativity. Laws 11(1):1–20. https://doi.org/10.3390/laws11010001

Robson R (2009) Compulsory matrimony. In: Fineman MA, Jackson JE, Romero AP (eds) Feminist and queer legal theory. Intimate encounters, uncomfortable conversations. Ashgate, pp 313–328

Romero AP (2009) Methodological descriptions: "feminist" and "queer" legal theories. In: Fineman MA, Jackson JE, Romero AP (eds) Feminist and queer legal theory. Intimate encounters, uncomfortable conversations. Ashgate, pp 179–198

Spiers J (2007) Breaking the wedding vows: woman-centered critiques of breaking the wedding vows: woman-centered critiques of marriage, 1963–1982. All theses 81. Clemson University. https://open.clemson.edu/cgi/viewcontent.cgi?article=1081&context=all_theses

Waaldijk K (2024) Same-sex couples under the international right to marry: some recognition of their right but more recognition for their exclusion from it and for their existing marriages. In: Ziegler AR, Fremuth ML, Hernández-Truyol B-E (eds) The Oxford handbook of LGBTI law. https://doi.org/10.1093/oxfordhb/9780198847793.013.20

Ždralović A (2019) Savremene perspektive feminističkih teorija. In: Gavrić S, Ždralović A (eds) Rodna ravnopravnost. Teorija, pravo, politike. Uvod u rodne studije za studentice i studente društvenih nauka u BiH. University of Sarajevo – Faculty of Law and Sarajevo Open Centre, Sarajevo, pp 39–56

Damir Banović (1983) is an associate professor at the University in Sarajevo – Faculty of Law (Department for State and Public International Law). He teaches Introduction to Law and Philosophy of Law. His main research focus is on the contemporary socio-legal theory, theory of collective rights, minority rights, consocialism, and comparative federalism. He has published many peer-reviewed articles in academic journals as well as monographs, including *The Political System of Bosnia and Herzegovina. Institutions – Actors – Processes,* Springer Nature, 2021; *Ethnic Diversity, Plural Democracy and Human Dignity. Challenges to the European Union and Western Balkans,* Springer Nature, 2022; *Realist Theory of Law – Essays on Legal Realism, Conventionalism and Naturalization in Law* (*Realistička teorija prava: ogledi o pravnom realizmu, konvencionalizmu i naturalizaciji u pravu*), Univerzitet u Sarajevu – Pravni fakultet, 2023; *Law* in *Max Planck Encyclopedia of Comparative Constitutional Law*, Oxford University Press, 2023; Queer Legal Theory in *Feminist Approaches to Law: Theoretical and Historical Insights,* Springer Nature, 2023.

MIX
Papier aus verantwortungsvollen Quellen
Paper from responsible sources
FSC® C105338

If you have any concerns about our products,
you can contact us on
ProductSafety@springernature.com

In case Publisher is established outside the EU,
the EU authorized representative is:
Springer Nature Customer Service Center GmbH
Europaplatz 3, 69115 Heidelberg, Germany

Printed by Libri Plureos GmbH
in Hamburg, Germany